The Clinician's Guide to Cognitive-Behavioral Therapy for Childhood Obsessive-Compulsive Disorder

The Clinician's Guide to Cognitive-Behavioral Therapy for Childhood Obsessive-Compulsive Disorder

Edited by

Eric A. Storch

Joseph F. McGuire

Dean McKay

ACADEMIC PRESS

An imprint of Elsevier

ELSEVIER

Academic Press is an imprint of Elsevier
125 London Wall, London EC2Y 5AS, United Kingdom
525 B Street, Suite 1800, San Diego, CA 92101-4495, United States
50 Hampshire Street, 5th Floor, Cambridge, MA 02139, United States
The Boulevard, Langford Lane, Kidlington, Oxford OX5 1GB, United Kingdom

Library of Congress Cataloging-in-Publication Data
A catalog record for this book is available from the Library of Congress

British Library Cataloguing-in-Publication Data
A catalogue record for this book is available from the British Library

ISBN: 978-0-12-811427-8

For information on all Academic Press publications
visit our website at https://www.elsevier.com/books-and-journals

Publisher: Nikki Levy
Acquisition Editor: Dennis McGonagle
Editorial Project Manager: Karen R. Miller
Production Project Manager: Punithavathy Govindaradjane
Cover Designer: Mark Rogers

Typeset by SPi Global, India

To those struggling with OCD either in themselves or a loved one; it is my great hope that this book can make a difference in your lives. And, for my loved ones who inspire and support me each day (JFS, MLS, NRS, and EMS).

—Eric A. Storch

For Ariel and Lilly, my unwavering sources of support, and for all of the children and families who have served as the sources of inspiration for this book.

—Joseph F. McGuire

For my mentors, in graduate school and in the academy.

—Dean McKay

Contents

Contributors

R. Lindsey Bergman, University of California; UCLA Semel Institute for Neuroscience and Human Behavior, Los Angeles, CA, United States

Joseph Berryhill, Bradley Hospital, Riverside, RI, United States

Shannon M. Blakey, University of North Carolina, Chapel Hill, NC, United States

Michael H. Bloch, Yale University, New Haven, CT, United States

Elle Brennan, Kent State University, Kent, OH, United States

Nicholas R. Farrell, Rogers Memorial Hospital, Oconomowoc, WI, United States

Christopher A. Flessner, Kent State University, Kent, OH, United States

Sarah Francazio, Kent State University, Kent, OH, United States

Jenny Herren, Alpert Medical School of Brown University, Providence; Bradley Hospital, Riverside, RI, United States

Tord Ivarsson, Center for Child and Adolescent Mental Health, Eastern and Southern Norway, Oslo, Norway

Amita Jassi, South London and Maudsley NHS Foundation Trust, London, United Kingdom

Carly Johnco, Macquarie University, Sydney, NSW, Australia

Cary Jordan, St. Elizabeth Boardman Hospital, Youngstown, OH, United States

Georgina Krebs, South London and Maudsley NHS Foundation Trust; King's College London, London, United Kingdom

Eli R. Lebowitz, Yale Child Study Center, New Haven, CT, United States

Angela Lewis, South London and Maudsley NHS Foundation Trust, London, United Kingdom

Rachel E. Mathews, Kent State University, Kent, OH, United States

Joseph F. McGuire, Johns Hopkins University, Baltimore, MD; University of California, Los Angeles, CA, United States

Dean McKay, Fordham University, New York, NY, United States

Yolanda E. Murphy, Kent State University, Kent, OH, United States

Ella L. Oar, Macquarie University, Sydney, NSW, Australia

Tara S. Peris, University of California, Los Angeles, Los Angeles, CA, United States

Stacey Rice Dobrinsky, McLean Hospital, Belmont, MA, United States

Michelle Rozenman, University of California; UCLA Semel Institute for Neuroscience and Human Behavior, Los Angeles, CA, United States

Gudmundur Skarphedinsson, Sorlandet Hospital, Kristiansand, Norway

Eric A. Storch, University of South Florida, St. Petersburg, FL, United States

Michael L. Sulkowski, University of Arizona, Tucson, AZ, United States

Benjamin E. Thomas, Rogers Memorial Hospital, Oconomowoc, WI, United States

Cynthia M. Turner, University of Queensland, Brisbane, QLD, Australia

Allison Vreeland, Vanderbilt University, Nashville, TN, United States

Bernhard Weidle, Norwegian University of Science and Technology; St. Olavs University Hospital, Trondheim, Norway

Tim I. Williams, University of Reading, Reading, United Kingdom

Chapter 1

Introduction

Eric A. Storch*, Joseph F. McGuire[†,‡] and Dean McKay[§]
**University of South Florida, St. Petersburg, FL, United States, †Johns Hopkins University, Baltimore, MD, United States, ‡University of California, Los Angeles, CA, United States, §Fordham University, New York, NY, United States*

Pediatric obsessive-compulsive disorder is a debilitating condition that affects approximately 1% of children worldwide at any time (Zohar, 1999). This condition confers great impairment across home, social and family domains (Piacentini, Bergman, Keller, & McCracken, 2003), and negatively impacts quality of life (Lack et al., 2009). Without intervention, symptoms tend to persist over time and escalate in severity (Bloch et al., 2009), often presenting with other cooccurring problems (Storch et al., 2008). Fortunately, there are two effective treatments that have been widely studied: cognitive behavioral therapy (CBT) that involves exposure and response prevention, and medication management with serotonin reuptake inhibitors (SRI). Although both interventions are effective, evidence suggests that CBT alone or together with SRI medications is the most effective treatment approach (Franklin et al., 2015; McGuire et al., 2015) with the specific approach depending on the severity of the child's condition as well as other clinical factors (AACAP, 2012).

Despite the strong efficacy of CBT, dissemination and access to treatment is a particular problem. Many children do not receive this form of psychotherapy at all or have to wait long periods until proper diagnosis and treatment is provided (Marques et al., 2010). Even when CBT is available, there may be considerable variability in its implementation due to the knowledge base and experience of the available providers. To address this critical dissemination gap, substantial efforts have been made. Training institutes (e.g., International OCD Foundation's Behavior Therapy Training Institute) have been designed with the goal of broadening the base of providers with expertise in CBT for childhood OCD. A second approach has involved developing treatment manuals that are published and made widely available. In this regard, several manuals have been published building on the initial seminal work by March and Mulle (1998), Freeman and Reinecke (1993), Piacentini, Langley, and

The Clinician's Guide to Cognitive-Behavioral Therapy for Childhood Obsessive-Compulsive Disorder
http://dx.doi.org/10.1016/B978-0-12-811427-8.00001-0

Roblek (2007). These manuals provide structured, evidence-based treatment approaches for helping children with OCD and their families overcome the condition. While the linear nature of these texts is a strength and therapeutic concepts well described, it may be difficult for texts of this nature to go into great detail about a particular topic. For example, what are the exact words that one can say when providing education to a child and their family? Or, how exactly does one create a detailed hierarchy for the multitude of problems a child experiences? And, how might one contend with the myriad of clinical complexities that so often occur in this population (e.g., resistance, comorbidity)? With this in mind, we sought to compile a group of leading experts in the field of childhood OCD to write about—in a practical, "how to" fashion—conducting many of the skills essential to treating children with OCD.

We have divided the book into two overall sections: (1) assessment and treatment of childhood OCD and (2) special considerations in working with this population. The first section starts with chapters dealing with diagnosing OCD and comorbid problems, as well assessing the presence and severity of obsessive-compulsive and comorbid symptoms using evidence-based assessment instruments. Next, a chapter on psychoeducation for children and their family members details how to discuss with families theoretical models of OCD, the treatment model, and nature of treatment. Clear examples are given as to how to convey this information in a ready-to-use format. Following this, the core of the CBT treatment approach is described across two chapters. There is an in-depth discussion on how to create an exposure hierarchy with multiple examples detailing this approach for varied symptoms. The chapter after discusses designing and implementing successful exposures for a variety of symptom presentations. Real-world examples are given as well as tips for implementing creative, child-oriented exposure, and response prevention tasks. Following this, a chapter discusses cognitive therapeutic approaches to complement exposure work. Detailed examples are provided to facilitate this treatment approach and integrate it within an exposure-based treatment model. The next chapter focuses on working with families in the context treatment. Earlier models of treatment seem to isolate the child with more limited family involvement. Our belief, in contrast, is that family should be intimately involved in treatment with a default position of including the parents in sessions as clinically appropriate so that they can learn how to implement therapeutic skills (Storch et al., 2007). We have found this to be not only very effective but also widely acceptable to family members who often typically want to be readily engaged in their child's care and understand how to best help them. To this end, this chapter discusses methods of integrating family members into treatment. There is a special focus on targeting family accommodation, which is a ubiquitous construct when working with children with OCD (Caporino et al., 2012), as well as how to enhance compliance with treatment. A chapter on relapse prevention strategies is included in which a clear relapse prevention plan is articulated to optimize the chance therapeutic gains are maintained. Importantly, this chapter also addresses the sensitive topic what to do if the child that you are working with experiences relapse. A clear, well laid out plan is included for implementation. Finally, a chapter on medication management for childhood OCD is included given the efficacy of this approach. This chapter highlights evidence-based pharmacotherapy practice as well as when to consider medication management combined with CBT.

The second section of the book has a variety of chapters that go into further detail necessary for the complexity of working with this population. The purpose of this section is to spend time discussing critical features related to working with children with OCD. The section starts with discussing common myths and misconceptions in treating childhood OCD including misperceptions about exposure therapy, symptom return, and multiple other aspects. Next, a chapter focused on understanding OCD within school settings and how to manage it within school is provided. This chapter provides clear examples for ensuring that the child is ultimately successful in school, and the more severe cases are able to return to school effectively. The next chapter focuses on addressing significant family accommodation. As noted, virtually all families engage in some level of accommodation of the child's symptoms. This chapter talks about addressing accommodation, especially when such behaviors are entrenched and significant. This chapter is also unique in presenting a treatment model for what to do when a child is unwilling to engage in addressing their symptoms (Lebowitz, Omer, Hermes, & Scahill, 2014). Two chapters are included to discuss working with challenging patients and families. The focus of these chapters addresses increasing motivation through reinforcement systems and working with family member issues such as parental anxiety. The second chapter describes how to manage the most commonly cooccurring conditions such as comorbid anxiety, disruptive behavior, and attentional problems to name several. Following this chapter, a chapter on working with young children with OCD is included given the frequency with which symptoms onset in early childhood. The core treatment components of exposure and response prevention remain the same, but the application of this and other therapeutic concepts can differ in many ways. This chapter focuses on describing how to work with a young child and her/his family in addressing OCD. The final chapter presents an algorithm for managing the patient's care should they not be responsive to the initial trial of CBT and/or a first-line medication.

We anticipate that this book could be used in many ways. For practitioners who are newer to treating childhood OCD, this book can serve as a practical, "how to" manual for addressing symptoms in an affected child. We believe that the core of treatment includes exposure and response prevention; after conducting a thorough assessment over one to two sessions followed by providing psychoeducation over a session, the bulk of treatment will consist of exposure and response prevention. Studies have suggested that 12–14 sessions of exposure and response prevention may not be sufficient to gain an optimal response and that additional sessions may help optimize outcome (Skarphedinsson et al., 2015); it is reasonable to expect that some children will get better in a relatively short period of time but that others will need a significantly longer course. In the present approach, cognitive therapy is a complementary technique to exposure and response prevention; we believe that the majority of treatment should focus on exposure therapy. As the child progresses in treatment, it would follow that sessions are tapered and a relapse prevention plan is set in place. For clinicians who are more experienced, this text may provide more detailed information on core treatment components or addressing clinical complexities.

In closing, it is our hope that this book contributes by providing individuals who are interested in conducting CBT for childhood OCD with a practical framework and resource for implementing the core elements of this intervention. Further, we hope that this book can be useful for parents of an affected child; perhaps as a complement to ongoing treatment, or as a reference to ensure that appropriate treatment is being provided. Ultimately, it is our central goal that CBT for childhood OCD becomes available to all children who are affected with this problem to improve their quality of life and happiness as well as that of their family.

REFERENCES

AACAP. (2012). Practice parameter for the assessment and treatment of children and adolescents with obsessive-compulsive disorder. *Journal of the American Academy of Child and Adolescent Psychiatry*, *51*(1), 98–113. http://dx.doi.org/10.1016/j.jaac.2011.09.019.

Bloch, M. H., Craiglow, B. G., Landeros-Weisenberger, A., Dombrowski, P. A., Panza, K. E., Peterson, B. S., et al. (2009). Predictors of early adult outcomes in pediatric-onset obsessive-compulsive disorder. *Pediatrics*, *124*(4), 1085–1093.

Caporino, N. E., Morgan, J., Beckstead, J., Phares, V., Murphy, T. K., & Storch, E. A. (2012). A structural equation analysis of family accommodation in pediatric obsessive-compulsive disorder. *Journal of Abnormal Child Psychology*, *40*(1), 133–143.

Franklin, M. E., Kratz, H. E., Freeman, J. B., Ivarsson, T., Heyman, I., Sookman, D., et al. (2015). Cognitive-behavioral therapy for pediatric obsessive-compulsive disorder: Empirical review and clinical recommendations. *Psychiatry Research*, *227*(1), 78–92.

Freeman, A., & Reinecke, M. A. (1993). *Cognitive therapy of suicidal behavior: A manual for treatment.* New York, NY: Springer Publishing Co.

Lack, C. W., Storch, E. A., Keeley, M. L., Geffken, G. R., Ricketts, E. D., Murphy, T. K., et al. (2009). Quality of life in children and adolescents with obsessive-compulsive disorder: Base rates, parent–child agreement, and clinical correlates. *Social Psychiatry and Psychiatric Epidemiology*, *44*(11), 935–942.

Lebowitz, E. R., Omer, H., Hermes, H., & Scahill, L. (2014). Parent training for childhood anxiety disorders: The SPACE program. *Cognitive and Behavioral Practice*, *21*(4), 456–469.

March, J. S., & Mulle, K. (1998). *OCD in children and adolescents: A cognitive-behavioral treatment manual.* New York: Guilford Press.

Marques, L., LeBlanc, N. J., Weingarden, H. M., Timpano, K. R., Jenike, M., & Wilhelm, S. (2010). Barriers to treatment and service utilization in an internet sample of individuals with obsessive–compulsive symptoms. *Depression and Anxiety*, *27*(5), 470–475.

McGuire, J. F., Piacentini, J., Lewin, A. B., Brennan, E. A., Murphy, T. K., & Storch, E. A. (2015). A meta-analysis of cognitive behavior therapy and medication for child obsessive–compulsive disorder: Moderators of treatment efficacy, response, and remission. *Depression and Anxiety, 32*(8), 580–593.

Piacentini, J., Bergman, R. L., Keller, M., & McCracken, J. (2003). Functional impairment in children and adolescents with obsessive-compulsive disorder. *Journal of Child and Adolescent Psychopharmacology, 13*(2, Suppl. 1), 61–69.

Piacentini, J., Langley, A., & Roblek, T. (2007). *Cognitive behavioral treatment of childhood OCD: It's only a false alarm therapist guide.* New York, NY: Oxford University Press.

Skarphedinsson, G., Weidle, B., Thomsen, P. H., Dahl, K., Torp, N. C., Nissen, J. B., et al. (2015). Continued cognitive-behavior therapy versus sertraline for children and adolescents with obsessive–compulsive disorder that were non-responders to cognitive-behavior therapy: A randomized controlled trial. *European Child & Adolescent Psychiatry, 24*(5), 591–602.

Storch, E. A., Geffken, G. R., Merlo, L. J., Mann, G., Duke, D., Munson, M., et al. (2007). Family-based cognitive-behavioral therapy for pediatric obsessive-compulsive disorder: Comparison of intensive and weekly approaches. *Journal of the American Academy of Child and Adolescent Psychiatry, 46*(4), 469–478.

Storch, E. A., Larson, M. J., Merlo, L. J., Keeley, M. L., Jacob, M. L., Geffken, G. R., et al. (2008). Comorbidity of pediatric obsessive–compulsive disorder and anxiety disorders: Impact on symptom severity and impairment. *Journal of Psychopathology and Behavioral Assessment, 30*(2), 111–120.

Zohar, A. H. (1999). The epidemiology of obsessive-compulsive disorder in children and adolescents. *Child and Adolescent Psychiatric Clinics of North America, 8*, 445–460.

Chapter 2

Diagnosing Childhood OCD

Ella L. Oar*, Carly Johnco*, and Cynthia M. Turner†
**Macquarie University, Sydney, NSW, Australia, †University of Queensland, Brisbane, QLD, Australia*

The Diagnostic and Statistical Manual of Mental Disorders 5th Edition (DSM-5) criteria for obsessive-compulsive disorder (OCD) requires the presence of obsessions and/or compulsions (APA, 2013). Obsessions are characterized by recurrent and persistent thoughts, urges, or images that are experienced (at some time) as intrusive and unwanted. These cognitive intrusions cause marked anxiety or distress for most individuals. Youth (particularly younger children) may lack the insight and/or verbal ability to communicate their obsessional experiences, sometimes simply describing a "need" to do something until it feels "just right." Hence, for children and adolescents it can be particularly helpful to use a symptom checklist measure (e.g., Children's Yale-Brown Obsessive-Compulsive Scale [CY-BOCS]; Scahill et al., 1997) that provides prompts for a range of common obsessional symptoms and content areas when conducting an initial assessment (e.g., Are you concerned about contamination [or getting germs on you] from touching animal/insects; Are you concerned that you will get/make others ill by spreading contaminants/germs). Clinician prompting facilitates diagnosis in three key ways. First, prompting maximizes the potential for youth to endorse symptoms by helping them to articulate their internal experiences. Second, youth often show limited insight into the excessive nature of their symptoms, and as such, do not spontaneously report these symptoms. Prompting may also help to identify symptoms that the child does not recognize as problematic. Finally, prompting has the potential to help to reduce shame or embarrassment about particular symptoms by validating them as common to OCD, rather than the symptom being a sign that the young person is weird, defiant, or abnormal.

The CY-BOCS provides prompts to help assess duration (i.e., persistence), interference, distress, resistance, and control over obsessions (e.g., How much time do you spend thinking about these things/what is the longest amount of time each day that you are not bothered by these thoughts? How much do these thoughts bother or upset you? How hard do you try to stop the thoughts or ignore them? Are you able to control the thoughts? Goodman et al., 1989).

The Clinician's Guide to Cognitive-Behavioral Therapy for Childhood Obsessive-Compulsive Disorder
http://dx.doi.org/10.1016/B978-0-12-811427-8.00002-2

Assessing these clinical features of intrusive thoughts is important to help with differential diagnosis.

Compulsions are characterized by repetitive behaviors (e.g., hand washing, ordering, checking) or mental acts (e.g., praying, counting, repeating words silently) that the child feels driven to perform in response to an obsession or according to rules that must be applied rigidly (APA, 2013). The goal of these behaviors is to prevent or reduce distress, to be rid of the intrusive thoughts, and/or to prevent some negative outcome from occurring. However, these behaviors are clearly excessive compared to the objective level of threat, or they may not be connected in a realistic way with what they are designed to neutralize or prevent (APA, 2013). Compulsions are not performed for pleasure, although some individuals do experience emotional relief from feelings of anxiety, distress, discomfort, or incompleteness. The DSM-5 includes a developmental specifier for young children, noting that they may not be able to articulate the goals of these behaviors or mental acts; however, this is also a common clinical experience in older children. Although missing from the DSM-5, the previous diagnostic manual (DSM-IV-TR) noted that in addition to difficulty communicating the function of their compulsions, youth also commonly fail to recognize the excessive nature of their compulsive behaviors (APA, 2000). Even when youth do have sufficient insight, their compulsive behaviors often become habitual over time, and as a result they may fail to report certain symptoms. Similar to obsessions, it can be useful to use a structured measure like the CY-BOCS to assess compulsive behaviors to ensure adequate assessment of common compulsive phenotypes.

Criterion B for OCD specifies that obsessions or compulsions need to be time consuming (e.g., take more than 1 h per day) or cause clinically significant distress or impairment in social, occupational, or other important areas of functioning. Intrusions are a common phenomenon, with almost all people experiencing at least the occasional intrusive thought (Crye, Laskey, & Cartwright-Hatton, 2010). These criteria help to differentiate occasional and normative intrusive thoughts from clinically significant intrusive thoughts. Although a time-based minimum of 1 h is noted in the diagnostic criteria, the frequency and duration of OCD symptoms can vary between youth. Symptom duration of 1–3 h per day is generally considered mild to moderate severity, although some individuals may experience almost constant symptom presence (more than 8 h per day).

Diagnosis can be challenging when, even in the context of severe OCD pathology, families or children report that their symptoms occupy less than 1 h per day. This is especially common in circumstances where a young person is avoiding particular items/situations that may "trigger" their obsessions, or when families are accommodating the child's OCD symptoms. Common accommodating behaviors that family members may engage in include providing excessive reassurance; participating in rituals (e.g., facilitating the child completing a compulsion; completing or avoiding a particular behavior at the request of the child); providing the child with items needed to complete their compulsions (e.g., decontaminants); allowing the child to avoid situations that may trigger their OCD; completing tasks or chores for the child (e.g., dressing, making the child's bed) to avoid triggering OCD; and altering family functioning (e.g., avoiding certain activities, allowing the child to dictate the arrangement of furniture in the house) (Calvocoressi et al., 1995; Wu et al., 2016). Families engage in these behaviors to prevent the child's OCD symptoms from being triggered or to reduce the child's distress. When diagnosing OCD, it is important to consider how OCD may be impacting on family members, as family accommodation may be reducing other clinically relevant factors (e.g., time spent, distress).

Youth with OCD can present with limited insight into the excessive or dysfunctional nature of their beliefs (Adelman & Lebowitz, 2012). It is not unusual for a child to endorse symptoms as "normal," when these are actually behavioral excesses or obsessional in nature. For example, children may report feeling strongly that certain clothing be worn on specific days. Parents may report that this belief is firmly held, but the child may report it as a highly desired preference. Clinicians can struggle to determine whether this constitutes merely a preference or a behavioral problem. Therefore clinical knowledge of the phenomenology of OCD (e.g., that individuals may display an inflated sense of responsibility for preventing harm, magical thinking about the capacity for special actions to prevent negative outcomes, excessive concern with controlling thoughts, or perceiving that having a thought is equivalent to acting on it, etc.) can aid diagnosis. Diagnostic specifiers can be used to note the level of insight displayed by the young person (e.g., "with good or fair insight," "with poor insight," and "with absent insight/delusional beliefs"). Regardless of the child's level of insight clinicians should routinely consult with parents during the assessment process, as this will greatly aid in determining whether behaviors are dysfunctional or excessive. Given the high level of comorbidity with tic disorders (Leckman et al., 2010), and the potentially different pattern of comorbidity, course, and familial history of youth with comorbid OCD and tics (APA, 2013), a "tic-related" specifier may also be given when youth have a current or lifetime diagnosis of a tic disorder. Finally, as with most mental health concerns, symptoms need to be differentiated from the effects of a substance or medical condition, and cannot be better explained by another mental disorder (refer to "Differential Diagnosis and Comorbidity" section).

DEVELOPMENTAL CONSIDERATIONS

Children often display a number of ritualistic and/or repetitive behaviors that can appear compulsive in nature. Differentiating between normative and pathological rituals is relevant when diagnosing OCD. By the age of 2, around 60% of children display some form of ritualistic behavior, with strong attachment to a favorite object commonly emerging around 14 months; bedtime routines around 16–17 months; being "very concerned with dirt, cleanliness or neatness" around 22 months; and lining up objects around 24 months (Evans et al., 1997). Although many of these rituals subside over time as children become more flexible, others (e.g., bedtime rituals) often remain, and superstitious beliefs can emerge in later childhood. Leonard, Goldberger, Rapoport, Cheslow, and Swedo (1990) describe a number of common age-normative rituals and beliefs during childhood. For example, children often play a game of "jinx" where one child can be silenced if two children speak the same word simultaneously; young children may fear being contaminated by "cooties" if touched by a child of the opposite sex; common childhood hobbies may be focused around acquiring (or "hoarding") large quantities of figurines, stamps, coins, or memorabilia related to popular culture; and children often play games where they avoid stepping on surface cracks (step on a crack and break your mother's back). It is normal for children to believe in more magical and mythical constructs (e.g., the tooth fairy, Santa), while adolescents typically do not. Although onset of OCD commonly occurs during childhood, it is important to consider whether the child's beliefs and behaviors are normative given their age and stage of development. The clinical dimensions of duration, interference, distress, resistance, and level of control related to the thoughts and behaviors being assessed aid in diagnosis.

COMMON OCD SYMPTOM PRESENTATIONS

Although core symptom features (obsessions and/or compulsions) remain similar across individuals, the clinical presentation of OCD can vary widely. There are a number of well-recognized OCD symptom subtypes or dimensions that youth can present with, with many individuals presenting with symptoms in more than one symptom cluster (Mataix-Cols, Nakatani, Micali, & Heyman, 2008).

Contamination (Contamination Obsessions and Cleaning Compulsions)

Youth with contamination OCD are typically preoccupied with fears of illness or death as a result of exposure to germ or chemical contamination. These obsessions often drive compulsive washing or cleaning behaviors (e.g., prolonged or excessive hand washing or showering; sterilization of objects, surfaces, and people). They also typically lead to avoidance of particular surfaces (e.g., door handles, trash cans), objects (e.g., crockery, cutlery, pens, toys), people (e.g., siblings), food (e.g., sushi), and situations (e.g., public transport, movie theaters). The dominant emotions in contamination-based OCD are fear and disgust.

Symmetry (Symmetry Obsessions and Repeating, Ordering and Counting Compulsions)

The symmetry symptom dimension is characterized by a preoccupation with evenness and symmetry. Symptoms can present in different ways. For example, arranging possessions in a particular order or pattern, or needing body parts to "feel even" if touched or when touching surfaces (e.g., feet on floor). Repetitive compulsions fall within this dimension and can include verbal repetition (e.g., words, phrases) or repeated activities (e.g., reading and rereading, writing and rewriting, retracing steps, turning handles or switches repetitively). Counting compulsions are also common. Unlike other symptom dimensions, individuals with these symptoms do not tend to report a fear of negative outcomes occurring from a lack of order or symmetry. Rather, there can be a strong urge for uniformity, perfectionism, feeling "right" or "even," and these symptoms have been termed "not just right experiences" (Coles, Frost, Heimberg, & Rhéaume, 2003; Schubert, Ravid, & Coles, 2016).

Forbidden or Taboo Thoughts (Aggressive, Sexual, or Religious Obsessions and Related Compulsions)

Unacceptable or "repugnant" obsessions typically refer to obsessions that contain aggression, harm, sexual, or religious content. Aggressive (or harm) obsessions involve distressing, unwanted thoughts, or images about purposefully or unintentionally causing harm to oneself or others (e.g., Moulding, Aardema, & O'Connor, 2014). For example, images, thoughts, or urges to push a friend off a balcony, stab a sibling, or step in front of a car. While compulsions may involve avoidance strategies (e.g., of objects, people, or environments) in order to "prevent" the child from engaging in the behavior, checking compulsions (e.g., recurrent calling or texting), and/or other ritualized behaviors aimed at "undoing" or preventing the risk of harm.

Sexual obsessions refer to unwanted sexual thoughts, often focused on family members, friends, or other children. These obsessions can include violent or homosexual acts, or bestiality. Similar to harm obsessions, behavioral responses tend to involve avoidance and/or engaging in compulsive rituals that either "un-do" or "compensate" and "make up" for their obsession (Fernández de la Cruz et al., 2013). These obsessions are often highly shameful and children may be reluctant to disclose such symptoms. There is no evidence to suggest that the experience of sexual obsessions is linked to the child sexual abuse.

Religious obsessions (referred to as scrupulosity) tend to involve preoccupations with blasphemy, death, (unwarranted) fears of having sinned, and religious or moral judgment focused on narrow/insignificant aspect of religious doctrines or moral standards (Miller & Hedges, 2008). Compulsions often involve ritualized, repetitive, and excessive use of religious behaviors (e.g., prayer, confession, self-punishment) or excessive use of behaviors that are perceived to "un-do" or "make up" for their sin (e.g., volunteer, donate, help others).

Hoarding

Although compulsive hoarding has historically been considered a symptom cluster within OCD, Hoarding disorder is now categorized separately (APA, 2013). However, many individuals with OCD may still display hoarding symptoms, despite not meeting criteria for hoarding disorder comorbidity (Morris, Jaffee, Goodwin, & Franklin, 2016; Pertusa et al., 2008). Hoarding behavior refers to a pattern of saving or acquiring items, with persistent difficulty discarding them, regardless of their actual value. Hoarding behavior may be limited or moderated by adults, given young people typically live with parents/adult caregivers. Youth may refuse to discard old toys, clothes, or items of no value (e.g., packaging, string, rubber bands), often with a belief focused on the potential "need" for the item at a later time, sentimentality related to the object (e.g., the item reminds the child of a particular event or experience), anthropomorphism, or a concern about "waste." In the context of OCD, hoarding is usually the direct consequence of obsessions or compulsions. Feelings on incompleteness and needing to preserve memories and meaning are the most common OCD symptom associated with hoarding, although acquisition may also be the result of avoiding other OCD-related triggers (e.g., not discarding to avoid washing or checking).

Other Miscellaneous Symptoms

There are several other common OCD symptoms that do not fit neatly within the symptom dimensions discussed earlier. These can include obsessional doubting (i.e., worries of having done something wrong) that usually relate to compulsive reassurance seeking or confessing (i.e., a need to tell or report all activities, thoughts, or perceived wrongdoings), superstitious fears (e.g., fears of certain numbers or colors, stepping on a crack); fear of losing things that can relate to obsessional checking or list making; transformation obsessions (e.g., fears of morphing or acquiring negative characteristics), and intrusive (nonviolent) images, songs, or music (e.g., theme songs).

DIFFERENTIAL DIAGNOSIS AND COMORBIDITY

In addition to high levels of comorbidity between OCD and other disorders, symptoms of OCD can "overlap" with some of these conditions. Assessments should incorporate multiple methods (e.g., clinical/diagnostic interview, behavioral observation, self-, and parent-report questionnaires) and multiple informants (e.g., child, parent, and teacher) to gain a complete picture of the youth across contexts and settings. Chapter 4 provides a comprehensive review of evidence-based assessment measures for OCD and differential/comorbid diagnoses. Therefore the focus here is on clinical guidance related to differentiating symptoms of OCD from other disorders that share commonalities in their clinical presentation. Table 1 provides an overview of the common features of these disorders, along with relevant clinical features that may help to differentiate symptoms.

TABLE 1 Shared and Differential Features Between OCD and Its Common Cooccurring Disorders

Differential Diagnosis	Shared Features	Distinguishing Features
Generalized anxiety disorder	• Repetitive thoughts • Maladaptive perfectionism • Intolerance of uncertainty • Cognitive avoidance • Compulsive checking and reassurance seeking	GAD • Cognitions: Ego-syntonic and abstract/verbal in nature • Compulsions: Performed at a low frequency; more flexible; more logical connection between thought and behavior; performed to prevent to directly prevent negative outcome OCD • Cognitions: ego-dystonic and image based • Thought-action fusion • Compulsions: Performed at a higher frequency; more rigid performance; stretched logic between thoughts and behavior; performed to reduce distress associated with obsessions
Illness/health anxiety and emetophobia	• Repetitive thoughts • Preoccupation with illness and vomiting • Superstitious or magical thinking • Overestimation of the likelihood of danger • Compulsive behaviors—Checking, reassurance seeking, and hand washing • Avoidance	Illness/health anxiety and emetophobia • Fear circumscribed to health or vomiting OCD • Cognitions: Illness-related thoughts experienced as more intrusive and ego-dystonic • Typically present with a varying range of obsessions and compulsive behaviors

Continued

TABLE 1 Shared and Differential Features Between OCD and Its Common Cooccurring Disorders—cont'd

Differential Diagnosis	Shared Features	Distinguishing Features
Body dysmorphic disorder	• Repetitive thoughts • Maladaptive perfectionism • Over importance of thoughts • Beliefs related to importance of controlling ones thoughts • Avoidance • Compulsive behaviors	BDD • Preoccupation focused on appearance • Compulsions performed in an attempt to check, hide, or improve their perceived defect • Poor insight • Comorbidity: Increased rates of depression, substance use problems, risk of suicidality OCD • Greater insight • Compulsion performed in an effort to relieve distress related to obsessional thoughts
Eating disorders (i.e., anorexia nervosa, binge eating disorder, bulimia)	• Preoccupation/repetitive thoughts associated with feared stimuli • Maladaptive perfectionism • Decision-making deficits • Compulsive behaviors • Potential to lead to significant weight loss	Eating disorders • Cognitions: Thoughts related to food, body shape/weight (e.g., drive for thinness) • Thoughts ego-syntonic and not viewed as intrusive or unwanted • Compulsive behaviors aimed at controlling or losing weight • Performance of compulsive behaviors not viewed as excessive or irrational OCD • Cognitions: Related to contamination; fears about choking, vomiting, or being poisoned by chemicals; or intrusive (grotesque) images • Repetitive thoughts ego-dystonic and oftentimes neutralized or suppressed
Tic disorders	• Repetitive behaviors	Tic disorder • History of simple tics • Presence of premonitory urges

TABLE 1 Shared and Differential Features Between OCD and Its Common Cooccurring Disorders—cont'd

Differential Diagnosis	Shared Features	Distinguishing Features
		• Repetitive behaviors: Brief, simplistic movements, perceived as involuntary, performed to relive sensory urge or physical tension OCD • History of anxiety • Associated with feelings of anxiety and distress and threat-based cognitions • Compulsions aimed at relieving distress related to obsessional thoughts
Autism spectrum disorder	• Preoccupying/repetitive thoughts • Repetitive behaviors	ASD • History of social interaction problems, fixated interests, and other repetitive behaviors • Repetitive thoughts: Content focused on a particular interest of the child, only leading to distress if the child needs to stop thinking the thoughts • Repetitive behaviors: Not preceded by a specific thought, reinforcing, only cause distress when the child is unable to perform the behavior OCD • Repetitive thoughts: Cause significant distress, unwanted, ego-dystonic • Compulsions aimed at relieving distress related to obsessional thoughts

Generalized Anxiety Disorder

Perhaps not surprisingly, a high degree of overlap exists between OCD and the anxiety disorders. Anxiety disorders are one of the most common comorbid conditions in childhood OCD, with 26%–75% of youth meeting criteria for a cooccurring anxiety disorder diagnosis (Langley, Lewin, Bergman, Lee, & Piacentini, 2010). Differential diagnosis between generalized anxiety disorder (GAD) and OCD is often the most complex given similarities in the phenotypic presentation of the disorders. GAD is characterized by excessive and uncontrollable worry about a range of events and/or activities (e.g., school, performance, health, family, and world events; APA, 2013). To meet diagnostic criteria, children and adolescents must worry most days, for at least 6 months, and worry must be associated with at least one physiological symptom (e.g., restlessness, fatigue, difficulty concentrating, irritability, tense muscles, and sleep disturbance).

OCD and GAD share a number of common symptoms such as repetitive and persistent thoughts that focus upon future events, in addition to other cognitive processes (e.g., perfectionism, intolerance of uncertainty, cognitive avoidance). There are also a number of shared safety-seeking behaviors (e.g., mental rituals, reassurance seeking, checking; Comer, Kendall, Franklin, Hudson, & Pimentel, 2004). One of the most common sources of diagnostic confusion between OCD and GAD is the overlap between obsessions and worries. To assist with differential diagnosis, clinicians can probe for further information relating to the content of the cognitions. Generalized worry tends to focus on more everyday concerns, such as parental health or well-being (Weems, Silverman, & La Greca, 2000). Obsessions are often more unusual or bizarre in nature, or the child may believe she or he has a pivotal role in preventing the feared outcome from occurring, such as fearing a parent may die if a child touches their food without washing his or her hands. Examining the form of the cognitions may also help clinicians to distinguish between the disorders. GAD has been found to be associated with thoughts that are more verbal in nature, whereas obsessions can also be image based or urge related (Langlois, Freeston, & Ladouceur, 2000).

Beliefs related to the meaning and significance of intrusive thoughts may also differentiate OCD and GAD, as research suggests that people with OCD are more likely to misinterpret the meaning of their thoughts (Purdon, 2004). For example, thought-action fusion (TAF) has been found to successfully discriminate between obsessive features and worry in adults, with TAF most strongly related to obsessions (Coles, Mennin, & Heimberg, 2001). TAF involves either a morality bias, where the individual believes that thinking about immoral behavior (e.g., harming a loved one) is morally equivalent to engaging in the behavior, and/or a likelihood bias whereby the individual believes that thinking about an aversive event (e.g., a loved one being in a car accident) actually increases the chance of that event occurring.

Ritualized or repetitive behaviors may be present in both GAD and OCD. For example, children with GAD may repeatedly check they have packed everything for school, rewrite/erase work, or seek reassurance from family members. Some authors have suggested that worry in GAD may be analogs to mental rituals in OCD, in that it is negatively reinforcing, provides relief from distress and regulates emotions (Vrana, Cuthbert, & Lang, 1986). Repetitive behaviors in OCD and GAD have been proposed to be distinguishable based upon the following key factors: (1) incidence—youth with OCD engage in compulsive behaviors more frequently than those with GAD; (2) flexibility—youth with OCD tend to be more rigid in the performance of their behaviors (i.e., OCD rituals are highly rule-bound, and often repeated unless done in exactly the "right" way); and (3) nature—the logic that connects the performance of the behavior to the thought in youth with OCD may be tenuous or magical (e.g., if I avoid stepping on cracks nothing bad will happen; Comer et al., 2004). These proposed differences in compulsive behaviors between GAD and OCD have not yet been empirically examined; however, they provide a heuristic for clinical decision-making.

Illness/Health-Related Anxiety and Emetophobia

There are several areas of symptom overlap between OCD and both illness/health anxiety and emetophobia. While the rates of comorbidity between the disorders are unknown in children and adolescents, comorbidity in adults is high, with 8.2%–15% of adults with OCD presenting with comorbid hypochondriasis, and 13% of adults with emetophobia presenting with comorbid OCD (du Toit, van Kradenburg, Niehaus, & Stein, 2001; Sykes, Boschen, & Conlon, 2016). Illness/health anxiety is a broad term that relates to anxiety associated with a fear of developing a serious illness (Asmundson, Abramowitz, Richter, & Whedon, 2010). In comparison, emetophobia is a type of specific phobia that is characterized by an extreme fear of vomiting (Boschen, 2007).

Both hypochondriasis and emetophobia are characterized by repetitive thoughts, which focus on illness and bodily sensations, in addition to behavioral symptoms such as checking, reassurance seeking, and hand washing (APA, 2013; Veale, Hennig, & Gledhill, 2015). Contamination-based OCD, one of the most common OCD subtypes, is similarly associated with obsessive thoughts related to illness and germs, compulsive washing or cleaning rituals, and avoidance of "contaminated" objects or situations. The cognitive processes that underlie these disorders also appear to overlap. For example, intolerance of uncertainty has been found to be associated with both OCD and health anxiety, and superstitious and magical thinking (e.g., repeating a phrase to prevent feared outcome occurring) has been observed in both OCD and emetophobia (Veale et al., 2015).

Two key considerations that are useful when determining an OCD diagnosis is whether the feared outcome is circumscribed to health/illness or vomiting, or involves a range of other fears or superstitions, and whether the behavioral symptoms are representative of magical thinking, or a well aligned to the fear. Moreover, in distinguishing health anxiety and OCD, those with OCD tend to experience illness-related thoughts as more intrusive and ego-dystonic in nature, and focus on *contracting* an illness as opposed to already *having* an illness (APA, 2013). The CY-BOCS can help clinicians determine whether the child endorses multiple OCD symptom subtypes or only concerns related to health/illness or vomit.

Body Dysmorphic Disorder

Body dysmorphic disorder (BDD) is a debilitating condition that involves a preoccupation with perceived defects or flaws in one's physical appearance, and associated repetitive behaviors or mental acts in response to these appearance concerns (APA, 2013). Between 6% and 78% of adolescents and adults with BDD present with comorbid OCD, and conversely, 3%–37% of those with OCD meet criteria for cooccurring BDD (Conceição Costa et al., 2012; Veale et al., 1996). Both OCD and BDD are characterized by recurrent, intrusive, distressing thoughts and share underlying cognitive processes such as perfectionism, beliefs related to the importance of thoughts and controlling thoughts (Lavell, Farrell, & Zimmer-Gembeck, 2014). Avoidance, time-consuming repetitive behaviors such as checking and reassurance seeking are also characteristic of both disorders.

Importantly, in BDD, the focus of the thoughts and behaviors tends to be exclusively in relation to physical appearance. For example, thoughts may be about a facial/body feature, skin or hair, or general appearance (ugliness), while behaviors may be focused on disguising, hiding, improving, or checking their physical defect (e.g., wearing heavy makeup, checking mirror, or seeking cosmetic surgery). When appearance is the focus of concern in OCD, metacognitive processes (e.g., TAF) tend to result in youth believing that their thought will magically "cause" a physical defect (e.g., increase in pimples), and compulsions are aimed at neutralizing or undoing this. Furthermore, adults (and anecdotally adolescents) with BDD have also been found to have poorer insight into their psychopathology, including a stronger conviction that their beliefs are accurate, and a decreased willingness to believe their concerns have a psychological cause in comparison to those with OCD (Eisen, Phillips, Coles, & Rasmussen, 2004). BDD is often considered a "silent disorder," as individuals with appearance concerns rarely seek treatment as a result of shame, embarrassment, or fear of negative evaluation from others (e.g., that others will think they're vain). Importantly, when conducting an OCD assessment with young people, clinicians should routinely screen for BDD, as this diagnosis may otherwise be missed.

Eating Disorders

OCD commonly cooccurs with eating disorders (EDs) (i.e., anorexia nervosa, bulimia nervosa, binge eating disorder), and in adolescent and adult ED samples, OCD prevalence can be as high as 79% (Lewin, Menzel, & Strober, 2013). In contrast, 3%–17% of adult OCD samples report a history of an ED (Altman & Shankman, 2009). In a recent study examining restrictive eating patterns in children and adolescents with OCD, 25% ($n=101$) endorsed engaging in ritualistic eating patterns during their initial assessment (Jassi, Patel, Lang, Heyman, & Krebs, 2016).

OCD and EDs can share a number of phenomenological and functional similarities including a preoccupation with a feared stimulus (e.g., food), avoidance of food, and the performance of various rule-bound behaviors (e.g., dietary restriction, ritualistic eating behaviors, body checking, purging) in order to alleviate distress. Moreover, the disorders share underlying cognitive deficits in decision-making and maladaptive perfectionism (Boisseau, Thompson-Brenner, Pratt, Farchione, & Barlow, 2013). To ascertain whether a child or adolescent is presenting with OCD or an ED, the therapist needs to closely examine the rationale for the child's performance of rituals and the content of related cognitions. The hallmark feature of EDs is a persistent disturbance of eating behaviors that leads to an altered consumption of food, with subsequent physical health problems and impairment in functioning (APA, 2013). For example, a child with an ED is likely to be preoccupied with thoughts related to body weight/shape (e.g., fear of fatness or a desire for particular body parts to be thinner), such thoughts are likely to be ego-syntonic, and their food-related behaviors are likely to be performed in order to achieve a weight or body-related goal. Youth with ED may not perceive their performance of compensatory behaviors (e.g., dieting, ritualized eating, exercising) to be excessive or irrational (Lewin et al., 2013). In comparison, a child with OCD may avoid eating due to ego-dystonic fears of contamination, choking, vomiting, or being poisoned, or concerns associated with other intrusive images (e.g., seeing food may trigger intrusive grotesque thoughts; Jassi et al., 2016).

Tic Disorders

Substantial overlap exists between OCD and tic disorders, with approximately 10%–40% of youth with OCD presenting with comorbid tics, and 20%–60% of youth presenting with tics also meeting criteria for OCD (Leckman et al., 2010). Indeed, the high overlap between the disorders resulted in the inclusion of a tic-related OCD specifier in DSM-5 (APA, 2013). Tics are defined as a sudden, rapid, and repetitive motor movements or vocalizations (APA, 2013). Three diagnostic categories of tic disorders have been described within DSM-5. To meet criteria for Tourette's Disorder the presence of at least two motor tics and at least one vocal tic is required, and if these criteria are not met, then a diagnosis of Persistent (Chronic) Motor or Vocal Tic Disorder is given. As tics commonly wax and wane in frequency, for a diagnosis to be made they must persist for longer than 1 year. Tics vary considerably in their presentation and are often categorized into "simple tics" which are brief in duration (e.g., sniffing, eye blinks, shoulder shrugging) or "complex tics" which are longer in duration, often involve a variety of muscle groups, and may involve multiple simple tics (Cohen, Leckman, & Bloch, 2013). It is usually complex tics that are confused with compulsions, given that complex tics can often involve repetitive sequences of behaviors.

For some behaviors, there is a high degree of phenotypic overlap that can make distinguishing between tics and compulsions complex. For example, eye blinking and staring or repetitive touching, tapping or rubbing may all be indicative of OCD or tic phenomenon. Many youth also describe that these behaviors are performed in response to a strong urge, and distinguishing between an obsessional urge in OCD and a premonitory urge in a tic disorder can be difficult. Repetitive behaviors that are brief, involve simplistic movements, do not have a purpose and are perceived as involuntary are suggestive of a tic (Kircanski, Peris, & Piacentini, 2013). Kircanski et al. (2013) recommend the use of a sneeze or itch analogy to describe the concept of the involuntary nature of tics with youth. The therapist can explain that a tic is similar to a sneeze in that is involuntary and has to be performed, while a compulsion is like an itch in that it is compelling and distressing, but voluntary as to whether we choose to scratch it or ignore it. Of note, however, some children with tics may interpret the fact that they respond to the premonitory urge as indicating their response is voluntary.

To assist with differentiating between a tic disorder and OCD, the clinician should complete a thorough assessment and history. Tic disorders typically onset between 5 and 8 years of age, with simple facial or vocal tics being the first symptoms noted, and tics then progressing to different body parts and more complex tics. It is rare for a child or adolescent to present with complex tics alone (Lewin & Piacentini, 2010). Thus if a child presents with behaviors that resemble complex tics, but does not have a history of simple tics, the child's symptoms may be more representative of OCD. Furthermore, if the child has a history of anxiety and well-defined obsessions and compulsions, this may suggest that the repetitive behaviors being observed are OCD related (Lewin & Piacentini, 2010).

Clinicians need to carefully assess the sensory, affective, and cognitive experiences that the young person experiences immediately prior to engaging in the symptomatic behavior, as this information is the most pertinent to determining which diagnosis is most appropriate (Lewin & Piacentini, 2010). The function of the child's symptomatic behavior can also be examined to assist in differentiating between the disorders. In the context of a tic disorder, the purpose of performing the tic is to relive the sensory urges or physical tension in a bodily part. While in those with OCD, the purpose of the behavior is more often related to relieving distress and anxiety-associated obsessions, although the exception to this is the "not just right behaviors" which tend to be OCD symptoms without accompanying anxiety (Kircanski et al., 2013; Lewin & Piacentini, 2010; Schubert et al., 2016). Lewin and Piacentini (2010) suggest that clinicians should explore with children the consequences of not performing their repetitive behavior. If children report responses along the line of "*something bad might happen*" or "*It would all be wrong*" this might be more indicative of OCD, while a response such as "*I would not be able to stop it*" (e.g., the urge would increase) or "*nothing would happen, I just have to do it*" may be more likely to be associated with a tic presentation.

Autism Spectrum Disorder

Autism Spectrum Disorder (ASD) and OCD are highly comorbid. In samples of youth with ASD, rates of cooccurring OCD range from 2% to 37%, and a median incidence of 10%, placing children with ASD at significantly higher risk of developing OCD than typically developing children (Neil & Sturmey, 2014). Persistent social communication and interaction deficits, and repetitive and restricted patterns of behaviors, interests, or activities are hallmark features of ASD (APA, 2013). To meet diagnostic criteria children must display at least two of the following restricted, repetitive interests or activities: (1) repetitive motor movements, use of objects, or speech; (2) insistence on sameness, inflexibility, and adherence with routines or particular patterns of behavior; (3) restricted interests that are abnormal in their intensity or focus; and (4) abnormal reactivity to sensory experiences (e.g., hyper or hyposensitivity) or an unusual focus on sensory experiences in the environment (APA, 2013). These symptoms must be pervasive, beginning in early development; however, an individual may not receive a diagnosis until social demands exceed their capabilities in later childhood.

The two key areas of overlap between ASD and OCD are repetitive stereotyped behaviors and obsessional thoughts/interests. If ASD is suspected, the clinician needs to obtain a thorough developmental history for the child, screening for difficulties in social interactions; problems reading social cues; and repetitive behaviors, fixated interests, or atypical preoccupations as this will assist with differential diagnosis (Lewin & Piacentini, 2010). As repetitive thoughts are a key feature of ASD and OCD diagnostic criteria, it can be difficult to distinguish between the disorders. In children who have OCD, obsessions are experienced as highly distressing and intrusive, ego-dystonic, and cause significant anxiety. In comparison, children with ASD tend to have repetitive thoughts that are ego-syntonic, related to a particular interest of the child (e.g., protecting the environment, Pokemon, trains, space), and not generally causing distress unless the child is required to stop thinking about them (Wu, Rudy, & Storch, 2014). Hence, examining the content of the child's repetitive thoughts (e.g., *is the content related to a restricted interest of the child?*) and their emotional reaction to these thoughts (e.g., *does the child experience the thought as highly distressing, intrusive, and ego-dystonic?*) may assist in distinguishing between the disorders (Wu et al., 2014).

Completing a functional analysis of repetitive behaviors can additionally aid differential diagnosis of these symptoms. As noted earlier, in the context of

OCD, compulsive behaviors are usually performed to relieve the anxiety and distress, while in ASD, repetitive behaviors are generally not preceded by a specific distressing thought. In contrast, engaging in these behaviors may be reinforcing and self-stimulating (e.g., comforting, soothing) for the child, with distress experiences only when the behaviors need to be stopped or are unable to be performed (Wu et al., 2014). Thus from an observer perspective, ASD-related repetitive behaviors and OCD compulsions may appear the same; however, they serve very different functions. Treatment of OCD in children with ASD is often more complex than treatment of OCD in youth without ASD, and clinicians need to ensure ongoing assessment of behaviors to determine those that are the focus of change, from those that are inherent to the ASD presentation.

OTHER ISSUES IN DIAGNOSIS

A number of developmental considerations related to diagnosing OCD in youth have been discussed earlier, including the role of family accommodation, limited insight, and overlapping symptomatology. There are two other key issues that clinicians need to be aware of when diagnosing OCD in youth, namely, how to conduct a risk assessment (e.g., in the context of violent, aggressive or sexual thoughts, or thoughts related to harming themselves), and considerations relating to the pediatric acute-onset neuropsychiatric syndrome (PANS) phenotype of OCD.

Risk Assessment

A significant proportion of children and adolescents who suffer from OCD experience intrusive violent, sexual, and death-related thoughts. A sound knowledge of OCD phenomenology is needed to be able to distinguish between the thoughts and urges of those who have OCD, in comparison to the thoughts experienced by those who may be sexual or violent offenders, or people whom are actively suicidal (Veale, Freeston, Krebs, Heyman, & Salkovskis, 2009). Of importance, in those who have OCD, the risk that they will carry out their obsession is almost negligible. By definition obsessions are intrusive and *unwanted* thoughts, which are *ego-dystonic*, and represent a fear that the person wants to avoid at all costs. Veale et al. (2009) provide a comprehensive discussion of factors that should be considered when assessing a child or adolescent with aggressive or sexual obsessions. In sum, these include: (1) Does the child/adolescent experience the thoughts as intrusive or unwanted? (2) Does the youth try to avoid situations/objects/people that trigger the thoughts? (3) Does the child attempt to suppress or neutralize the thoughts? (4) When the child has the thought what do they feel (e.g., anxiety, distress, guilt vs pleasure)? (5) Does the child report any other OCD symptoms? (6) Is the child/adolescent motivated to seek help? and (7) Does the youth have any history of harming themselves?

Where an assessment has indicated that symptoms are consistent with OCD, prolonged risk assessment can actually be harmful, and a clear message that the symptoms do not indicate risk can be helpful.

Secondary risk of harm is a far more common issue in OCD. Secondary risk of harm arises as an unintended consequence of engaging in compulsions and urges, for example, significant weight loss or health consequences as a result of restricting food or fluid intake due to contamination fear, or stepping onto a road as part of a repeating compulsion. Clinicians also need to be aware that while some children and adolescents may present with *obsessions* related to harming themselves (e.g., jumping off a balcony or walking in front of a car), there is still a possible *secondary* risk of suicidal ideation, often but not always due to comorbid depression and hopelessness that can arise as secondary to having OCD. By way of an example, a child or adolescent with OCD may choose to hurt themselves rather than endure the obsessional belief that they might hurt someone else (Milliner-Oar, Cadman, & Farrell, 2016).

Pediatric Acute-Onset Neuropsychiatric Syndrome

An increasing body of research has examined the PANS subtype of OCD. Key clinical features of PANS-related OCD symptoms include an abrupt or dramatic onset of OCD and/or tics symptoms, restricted food intake, sensory hypersensitivity (e.g., sensitivity to light and sounds, dystonia, tremors, stereotypies), sudden regression in handwriting and math abilities, increased urinary frequency (Chang et al., 2015; Murphy, Gerardi, & Leckman, 2014). While the exact prevalence of PANS is unknown, some suggest that of those who experience OCD, as many as 10% may meet criteria for the PANS subtype (Murphy et al., 2014) although this requires additional study. The etiology and casual mechanisms of PANS are still being explored. However, research suggests that this subtype of OCD is triggered by infections. One subtype of PANS is referred to as pediatric autoimmune neuropsychiatric disorder associated with streptococcal infections. Other infections that can trigger PANS include varicella, mycoplasma pneumonia, and Lyme disease (Chang et al., 2015; Murphy et al., 2014). Clinicians should screen for PANS subtype of OCD given that treatment may include a concurrent course of antibiotics for an infection. If a PANS subtype of OCD is suspected, the clinician should promptly refer the child for a physical and medical evaluation with a general practitioner, pediatrician, or child psychiatrist.

CONCLUSIONS

Assessing and diagnosing OCD in children and young people can be a complex task and requires a sound knowledge of the phenomenology of OCD. It is a normal experience for young people to have thoughts that make them feel anxious, scared, or worried. A variety of ritualized and rule-bound behaviors are also quite typical for children at certain developmental stages. Clinicians therefore need to consider key criteria including the time spent preoccupied with thoughts or rituals, the level of interference caused to everyday functioning, the distress caused to the child, and whether the thoughts and rituals can be easily managed by the child or whether the child experiences them as uncontrollable. The way that families respond to, or accommodate, a young person's thoughts and rituals is important as well. If families accommodate the symptoms to such an extent that they are no longer distressing or interfering to the child, then this needs to be factored in to clinical decision-making.

Perhaps more than any other childhood mental health disorder, OCD is highly heterogeneous. Many clinicians will recognize some of the more common OCD symptom presentations, such as contamination fears and associated washing or cleaning rituals, or fears for safety and associated checking behaviors. However, there are many other less well-recognized symptom presentations that require careful assessment. These include urge-related obsessions; touching, tapping, or rubbing behaviors; preoccupations with order and symmetry; intrusive thoughts that are aggressive, sexual, or religious in nature, or strongly held bizarre (e.g., transformation) or superstitious beliefs (e.g., stepping on cracks or joins on surfaces). There is a high degree of overlap between symptoms of OCD and other disorders that are commonly comorbid with OCD. Awareness of key features of these disorders aids differential diagnosis and diagnosis of potentially comorbid conditions.

Intrusive thoughts of an aggressive, sexual, or bizarre nature are unfortunately fairly commonly experienced by young people who suffer from OCD. These experiences are highly distressing and shameful for young people. Accurate diagnosis ensures that concerns regarding risk to self or others are quickly allayed. Repeated or in-depth risk assessments can potentially do more harm than good. The concept of secondary risk is perhaps a more pertinent issue in OCD than primary risk. Secondary risk refers to the unintended negative consequences associated with a young person's OCD symptoms, for example, jeopardizing health as a result of engaging in compulsive behaviors, or significant feelings of low self-worth and suicidal ideation due to the experience of repugnant obsessions. While there are many sobering issues to be mindful of when assessing OCD in young people, it is equally important to remember that OCD is a treatable condition, and accurate diagnosis paves the way for clinicians to implement evidence-based interventions, which are further discussed in this volume.

REFERENCES

Adelman, C. B., & Lebowitz, E. R. (2012). Poor insight in pediatric obsessive compulsive disorder: Developmental considerations, treatment implications, and potential strategies for improving insight. *Journal of Obsessive-Compulsive and Related Disorders*, *1*(2), 119–124. http://dx.doi.org/10.1016/j.jocrd.2012.02.003.

Altman, S. E., & Shankman, S. A. (2009). What is the association between obsessive–compulsive disorder and eating disorders? *Clinical Psychology Review*, *29*(7), 638–646. http://dx.doi.org/10.1016/j.cpr.2009.08.001.

American Psychiatric Association (APA). (2000). *Diagnostic and statistical manual of mental disorders—Text revision (DSM-IV-TR)* (4th ed.). Washington, DC: American Psychiatric Publishing.

American Psychiatric Association (APA). (2013). *Diagnostic and statistical manual of mental disorders (DSM-5)* (5th ed.). Washington, DC: American Psychiatric Association Task Force.

Asmundson, G. J. G., Abramowitz, J. S., Richter, A. A., & Whedon, M. (2010). Health anxiety: Current perspectives and future directions. *Current Psychiatry Reports*, *12*(4), 306–312. http://dx.doi.org/10.1007/s11920-010-0123-9.

Boisseau, C. L., Thompson-Brenner, H., Pratt, E. M., Farchione, T. J., & Barlow, D. H. (2013). The relationship between decision-making and perfectionism in obsessive-compulsive disorder and eating disorders. *Journal of Behavior Therapy and Experimental Psychiatry*, *44*(3), 316–321. http://dx.doi.org/10.1016/j.jbtep.2013.01.006.

Boschen, M. J. (2007). Reconceptualizing emetophobia: A cognitive–behavioral formulation and research agenda. *Journal of Anxiety Disorders*, *21*(3), 407–419. http://dx.doi.org/10.1016/j.janxdis.2006.06.007.

Calvocoressi, L., Lewis, B., Harris, M., Trufan, S. J., Goodman, W. K., McDougle, C. J., et al. (1995). Family accommodation in obsessive-compulsive disorder. *American Journal of Psychiatry*, *152*(3), 441–443.

Chang, K., Frankovich, J., Cooperstock, M., Cunningham, M. W., Latimer, M. E., Murphy, T. K., et al. (2015). Clinical evaluation of youth with pediatric acute-onset neuropsychiatric syndrome (PANS): Recommendations from the 2013 PANS consensus conference. *Journal of Child and Adolescent Psychopharmacology*, *25*(1), 3–13. http://dx.doi.org/10.1089/cap.2014.0084.

Cohen, S. C., Leckman, J. F., & Bloch, M. H. (2013). Clinical assessment of Tourette syndrome and tic disorders. *Neuroscience and Biobehavioral Reviews*, *37*(6), 997–1007. http://dx.doi.org/10.1016/j.neubiorev.2012.11.013.

Coles, M. E., Frost, R. O., Heimberg, R. G., & Rhéaume, J. (2003). "Not just right experiences": Perfectionism, obsessive–compulsive features and general psychopathology. *Behaviour Research and Therapy*, *41*(6), 681–700. http://dx.doi.org/10.1016/S0005-7967(02)00044-X.

Coles, M. E., Mennin, D. S., & Heimberg, R. G. (2001). Distinguishing obsessive features and worries: The role of thought–action fusion. *Behaviour Research and Therapy*, *39*(8), 947–959. http://dx.doi.org/10.1016/S0005-7967(00)00072-3.

Comer, J. S., Kendall, P. C., Franklin, M. E., Hudson, J. L., & Pimentel, S. S. (2004). Obsessing/worrying about the overlap between obsessive–compulsive disorder and generalized anxiety disorder in youth. *Clinical Psychology Review*, *24*(6), 663–683. http://dx.doi.org/10.1016/j.cpr.2004.04.004.

Conceição Costa, D. L., Chagas Assunção, M., Arzeno Ferrão, Y., Archetti Conrado, L., Hajaj Gonzalez, C., Franklin Fontenelle, L., et al. (2012). Body dysmorphic disorder in patients with obsessive-compulsive disorder: Prevalance and clinical correlates. *Depression and Anxiety*, *29*(11), 966–975. http://dx.doi.org/10.1002/da.21980.

Crye, J., Laskey, B., & Cartwright-Hatton, S. (2010). Non-clinical obsessions in a young adolescent population: Frequency and association with metacognitive variables. *Psychology and Psychotherapy: Theory, Research and Practice*, *83*(1), 15–26.

du Toit, P. L., van Kradenburg, J., Niehaus, D., & Stein, D. J. (2001). Comparison of obsessive-compulsive disorder patients with and without comorbid putative obsessive-compulsive spectrum disorders using a structured clinical interview. *Comprehensive Psychiatry*, *42*(4), 291–300. http://dx.doi.org/10.1053/comp.2001.24586.

Eisen, J. L., Phillips, K. A., Coles, M. E., & Rasmussen, S. A. (2004). Insight in obsessive compulsive disorder and body dysmorphic disorder. *Comprehensive Psychiatry*, *45*(1), 10–15. http://dx.doi.org/10.1016/j.comppsych.2003.09.010.

Evans, D. W., Leckman, J. F., Carter, A., Reznick, J. S., Henshaw, D., King, R. A., et al. (1997). Ritual, habit, and perfectionism: The prevalence and development of compulsive-like behavior in normal young children. *Child Development*, *68*(1), 58–68. http://dx.doi.org/10.2307/1131925.

Fernández de la Cruz, L., Barrow, F., Bolhuis, K., Krebs, G., Volz, C., Nakatani, E., et al. (2013). Sexual obsessions in pediatric obsessive compulsive disorder: Clinical characteristics and treatment outcomes. *Depression and Anxiety*, *30*(8), 732–740. http://dx.doi.org/10.1002/da.22097.

Goodman, W. K., Price, L. H., Rasmussen, S. A., Mazure, C., Fleischmann, R. L., Hill, C. L., et al. (1989). The Yale-Brown obsessive compulsive scale. I. Development, use, and reliability. *Archives of General Psychiatry*, *46*, 1006–1011. http://dx.doi.org/10.1001/archpsyc.1989.01810110048007.

Jassi, A. D., Patel, N., Lang, K., Heyman, I., & Krebs, G. (2016). Ritualised eating in young people with obsessive compulsive disorder; clinical characteristics and treatment outcomes. *Journal of Obsessive-Compulsive and Related Disorders*, *8*, 1–8. http://dx.doi.org/10.1016/j.jocrd.2015.11.002.

Kircanski, K., Peris, T. S., & Piacentini, J. (2013). Assessment of tics and comorbid obsessive–compulsive symptoms. In D. McKay & A. E. Storch (Eds.), *Handbook of assessing variants and complications in anxiety disorders* (pp. 63–75). New York, NY: Springer New York.

Langley, A. K., Lewin, A. B., Bergman, R. L., Lee, J. C., & Piacentini, J. (2010). Correlates of comorbid anxiety and externalizing disorders in childhood obsessive compulsive disorder. *European Child and Adolescent Psychiatry*, *19*(8), 637–645. http://dx.doi.org/10.1007/s00787-010-0101-0.

Langlois, F., Freeston, M. H., & Ladouceur, R. (2000). Differences and similarities between obsessive intrusive thoughts and worry in a non-clinical population: Study 1. *Behaviour Research and Therapy*, *38*(2), 157–173. http://dx.doi.org/10.1016/S0005-7967(99)00027-3.

Lavell, C. H., Farrell, L. J., & Zimmer-Gembeck, M. J. (2014). Do obsessional belief domains relate to body dysmorphic concerns in undergraduate students? *Journal of Obsessive-Compulsive and Related Disorders*, *3*(4), 354–358. http://dx.doi.org/10.1016/j.jocrd.2014.10.001.

Leckman, J. F., Denys, D., Simpson, H. B., Mataix-Cols, D., Hollander, E., Saxena, S., et al. (2010). Obsessive-compulsive disorder: A review of the diagnostic criteria and possible subtypes and dimensional specifiers for DSM-V. *Depression and Anxiety*, *27*(6), 507–527. http://dx.doi.org/10.1002/da.20669.

Leonard, H. L., Goldberger, E. L., Rapoport, J. L., Cheslow, D. L., & Swedo, S. E. (1990). Childhood rituals: Normal development or obsessive-compulsive symptoms? *Journal of the American Academy of Child and Adolescent Psychiatry*, *29*(1), 17–23. http://dx.doi.org/10.1097/00004583-199001000-00004.

Lewin, A. B., Menzel, J., & Strober, M. (2013). Assessment and treatment of comorbid anorexia nervosa and obsessive–compulsive disorder. In A. E. Storch & D. McKay (Eds.), *Handbook of treating variants and complications in anxiety disorders* (pp. 337–348). New York, NY: Springer New York.

Lewin, A. B., & Piacentini, J. (2010). Evidence-based assessment of child obsessive compulsive disorder: Recommendations for clinical practice and treatment research. *Child & Youth Care Forum*, *39*(2), 73–89. http://dx.doi.org/10.1007/s10566-009-9092-8.

Mataix-Cols, D., Nakatani, E., Micali, N., & Heyman, I. (2008). Structure of obsessive-compulsive symptoms in pediatric OCD. *Journal of the American Academy of Child and Adolescent Psychiatry*, *47*(7), 773–778. http://dx.doi.org/10.1097/CHI.0b013e31816b73c0.

Miller, C. H., & Hedges, D. W. (2008). Scrupulosity disorder: An overview and introductory analysis. *Journal of Anxiety Disorders*, *22*(6), 1042–1058. http://dx.doi.org/10.1016/j.janxdis.2007.11.004.

Milliner-Oar, E. L., Cadman, J. H., & Farrell, L. J. (2016). Treatment of aggressive obsessions in childhood obsessive-compulsive disorder. In E. A. Storch & A. B. Lewin (Eds.), *Clinical handbook of obsessive-compulsive and related disorders* (pp. 149–169). Switzerland: Springer International Publishing.

Morris, S. H., Jaffee, S. R., Goodwin, G. P., & Franklin, M. E. (2016). Hoarding in children and adolescents: A review. *Child Psychiatry and Human Development*, *47*(5), 740–750. http://dx.doi.org/10.1007/s10578-015-0607-2.

Moulding, R., Aardema, F., & O'Connor, K. P. (2014). Repugnant obsessions: A review of the phenomenology, theoretical models, and treatment of sexual and aggressive obsessional themes in OCD. *Journal of Obsessive-Compulsive and Related Disorders*, *3*(2), 161–168. http://dx.doi.org/10.1016/j.jocrd.2013.11.006.

Murphy, T. K., Gerardi, D. M., & Leckman, J. F. (2014). Pediatric acute-onset neuropsychiatric syndrome. *Psychiatric Clinics of North America*, *37*(3), 353–374. http://dx.doi.org/10.1016/j.psc.2014.06.001.

Neil, N., & Sturmey, P. (2014). Assessment and treatment of obsessions and compulsions in individuals with autism spectrum disorders: A systematic review. *Review Journal of Autism and Developmental Disorders*, *1*(1), 62–79. http://dx.doi.org/10.1007/s40489-013-0006-1.

Pertusa, A., Fullana, M. A., Singh, S., Alonso, P., Menchón, J. M., & Mataix-Cols, D. (2008). Compulsive hoarding: OCD symptom, distinct clinical syndrome, or both? *American Journal of Psychiatry*, *165*(10), 1289–1298.

Purdon, C. (2004). Cognitive-behavioral treatment of repugnant obsessions. *Journal of Clinical Psychology*, *60*(11), 1169–1180. http://dx.doi.org/10.1002/jclp.20081.

Scahill, L., Riddle, M. A., McSwiggin-Hardin, M., Ort, S. I., King, R. A., Goodman, W. K., et al. (1997). Children's Yale-Brown obsessive compulsive scale: Reliability and validity. *Journal of the American Academy of Child and Adolescent Psychiatry*, *36*(6), 844–852. http://dx.doi.org/10.1097/00004583-199706000-00023.

Schubert, J., Ravid, A., & Coles, E. M. (2016). Treatment of "not-just-right experiences" in childhood obsessive-compulsive disorder. In A. E. Storch & B. A. Lewin (Eds.), *Clinical handbook of obsessive-compulsive and related disorders: A case-based approach to treating pediatric and adult populations* (pp. 197–210). Cham: Springer International Publishing.

Sykes, M., Boschen, M. J., & Conlon, E. G. (2016). Comorbidity in emetophobia (specific phobia of vomiting). *Clinical Psychology & Psychotherapy*, *23*(4), 363–367. http://dx.doi.org/10.1002/cpp.1964.

Veale, D., Boocock, A., Gournay, K., Dryden, W., Shah, F., Willson, R., et al. (1996). Body dysmorphic disorder. A survey of fifty cases. *The British Journal of Psychiatry*, *169*(2), 196–201. http://dx.doi.org/10.1192/bjp.169.2.196.

Veale, D., Freeston, M. H., Krebs, G., Heyman, I., & Salkovskis, P. (2009). Risk assessment and management in obsessive–compulsive disorder. *Advances in Psychiatric Treatment*, *15*(5), 332–343. http://dx.doi.org/10.1192/apt.bp.107.004705.

Veale, D., Hennig, C., & Gledhill, L. (2015). Is a specific phobia of vomiting part of the obsessive compulsive and related disorders? *Journal of Obsessive-Compulsive and Related Disorders*, *7*, 1–6. http://dx.doi.org/10.1016/j.jocrd.2015.08.002.

Vrana, S. R., Cuthbert, B. N., & Lang, P. J. (1986). Fear imagery and text processing. *Psychophysiology*, *23*(3), 247–253. http://dx.doi.org/10.1111/j.1469-8986.1986.tb00626.x.

Weems, C. F., Silverman, W. K., & La Greca, A. M. (2000). What do youth referred for anxiety problems worry about? Worry and its relation to anxiety and anxiety disorders in children and adolescents. *Journal of Abnormal Child Psychology*, *28*(1), 63–72. http://dx.doi.org/10.1023/a:1005122101885.

Wu, M. S., McGuire, J. F., Martino, C., Phares, V., Selles, R. R., & Storch, E. A. (2016). A meta-analysis of family accommodation and OCD symptom severity. *Clinical Psychology Review*, *45*, 34–44. http://dx.doi.org/10.1016/j.cpr.2016.03.003.

Wu, M. S., Rudy, B. M., & Storch, E. A. (2014). Obsessions, compulsions, and repetitive behavior: Autism and/or OCD. In T. E. Davis, III,, S. W. White, & T. H. Ollendick (Eds.), *Handbook of autism and anxiety* (pp. 107–120). Cham: Springer International Publishing.

Chapter 3

Psychoeducation for Children, Parents, and Family Members About Obsessive-Compulsive Disorder and Cognitive Behavior Therapy

Gudmundur Skarphedinsson* **and Bernhard Weidle**[†,‡]
**Sorlandet Hospital, Kristiansand, Norway,* [†]*Norwegian University of Science and Technology, Trondheim, Norway,* [‡]*St. Olavs University Hospital, Trondheim, Norway*

Psychoeducation is the most important task in order to establish a common understanding of the nature of obsessive-compulsive disorder (OCD) and its treatment between therapist, child, and parents. Treatment of OCD in terms of exposure and response prevention (E/RP) is more challenging than other psychotherapies, because it depends on compliance with anxiety-provoking exposure exercises. Understanding the treatment rationale and compliance with exposure instructions is significantly related to lower posttreatment OCD symptom severity in an adult sample, which suggests that a strong emphasis on psychoeducation may lay the groundwork for subsequent success (Abramowitz, Franklin, Zoellner, & DiBernardo, 2002). The main aim of psychoeducation is to build a model of understanding the symptoms and the treatment allowing all parties involved to work together as a team. To reach this goal, information should be balanced and based on current research and clinical experience. This chapter describes a step-by-step process and instructions for therapists on how to provide psychoeducation to children and adolescents with OCD and their caretakers or relatives. In this chapter we use the term children referring to children and adolescents. When children and adolescents are distinguished, this is indicated. We also use the term parents referring to all caretakers and relatives involved in the therapeutic process.

The Clinician's Guide to Cognitive-Behavioral Therapy for Childhood Obsessive-Compulsive Disorder
http://dx.doi.org/10.1016/B978-0-12-811427-8.00003-4

OCD INFORMATION

Basic Principles

Initially it is important to build rapport with the child and the parents. Among the strategies to initiate the process would be to investigate the strengths and interests of the child and to let the child tell about hobbies or other activities she or he likes or masters. This process may reduce anxiety and contributes to a relaxed atmosphere. In addition, the therapist may identify skills which could be helpful and later used as examples and metaphors during the treatment. For example, if a child excels in sport, music, gaming, etc., the therapist can ask how she learned these skills. The likely answer is by practicing or training a lot, a model which subsequently can be used as parallel to exposure exercises. After the foundations for rapport are laid, basic information about OCD is provided. How much information the child and the parents have may vary a lot. Therefore a good starting point for a discussion is to ask what the family knows about the disorder so far, including their ideas of treatment. The parents may have misconceptions about OCD that may be necessary to correct, for example, that OCD is just a bad habit or a lack of willpower. Children might be afraid of "losing their mind or turning crazy," as they experience the intrusiveness of the obsessions. An initial exploration of the family's knowledge and ideas about OCD is crucial in order to adjust information to their concepts and level of understanding. Based on the families' level of knowledge, information about the nature of OCD and its treatment is provided. The therapist should convey hope and optimism communicating an expectation that the patient will improve as a result of the treatment. Using humor links OCD to a different affect and helps alleviate the embarrassment and demoraliziation children often feel as a result of OCD. Since children are frequently secretive about their symptoms, laughing at ridiculous aspects of OCD (not at the child) can help children discuss OCD in a less threatening context and contribute to a trustful therapeutic relation. We think it is important to present information in tune with the family's conversational style, for example, using a lay-language format. Not all children with OCD identify the associated unpleasant feelings as anxiety. If the child's experience is disgust or that something is "just not right," it is important to adjust the terminology used to the child's description. A quality indicator for the information given is to make sure that it is relevant for the addressee by relating it to the child's symptoms, and encouraging reflection upon how information such as this represents the family's own experience with OCD. Another important tool to reassure that information is absorbed by the child and the parents is repetition of the most relevant clues (take home massage) applied to different situations and illustrated from different angles, when appropriate. This is relevant not only for the initial psychoeducation process described in this chapter but also for all subsequent sessions throughout therapy.

Developmental Concerns

In general, all information should be provided in a developmentally appropriate manner. Therefore in the first sessions the therapist needs to evaluate the child's cognitive and social skills to adjust psychoeducation accordingly. Psychoeducation is different for a 7-year-old compared to a 15-year-old teenager, although the general structure could be the same. The therapist uses examples and metaphors fitting with the child's developmental level, social temperament, and attention span. Younger children usually have different emotional needs and shorter attention span. They will need more supervision and time for play and activities. Older children are probably more focused on peers' attitudes, and the therapist should be prepared for more discussion and debate. The therapist should keep in mind that a working alliance with the child is a crucial part of the therapy. Therefore significant efforts to promote this alliance are important and should not be missed. This means to address the most relevant parts of the information directly to the child. Depending on the families' relations, often it is an advantage to give information to the child and his/her parents together, where questions and explanations could be directed toward the child as much as possible. Most parents are pleased to see the therapist give this information to their child and are content to get informed by "listening in." They, of course, should also be given an opportunity to ask questions and to receive more complicated information in a separate part of the session. Younger children may, for example, be asked to engage in play or wait outside while the therapist discusses controversial or sophisticated (boring) topics with the parents. This is especially true in case of conflicts which may be related to OCD or not, for example, when parents are reluctant to reveal in front of the child that their perception of symptoms is much more severe than the child's. Also for older youth, communication might work best without the presence of the parents, especially if they have a tendency "to take over" or to correct the conversation with the adolescent. If there are no conflicts, for younger children the continuous presence of the parents in the session is often an advantage, as parents may subsequently repeat and refine the information to the child in a manner which is adjusted to the needs of their particular child. The dialog examples in this chapter are predominantly adjusted to younger children as it is the most difficult to find the correct wording for that age group. The therapist needs to be aware of that and adjust the dialog when treating adolescents in order to create the right climate for cooperation. In general, the dialog samples are intended to encourage exploring the child's perspective and inviting to a discussion where a common perspective is developed step by step.

Define OCD: Sample Dialog: Basic Information

Obsessions are disturbing thoughts, images, feelings, or impulses which are coming into your mind again and again, even when you don't want to have them. They may make you anxious, distressed, upset, or feeling disgusted. Kids with OCD are often afraid of dirt or germs, or that something terrible will happen, for example, that they or their parents or siblings may be hurt or die. (The therapist illustrates the theoretical explanation with the actual symptoms of the child or gives examples from other children with OCD.)

Obsessions are usually so unpleasant, that kids and even adult people try to make them disappear by doing things that they think would help, for example, washing frequently, checking things, or repeat things again and again until they feel more comfortable. These actions you do to make the disturbing thoughts go away are called compulsions, for example, when you are washing your hands again and again (use examples from the child's symptoms). Kids often call their behaviors/ compulsions names: habits, rituals, etc. What do you call yours?

Normalize OCD

Some children may be reluctant to talk about their OCD and they underreport symptoms, because they feel ashamed. To address this problem, the therapist can provide background facts about OCD as prevalence, gender ratio, typical course, etc. Another way to "normalize" the disorder is to ask the child about rituals of other family members, friends, etc., or describe a situation where he/ she might perform a compulsion him or herself. A variety of famous people have informed about their rituals; for example, sport professionals, like David Beckham, who performed rituals related to important soccer matches. If a child may know some sports professionals who have rituals, this could be another clue to make OCD less dangerous. Such a discussion can also be used to explain the difference between "normal rituals" and OCD, where the first are not time consuming or in other ways interfering with daily life and can be easily omitted if necessary. Probably the best technique to talk about OCD with a child who denies or underreports symptoms is to tell about other kids with the same or resembling symptoms.

Sample Dialog: Normalize OCD

Research suggests that one or two children out of every one hundred may have OCD. Do you know anybody in your school who has OCD? Do you know anybody from somewhere else that may have OCD? How many kids are in your school? So there may be X children that may have OCD. The reason that you don't know anybody with OCD is probably that they don't tell others about their OCD, just like you. Maybe it is also interesting for you to know that most people may have obsessive thoughts once in a while. For example, sometimes when I am leaving my house, there might come thoughts into my mind whether I have locked the door or not. Sometimes I even go back to check it out. Double checking might be a good thing and prevents you to do mistakes like leaving the door unlocked. But if such thoughts would come again and again and I would have to check the door three, four, or even more times causing that I lose a lot of time and come too late to my job or to a meeting, then it would be a disorder. The problem is not that you have thoughts like this, but that OCD stick these thoughts in your head so you can't leave them and feel very anxious or uncomfortable about them.

Anxiety Response

For all youth, and especially the youngest children, it is immensely important to explain OCD behavior in a way that they understand it. For instance, talking about the anxiety response as a normal and an adaptive response that helps us in various situations and has helped mankind from prehistoric times is helpful to foster insight and compliance. A conclusion where the child and the therapist together find out what the difference is between a normal anxiety response and OCD-driven anxiety reframes OCD and prepares for the understanding of the irrational nature of the anxiety.

Sample Dialog: Anxiety Response Is Adaptive and Helped Humans to Survive

All people experience anxiety or being scared or nervous sometimes. Anxiety is a normal and actually important feeling, which helps us to guard us against dangers. Without feeling anxious we would be doing all sorts of dangerous things. What do you think would happen to someone walking into a busy street without being afraid of or thinking about whether cars were coming? Of course he might be hit by a car. That is obviously not good. Anxiety is a part of us humans. So it has been with us from the beginning. In fact, feeling anxious is what protects us from dangerous things in the wilderness. In Stone Age being afraid helped people to survive. For instance, in this story from prehistoric times, two humans saw a lion nearby. One gets afraid and runs as quickly as possible away but the other is not afraid and does not run or try to defend himself with weapons. What do you think that happens to the guy who was not afraid? He probably gets eaten by the lion.

So anxiety is a good thing because it makes you do things that are necessary to protect you, for example, look out for cars before you cross the street. What do you think is the difference between the anxiety for fast approaching cars or lions and anxiety caused by OCD? Kids with OCD get afraid or anxious about things that in fact are not dangerous at all or only a little bit dangerous. OCD makes them think that something is very dangerous, but when they think about it, it really is not so dangerous. So the difference is that you have the anxiety, but there is no lion or car or any other real danger approaching you.

False Alarm

Although the anxiety response is normal and adaptive as we have talked about, the anxiety response in people with OCD is not working adaptively. An often used and helpful metaphor for the anxiety response experienced in OCD is a false fire alarm.

Sample Dialog: Anxiety as a False Alarm

Do you know what a fire alarm is used for? A fire alarm is a detector that tells us if a fire has started, for example, at your home or at your school. Have you heard a fire alarm go off? A really unpleasant sound that make us take action immediately. When you heard the fire alarm, was it because of a fire? Ok sometimes the fire alarm goes off without indicating a fire? For example, if someone has cooked a meal or lighted a cigarette too close to the detector. Ok, what is this called? A false alarm. OCD is like a fire alarm that goes off without any fire present. For instance, when someone with OCD gets scared or unpleasant feelings because of a thought, it is like a false alarm. You can think about OCD as an error in your detector for dangers. Just like the fire alarm that gives false alarm, you get alarms of danger, when there is in fact nothing dangerous happening. To reset these false alarms you need to experience and teach your mind that nothing bad will happen, when you ignore your scary or unpleasant feelings.

Externalizing OCD

Many therapeutic manuals emphasize that OCD as a disorder should be externalized in order to make OCD distinct from the child itself (White & Epston, 1990). Externalizing is the process in which the therapist describes and personifies OCD as an "intrusive" phenomenon external to the child in order to reinforce the child's perception of his or her identity as independent from OCD. Externalizing separates OCD also linguistically from the child, referring to a medical condition, while the child is described as normal functioning except from the OCD area. The therapist can, for instance, ask the child to give OCD a bad nickname to underline the view of OCD as a discrete enemy allowing the child and the parents to stand together as allies against OCD rather than fighting or blaming each other. Younger children often like this approach and call their OCD names such as "Bad guy," "Silly," "Super fool" (Fig. 1). It is recommended to discourage the use of nicknames of heroes or symbols with great power, signalizing they might be difficult to defeat. Children who like drawing can be asked to make an illustration of the externalized and personified foe. Adolescents may find this childish, and they often refer to OCD by its medical name. However, the principle of externalizing OCD is the same.

CAUSES OF OCD

As a principle, the therapist should be prepared for a detailed discussion of OCD as a neurobehavioral disorder and its causes with both children or adolescents and parents, but it is important to adjust both amount and content to the situation, the need, and the capacity of the family. An overload of information which the family is not able to absorb might lead to as much confusion as a lack of information. In the following paragraph, we present the most recent scientific representation on different etiological models of OCD to constitute a background for the therapist's discussion with the family and for answering potential questions. A sample dialog for how this information can be reduced and applied in clinical praxis is provided as well.

FIG. 1 Externalizing OCD: Super fool commanding "Do as I say" (Alternative 1) and Mr. White whispering obsessions and anxious thoughts (Alternative 2).

The vast majority of parents and many young people want to know why OCD developed or they have their own concepts about the causes. It is very helpful to explore their personal ideas and beliefs on what caused OCD. This approach will allow to confirm or, if needed, to correct and modify their understanding. In addition, the therapist can adjust the amount and language style of psychoeducation to the level which is most appropriate for this individual family.

Biological Model

Several neurobiological models of OCD pathogenesis have been proposed (Huey et al., 2008), all of which suggest that several substructures within the frontal-striatal-thalamic-cortical networks (Alexander, DeLong, & Strick, 1986) play a role in OCD. Presumably, the networks involve both routine- and goal-directed behaviors, more specifically motor control, procedural learning, cognition, emotion, and motivation (Huey et al., 2008; Menzies et al., 2008). In the prefrontal cortex, these include the orbitofrontal cortex (possibly the source of obsessions and intentions of rituals), anterior cingulate cortex (signaling whether behavior has reached its intended goal), and dorsolateral prefrontal cortex (cognitive flexibility and response inhibition) (Brem et al., 2012; Huey et al., 2008). Several researchers have proposed that the basal ganglia, which project inhibitory and excitatory control to the cortex in order to balance behaviors and cognitions, are overactive in OCD patients and project excessive excitatory signals to the cortex (Abramowitz, Taylor, & McKay, 2009; Huyser, Veltman, de Haan, & Boer, 2009; MacMaster, O'Neill, & Rosenberg, 2008). In addition, different neurotransmitters modulate activities within these loops (e.g., serotonin, dopamine, glutamate, and gamma-aminobutyric acid) (MacMaster, 2010; MacMaster et al., 2008; Menzies et al., 2008; Rosenberg & Keshavan, 1998). Other areas may also play a role in OCD, such as the brainstem (Jenike et al., 1996; Szechtman & Woody, 2004), the amygdala (Szeszko et al., 2004), and the corpus callosum (Rosenberg et al., 1997). However, we don't know for sure whether these neurobiological abnormalities are the cause of OCD or if they simply initiate following OCD onset. Research in this field continues and we will receive more knowledge in the future.

For the parent and the youth, the important message is that OCD is a neurobehavioral disorder and not, for example, a bad habit. The therapist can use analogies to medical illnesses such as asthma or diabetes. Conceptualizing OCD as a medical disorder reduces stigma and minimizes possible blame toward the child for the symptoms. The analogy to a somatic disorder applies also to the therapeutic approach: OCD is rooted in disordered information processing in the brain. Therefore changes in symptoms brought by cognitive behavior therapy (CBT) should reflect changes in brain function, which has been supported by research. For instance, researchers studying the effect of both CBT and selective serotonin reuptake inhibitor (SSRI) found revolutionary changes in brain function before and after treatment (Baxter et al., 1996; Schwartz, Stoessel, Baxter, Martin, & Phelps, 1996). So people with OCD can be approached similarly as people with, for instance, diabetes—the only thing that differs is the target organ (pancreas's failure to produce enough insulin for juvenile diabetes vs dysfunctional brain processes for OCD) and symptoms (high blood sugar levels for diabetes vs obsessions and compulsions for OCD). The treatment for both disorders is correction of the lacking regulation function either by substituting insulin in diabetes or reestablish appropriate anxiety regulation with CBT. As appropriate metaphors to explain OCD to children, CBT manuals have described obsessions as hiccups in the brain or problems with the volume control knob (March & Mulle, 1998), reflecting the analogy to the somatic disorders as outlined earlier. For many children it is attractive to use technical metaphors, for example, that obsessions are like a worry computer chip that sends fear cues inappropriately when no threat is present. Obsessions could be described as OCD causing the brain to turn up the volume of fear resulting in the need to respond to cues that do not deserve any attention.

In cases where information as outlined earlier is not enough to convince parents or children with regard to the benefits of treatment, results of neuroimaging studies showing and explaining pet scan changes from pre- to posttreatment (e.g., from Baxter et al., 1996) could be helpful.

Sample Dialog: Biological Model

We do not exactly know what causes OCD. But, scientists and doctors believe that different factors like genetics and environmental factors together cause OCD and these factors might differ from one person to another. You can look at OCD as any other medical illness. Do you have heard about diabetes? It is a regulation problem in the body. An organ called pancreas does not produce enough of a stuff called insulin which is necessary to keep blood sugar levels in the right range. So it is a problem with the regulation technique. In the same way you can view OCD as a regulation problem in the brain. Imagine your brain as a computer and OCD like a chip sending out error messages to the rest of the computer. This means that a part of your brain sends out wrong messages about things that are dangerous which should not be sent at all. Or it may send out messages that things are very dangerous, instead of a message that this is just a little bit dangerous. It is like the false fire alarms we talked about previously. Do you remember? You get a fire alarm in your brain, when it is in fact only a candle lit, but not a real fire. You may think of it as a problem like the volume regulation of a music device: the volume control knob has stopped working or is stuck causing a very high sound instead of a proper sound level. OCD gives you messages about real big dangers, when there is no danger at all or only a little bit danger. For example, when you go to a public restroom, OCD sends a message that you have to wash your hands many times, if not you will die due to dangerous germs (use example from the child's symptoms). So these erroneous messages cause your feelings of anxiety or disgust. These erroneous messages are what we called obsessions, and the actions you perform to make these thoughts go away (like washing hands over and over again) are what we called compulsions.

Cognitive Behavioral Model

CBT for obsessive-compulsive disorder includes the assumption that the child has learned dysfunctional behavioral patterns regarding obsessional fears. The primary model of OCD as learned behavior (Mowrer, 1960) suggests that (1) obsessional fear develops when a neutral stimulus is paired with an aversive stimulus (classical conditioning), and (2) avoidance behavior develops in order to reduce obsessional anxiety (operant conditioning; negative reinforcement). Thus exposure to obsessional and feared stimuli, such as physical objects or thoughts that are distressful, cause anxiety (or disgust). The role of the rituals is to neutralize or to prevent the negative emotions which then maintain this pattern (negative reinforcement) (Abramowitz, Taylor, & McKay, 2007). However, empirical research does not support the role of classical conditioning in explaining the development of obsessional fear. The onset of OCD is usually gradual and not immediate, which would not be predicted by classical conditioning. Patients do not usually ascribe the onset of OCD to any specific conditioning event. In addition, OCD usually does not include a single type of obsessional fear but rather multiple types of obsessions and fears. Furthermore, new types of obsessions that are not related to previous obsessions tend to develop (Abramowitz et al., 2007). However, the theory explains the maintenance of obsessional fear quite well (Rachman, De Silva, & Roper, 1976; Roper, Rachman, & Hodgson, 1973) and this model has led to the effective treatment of E/RP (McGuire et al., 2015; Ost, Riise, Wergeland, Hansen, & Kvale, 2016).

Cognitive components may also contribute to OCD etiology (Foa & Kozak, 1985; Rachman, 1997; Reed, 1985; Salkovskis, 1985) suggesting that dysfunctional interpretations of normal but intrusive thoughts lead to obsessions and compulsions. These normal thoughts develop into distressing and time-consuming obsessions when they are interpreted as very significant and as a personal responsibility, for example, to avoid harm to self or others. One becomes preoccupied with the thought and tries to control it in any way possible. Compulsions and avoidance behaviors are perceived as maladaptive ways to prevent or remove these thoughts; several examples of distorted thoughts have been identified, including inflated responsibility, distorted interpretations, pathological doubt, overestimation of threat, overimportance of thoughts, and the need to control thoughts (Rachman, 1997).

Sample Dialog: Cognitive Behavior Model/Habituation

There is another important aspect of OCD. If you do something again and again, for example, your OCD rituals, they get stronger. You are in fact teaching your body that it helps to do certain rituals when you get scary or unpleasant thoughts. CBT will teach you how to send a new and better message to your body to make your anxiety go away and why it is important not doing the rituals. By resisting doing rituals you will send the message that nothing bad will happen, even when you don't do the rituals. For every time you send this message, it will make OCD weaker.

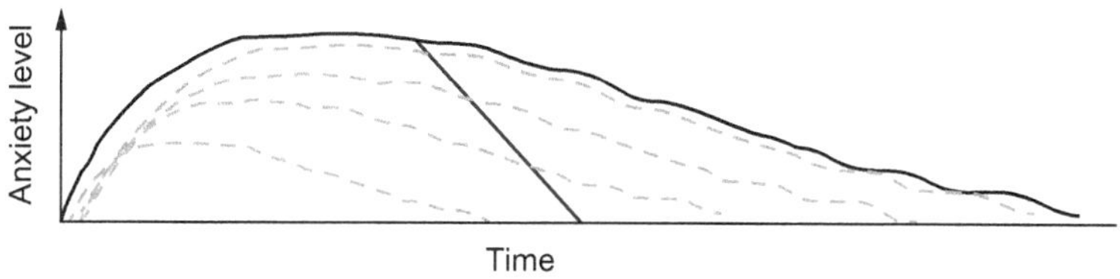

FIG. 2 The anxiety curve.

What do you think will happen if you would not do your ritual [use the description from the child]? Very often your OCD will make you think that the feeling of anxiety [disgust, etc.] will just go higher and higher without stopping. But this is not correct. Usually what happens is that the feeling of anxiety [disgust] will go away after time. Sometimes really fast, sometimes it may take a longer time. Look at Fig. 2. It shows what happens to anxiety, when a ritual is performed (broken line) and if you don't do the ritual (black line). Anxiety comes down either way, because you are not able to be constantly alarmed over long time, except when new threats are coming all the time. Without rituals, it may take much longer time. But the good thing is that it will take less and less time, the more you are practicing of resisting your rituals (dotted line). This means that you will be stronger and stronger and OCD weaker and weaker, if you practice your exposures. And in the end OCD will be so weak that it will not bother you any longer.

Genetic Model

OCD aggregates in families suggesting that members of the family may share both genetic and environmental risk factors. Twin studies indicate an estimated heritability of OCD in the range of 45%–65% (van Grootheest, Cath, Beekman, & Boomsma, 2005). Genetic association studies have investigated more than 200 polymorphisms. The aggregated results demonstrate that multiple genes are associated with OCD (particularly genes related to serotonin regulation and catecholamine modulation) that incrementally increase the likelihood of developing OCD (Taylor, 2013). However, in the most recent metaanalysis the association between genes and OCD was much lower than previously expected (Taylor, 2013) leaving a very large part of the explanation of OCD expression to the environment. However, it might be helpful to ask parents for the presence of OCD symptoms in other family members and to discuss both genetic and learning theories, explaining that OCD can run in families and that the genetic and environmental factors together cause OCD. It is important to emphasize that, although family factors are associated with OCD, it is not parents that cause OCD. On the other hand, OCD is not simply a behavior that is learned and it is neither the parents nor the child's fault.

Sample Dialog: Genetic Model/Familial Causes

Research suggests that OCD has a genetic predisposition. This means that people with OCD have an inherited general tendency to obsessional fear or disgust. So children with a genetic tendency toward OCD are more vulnerable to develop a pattern that leads to OCD than children without this genetic tendency. This means also that OCD may be seen in other family members or in previous generations. However, environmental factors contribute to the outbreak of the disorder. (The therapist should explain that OCD in the child is not the parents fault; although it runs in families the parents did not cause it. So there is no one to blame as less as in the mentioned analogy of a somatic disorder like diabetes.)

Integrated Model: Neurobiological Behavior Model

It is widely acknowledged that an integrated neurobehavioral model where OCD is explained by integrating all the three models: neurobiological, cognitive behavioral, and genetic/familial, gives the patients the currently most accurate knowledge on OCD. OCD is explained as interplay between genetic/familial, cognitive behavioral, and biologic factors: Concrete environmental events trigger unpleasant thoughts (obsessions), eliciting signals of danger and anxiety, which are reinforced by avoiding behavior and compulsions. Exaggerated thoughts about danger and catastrophe (or sometimes disgust or other intolerable feelings) lead to actions which should reduce worry and discomfort. However, OCD symptoms are often so strong that it is difficult to evaluate the situation realistically. Even when the danger is not real, the alarm system is activated. Information about the different aspects of OCD integrating these models as outlined earlier supports the main goal for psychoeducation, namely, engagement in treatment.

CBT RATIONALE AND DEFINITIONS

Treatment Rationale

Motivation to engage in and to comply with therapeutic exposure tasks is crucial for successful treatment of OCD. Understanding the treatment rationale and compliance with exposure instructions was significantly related to lower post-treatment OCD symptom severity in a study with adults with OCD (Abramowitz et al., 2002). Although not studied explicitly in children, this is likely to apply for pediatric OCD as well. If the therapist succeeds in convincing the child that the task is both rational and achievable and the best choice, all subsequent therapeutic work will be easier to accomplish. The mere explanation of an exposure constitutes a mental exposure and might elicit potential distress interfering with both the child's attention and ability to converse with the therapist. On the other hand, it is important to convey an attitude that anxiety is not dangerous without communicating exaggerated reassurance by the therapist. To balance between these ambiguities, it is important to explore and tune in to the child's worries and expectations and adjust psychoeducation appropriately.

Sample Dialog: Rationale for CBT With E/RP and "Habituation"

I want to help you to learn how you can deal with your OCD and not respond to these false alarms, I mean not being anxious or distressed when you don't need to. But what you need to do is to hear the false fire alarm again and again to see that nothing dangerous is happening, even when you don't do your rituals (example from the child). This is what CBT is about. I will help you not to do all these things OCD want you to do and probably a part of you will feel a bit anxious or uncomfortable. It is called exposure. But the other part of you will be proud and glad and you will see that being anxious or afraid because of false alarms is not dangerous.

Exposure and Response Prevention

Exposure means that the child exposes him or herself to feared objects, situations, or thoughts. Response prevention means that the child does not perform the rituals or compulsions. Exposure can be done as defined exercises, for example, can the child touch a "dirty" door handle without washing the fingers afterward. Mental exposure means that the child imagines an anxiety-provoking situation. This can be done, for example, by describing such a situation in detail or by role-play. The most important part of the exposure is that the child experiences that anxiety either diminishes (habituation) or that he/she is able to tolerate the anxiety without performing rituals. To promote this experience the child has to be encouraged to remain long enough in the frightening situation. Previous research on CBT mainly focused on the habituation process, based on the *emotional processing theory* (Foa & Kozak, 1986). The assumption here is that anxiety level will be reduced for every time an exposure is performed. However, the research of Craske et al. (2008) based on *Inhibitory learning theory* demonstrated, that even when exposure in general leads to habituation, anxiety reduction is not an absolutely necessary condition for improvement over time. This means that it is not required that anxiety diminishes during the exercise in order to lead to a successful exposure and to improvement of OCD. If a child experiences that anxiety remains unchanged during exposure, it is important to change the focus. Training to seek out and tolerate anxiety-provoking situations, the child will learn that tolerating anxiety provoked by false alarm might be very unpleasant but is not dangerous. An example is again a child who is avoiding touching the door handle because of fear of contamination and germs. In this case the exposure exercise will be to touch the handle until the anxiety is either reduced or tolerated. However, children and adolescents with OCD may have impaired inhibitory learning and contingency awareness in extinction (see McGuire et al., 2016).

Sample Dialog: Exposure and Response Prevention

I will be your coach for the next weeks teaching you how you can overcome OCD. We will work together meeting every week and then you will train things you have learned at home in between our sessions. How does this sound for you?

If you want to get rid of OCD we have two important tools, the first is called exposure and the second is called response prevention. Exposure happens when you are doing things that OCD says you should not do; for example, touch a door knob on a public restroom. Response prevention happens if you tolerate anxiety or other unpleasant feelings without performing compulsions or rituals; for example, don't wash your hands over and over again. Maybe you think that the anxiety will increase and you will not be able to tolerate these feelings? But what actually will happen, if you don't do your rituals is the following: Either will anxiety and the unpleasant feeling decrease until there is only a little bit or no anxiety at all left, which is very good, of course. The other possibility is that you experience that tolerating anxiety is not dangerous, just unpleasant, which is an important experience as well.

Did you ever use a reset button on an electronic device? What happened? Remember the false alarms we were talking about previously? There is a way to reset the stuck volume control button that sends all these false alarms to your brain. You have to send the right message to your brain, that these false alarms are not dangerous. By sending the message "I know inside, this is a false alarm and there is no danger" again and again, eventually your brain and your body will believe in the right message and your obsessions fade away. This is a little bit like a roller coaster in an adventure park. The first time most kids are a bit scared, but if you take the same roller coaster again and again it isn't scaring at all anymore. In this treatment you are the one who decides how fast we move on and how much exercise you are able to do. If I would force you to do exercises, it wouldn't work. How does this sound?

There is another important point: Remember, I said you are the one who decides how fast we move on, but is important to move on continuously. It is okay to handle OCD step by step, but it is not a good idea to stop challenging OCD, because then OCD can win. Therefore we will not stop working, and my job is to motivate you to continue with your efforts in order to assure that you are the one who wins over OCD and not the other way round. Do you think this sounds possible?

Beginning the exposure exercises may feel like going into a swimming pool or the sea at the beach. Have you done that? It feels rather uncomfortable to dip your toes into it for the first time. It feels cold. But guess what happens after a while? You get used to it and it doesn't feel cold anymore. In CBT you and I will do all these things that feel scary. But we will together find out the things that are only a little bit scaring and start with them. When you have done it a few times it gets easier. When that happens we can start to do things that are more difficult.

To perform an easy "test exercise" demonstrates the task for the child probably better than any explanation. In addition, this will allow assessing the patient's ability to tolerate anxiety, his or her insight, motivation and will to comply with the treatment.

Experiences from test exposure establish the base for the next exposure level in order to avoid initial exercises that are too difficult. After the child is succeeding in his resistance against OCD, exercises from the upper range of the symptom hierarchy may be approached.

Sample Dialog: Exposure Demonstration

Let us test how this is working. Look here is my trash can. Would it be difficult for you to touch it outside? (Inside, remove a piece from it, etc.; the therapist chose an exposure exercise from the child's actual symptoms, which should be easily to accomplish, just to show how exposure works). If all suggestions for exposure demonstration are too frightening for the child, a symbolic exposure is chosen; for example, keep the fingers 4 in. (or more) above the trash can. In this situation it is important to praise the effort reframing the situation: Wow, I saw this was really difficult for you, but you were brave and kept your fingers very close to the trash can. If there is no situation or surface at the office eliciting symptoms, a mental exposure, i.e., talking through a situation in which OCD symptoms were present and planning how to do an exposure in the next session, is an alternative choice.

Disgust

The concept of disgust and its role vs anxiety in OCD is to a certain degree investigated in adults, while there is still little research concerning children and adolescents (Ludvik, Boschen, & Neumann, 2015; McKay & Tsao, 2005; Taboas, Ojserkis, & McKay, 2015). As mentioned earlier, some children do not experience anxiety as a consequence of their obsessions, but only disgust. They might, for example, exhibit extreme avoidance behavior or excessive cleaning, not because they are afraid of any dangerous diseases or other catastrophes, but they experience a surface or a place as intolerably disgusting. It is helpful to discuss the physiologic function of disgust which is to prevent humans from consuming rotten food. The child may easily acknowledge that disgust may be exaggerated without decaying biological material being present in analogy to the model of exaggerated anxiety due to false alarm. However, it takes often much longer time to habituate to feelings of disgust than to anxiety (Mason & Richardson, 2012; Olatunji, Wolitzky-Taylor, Willems, Lohr, & Armstrong, 2009). Therefore it is helpful preparing the patient that exposure not necessarily will result in a fast reduction of disgust, but rather fade away gradually by time, if the brain learns that exposure to disgusting items is not dangerous and can be tolerated.

Metacognitive Perspective

When a child is exposed to a feared cue and resists performing the usual compulsive response, he or she will invariably experience increased anxiety and must therefore be prepared to expect and tolerate that anxiety. To tolerate unpleasant feelings like anxiety is in general more difficult for children than for adults. A common agreement that the demands to the child should be realistic and achievable is important for treatment motivation. In addition, the therapist can make sure that treatment will proceed at the child's chosen pace (i.e., the "allies" won't suddenly become enemies by asking the child to do the impossible). If these conditions fail to motivate the child to engage in exposure exercises, it can be helpful to explore the metacognitive aspects of compulsions (Fisher & Wells, 2008; Simons, Schneider, & Herpertz-Dahlmann, 2006), for example, by discussing the differences between obsessive thoughts and normal thoughts. To help the child to find out, that the only difference is the significance the child is giving the thoughts might be relieving. Subsequently, it might become easier tolerating and ignoring the unwanted thoughts. This technique is especially helpful, if the child has predominantly obsessions without or with only few compulsions. See Chapter 7 for further discussion of cognitive skills for OCD.

Sample Dialog: Metacognition/Normal Thoughts

What is the difference between normal thoughts, let us say "the house over there is gray" (or any other example) and your obsession (example from the child)? Ok, the one is frightening and the other not. What makes this thought frightening? Will all children/people think this is frightening? Will I think this thought is frightening? Ok, it is because you think this thought is frightening. So, not the thoughts are the problem but that you think they are a problem and that you do what they want you to do. People have a lot of strange thoughts in their mind. There is sex and crime and rock "n" roll all the time, but people do not act out all thoughts coming in mind. People without OCD do not pay attention to these thoughts and just let them come and go. Not that you have these thoughts is the problem but that they get stuck and bother you. OCD wants you to be 100% certain, but nothing in life is 100% certain. Theoretically a roof tile can fall down from the roof and hit my head, when I leave my house. Still, I and most other people choose to take that risk and go out every day. What do you think about taking the risk?

CBT AND MEDICATIONS

It is recommended to combine CBT and medication, predominantly SSRIs for youth with moderate to severe OCD (Geller & March, 2012). Although, there is some evidence that the sequential application of SSRI+CBT vs pill CBT alone does not differ significantly (Ivarsson et al., 2015; Storch, Bussing, et al., 2013). The combination of CBT and SSRI is also recommended when CBT is not (sufficiently) effective (Geller & March, 2012), although continuing CBT might be as effective (Skarphedinsson et al., 2014) (see also Chapter 9). In a study with adults (Tolin, Maltby, Diefenbach, Hannan, & Worhunsky, 2004) responders to a combination of medication and CBT had reduced risk for relapse, compared to those who used medication only, which is known to be associated with high relapse rates. When CBT is combined with medication it is important to explain the potential synergy between CBT and the drug. The therapist underlines that medication is an auxiliary tool which probably will help to reduce the level of anxiety. The child needs to take advantage of this situation, allowing performing exposure exercises, which previously were impossible. Another important point to mention is the need to intensify CBT/exposure work during the process of gradual cessation of medication, after treatment response is obtained, in order to prevent relapse. Sometimes children attribute all treatment effects exclusively to the medication, depreciating their own contribution. Such an attitude may lead to lower self-confidence during discontinuation of medication, causing higher levels of anxiety that OCD might relapse completely. Therefore the therapist emphasizes the role of medication as a helping tool to turn down the volume of the false alarm in the brain, but E/RP serves to reset it. If the child has succeeded with exposures, medication cessation will be much easier.

The child's and the parents' compliance with medication treatment is crucial. In the same way as CBT, also medication is a collaboration project with the family. To understand the treatment rationale improves motivation for treatment. In terms of psychoeducation, the contribution of medication as auxiliary tool in order to enable exposure can be illustrated metaphorically like using water wings in order to learn to swim. Just as water wings are helpful when first learning to swim, medications are helpful when implementing CBT and exposure exercises and can later be withdrawn when they are no longer needed.

Sample Dialog: Water Wings

Can you swim? Do you remember how you learned to swim? Did you learn it in school or from your parents? Some kids learn swimming right away with a trainer or a parent supporting them from beyond and helping them to keep the nose out of the water. Do you remember how you did it? Do you have seen water wings or floaties that you can blow up and fix around the arms? Some kids use water wings to learn to swim, especially those who are very afraid. Just as water wings are helpful when you start learning to swim, medications can help to get your anxiety down and to start practicing swimming movements. Exactly in the same way as with water wings it is important to practice and to get skilled, that you can later remove them when they are no longer needed. If kids don't practice the movements, they will not learn the swimming skills. Some kids gradually inflate the wings with smaller amounts of air, as they become more and more skilled in swimming. Likewise we reduce the medication gradually, when you have practiced your exposure skills enough and are able to continue without medication aid.

CHALLENGING/COMPLEX ISSUES

For the majority of children, psychoeducation about the treatable nature of the disorder provided individually according to the principles described earlier and the desire to obtain better quality of life are sufficient motivators to comply with treatment recommendations. However, in a considerable number of young patients presenting for assessment of OCD, treatment motivation is very low or lacking completely. In contrast to adult patients who have to make a decision to seek help, children may be brought to treatment by their parents without actually wishing it. In these circumstances psychoeducation has to address complex issues like lacking motivation or ambivalence to therapy, poor insight, low compliance, poor family function including high family accommodation or low parent support and most of all presence of comorbidity which is frequent in OCD. The next two paragraphs review briefly the most common challenges and give suggestions for how to adjust psychoeducation to complex issues and comorbidity and how to solve problems. Sometimes only one of the following factors may be present; unfortunately in clinical praxis a combination of several of these factors is more likely and has to be dealt with, for example, in a child with OCD, comorbid attention deficit hyperactivity disorder (ADHD), frequent rage outbursts, and poor insight due to limited cognitive capacity.

Family Function/Family Accommodation

As outlined earlier family members have an important role as supporters for the child during the treatment course. Family factors such as conflict, blame, and poor cohesion have been found to influence response to CBT in pediatric OCD (Peris et al., 2012). Family issues such as conflicts, blame, rearing style, accommodation to OCD, or lacking encouragement to conduct exposure, for example, if parents have their own OCD symptoms should be assessed and addressed. For example, if parents accommodate all compulsive needs of the child and the whole family engages in avoidance behavior and cleaning routines, the child has little incentives to engage in demanding exposure exercises. In these cases additional sessions with psychoeducation for the parents alone might be essential, allowing them to understand that despite of good intentions, they help OCD, but not their child. Depending on the nature and the reasons for insufficient or lacking support from family members, additional psychoeducation or other measures dealing with the actual family problem might be required.

Poor Motivation

Motivation to engage in exposure task is crucial for the outcome of the therapy. Poor motivation may be caused by a variety of reasons such as not believing that the treatment will help, lack of self-confidence for being able to comply with exposure, anxiety about potential negative consequences of engaging in treatment (e.g., high workload or high level of anxiety), and the presence of comorbid disorders. The reasons for lacking motivation should be investigated and removed or dealt with, for example, by adding motivational strategies to psychoeducation (Weidle & Skarphedinsson, 2016).

Poor Insight

Some children show poor insight into the irrational and unreasonable nature of the obsessions as specified in the diagnostic categories "poor or absent insight" in the DSM-5 (American Psychiatric Association, 2013). Poor insight is associated with earlier age at onset, greater symptom severity, and near-delusional processes (Catapano et al., 2010; Kozak & Foa, 1994). Also comorbid autism spectrum disorder (ASD) or subclinical autistic traits may reduce insight, due to impaired ability to introspection, literal perception of language (e.g., exaggerated alerts of danger in the media) and impaired social judgment (Kozak & Foa, 1994). The youngest patients may lack insight into the exaggerated nature of their obsessions and the irrationality of their compulsive behavior due to immaturity of their cognitive development. Sometimes more and repeated psychoeducation including CBT techniques like "socratic" questioning, thought experiments, calculations of likelihood, and exploration of cognitions might be helpful to enhance insight. However, a strategy of emphasizing exposure with practical examples as described in the next paragraph and deemphasizing cognitive models might be more fruitful.

Limited Cognitive Capacity

Limited cognitive capacity may be present due to a variety of reasons, namely, low age, intellectual disability, attention deficit, and other developmental disorders. As outlined earlier adjustment to the actual cognitive capacity of the child includes modifying language to the level of understanding of the child and a reduction of psychoeducation to the most important points, emphasizing practical examples of E/RP. By showing in practice how exposure works with easily conductible and concrete examples and multiple repetitions the child will gradually be socialized to the exposure model. Psychoeducative clues are added in small chunks and related to the exposure situation reinforcing the exposure model by explaining and describing and reframing what is happening under exposure.

Sample Dialog During Exposure

Yes, now you are doing exactly what we were talking about. You have the unpleasant feeling of ..., but you are still here tolerating it. Now you are sending this signals which will reset the false alarm, very good, continue.

Comorbidity

Comorbid disorders or subclinical symptoms are frequent in OCD (Ivarsson, Melin, & Wallin, 2008; Storch et al., 2008). If a child has no energy or feels hopeless due to depression, has no goal directedness and low executive functioning due to ADHD, or has poor insight into the OCD disorder due to an ASD, then he or she may be far less motivated to engage in treatment and/or be compliant with treatment requirements. In general, comorbid disorders should be assessed and, if they would likely impede treatment of OCD, they may need to be treated before addressing OCD to improve the final outcome (Storch et al., 2008). To treat comorbidity first, seems to be particularly important, when effective treatments are available. In the following paragraphs we discuss three comorbid conditions which are frequently presenting together with OCD usually requiring adjustments of psychoeducation, either treated or not.

Attention Deficit Hyperactivity Disorder

In children with OCD and comorbid ADHD, the need for medication for the attention deficit should be evaluated before starting with CBT in order to foster better compliance during CBT. However, in any case it will be necessary to adjust the content and amount of psychoeducation to the attention span of the child, focusing on the most important clues, motivating and preparing the child for exposure exercises. In view of the deficits in executive functioning, it is necessary to allow additional time and repeated explanations over time and in different situations with practical examples to allow the child to grasp the clues, which should include checking whether the content was understood or not. In addition, a discussion on how to assure that homework exercises will be performed, for example, with the help of Smartphone alerts and other technical facilities or involving parents to a greater extent in supervising exposure exercises should be a part of the psychoeducational process.

Autism Spectrum Disorders

Between 8% and 37% of individuals with ASD fulfill diagnostic criteria for comorbid OCD (Leyfer et al., 2006; Simonoff et al., 2008). Compulsions and obsessions add significantly to the burden of impairment in ASD (Russell, Mataix-Cols, Anson, & Murphy, 2005). There is growing evidence that CBT, modified and adjusted to the needs of individuals with ASD, might be an effective treatment option (Russell et al., 2013; Storch, Arnold, et al., 2013; Storch, Bussing, et al., 2013). Also subclinical ASD symptoms are found to be common (10%–17%) in children with OCD (Arildskov et al., 2015). Psychoeducation in children with ASD or subsyndromal traits needs to be adjusted to the patients' style of communication, their areas of interest, deficits in executive functioning, social development, and their perception of the environment.

Communication needs to be clear and concrete without ambiguity. Sentences with metaphors and implicit messages can be interpreted literally and should be explained explicitly. Small talk should be avoided. Precise communication in few words with a focus on the essential messages with a clear expression of what is expected helps the child to understand the processes during therapy. An important reward for children with OCD without ASD engaging in successful E/RP is allowing them to participate in the social life with friends and peers again, which is often hampered by OCD. Children with ASD and limited social motivation may not perceive a symptom reduction per se as rewarding. Therefore assessing individual motivation factors, beyond just getting better from OCD, is important. Examples can be that the child will be able to avoid stress when accidentally in contact with germs, to avoid fuss from parents, or to gain more time for the areas of interest, when OCD is conquered. In addition, rewards using areas of special interest or other ways to make therapy interesting; for example, reframing and modeling exposure as "scientific experiment" can be helpful.

Disruptive Behavior

Clinical and subclinical disruptive behavior disorders, for example, oppositional defiant disorder (ODD) and conduct disorder (CD) are associated with increased severity of OCD symptoms and poorer treatment outcome (Storch, Lewin, Geffken, Morgan, & Murphy, 2010; Torp et al., 2015). However, anger outbursts are quite frequent in children with OCD also without comorbid disruptive behavior, often involving limit-setting situations (Storch et al., 2012). In general, the base of aggression in ODD and OCD is different. In ODD the child refuses to recognize authority mainly with the goal to engage in pleasurable activities, while in OCD aggressive behavior usually is provoked by authorities interfering with the need to perform rituals. It is important to differentiate between comorbid ODD/CD and aggression motivated by the need to perform compulsions. Comorbid ODD/CD is associated with high levels of aggression, negativity, and hostility challenging the therapeutic alliance. A solution is first to treat the comorbid ODD or CD, for example, with Parent Management Training (Sukhodolsky, Gorman, Scahill, Findley, & McGuire, 2013), allowing for building an alliance subsequently. In the second case when aggressive behavior is motivated by the need to conduct rituals without interfering by others, reframing and directing anger against OCD and not parents is a helpful psychoeducative technique.

CONCLUSIONS

A strong emphasis on psychoeducation to both the young patients and caregivers involved in the treatment may lay the groundwork for a common understanding of the symptoms and the treatment process. Common understanding is a prerequisite to establish a working alliance as a team. Understanding the treatment rationale and compliance with exposure instructions is vital for the treatment of OCD and directly related to outcome. In case of comorbidity or other circumstances interfering with understanding of the disorder or the treatment, psychoeducation has to be tailored individually and adjusted to the need of the particular family.

REFERENCES

Abramowitz, J. S., Franklin, M. E., Zoellner, L. A., & DiBernardo, C. L. (2002). Treatment compliance and outcome in obsessive-compulsive disorder. *Behavior Modification*, *26*(4), 447–463.

Abramowitz, J. S., Taylor, S., & McKay, D. (2007). Psychological theories of obsessive-compulsive disorder. In E. A. Storch, G. R. Geffken, & T. K. Murphy (Eds.), *Handbook of child and adolescent obsessive-compulsive disorder* (pp. 109–129). Mahawah, NJ: Lawrence Erlbaum Associates.

Abramowitz, J. S., Taylor, S., & McKay, D. (2009). Obsessive-compulsive disorder. *The Lancet*, *374*(9688), 491–499. http://dx.doi.org/10.1016/S0140-6736%2809%2960240-3.

Alexander, G. E., DeLong, M. R., & Strick, P. L. (1986). Parallel organization of functionally segregated circuits linking basal ganglia and cortex. *Annual Review of Neuroscience*, *9*, 357–381.

American Psychiatric Association. (2013). *Diagnostic and statistical manual of mental disorders (DSM-5)* (5th ed.). Washington, DC: American Psychiatric Publishing.

Arildskov, T. W., Hojgaard, D. R., Skarphedinsson, G., Thomsen, P. H., Ivarsson, T., Weidle, B., et al. (2015). Subclinical autism spectrum symptoms in pediatric obsessive-compulsive disorder. *European Child & Adolescent Psychiatry*, *25*, 711–723. http://dx.doi.org/10.1007/s00787-015-0782-5.

Baxter, L. R., Jr., Saxena, S., Brody, A. L., Ackermann, R. F., Colgan, M., Schwartz, J. M., et al. (1996). Brain mediation of obsessive-compulsive disorder symptoms: Evidence from functional brain imaging studies in the human and nonhuman primate. *Seminars in Clinical Neuropsychiatry*, *1*(1), 32–47. http://dx.doi.org/10.1053/SCNP00100032. 00100032 [pii].

Brem, S., Hauser, T. U., Iannaccone, R., Brandeis, D., Drechsler, R., & Walitza, S. (2012). Neuroimaging of cognitive brain function in paediatric obsessive compulsive disorder: A review of literature and preliminary meta-analysis. *Journal of Neural Transmission*, *119*(11), 1425–1448. http://dx.doi.org/10.1007/s00702-012-0813-z.

Catapano, F., Perris, F., Fabrazzo, M., Cioffi, V., Giacco, D., De Santis, V., et al. (2010). Obsessive-compulsive disorder with poor insight: A three-year prospective study. *Progress in Neuro-Psychopharmacology and Biological Psychiatry*, *34*(2), 323–330.

Craske, M. G., Kircanski, K., Zelikowsky, M., Mystkowski, J., Chowdhury, N., & Baker, A. (2008). Optimizing inhibitory learning during exposure therapy. *Behaviour Research and Therapy*, *46*(1), 5–27. http://dx.doi.org/10.1016/j.brat.2007.10.003.

Fisher, P. L., & Wells, A. (2008). Metacognitive therapy for obsessive-compulsive disorder: A case series. *Journal of Behavior Therapy and Experimental Psychiatry*, *39*(2), 117–132.

Foa, E. B., & Kozak, M. J. (1985). Treatment of anxiety disorders: Implications for psychopathology. In A. H. Tuma & J. D. Maser (Eds.), *Anxiety and the anxiety disorders* (pp. 451–452). Hillsdale, NJ: Erlbaum.

Foa, E. B., & Kozak, M. J. (1986). Emotional processing of fear: Exposure to corrective information. *Psychological Bulletin*, *99*(1), 20–35.

Geller, D., & March, J. (2012). Practice parameter for the assessment and treatment of children and adolescents with obsessive-compulsive disorder. *Journal of the American Academy of Child and Adolescent Psychiatry*, *51*(1), 98–113. http://dx.doi.org/10.1016/j.jaac.2011.09.019.

Huey, E. D., Zahn, R., Krueger, F., Moll, J., Kapogiannis, D., Wassermann, E. M., et al. (2008). A psychological and neuroanatomical model of obsessive-compulsive disorder. *The Journal of Neuropsychiatry and Clinical Neurosciences*, *20*(4), 390–408. http://dx.doi.org/10.1176/appi.neuropsych.20.4.390.

Huyser, C., Veltman, D. J., de Haan, E., & Boer, F. (2009). Paediatric obsessive-compulsive disorder, a neurodevelopmental disorder? Evidence from neuroimaging. *Neuroscience and Biobehavioral Reviews*, *33*(6), 818–830. http://dx.doi.org/10.1016/j.neubiorev.2009.01.003. pii: S0149-7634(09)00005-0.

Ivarsson, T., Melin, K., & Wallin, L. (2008). Categorical and dimensional aspects of co-morbidity in obsessive-compulsive disorder (OCD). *European Child & Adolescent Psychiatry*, *17*(1), 20–31. http://dx.doi.org/10.1007/s00787-007-0626-z.

Ivarsson, T., Skarphedinsson, G., Kornor, H., Axelsdottir, B., Biedilae, S., Heyman, I., et al. (2015). The place of and evidence for serotonin reuptake inhibitors (SRIs) for obsessive compulsive disorder (OCD) in children and adolescents: Views based on a systematic review and meta-analysis. *Psychiatry Research*, *227*(1), 93–103. http://dx.doi.org/10.1016/j.psychres.2015.01.015.

Jenike, M. A., Breiter, H. C., Baer, L., Kennedy, D. N., Savage, C. R., Olivares, M. J., et al. (1996). Cerebral structural abnormalities in obsessive-compulsive disorder. A quantitative morphometric magnetic resonance imaging study. *Archives of General Psychiatry*, *53*(7), 625–632.

Kozak, M. J., & Foa, E. B. (1994). Obsessions, overvalued ideas, and delusions in obsessive-compulsive disorder. *Behaviour Research and Therapy*, *32*(3), 343–353.

Leyfer, O. T., Folstein, S. E., Bacalman, S., Davis, N. O., Dinh, E., Morgan, J., et al. (2006). Comorbid psychiatric disorders in children with autism: Interview development and rates of disorders. *Journal of Autism and Developmental Disorders*, *36*(7), 849–861. http://dx.doi.org/10.1007/s10803-006-0123-0.

Ludvik, D., Boschen, M. J., & Neumann, D. L. (2015). Effective behavioural strategies for reducing disgust in contamination-related OCD: A review. *Clinical Psychology Review*, *42*, 116–129.

MacMaster, F. P. (2010). Translational neuroimaging research in pediatric obsessive-compulsive disorder. *Dialogues in Clinical Neuroscience*, *12*(2), 165–174.

MacMaster, F. P., O'Neill, J., & Rosenberg, D. R. (2008). Brain imaging in pediatric obsessive-compulsive disorder. *Journal of the American Academy of Child and Adolescent Psychiatry*, *47*(11), 1262–1272. http://dx.doi.org/10.1097/CHI.0b013e318185d2be. S0890-8567(08)60118-5 [pii].

March, J. S., & Mulle, K. (1998). *OCD in children and adolescents: A cognitive-behavioral treatment manual*. New York: Guilford Press.

Mason, E. C., & Richardson, R. (2012). Treating disgust in anxiety disorders. *Clinical Psychology: Science and Practice*, *19*(2), 180–194. http://dx.doi.org/10.1111/j.1468-2850.2012.01282.x.

McGuire, J. F., Orr, S. P., Wu, M. S., Lewin, A. B., Small, B. J., Phares, V., et al. (2016). Fear conditioning and extinction in youth with obsessive-compulsive disorder. *Depression and Anxiety*, *33*(3), 229–237.

McGuire, J. F., Piacentini, J., Lewin, A. B., Brennan, E. A., Murphy, T. K., & Storch, E. A. (2015). A meta-analysis of cognitive behavior therapy and medication for child obsessive-compulsive disorder: Moderators of treatment efficacy, response, and remission. *Depression and Anxiety*, *32*(8), 580–593.

McKay, D., & Tsao, S. D. (2005). A treatment most foul: Handling disgust in cognitive-behavior therapy. *Journal of Cognitive Psychotherapy*, *19*(4), 355–367. http://dx.doi.org/10.1891/jcop.2005.19.4.355.

Menzies, L., Chamberlain, S. R., Laird, A. R., Thelen, S. M., Sahakian, B. J., & Bullmore, E. T. (2008). Integrating evidence from neuroimaging and neuropsychological studies of obsessive-compulsive disorder: The orbitofronto-striatal model revisited. *Neuroscience and Biobehavioral Reviews*, *32*(3), 525–549. http://dx.doi.org/10.1016/j.neubiorev.2007.09.005. S0149-7634(07)00114-5 [pii].

Mowrer, O. H. (1960). *Learning theory and behavior*. New York: Wiley.

Olatunji, B. O., Wolitzky-Taylor, K. B., Willems, J., Lohr, J. M., & Armstrong, T. (2009). Differential habituation of fear and disgust during repeated exposure to threat-relevant stimuli in contamination-based OCD: An analogue study. *Journal of Anxiety Disorders*, *23*(1), 118–123.

Ost, L. -G., Riise, E. N., Wergeland, G. J., Hansen, B., & Kvale, G. (2016). Cognitive behavioral and pharmacological treatments of OCD in children: A systematic review and meta-analysis. *Journal of Anxiety Disorders*, *43*, 58–69.

Peris, T. S., Sugar, C. A., Bergman, R. L., Chang, S., Langley, A., & Piacentini, J. (2012). Family factors predict treatment outcome for pediatric obsessive-compulsive disorder. *Journal of Consulting and Clinical Psychology*, *80*(2), 255–263. http://dx.doi.org/10.1037/a0027084.

Rachman, S. (1997). A cognitive theory of obsessions. *Behaviour Research and Therapy*, *35*(9), 793–802.

Rachman, S., De Silva, P., & Roper, G. (1976). The spontaneous decay of compulsive urges. *Behaviour Research and Therapy*, *14*(6), 445–453.

Reed, G. (1985). *Obsessional experience and compulsive behavior: A structural approach*. Orlando, FL: Academic Press.

Roper, G., Rachman, S., & Hodgson, R. (1973). An experiment on obsessional checking. *Behaviour Research and Therapy*, *11*(3), 271–277.

Rosenberg, D. R., & Keshavan, M. S. (1998). A.E. Bennett Research Award. Toward a neurodevelopmental model of obsessive–compulsive disorder. *Biological Psychiatry*, *43*(9), 623–640. pii: S0006322397004435.

Rosenberg, D. R., Keshavan, M. S., Dick, E. L., Bagwell, W. W., MacMaster, F. P., & Birmaher, B. (1997). Corpus callosal morphology in treatment-naive pediatric obsessive compulsive disorder. *Progress in Neuro-Psychopharmacology and Biological Psychiatry*, *21*(8), 1269–1283. pii: S0278584697001632.

Russell, A. J., Jassi, A., Fullana, M. A., Mack, H., Johnston, K., Heyman, I., et al. (2013). Cognitive behavior therapy for comorbid obsessive-compulsive disorder in high-functioning autism spectrum disorders: A randomized controlled trial. *Depression and Anxiety*, *30*(8), 697–708. http://dx.doi.org/10.1002/da.22053.

Russell, A. J., Mataix-Cols, D., Anson, M. A., & Murphy, D. G. (2005). Obsessions and compulsions in Asperger syndrome and high-functioning autism. *The British Journal of Psychiatry*, *186*, 525–528.

Salkovskis, P. M. (1985). Obsessional-compulsive problems: A cognitive-behavioural analysis. *Behaviour Research and Therapy*, *23*(5), 571–583.

Schwartz, J. M., Stoessel, P. W., Baxter, L. R., Jr., Martin, K. M., & Phelps, M. E. (1996). Systematic changes in cerebral glucose metabolic rate after successful behavior modification treatment of obsessive-compulsive disorder. *Archives of General Psychiatry*, *53*(2), 109–113.

Simonoff, E., Pickles, A., Charman, T., Chandler, S., Loucas, T., & Baird, G. (2008). Psychiatric disorders in children with autism spectrum disorders: Prevalence, comorbidity, and associated factors in a population-derived sample. *Journal of the American Academy of Child and Adolescent Psychiatry*, *47*(8), 921–929. http://dx.doi.org/10.1097/CHI.0b013e318179964f.

Simons, M., Schneider, S., & Herpertz-Dahlmann, B. (2006). Metacognitive therapy versus exposure and response prevention for pediatric obsessive-compulsive disorder. A case series with randomized allocation. *Psychotherapy and Psychosomatics*, *75*(4), 257–264.

Skarphedinsson, G., Weidle, B., Thomsen, P., Dahl, K., Torp, N. C., Nissen, J. B., et al. (2014). Continued cognitive behavior therapy versus sertraline for children and adolescents with obsessive-compulsive disorder that were non-responders to cognitive behavior therapy—A randomized controlled trial. In *Paper presented at the Nordic child and adolescent psychiatric (NordCAP) research meeting, Middelfart, Denmark.*

Storch, E. A., Arnold, E. B., Lewin, A. B., Nadeau, J. M., Jones, A. M., De Nadai, A. S., et al. (2013). The effect of cognitive-behavioral therapy versus treatment as usual for anxiety in children with autism spectrum disorders: A randomized, controlled trial. *Journal of the American Academy of Child and Adolescent Psychiatry. 52*(2). http://dx.doi.org/10.1016/j.jaac.2012.11.007. 132-142.e132.

Storch, E. A., Bussing, R., Small, B. J., Geffken, G. R., McNamara, J. P., Rahman, O., et al. (2013). Randomized, placebo-controlled trial of cognitive-behavioral therapy alone or combined with sertraline in the treatment of pediatric obsessive–compulsive disorder. *Behaviour Research and Therapy, 51*(12), 823–829. http://dx.doi.org/10.1016/j.brat.2013.09.007.

Storch, E. A., Jones, A. M., Lack, C. W., Ale, C. M., Sulkowski, M. L., Lewin, A. B., et al. (2012). Rage attacks in pediatric obsessive-compulsive disorder: Phenomenology and clinical correlates. *Journal of the American Academy of Child and Adolescent Psychiatry, 51*(6), 582–592. http://dx.doi.org/10.1016/j.jaac.2012.02.016.

Storch, E. A., Lewin, A. B., Geffken, G. R., Morgan, J. R., & Murphy, T. K. (2010). The role of comorbid disruptive behavior in the clinical expression of pediatric obsessive-compulsive disorder. *Behaviour Research and Therapy, 48*(12), 1204–1210. http://dx.doi.org/10.1016/j.brat.2010.09.004.

Storch, E. A., Merlo, L. J., Larson, M. J., Geffken, G. R., Lehmkuhl, H. D., Jacob, M. L., et al. (2008). Impact of comorbidity on cognitive-behavioral therapy response in pediatric obsessive-compulsive disorder. *Journal of the American Academy of Child and Adolescent Psychiatry, 47*(5), 583–592. http://dx.doi.org/10.1097/CHI.0b013e31816774b1.

Sukhodolsky, D. G., Gorman, B. S., Scahill, L., Findley, D., & McGuire, J. (2013). Exposure and response prevention with or without parent management training for children with obsessive-compulsive disorder complicated by disruptive behavior: A multiple-baseline across-responses design study. *Journal of Anxiety Disorders, 27*(3), 298–305. http://dx.doi.org/10.1016/j.janxdis.2013.01.005.

Szechtman, H., & Woody, E. (2004). Obsessive-compulsive disorder as a disturbance of security motivation. *Psychological Review, 111*(1), 111–127. http://dx.doi.org/10.1037/0033-295X.111.1.111.

Szeszko, P. R., MacMillan, S., McMeniman, M., Lorch, E., Madden, R., Ivey, J., et al. (2004). Amygdala volume reductions in pediatric patients with obsessive-compulsive disorder treated with paroxetine: Preliminary findings. *Neuropsychopharmacology, 29*(4), 826–832. http://dx.doi.org/10.1038/sj.npp.1300399. 1300399 [pii].

Taboas, W., Ojserkis, R., & McKay, D. (2015). Change in disgust reactions following cognitive-behavioral therapy for childhood anxiety disorders. *International Journal of Clinical and Health Psychology, 15*(1), 1–7. http://dx.doi.org/10.1016/j.ijchp.2014.06.002.

Taylor, S. (2013). Molecular genetics of obsessive-compulsive disorder: A comprehensive meta-analysis of genetic association studies. *Molecular Psychiatry, 18*(7), 799–805. http://dx.doi.org/10.1038/mp.2012.76.

Tolin, D. F., Maltby, N., Diefenbach, G. J., Hannan, S. E., & Worhunsky, P. (2004). Cognitive-behavioral therapy for medication nonresponders with obsessive-compulsive disorder: A wait-list-controlled open trial. *The Journal of Clinical Psychiatry, 65*(7), 922–931.

Torp, N. C., Dahl, K., Skarphedinsson, G., Compton, S., Thomsen, P. H., Weidle, B., et al. (2015). Predictors associated with improved cognitive-behavioral therapy outcome in pediatric obsessive-compulsive disorder. *Journal of the American Academy of Child and Adolescent Psychiatry*, *54*(3). http://dx.doi.org/10.1016/j.jaac.2014.12.007. 200–207.e201.

van Grootheest, D. S., Cath, D. C., Beekman, A. T., & Boomsma, D. I. (2005). Twin studies on obsessive-compulsive disorder: A review. *Twin Research and Human Genetics*, *8*(5), 450–458. http://dx.doi.org/10.1375/183242705774310060.

Weidle, B., & Skarphedinsson, G. (2016). Treatment of a child with obsessive-compulsive disorder with limited motivation: Course and outcome of cognitive-behavior therapy. *Journal of Clinical Psychology*, *72*, 1139–1151.

White, M., & Epston, D. (1990). *Narrative means to therapeutic ends*. New York: Norton.

Chapter 4

Assessment of Children With OCD

Michelle Rozenman*,† and R. Lindsey Bergman*,†
*University of California, Los Angeles, CA, United States, †UCLA Semel Institute for Neuroscience and Human Behavior, Los Angeles, CA, United States

Obsessive-compulsive disorder (OCD) is a remarkably heterogeneous condition with individual symptom presentations that tend to vary widely. Careful evidence-based assessment of OCD is critical in order to accurately understand each individual's symptoms and to identify appropriate psychosocial treatment targets. Assessment of OCD should include detailed information regarding past and current symptoms, associated impairment, family accommodation, youth insight, and comorbid psychopathology. The perspectives of both the youth and their parent should be obtained.

The goal of this chapter is to provide the practicing clinician with a framework for assessing OCD in children and adolescents. We begin with discussion of how to prepare for a clinical interview with a youth and parent(s). Next, we turn to the clinician-rated diagnostic and symptom assessment tools, and review common challenges and complex issues that may arise during the clinical interview. Then, we review youth- and parent-reported questionnaires for symptoms, impairment, insight and cognition, and family accommodation. It should be noted that, while hoarding disorder is now a separate diagnosis from OCD in DSM-5 (American Psychiatric Association [APA], 2013), clinician-, youth-, and parent-reported measures do include queries for hoarding; therefore we include some discussion of hoarding assessment.

INITIAL CONSIDERATIONS AND COMPONENTS OF ASSESSMENT

Careful assessment of pediatric OCD includes several components. At the time of initial contact, the clinician should obtain the youth's age, and preliminary information regarding the parent concerns and parent perceptions of youth concerns, and whether the youth discusses their symptoms with their parent (Lewin & Piacentini, 2010). This will provide the clinician with preliminary

The Clinician's Guide to Cognitive-Behavioral Therapy for Childhood Obsessive-Compulsive Disorder
http://dx.doi.org/10.1016/B978-0-12-811427-8.00004-6

information about how they might structure time spent during the assessment with child and parent together vs separately. The clinician should be sensitive to youth concerns about embarrassment, particularly as relevant for adolescents, and youth with OCD symptoms related to harm avoidance/aggression (e.g., thoughts or images of harming others), intrusive thoughts of a sexual nature (e.g., thoughts or images of touching self or others), etc. It may be possible that, while the parent has some indication that their child experiences difficulties, the youth may hide or minimize symptoms. Entirely separate interviews might be conducted with each youth and parent in instances where the youth reports embarrassment or shame, parent has minimal knowledge of symptoms, or youth requests to meet with the clinician alone. We discuss reconciliation of youth and parent reports near the end of this chapter.

At the start of the assessment, the clinician should begin with a clear description of their goals and assessment procedures to provide the family with a framework for the assessment visit. This includes a description of the purpose and components of the clinical interview to parent and child using developmentally appropriate language. During the assessment, psychoeducation about OCD (e.g., 1%–3% of youth experience the condition, experience of intrusive thoughts is common among nearly all individuals and not just those with OCD, etc.) may normalize the experience for families who have little knowledge about the disorder, or who feel stigma or shame about symptoms (see Chapter 3). This is especially useful in instances where obsessional themes include topics that may be embarrassing to discuss (e.g., harm, aggression, sexual obsessions), as well as when the youth engages in compulsions in a secretive manner or when the compulsions themselves may embarrass the youth (e.g., checking self for bodily fluid leakage).

The clinical interview should be conducted using evidence-based assessment, with differential diagnosis of other conditions, in order to provide accurate OCD diagnosis. During the interview, the clinician should clearly query each OCD symptom cluster (see Chapter 2). While querying, the clinician may even provide psychoeducation about and normalize experience of less commonly known symptom clusters or those that may be perceived as taboo (e.g., harm avoidance, intrusive sexual thoughts). In addition to a full psychiatric history, the American Academy of Child and Adolescent Psychiatry (AACAP) also recommends that a full medical, developmental, family, and school history be obtained (Geller & March, 2012). Youth- and parent-reported questionnaires may augment the clinical interview, particularly if either party feels embarrassment or shame about symptoms. We caution that questionnaires should be used as a supplement to, and not as a replacement for, the clinical interview. Such questionnaires have been developed for OCD symptomatology, impairment, insight and OCD-related cognition, and familial accommodation, each of which are described in more detail later. Note that there are no genetic, brain imaging, electrophysiological, neuropsychological, or other tests that provide OCD diagnosis at the present time. Thus the clinical interview is currently the only way to determine OCD diagnosis.

DETERMINING OCD DIAGNOSIS, COOCCURRING PSYCHOPATHOLOGY, AND DIFFERENTIAL DIAGNOSIS

As mentioned earlier, OCD is an extremely heterogeneous condition, and there are a wide variety of obsessional themes and resultant compulsions that may present. Thus the clinician must carefully query symptomatology in order to arrive at the accurate diagnosis, rule out differential diagnoses, and determine whether the youth meets criteria for other cooccurring problems. Clinicians with little experience in evidence-based assessment of OCD, in particular, are unlikely to be familiar with less common symptom presentations, and therefore may not probe for these symptoms. We therefore recommend that even if the entire measure or interview is not going to be completed, clinicians use one of the diagnostic or clinician-rated assessment tools discussed later for reference during the initial clinical interview.

Initial OCD Symptom Prompts

The primary purpose of the clinical interview is to determine whether OCD symptoms are present. Thus the clinician should be familiar with and able to clearly query the wide range of OCD symptoms that may present. To aid in this characterization of OCD symptomatology, researchers have classified OCD symptoms into subtypes or "clusters" of symptoms that tend to group together. Broadly, these include: (a) aggressive, sexual, religious, and somatic obsessions and checking compulsions; (b) symmetry obsessions and ordering, counting, and repeating compulsions; (c) contamination obsessions and cleaning/washing compulsions; and (d) hoarding, which consists of excessive acquisition and difficulty discarding items. However, youth may not necessarily endorse all symptoms within a cluster, and that many youth with OCD experience symptoms from more than one cluster.

A clear description of obsessions and compulsions should be provided to the youth and parent in developmentally appropriate language. It may be useful to provide examples of specific symptoms during these initial queries in order to provide a context for subsequent queries. For example, an initial query about obsessions might be: "Do you ever have thoughts or images that come into your mind that make you feel anxious or upset, and that you can't stop?" For younger children, the prompt might be simpler: "Do you ever have thoughts that scare you or make you upset? Is it hard to make them go away?" These can be followed with additional examples such as: "Sometimes kids have thoughts that just won't go away. These thoughts can be about germs, doing something bad, hurting themselves or someone else, wanting things to feel just right ..." and so forth. An initial query about compulsions might be: "Do you have to do things over and over to make thoughts or images go away, or because if you don't do them something doesn't feel right?" with subsequent queries including "Sometimes kids have to keep washing their hands over and over, or asking their parents if things are going to be ok, or checking to make sure that they didn't do something wrong." Additional prompts for assessing obsessions and compulsions can be found in the AACAP Practice Parameters (Geller & March, 2012) and in Conelea, Freeman, and Garcia (2012). In brief, these include asking about thoughts that won't go away on their own and habits or behaviors that the child does to relieve worry or upset feelings. Supplemental questions might include how the child feels that the two (obsessions and compulsions) might be related, and what would happen if the child was not able to do the compulsion.

OCD Diagnosis

Per the DSM-5 (APA, 2013), a diagnosis of OCD requires presence of obsessions and/or compulsions that are time consuming (e.g., 1+h per day) or cause distress and/or impairment in functioning, and are not due to physiological effects of a substance or another medical or mental health condition. Children may not necessarily be able to articulate or specify the rationale for why they engage in compulsions and may still meet diagnostic criteria for OCD. Further, a change from the prior editions of the DSM, it is not necessary that youth recognize obsessions to be illogical, nonsensical, or unrealistic. Finally, specific OCD symptoms may wax and wane over the course of development. It is not the content of obsessions or the specific compulsions that dictate whether a youth meets for diagnosis. Rather, it is the experience of intrusive unwanted thoughts and engagement in ritualistic behaviors in attempts to relieve the distress of those thoughts, which constitutes this form of psychopathology.

In considering the OCD diagnosis, the clinician should be mindful that the core feature of obsessions is that they are unwanted, distressing, or upsetting, and that these thoughts are difficult to ignore. Compulsions are conducted in attempts to relieve distress associated with obsessions. The clinician should also be mindful that while some compulsions are observable (e.g., hand washing, rewriting, tapping, checking), mental compulsions are not necessarily observable (e.g., counting to a certain number, replacing a "bad" thought with a "good" thought). Youth may also engage in compulsions in order to "feel just right" and not as related to a specific obsession other than a feeling of incompleteness. Additionally, while some obsessions and compulsions can be logically linked (e.g., obsessions about germs and getting sick may be followed by hand washing compulsions), others may not appear to follow a logical progression (e.g., an obsession about offending God may be followed by counting to the number seven, several times in a row). Moreover, some youth engage in significant avoidance of OCD triggers (e.g., not touching contaminated surfaces, avoidance of homework so that they do not need to reread/rewrite), confessing thoughts, or reassurance seeking from family members in order to experience relief from distress associated with obsessions; each of these should be considered as potentially contributing to the OCD cycle while conducting assessment of compulsions.

It is also important to establish that a youth's OCD symptoms cause them to experience significant distress and/or impairment to meet diagnostic criteria. To assess these, the clinician might begin with broad queries about how symptoms cause the child to feel anxious or upset, and areas in which symptoms interfere. Queries might then become more specific about whether and how symptoms interfere in functional domains (i.e., school, social, home). For example, for school, does it take significantly longer to complete school assignments because of rereading/rewriting symptoms? Does the child have difficulties with class participation and attention because they experience intrusive harm-related thoughts? Have teachers or other youths commented on the child's behaviors? Socially, has the child begun to avoid peers, either because peers trigger symptoms or because the child does not want to be embarrassed? At home, is there increasing conflict because parents must participate in compulsions, provide reassurance, remove OCD-related triggers, or because the child constantly confesses their thoughts to a parent? In instances where youth report little distress or impairment because they typically do not attempt to refrain from engaging in compulsions, the clinician should query "what might happen" (i.e., how would the youth feel? what would they do?) if they were unable to complete a compulsion.

Clinical observation during the interview can also be used to aid in determining impairment. For example, does the child tap or touch objects until it feels "just right" as they walk into the room and sit down? Does the clinician observe the youth engaging in compulsions or asking their parent for reassurance during the interview? Is the child able to touch the door handle to the office and use a pen provided by the clinician?

Equally important, the clinician should consider the youth's symptoms in the context of what is considered developmentally normative. Many fears and behaviors that might be symptomatic in an adolescent would not be considered symptomatic in a much younger child. Both chronological and cognitive development should be considered, particularly related to parent reports about behaviors that may be within the normal range for young children. For example, young children may engage in bedtime or goodbye rituals with their parent or be rigid about following rules, which would not necessarily be symptomatic depending on the degree to which they engage in these behaviors and their age. As an aside, many individuals—youth and adults alike—engage in superstitious (e.g., wearing same socks to all baseball games) or otherwise idiosyncratic behavior (e.g., wanting shoes lined up to be a particular way); such behavior in and of itself does not constitute OCD. However, if this behavior significantly interferes in the individual's life (e.g., spending hours lining up shoes in the closet), and is accompanied by other symptoms, then an OCD diagnosis may be warranted.

Hoarding Disorder

Previously considered part of OCD, hoarding disorder is now its own diagnosis within the obsessive-compulsive spectrum disorders in DSM-5 (APA, 2013).

However, as mentioned later, the recommended evidence-based assessment tools for youth do not yet reflect this change, and hoarding symptoms are queried as part of OCD. Therefore the clinician should be aware of diagnostic criteria for hoarding disorder: difficulty discarding possessions regardless of their value due to a perceived need for or assignment of importance to the items, with accumulation of items that leads to clutter or compromised living conditions. As with OCD, hoarding must cause distress and/or impairment, and must not be due to physiological effects of a substance or another medical or mental health condition. It should be noted that children may meet for a hoarding diagnosis even if there is not accumulation of clutter or compromised home environment, as youth may not have the means or ability to acquire and bring objects into the home or parents may discard objects. Thus when querying hoarding symptoms, the clinician should take care to ask whether and what kinds of behaviors parents engage in (e.g., not allowing their child to remove anything from restaurants or parks, throwing items away while the child sleeps) to reduce or prevent clutter from accruing in the home.

Differential Diagnosis and Cooccurring Psychopathology

Careful diagnostic assessment is critical in order to ensure that the youth's symptoms are not better accounted for by another condition. Differential diagnosis can be especially difficult, as the symptoms of OCD and other disorders (e.g., anxiety, depression, autism spectrum, tic disorders) may appear similar. To further complicate diagnostic assessment, OCD has been shown to be comorbid with anxiety, depression, ADHD, and tics (Coskun, Zoroglu, & Ozturk, 2012; Garcia et al., 2009; Huang et al., 2014; Ivarsson, Melin, & Wallin, 2007; Masi et al., 2010). The clinician should assess for the full range of psychopathology in order to understand the factors that may complicate OCD presentation and its treatment. For example, a youth with OCD and cooccurring uncontrolled ADHD may have especial difficulty attempting to refrain from compulsions due to problems with impulse control, while a youth with OCD and depression may feel hopeless and therefore lack motivation to complete exposures in treatment. Of especial importance, differential diagnosis between OCD and trauma/stressor-related disorders must be done with sensitivity and careful queries; a youth with trauma-related symptoms must report experience of a traumatic event, while a youth with sexual intrusive thoughts, related compulsions or avoidance, and no history of trauma will likely meet criteria for OCD. While a comprehensive review of queries to determine differential diagnosis from other conditions is outside of the scope of this chapter, clinicians can review Lewin and Piacentini (2010) for additional information.

Diagnostic and Symptom Severity Assessment Tools

Two commonly used clinician-administered diagnostic interviews for youth with OCD, and a clinician-administered OCD symptom severity scale, are described in detail later. These are semistructured tools whereby interview prompts are used to query initial symptoms and then, if the initial inquiry is endorsed, additional questions are pursued. Youth and parents are typically interviewed separately, and the clinician uses clinical judgment to combine reports and determine diagnoses and severity scores. The interview can take anywhere from 30 min to 2 h, depending on the presenting problem(s) and informant response styles. It should be noted that the developers of these assessment tools recommend that clinicians obtain specialized training to ensure that these measures are used appropriately. As mentioned earlier, hoarding symptoms are included within the OCD sections of these diagnostic tools, given that hoarding was previously considered part of OCD in earlier versions of the DSM when these assessments were developed.

Anxiety Disorders Interview Schedule for DSM-IV: Child and Parent Versions (ADIS; Silverman & Albano, 1996) is a semistructured psychiatric diagnostic interview. The ADIS assesses anxiety disorders (separation, social generalized, panic, social phobia, specific phobia), OCD, PTSD, mood disorders, tic disorders, ADHD and disruptive behavior disorders, and psychosis. The anxiety and OCD sections of the ADIS are well validated, and the measure has been used in many anxiety and OCD treatment outcome studies. Therefore we recommend it as the preferred diagnostic tool when OCD is suspected.

Schedule for Affective Disorders and Schizophrenia for School-Age Children (K-SADS; Kaufman et al., 1997) is a semistructured psychiatric diagnostic interview. The K-SADS' strength lies in its sections on mood disorders, psychosis, and ADHD and disruptive behavior disorders, although it also has sections for anxiety, OCD, PTSD.

OCD Severity

The *Children's Yale-Brown Obsessive-Compulsive Scale* (CYBOCS; Scahill et al., 1997) is a dimensional, clinician-rated semistructured measure of OCD symptoms and severity in the past week. Parent and youth reports are reconciled using clinical judgment. The CYBOCS has demonstrated strong psychometric properties in youths ages 8–18 (Gallant et al., 2008; Storch et al., 2004). Preliminary support for its psychometric properties and sensitivity to treatment effects have also been found in early childhood (ages 4–8; Freeman, Flessner, & Garcia, 2011). The CYBOCS is not a diagnostic tool, and its total severity score may not be reflective of symptom severity for youth who only report obsessions or compulsions (Merlo, Storch, Murphy, Goodman, & Geffken, 2005). However, the CYBOCS is considered the gold-standard measure for assessing OCD severity in youth and can be valuable as a primary measure of OCD symptoms and severity during the clinical interview.

The CYBOCS is divided into two sections: a 60-item obsession and compulsion symptom checklist and 10 global items assessing severity of obsessions and compulsions. The symptom checklist is reviewed first and categorized by symptom cluster theme for each obsessions and compulsions.

While administering the checklist, the clinician might also query the youth and parent about the youth's specific fears/discomfort in regards to obsessions, and how they believe the compulsion will relieve distress associated with the obsession; this will aid the clinician in full understanding the youth's symptom presentation. For example, one youth might have fear of germs and engage in hand washing because there are afraid that they will get sick and die and believe that hand washing will prevent illness. Conversely, another youth may fear germs and engage in hand washing because they worry that germs will make them "gross" and hand washing relieves the feelings of disgust. While such distinction may appear to be negligible to the untrained clinician, it is critical to devising appropriate exposures in treatment that will trigger the specific youth's obsessions.

The clinician should be aware that only the more common OCD symptoms are listed in the CYBOCS symptom checklist and that some youth may present with symptoms that are not listed. For example, fears of emotional contamination (e.g., fears that youth will acquire negative traits from an undesirable person), transformation (e.g., fears that youth will transform into or become more like another person), and excessive checking of undergarments or private parts for urine/feces are not listed within the checklist, but are OCD symptoms that are not uncommon. Therefore the clinician should ask at the end of each obsession and compulsion checklists "Are there any other things that I haven't asked you about but that you have upsetting thoughts about/do over and over?" These can be listed in the "other" space provided within the checklist and should be queried when completing the severity items.

Once the clinician has completed the symptom checklist, they complete the 10 obsessions severity (5 items) and compulsions severity (5 items) queries. These items include amount of time spent on obsessions or compulsions, distress associated with obsessions or compulsions, whether and how much the youth is able to refrain from engaging in obsessions or compulsions, perceived control over obsessions or compulsions, and interference in domains of functioning. Each item is rated on a 5-point Likert scale ranging from none (score = 0) to extreme (score = 4), and these 10 items are then summed for the total severity score (range 0–40).

CYBOCS total scores should reflect illness severity. The AACAP Practice Parameters (Geller & March, 2012) suggest that total severity scores of 8–15 represent mild illness, 16–23 represent moderate illness, and 24+ represent severe illness. CYBOCS total severity scores can also be compared against the Clinician Global Impressions—Severity (Guy, 1976) scores, such that CYBOCS scores of 5–13 correspond to a CGI-S of 2 (mild symptoms with little functional impairment), scores of 14–24 correspond to a CGI-S of 3 (moderate symptoms with effort to function), scores of 25–30 correspond to a CGI-S of 4 (moderate-to-severe symptoms with limited functioning), and scores above 30 corresponding with a CGI-S of 5 or 6 (severe symptoms and functioning primarily with assistance) (Lewin et al., 2014). Additionally, prior research has identified CYBOCS cutoffs for treatment response (Storch, Lewin, De Nadai, & Murphy, 2010) such that a CYBOCS reduction of 25% indicates response to CBT, and either 45%–50% reduction or a raw score of 14 at posttreatment indicates symptom remission.

Organization of the Clinical Interview—Diagnostic and OCD Severity Assessments

Due to the overlap between symptoms of OCD and other conditions, it is recommended that the diagnostic interview be conducted prior to the CYBOCS. Once the diagnostic interview is completed, and the clinician has a full understanding of current symptoms and the diagnostic categories those symptoms fit within, the clinician can then use this information to complete the CYBOCS with the youth and parent (again, either together or separately). In addition, because these interviews can be tiresome and may even be emotionally difficult for families, it is recommended that the clinician use their judgment when querying CYBOCS symptoms that have already been endorsed during the diagnostic interview. For example, if a youth already endorsed symmetry symptoms during the ADIS, then the clinician might state during the arranging/symmetry section of the CYBOCS, "You already told me that your items at home need to be arranged in a particular way until it feels "just right." Just to confirm, you've had thoughts about or the desire to arrange your books and items in your desk in the last week?" Similarly, information obtained during the diagnostic interview about interference, distress, time spent, and difficulties resisting can be applied to the CYBOCS severity items, with confirmation from the youth/parent, as long as the clinician confirms that the severity item endorsement is for the past week.

CHALLENGES AND COMPLEX ISSUES IN ASSESSMENT

Youth Age and Cognitive Development

As described earlier, the clinician should use sensitivity and clinical judgment when querying symptoms based on the youth's chronological age and their cognitive development. Studies of cognitive development suggest that abstract thinking begins to occur in mid-childhood/preadolescence (Kingery et al., 2006); thus younger children may not endorse symptoms unless they are queried in such a way that the child understands. For example, while an adolescent might be asked "do you have concerns about contamination?," a younger child might be asked "do you get upset if you have to touch something dirty or sticky?" or "do you worry about getting sick?" As younger children may have more difficulty discussing obsessions given the metacognition involved, some have suggested that for younger youth it may be useful to administer the CYBOCS compulsions checklist prior to the obsessions checklist

(Freeman et al., 2011). This would allow the clinician to then help the child link any thoughts to the compulsions that they have already endorsed.

Reconciling Youth and Parent Reports

Typical convention in assessment of youth mental health problems is to weigh parent report more heavily for younger children, and weigh youth report more heavily for adolescents and/or when youth have been reluctant to discuss symptoms with their parents (Freeman et al., 2011; Merlo et al., 2005). Younger children often deny experience of obsessions so it may appear that only compulsions are present. Parent report might also be weighed more heavily when the youth, regardless of age, minimizes, denies, or is reluctant to discuss symptoms with the clinician, or appears to have poor or limited insight into their symptoms. However, given that parents are not diagnosticians, they may describe behaviors as symptomatic of OCD when those behaviors actually are normative or reflective of another mental health problem (Lewin & Piacentini, 2010). For younger youth, or those who have difficulty articulating their thoughts, the majority of the interview might be conducted with parent and child together. The onus falls on the clinician to obtain as much information as possible from each informant and use clinical judgment to reconcile youth and parent reports.

Parental OCD or Other Mental Health Problems

Up to 70% of youth with OCD have one or more family members with a history of mental health problems (e.g., Calvo, Lázaro, Castro, Morer, & Toro, 2007). While not a formal part of the assessment measures described earlier, during the individual meeting with the parent, the clinician should query whether any immediate or extended family members have experienced mental health problems. In our clinical experience, parental psychopathology (particularly OCD or anxiety) may cause parental distress or interfere with parent follow-through during intervention, especially if parents are not able to tolerate seeing their child distressed (i.e., during exposures) and/or if the child's exposures are triggering for the parent (e.g., parent with contamination symptoms may become upset, disgusted, or encourage their child to wash their hands after the child with contamination symptoms participates in contamination exposures). The role of family members in OCD symptom maintenance is important to assess initially, as well as over the course of intervention.

Familial and Cultural Considerations

Family units can differ tremendously in their composition, interactions with one another and their communities, and religious and/or cultural practices. It then follows that OCD symptoms must be considered within the youth's environment and family belief system. The assessing clinician must demonstrate sensitivity for the family and their practices. This becomes especially relevant when considering whether certain behaviors are normative or problematic within the family's context. For example, a youth with scrupulosity symptoms may have been raised in a religious background in which the symptoms are either viewed as entirely pathological by parents (e.g., family has never been religious and does not understand the youth's symptoms) or viewed on a spectrum as aberrant from the family norms but still within the range of acceptable behavior (e.g., family is extremely religious, all family members pray at least once or more per day, etc.). For all symptoms, the clinician should determine what parental expectations are for the youth and any siblings in the home, as well as broader family and community connections that may have influence on the family's beliefs and/or practices.

YOUTH AND PARENT OCD SYMPTOM QUESTIONNAIRES

To initially screen for presence of OCD symptoms, or to supplement the clinical interview, a variety of symptom youth self- and parent reports are available. These are particularly useful for youth or parents who feel embarrassment or concern about describing symptoms during the clinical interview, and for tracking treatment progress over time. These measures, which are each somewhat distinct, are quickly and easily administered, and the clinician needs little training to interpret scores. Following we describe the most common youth self-report and parent-report symptom assessments, with some commentary and recommendations based upon prior research in the field. For additional information on the scientific evidence base for each questionnaire, see Iniesta-Sepúlveda, Rosa-Alcázar, Rosa-Alcázar, and Storch (2014).

OCD Symptoms and Severity

Children's Yale-Brown Obsessive-Compulsive Scale—Child and Parent Self-Reports (*CYBOCS-SR*; Piacentini, Langley, & Roblek, 2007) is a youth- and parent-rated OCD symptom and severity self-report. Modeled after the clinician-rated CYBOCS, the CYBOCS-SR is comprised of a 60-item checklist and 10 severity items (5 obsession impairment items, 5 compulsion impairment items) that are summed for a total score ranging from 0 to 40. A research study found the parent-reported CYBOCS-SR to correlate more strongly with the clinician-rated CYBOCS than the youth-reported CYBOCS-SR. This may be due to the fact that clinicians place more emphasis on parent reports than youth report when rating OCD symptom severity and impairment (Merlo et al., 2005). The CYBOCS-SR is a useful indicator of OCD severity, but it is cautioned that the self-report measures should be used in addition to, rather than in replacement of, the clinician-rated CYBOCS (Conelea, Schmidt, Leonard, Riemann, & Cahill, 2012). For example, following administration of the CYBOCS during clinical interview, the CYBOCS-SR may then be administered, and the clinician may review any discrepancies or additional symptoms mentioned in the CYBOCS-SR by parent and/or child that weren't mentioned in the clinical interview.

Children's Florida Obsessive-Compulsive Inventory (*C-FOCI*; Storch et al., 2009) is a youth- and parent-reported OCD symptom questionnaire developed specifically to be used as a screening tool for youth. The C-FOCI consists of a 17-item symptom checklist (Part A) that assesses presence (score of 1) or absence (score of 0) of common obsessions and compulsions experienced in the past month, and a 5-item severity scale (Part B) that queries time spent, distress, ability to control symptoms, avoidance, and interference rated on a 0- to 4-point scale similar to the CYBOCS. Obsession and compulsion subscale scores, as well as a total score, are obtained by summing the items in the 17-item checklist. The severity score is obtained by summing the five severity items. The C-FOCI is intended as a screener rather than a severity index and, as such, assesses for only the more commonly endorsed OCD symptoms.

Obsessive-Compulsive Inventory—Child Version (OCI-CV; Foa et al., 2010) is a youth-reported questionnaire assessing OCD symptoms over the past month. Developed from the Obsessive–Compulsive Inventory for adults (Foa, Kozak, Salkovskis, Coles, & Amir, 1998), the OCI-CV has demonstrated favorable psychometric properties in youth ages 7–17 (Foa et al., 2010; Jones et al., 2013). The 21 items of the OCI-CV are rated on a 3-point scale, from never (0) to always (2), with higher total scores (range 0–42) indicating more OCD symptoms and/or higher symptom frequency. One drawback to use of the OCI-CV is that a parent-reported version has not yet been published.

Child Behavior Checklist—Obsessive-Compulsive Scale (CBCL-OCS; Nelson et al., 2001) is a subscale from the CBCL (Achenbach & Rescorla, 2001), one of the most widely used and broad-based parent-reported symptom screening tools for youth. The CBCL consists of 118 parent-reported problem behaviors exhibited by the child in the last 6 months, with each item rated on a 3-point scale from "not true" (0) to "often true" (2). The CBCL-OCS subscale consists of eight items with the subscale total score ranging from 0 to 16. Prior research has found that a total subscale score of 5 or greater indicates good sensitivity and specificity for screening for OCD (Hudziak et al., 2006). It should be noted that these items broadly query unusual thoughts (e.g., "can't get his/her mind off certain thoughts," "feels might think or do something bad") and behavior (e.g., "repeats certain acts over and over," "strange behavior"). We recommend use of the CBCL-OCS if the clinician is interested in parent report of a variety of problem behaviors (not just OCD) and suggest that for scores of 5 or greater on the CBCL-OCS, clinical interview (including CYBOCS) and additional self- and parent reports should be administered that specifically query OCD (e.g., CYBOCS-SR, C-FOCI).

Children's Obsessional Compulsive Inventory—Revised (CHOCI-R; Uher, Heyman, Turner, & Shafran, 2008) is a self- and parent-reported questionnaire to assess OCD symptoms and severity in youth in the last month. The 32 items are divided into two sections for obsessions and compulsions, with each section consisting of 10 questions about the presence of symptoms, rated on a 3-point scale, followed by 6 questions rated on a 5-point scale assessing the severity and impairment associated with those symptoms. These provide subscales for obsessions (range 0–20), compulsions (0–20), a total score for OCD symptoms (obsessions = compulsions score), and an impairment score (range 0–24). While the CHOCI-R does provide ratings for severity and impairment of obsessions and compulsions, it only assesses the more common OCD symptoms and does not provide information about symptom subtypes.

Leyton Obsessional Inventory—Child Version (LOI-CV; Berg, Whitaker, Davies, & Flament, 1988) is a 20-item youth-reported questionnaire of OCD symptoms and severity. Symptoms are rated as either present or absent; for those items endorsed, follow-up questions assess interference of that particular symptom on a 4-point scale. A short version (Short LOI-CV; Bamber, Tamplin, Park, Kyte, & Goodyer, 2002) has also been developed based on the LOI-CV, with 11 of the original items retained. However, recent investigation has suggested that neither version of the LOI demonstrate sufficiently strong psychometric properties to assess pediatric OCD symptoms or severity (Storch, Park, et al., 2011); thus we do not recommend them.

Children's Saving Inventory (CSI; Storch, Muroff, et al., 2011) is a parent-reported measure of hoarding behavior in youth, based on the Saving Inventory—Revised (Frost, Steketee, & Grisham, 2004). The 23 items assess youth difficulties with acquisition and difficulty discarding items on a 5-point scale, with subscale scores provided for discarding, clutter, acquisition, and distress/impairment, as well as a total score. Any subscale score or total score averaging 2 points or higher is considered "moderate" for hoarding symptoms (Storch, Muroff, et al., 2011; Storch, Park, et al., 2011). As the CSI is currently the only questionnaire for hoarding symptoms in youth, we recommend it be used any time hoarding symptoms are endorsed during clinical interview or on one of the OCD self- or parent-reported questionnaires described earlier.

ASSOCIATED CHARACTERISTICS OF OCD: YOUTH AND PARENT REPORTS

As discussed earlier, associated characteristics of OCD (impairment, family functioning and accommodation, insight and beliefs about OCD) should be assessed during the clinical interview. However, there are also several self- and parent-reported measures of these associated traits that may supplement the interview and be tracked as part of treatment progress over time. These measures may provide additional information about youth and parent perceptions of the domains in which the youth is functionally impaired by OCD, maladaptive beliefs about OCD that the youth may experience as part of their symptom presentation, and the home environment and family climate.

Impairment

Child OCD Impact Scale—Revised (COIS-R; Piacentini, Peris, Bergman, Chang, & Jaffer, 2007) is a youth- and parent-reported questionnaire that measures the impairment caused by OCD in specific functional domains (home, academic, social) in the past month. The youth or parent responds to the prompt "how much trouble have you/your child had doing the following because of OCD?" and lists a variety of activities for each functional domain on a 4-point scale. The COIS-R is currently the only questionnaire for youth and parents that specifically assesses domains of impairment due to OCD symptomatology and is useful to supplement the clinical interview in order to understand the areas in which OCD interferes with the child's functioning.

Insight and Cognition

Obsessive Beliefs Questionnaire—Child Version (OBQ-CV; Coles et al., 2010) is a self-reported questionnaire assessing OCD-related beliefs, modified from the adult version of the questionnaire, and consisting of six core belief domains identified by the Obsessive Compulsive Cognitions Working Group (1997, 2001). The measure provides a total score, and three subscales: responsibility/threat estimation, perfectionism/certainty, and importance/control of thoughts. Findings for the OBQ-CV are mixed, as total scores have not always been shown to correlate with OCD symptoms and/or severity (Coles et al., 2010; Wolters et al., 2012). Nonetheless, this measure may be useful to administer to those youth who appear to exhibit maladaptive, irrational beliefs about their obsessions.

Child Assessment of Beliefs Scale (CABS; Storch et al., 2014) is a clinician-rated measure of OCD-related insight and beliefs, based on the Brown Assessment of Beliefs Scale (Eisen et al., 1998). The clinician interviews parent and child separately, and then makes a consensus rating for each of five items assessing the child's beliefs, including rationality of beliefs, perceptions of others' views of beliefs, fixity of beliefs, thoughts about the cause of problems, and perception of whether they are in need of help for the beliefs. The total score consists of the sum of each of these five items, which are scored on a scale of 0 (normal) to 4 (pathological). Although a newer scale, the CABS may be particularly useful as an assessment/intervention tool for the clinician and youth, particularly in challenging the veracity of obsessions by participating in exposures.

Other measures. Two additional questionnaires have been developed and tested for adults with OCD—each assesses a construct that has been found to correlate with OCD symptoms and severity in adults. The *Thought-Action Fusion Scale* (TAFS; Shafran, Thordarson, & Rachman, 1996) measures beliefs that thinking about something is comparable to engaging in that behavior (e.g., if I have a thought about hitting someone, it's just as bad as hitting them). The *Thought-Action Fusion Questionnaire for Adolescents* (TAFQ-A; Muris, Meesters, Rassin, Merckelbach, & Campbell, 2001) has been revised for use in adolescents. The *Responsibility Attitudes Scale* (RAS; Salkovskis et al., 2000) is a questionnaire designed to assess beliefs about responsibility. These scales have been used in a few studies with children and adolescents, although their psychometric properties have not been tested in youth samples to date. Additional research is needed to determine whether these questionnaires demonstrate adequate reliability and validity with youth and whether they may provide meaningful data for clinicians.

Family Functioning and Accommodation

OCD Family Functioning Scale (OFF; Stewart et al., 2011) is a 42-item youth- and family member-reported measure of OCD-related family functioning containing three parts: (1) family functioning impairment, (2) symptom-specific impairment, and (3) family role-specific impairment. Part 1 is scored on a scale of never (0) to daily (3), with a total potential score of 63, and Parts 2 and 3 are dichotomized such that scores of 1, 2, or 3 are considered a positive response. While the OFF has demonstrated strong psychometric properties (Stewart et al., 2011), and may provide useful and detailed information about each family member's perspective about the impact of the youth's OCD in the home, it is a relatively new measure and future research will determine how the scale should be used clinically.

Family Accommodation Scale (FAS; Calvocoressi et al., 1995) is a parent-reported questionnaire that assesses familial involvement in and accommodation of OCD symptoms in the last month. The 13 items query provision of reassurance, modification of expectations for the youth, and family routines, whether and how much family members aid the child in avoidance of OCD triggers, distress experienced by family members due to accommodation, and distress experienced by the child if/when family members do not participate in OCD. This parent-reported questionnaire may be particularly useful in augmenting the clinical interview with parent, as it provides detailed information about how the family responds to the youth's OCD and may even be involved in the OCD cycle.

Parental Attitudes and Behaviors Scale (PABS; Peris, Benazon, Langley, Roblek, & Piacentini, 2008) is a parent-reported questionnaire of attitudes and behaviors related to the child's OCD symptoms in the last 3 months. The PABS consists of 24 items rated on a 5-point scale from "not at all" (1) to "very often" (5), and provides a total score, as well as three subscale scores for blame, accommodation, and empowerment. The PABS may be particularly useful as an assessment and intervention tool in instances when the clinician is conducting family-based treatment for pediatric OCD and/or when parents report significant anger or criticism toward their child for their symptoms.

CONCLUDING REMARKS

As described throughout this chapter, the assessment of OCD in youth requires that the clinician be familiar with the heterogeneity of OCD symptom presentation and appropriately utilize extant evidence-based assessment tools. The clinical interview is the primary method of OCD assessment, and we strongly recommend use of the clinician-rated CYBOCS. Self- or parent reports should only be used to supplement the interview, and items denied during the clinician interview but endorsed on self/parent reports should be further queried in person. Accurate assessment is critical given that intervention selection hinges upon OCD diagnosis, and that assessment is the first step of intervention. Moreover, symptoms can be difficult or embarrassing for the family to discuss, the assessment may be the family's first contact with mental health and/or the first time they have discussed the youth's symptoms. Thus the clinician must be able to query symptoms in a way that is sensitive to each family member while normalizing the disorder. Clinicians should not be afraid to seek consultation, particularly when symptom presentations are unusual or unfamiliar to them and/or when symptom complexities may require difficult differential diagnoses. Use of the practices outlined in this chapter, along with empathy and good clinical judgment, will likely lead to precise diagnosis, case conceptualization, and treatment goal identification while simultaneously providing the family with a positive assessment experience.

REFERENCES

Achenbach, T. M., & Rescorla, L. A. (2001). *Manual for the ASEBA school-age forms & profiles*. Burlington, VT: University of Vermont, Research Center for Children, Youth, & Families.

American Psychiatric Association. (2013). *Diagnostic and statistical manual of mental disorders* (5th ed.). Arlington, VA: American Psychiatric Publishing.

Bamber, D., Tamplin, A., Park, R. J., Kyte, Z. A., & Goodyer, I. M. (2002). Development of a short Leyton obsessional inventory for children and adolescents. *Journal of the American Academy of Child and Adolescent Psychiatry*, *41*, 1246–1252.

Berg, C., Whitaker, A., Davies, M., & Flament, M. (1988). The survey form of the Leyton obsessional inventory—Child version: Norms from an epidemiological study. *Journal of the American Academy of Child and Adolescent Psychiatry*, *27*, 759–763.

Calvo, R., Lázaro, L., Castro, J., Morer, A., & Toro, J. (2007). Parental psychopathology in child and adolescent obsessive-compulsive disorder. *Social Psychiatry and Psychiatric Epidemiology*, *42*, 647–655.

Calvocoressi, L., Lewis, B., Harris, M., Trufan, S. J., Goodman, W. K., McDougle, C. J., et al. (1995). Family accommodation in obsessive-compulsive disorder. *American Journal of Psychiatry*, *152*, 441–443.

Coles, M. E., Wolters, L. H., Sochting, I., De Haan, E., Pietrefesa, A. S., & Whiteside, S. P. (2010). Development and initial validation of the obsessive belief questionnaire-child version (OBQ-CV). *Depression and Anxiety, 27*, 982–991.

Conelea, C. A., Freeman, J. B., & Garcia, A. M. (2012). Integrating behavioral theory with OCD assessment using the Y-BOCS/CY-BOCS symptom checklist. *Journal of Obsessive-Compulsive and Related Disorders, 1*, 112–118.

Conelea, C. A., Schmidt, E. R., Leonard, R. C., Riemann, B. C., & Cahill, S. (2012). The Children's Yale–Brown Obsessive Compulsive Scale: Clinician versus self-report format in adolescents in a residential treatment facility. *Journal of Obsessive-Compulsive and Related Disorders, 1*, 69–72.

Coskun, M., Zoroglu, S., & Ozturk, M. (2012). Phenomenology, psychiatric comorbidity and family history in referred preschool children with obsessive-compulsive disorder. *Child and Adolescent Psychiatry and Mental Health, 6*, 1–9.

Eisen, J. L., Phillips, K. A., Baer, L., Beer, D. A., Atala, K. D., & Rasmussen, S. A. (1998). The Brown Assessment of Beliefs Scale: reliability and validity. *American Journal of Psychiatry, 155*(1), 102–108.

Foa, E. B., Coles, M., Huppert, J. D., Pasupuleti, R. V., Franklin, M. E., & March, J. (2010). Development and validation of a child version of the obsessive compulsive inventory. *Behavior Therapy, 41*, 121–132.

Foa, E. B., Kozak, M. J., Salkovskis, P. M., Coles, M. E., & Amir, N. (1998). The validation of a new obsessive–compulsive disorder scale: The obsessive–compulsive inventory. *Psychological Assessment, 10*, 206.

Freeman, J., Flessner, C. A., & Garcia, A. (2011). The children's Yale-Brown obsessive compulsive scale: Reliability and validity for use among 5 to 8 year olds with obsessive-compulsive disorder. *Journal of Abnormal Child Psychology, 39*, 877–883.

Frost, R. O., Steketee, G., & Grisham, J. (2004). Measurement of compulsive hoarding: Saving inventory revised. *Behavior Research and Therapy, 42*, 1163–1182.

Gallant, J., Storch, E. A., Merlo, L. J., Ricketts, E. D., Geffken, G. R., Goodman, W. K., et al. (2008). Convergent and discriminant validity of the children's Yale-Brown obsessive compulsive scale-symptom checklist. *Journal of Anxiety Disorders, 22*, 1369–1376.

Garcia, A. M., Freeman, J. B., Himle, M. B., Berman, N. C., Ogata, A. K., Ng, J., et al. (2009). Phenomenology of early childhood onset obsessive compulsive disorder. *Journal of Psychopathology and Behavioral Assessment, 31*(2), 104–111.

Geller, D. A., & March, J. (2012). Practice parameter for the assessment and treatment of children and adolescents with obsessive-compulsive disorder. *Journal of the American Academy of Child & Adolescent Psychiatry, 51*, 98–113.

Guy, W. (1976). *Clinical global impressions ECDEU assessment manual for psychopharmacology*. Rockville, MD: National Institute for Mental Health.

Huang, L., Tsai, K., Wang, H., Sung, P., Wu, M., Hung, K., et al. (2014). Prevalence, incidence, and comorbidity of clinically diagnosed obsessive–compulsive disorder in Taiwan: A national population-based study. *Psychiatry Research, 220*(1–2), 335–341.

Hudziak, J. J., Althoff, R. R., Stanger, C., Beijsterveldt, C. V., Nelson, E. C., Hanna, G. L., et al. (2006). The obsessive compulsive scale of the child behavior checklist predicts obsessive-compulsive disorder: A receiver operating characteristic curve analysis. *Journal of Child Psychology and Psychiatry, 47*, 160–166.

Iniesta-Sepúlveda, M., Rosa-Alcázar, A. I., Rosa-Alcázar, Á., & Storch, E. A. (2014). Evidence-based assessment in children and adolescents with obsessive–compulsive disorder. *Journal of Child and Family Studies, 23*, 1455–1470.

Ivarsson, T., Melin, K., & Wallin, L. (2007). Categorical and dimensional aspects of co-morbidity in obsessive-compulsive disorder (OCD). *European Child & Adolescent Psychiatry*, *17*(1), 20–31.

Jones, A. M., De Nadai, A. S., Arnold, E. B., McGuire, J. F., Lewin, A. B., Murphy, T. K., et al. (2013). Psychometric properties of the obsessive compulsive inventory: Child version in children and adolescents with obsessive–compulsive disorder. *Child Psychiatry and Human Development*, *44*, 137–151.

Kaufman, J., Birmaher, B., Brent, D., Rao, U., Flynn, C., Moreci, P., et al. (1997). Schedule for affective disorders and schizophrenia for school-age children-present and lifetime version (K-SADS-PL): Initial reliability and validity data. *Journal of the American Academy of Child and Adolescent Psychiatry*, *36*(7), 980–988.

Kingery, J. N., Roblek, T. L., Suveg, C., Grover, R. L., Sherrill, J. T., & Bergman, R. L. (2006). They're not just. *Journal of Cognitive Psychotherapy*, *20*, 263–273.

Lewin, A. B., & Piacentini, J. (2010). Evidence-based assessment of child obsessive compulsive disorder: Recommendations for clinical practice and treatment research. *Child & Youth Care Forum*, *39*, 73–89.

Lewin, A. B., Piacentini, J., De Nadai, A. S., Jones, A. M., Peris, T. S., Geffken, G. R., et al. (2014). Defining clinical severity in pediatric obsessive-compulsive disorder. *Psychological Assessment*, *26*, 679–684.

Masi, G., Millepiedi, S., Perugi, G., Pfanner, C., Berloffa, S., Pari, C., et al. (2010). A naturalistic exploratory study of the impact of demographic, phenotypic and comorbid features in pediatric obsessive-compulsive disorder. *Psychopathology*, *43*(2), 69–78.

Merlo, L. J., Storch, E. A., Murphy, T. K., Goodman, W. K., & Geffken, G. R. (2005). Assessment of pediatric obsessive-compulsive disorder: A critical review of current methodology. *Child Psychiatry and Human Development*, *36*, 195–214.

Muris, P., Meesters, C., Rassin, E., Merckelbach, H., & Campbell, J. (2001). Thought–action fusion and anxiety disorders symptoms in normal adolescents. *Behaviour Research and Therapy*, *39*, 843–852.

Nelson, E. C., Hanna, G. L., Hudziak, J. J., Botteron, K. N., Heath, A. C., & Todd, R. D. (2001). Obsessive-compulsive scale of the child behavior checklist: Specificity, sensitivity, and predictive power. *Pediatrics*, *108*, e14.

Obsessive Compulsive Cognitions Working Group. (1997). Cognitive assessment of obsessive-compulsive disorder. *Behaviour Research and Therapy*, *35*, 667–681.

Obsessive Compulsive Cognitions Working Group. (2001). Development and initial validation of the obsessive beliefs questionnaire and the interpretation of intrusions inventory. *Behaviour Research and Therapy*, *39*, 987–1006.

Peris, T. S., Benazon, N., Langley, A., Roblek, T., & Piacentini, J. (2008). Parental attitudes, beliefs, and responses to childhood obsessive compulsive disorder: The parental attitudes and behaviors scale. *Child & Family Behavior Therapy*, *30*, 199–214.

Piacentini, J., Langley, A., & Roblek, T. (2007). *Cognitive-behavioral treatment of childhood OCD: It's only a false alarm. Therapist guide*. New York, NY: Oxford University Press.

Piacentini, J., Peris, T. S., Bergman, R. L., Chang, S., & Jaffer, M. (2007). Brief report: Functional impairment in childhood OCD: Development and psychometrics properties of the child obsessive-compulsive impact scale-revised (COIS-R). *Journal of Clinical Child and Adolescent Psychology*, *36*, 645–653.

Salkovskis, P. M., Wroe, A. L., Gledhill, A., Morrison, N., Forrester, E., Richards, C., et al. (2000). Responsibility attitudes and interpretations are characteristic of obsessive compulsive disorder. *Behaviour Research and Therapy*, *38*, 347–372.

Scahill, L., Riddle, M. A., Mcswiggin-Hardin, M., Ort, S. I., King, R. A., Goodman, W. K., et al. (1997). Children's Yale-Brown Obsessive Compulsive Scale: Reliability and validity. *Journal of the American Academy of Child and Adolescent Psychiatry*, *36*(6), 844–852.

Shafran, R., Thordarson, D. S., & Rachman, S. (1996). Thought-action fusion in obsessive compulsive disorder. *Journal of Anxiety Disorders*, *10*, 379–391.

Silverman, W., & Albano, A. (1996). *The anxiety disorders interview schedule for children–IV (child and parent versions)*. San Antonio, TX: Psychological Corporation.

Stewart, S. E., Hu, Y. P., Hezel, D. M., Proujansky, R., Lamstein, A., Walsh, C., et al. (2011). Development and psychometric properties of the OCD family functioning (OFF) scale. *Journal of Family Psychology*, *25*, 434.

Storch, E. A., De Nadai, A. S., Jacob, M. L., Lewin, A. B., Muroff, J., Eisen, J., et al. (2014). Phenomenology and correlates of insight in pediatric obsessive–compulsive disorder. *Comprehensive Psychiatry*, *55*, 613–620.

Storch, E. A., Khanna, M., Merlo, L. J., Loew, B. A., Franklin, M., Reid, J. M., et al. (2009). Children's Florida obsessive compulsive inventory: Psychometric properties and feasibility of a self-report measure of obsessive–compulsive symptoms in youth. *Child Psychiatry and Human Development*, *40*, 467–483.

Storch, E. A., Lewin, A. B., De Nadai, A. S., & Murphy, T. K. (2010). Defining treatment response and remission in obsessive-compulsive disorder: A signal detection analysis of the children's Yale-Brown obsessive compulsive scale. *Journal of the American Academy of Child and Adolescent Psychiatry*, *49*, 708–717.

Storch, E. A., Muroff, J., Lewin, A. B., Geller, D., Ross, A., McCarthy, K., et al. (2011). Development and preliminary psychometric evaluation of the children's saving inventory. *Child Psychiatry and Human Development*, *42*, 166–182.

Storch, E. A., Murphy, T. K., Geffken, G. R., Soto, O., Sajid, M., Allen, P., et al. (2004). Psychometric evaluation of the Children's Yale–Brown Obsessive-Compulsive Scale. *Psychiatry Research*, *129*, 91–98.

Storch, E. A., Park, J. M., Lewin, A. B., Morgan, J. R., Jones, A. M., & Murphy, T. K. (2011). The Leyton obsessional inventory-child version survey form does not demonstrate adequate psychometric properties in American youth with pediatric obsessive-compulsive disorder. *Journal of Anxiety Disorders*, *25*, 574–578.

Uher, R., Heyman, I., Turner, C. M., & Shafran, R. (2008). Self-, parent-report and interview measures of obsessive–compulsive disorder in children and adolescents. *Journal of Anxiety Disorders*, *22*, 979–990.

Wolters, L. H., Hogendoorn, S. M., Oudega, M., Vervoort, L., Haan, E., Prins, P. J. M., et al. (2012). Psychometric properties of the Dutch version of the meta-cognitions questionnaire–adolescent version (MCQ-A) in non-clinical adolescents and adolescents with obsessive–compulsive disorder. *Journal of Anxiety Disorders*, *26*, 343–351.

FURTHER READING

Selles, R. R., Storch, E. A., & Lewin, A. B. (2014). Variations in symptom prevalence and clinical correlates in younger versus older youth with obsessive–compulsive disorder. *Child Psychiatry and Human Development*, *45*, 666–674.

Chapter 5

Developing Exposure Hierarchies

Dean McKay
Fordham University, New York, NY, United States

DEVELOPING EXPOSURE HIERARCHIES

Treatment of obsessive-compulsive disorder (OCD) in children requires first developing hierarchies of stimuli that are the source of avoidance before initiating treatment. Effective treatment of OCD employing exposure with response prevention (ERP) is critically dependent on carefully crafted hierarchies of stimuli that are associated with avoidance.

Wolpe, in his classic work on behavior therapy, laid out the rationale for developing hierarchies in conducting systematic desensitization, which was to ensure that exposure to fear-producing stimuli was manageable, and that the relaxation skills that would be employed could overcome the provoked anxiety (Wolpe, 1990, chap. 5). When systematic desensitization gave way to exposure as the dominant method for fear reduction, the need for hierarchies remained as research showed that exposure to stimuli that provoked anxiety that was too intense would interfere with developing new neural structures that would produce effective fear reduction (Foa & Kozak, 1986).

A way to present this to parents/caregivers is through a physical conditioning metaphor. If someone were interested in beginning a physical fitness program, the first thing she or he would do is start with a level of exercise that could be readily tolerated and repeated each day without excessive fatigue. Further, it is worth presenting to parents that each fitness plan is calibrated to fit the individual needs of the person, but that many of these plans will share common features. Likewise for children beginning treatment with ERP for OCD, who have not practiced any tasks designed to interfere with their avoidance, which is by its very nature demanding. This will help parents/caregivers understand the incremental nature of ERP and to have a greater sense of how to expect change to take shape in their child over the course of treatment.

A way to present this to children can be through academic performance. When a child starts a new school year, the teacher presents new information

The Clinician's Guide to Cognitive-Behavioral Therapy for Childhood Obsessive-Compulsive Disorder
http://dx.doi.org/10.1016/B978-0-12-811427-8.00005-8

gradually, with additional material building on the prior work. Accordingly, the school year follows a pacing that hopefully is tolerated well. The same is the case for ERP. This will also help the child understand how treatment is likely to proceed, in a progression rather than with sudden gains.

GETTING ORIENTED: ASSESSING SYMPTOMS DOMAINS FOR HIERARCHY DEVELOPMENT

Before developing any hierarchies, it is essential to prioritize which symptoms should be the target of ERP (see also Chapter 4). One way to address this is through discussion with the parents/caregivers regarding symptoms that are observed most frequently or those that interfere most with daily activities. If treatment first targets these symptoms, there is likely to be greater "buy in" on conducting additional interventions later that aim to reduce overall OCD symptom severity. It is often useful to keep in mind that OCD is a highly complex and heterogeneous condition (McKay et al., 2006). Therefore it is necessary to determine the full scope of symptoms, those that cause regular interference in daily functioning as well as those that may be less apparent, but which could later create interference in functioning.

A Phenomenological Perspective on Hierarchies

In order to develop a detailed and useful hierarchy, it is essential for the clinician to understand the sources of avoidance through the child's perspective. Consider the following basic example: a child presents for treatment due to contamination fear with washing rituals. The task for the clinician is to determine the environmental sources of contamination fear, the nature of the washing rituals, and what features each possess that could be broken down into smaller units to place on a hierarchy. This by necessity requires the clinician to identify elements of shared experiences consistent with the tenets of phenomenology (Kaufer & Chemero, 2015). This means that the stimulus complex is being conceptualized as components of a larger whole (illustrated in Fig. 1). In the aforementioned case, this would entail careful consideration of settings where the child might feel at risk of being contaminated and include reports from the parents. The following brief transcript illustrates the approach to developing a phenomenological understanding of the child's sources of fear and avoidance:

> *Clinician*: Your parents said you often say you feel contaminated after playing with your friends. Which of your friends makes you feel most contaminated and why?
>
> *Youth*: Joe and Eric both make me feel contaminated. They both like to say yucky things, like talk about boogers and poop. Then I feel like I got some on me, even if there was none around. I want to wash so badly after they say things like that.

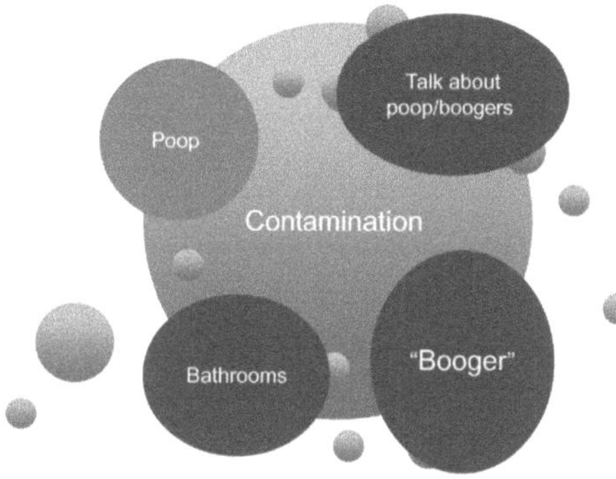

FIG. 1 Whole and constituent parts of stimulus complex. *Note*: Nonoverlapping bubbles represent other feared stimuli unrelated to contamination; overlapping bubbles represent components of feared stimuli not identified by therapist.

C: I see. Which is worse, boogers or poop?
Y: Both are yucky, but I guess poop is worse.
C: You said both words now. Is that easier than hearing someone else say these things?
Y: I don't like it, but since you are a doctor I think it is ok. But when Joe and Eric talk about it, they say so much more, it's really disgusting.
C: I see. So it is not just the words, but they say more stuff about boogers and poop.

In this brief exchange, the clinician is attempting to understand, from this young boy's perspective, the unique details of a single source of contamination fear for the child. While a common symptom of OCD involves contamination fear, it turns out that there are a variety of ways this specific problem may manifest. Getting this additional specific information helps the clinician create more potent and individualized hierarchies for later use in ERP. This topic will be addressed again later in the chapter when the complex hierarchies are discussed.

The Nuts and Bolts

So now that the major symptoms have been identified that will be targeted for treatment and have an emerging phenomenological understanding of the child's symptoms. There remains one more step before the hierarchy can be developed.

Developing the Subjective Units of Distress (SUDS) Scale

Essential in developing the hierarchy is identification of anticipation levels of distress the child will experience when exposed to different components of the feared stimulus complex. This necessarily requires defining the scale for the child, in particular the anchor points at each extreme. The following is an illustrative discussion with a child for defining the scale.

C: Can you tell me a time when you felt the most calm?
Y: When I first wake up in the morning, I usually feel really calm.
C: Ok, that is great. So we are going call that zero, on our distress meter. Now, can you tell me when you felt more afraid than ever?
Y: I was in the car, and I was playing with Joe and Eric and they were talking about poop boogers. My mom had to pick me up early because they kept making up stories about poop boogers, and I felt so yucky I couldn't take it.
C: Ok, thanks for telling me about that, you are so brave. Let's call that time a 100, the highest score on our distress meter.

This dialog is essential in order that all the future potential stimuli that will be discussed can be placed in a hierarchy. It may be necessary to adjust the scale, as will be discussed shortly. It is also sometimes helpful to draw a picture of the scale for the child or use a preprinted illustration. Further, the language used to describe the scale can be modified based on the child's needs. This means it can be called a thermometer, rating, scale, or based on any other metric. In some children, instead of using numbers, the scale can be designed based on different animals in levels of dangerousness. The following illustrates this last example:

C: Can you tell me when you felt the calmest?
Y: Yes, it is when I get up in the morning.
C: So getting up in the morning, you might feel like a sleepy kitten?
Y: Haha, yes, that is funny.
C: And what about the time you felt the most afraid. Can you tell me that?
Y: It was a time when I had to wait for my mom to get soap so I could wash after hearing a lot of yucky talk about boogers and poop.
C: So, maybe that time your fear was like a big scary lion roaring at you?
Y: Yes, it was that scary.

Fig. 2 illustrates two different SUDS options, with anchor points.

Developing the Hierarchy

Now that the extreme points on the scale have been established, and there is an emerging phenomenology of the symptoms of the child, it is time to develop the hierarchy. For the purpose of this illustration the example with contamination fear and washing rituals is used. What is known at this point about the child is that there is a fear of "boogers" and "poop," at least in discussion. What is not known is the reaction to actual bodily products. How does the child react to occasions where he defecates or blows his nose? Can the child use bathrooms outside the home? What kind of avoidance takes place, and how do the parents/caregivers accommodate these symptoms (see also Chapters 8, Involving Family Members and 13, Addressing Family Accommodation). These are all

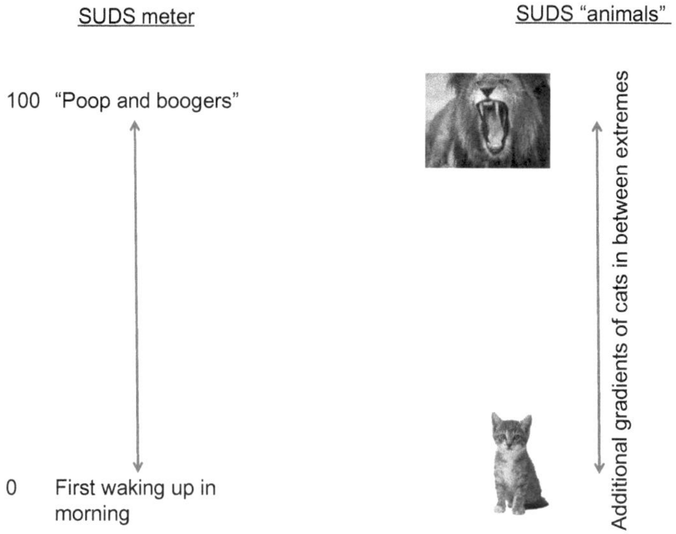

FIG. 2 Subjective units of distress anchor points.

essential areas to keep in mind while developing the hierarchy and will allow the clinician to develop a deeper phenomenological understanding of the child's symptoms. The following illustrates the discussion that might lead to the hierarchy for contamination fears.

C: You said before that when Joe and Eric talk about yucky stuff, especially boogers and poop, that you feel the most uncomfortable. But tell me, what happens when you have to go to the bathroom and make a poop?
Y: That is too yucky, I can't think about it.
C: Is that more yucky than talking about boogers and poop with your friends?
Y: Yes.
C: Oh, I see. Ok, so that means we might need to change our meter we made before. Would going to the bathroom to make poop be higher than talking about poop?
Y: Yes, that would be the highest.
C: Ok, but I can think of something yuckier. What if you got a little bit of poop on your hand. Would that be worse than just making poop?
Y: Oh, yes, that would be definitely be the worst!
C: I see. Can we change the meter we made before? I think our highest number of 100 should be if you ever got poop on your hand. Right?
Y: Definitely. That seems really scary.
C: Ok, so now, how scary would it be just to go to the bathroom, and poop, but with no poop getting on your hands.
Y: Hmmm, I think that might be an 80.

<the clinician, during this discussion, would be writing the responses on a scale to show the child>

C: Ah, ok. So now, what about talking about poop? How scary is that now?

Y: Maybe 70.

C: Great, you are doing fantastic!

So now the hierarchy is starting to take a very different shape than what was expected when the anchor points for the extreme ends of the scale were developed. In this instance, it is useful to consider how lower ends of the hierarchy might look.

> *C*: You've told me a lot about the really scary things. Can we talk about some things that might make you feel yucky, but are not too scary? Using our meter, how upset might you feel if you saw a picture of someone with a finger in their nose?
>
> *Y*: I wouldn't see a booger?
>
> *C*: No, just a finger in the nose.
>
> *Y*: That might be a 20. I see kids do that all the time in school.
>
> *C*: Ok, great. How about if the kid in class does that, and then pulls his finger out and quickly puts it in his mouth.
>
> *Y*: Ew, yuck. But if I don't see it, that would be a 30. I see that a lot too.
>
> *C*: Great job. Ok, now what if you walk into a bathroom and you know someone just pooped, but you don't see anyone or anything?
>
> *Y*: Ugh, that happens a lot. It's really yucky. That would be a 60.
>
> *C*: Ok, so then what if you see a kid leave, he clearly just pooped, and he walks out of the bathroom without washing?
>
> *Y*: Ewww!! That would be a 70.
>
> *C*: So I want to make sure I understand. That would be a 70, and so would a conversation with your friends about boogers and poop. Is that right?
>
> *Y*: Oh, hmmm. Well, I guess talking about boogers and poop is not as bad, maybe a 60.

This illustration represents something that commonly happens when developing a hierarchy, specifically, the initial estimates of the scariest stimuli drops in level once other more anxiety or distress-inducing stimuli are identified. The clinician would continue to identify additional stimuli or situations that provoke different levels of distress, including some that might be the same level as others (equal estimates of distress), and potentially further refinement of the upper and lower bounds of the scale. Table 1 presents the hierarchy developed from this transcript.

HIERARCHY DEVELOPMENT FOR COMPLEX SYMPTOMS

As noted earlier, OCD is a heterogeneous condition. Accordingly, there are many other symptom presentations that present serious challenges to the aforementioned phenomenological analysis. Nonetheless, it is important to begin to occupy the mind-set of the child in order to better understand how to assess the

TABLE 1 Illustrative Partial Hierarchy—Contamination Fear With Washing Rituals

Stimuli or Situation	SUDS (0–100)
Child with a finger in nose	20
Child with finger in nose, quickly removes and puts in mouth	30
Talking about poop	60
Go in bathroom, see someone come out who clearly pooped and did not wash hands	70
Uses bathroom to poop	80
Uses bathroom to poop, gets a little on hand	100

full range of stimuli and situations that provoke obsessions and compulsions. The following are several common symptom presentations that clinicians would confront in developing hierarchies.

All or Nothing Reports of Fear

This is a particularly common challenge that clinicians must contend with in developing hierarchies. Children often view any stimuli or situation that is related to their primary presenting obsession as maximally fear provoking. Addressing this requires careful consideration for two important reasons. First, the child may not possess the cognitive flexibility to understand different levels of fear. Therefore the clinician's task is to guide the child to stimuli that at least appear to be more or less fear provoking. The following brief exchange illustrates this point:

> *C*: You mentioned before that hearing Joe and Eric discuss poop and boogers would be a 100 on the meter. What would you rate it, on our meter, if you had to use the bathroom yourself.
> *Y*: That would be a 100, too.
> *C*: I want to just make sure I understand you. Talking about poop and boogers *is the same as* going to the bathroom, where you produce poop?
> *Y*: Um, I'm not sure.
> *C*: Think for just a moment. Talking about it, where you don't see it at all, is the same as going to the bathroom, where you might see it, might smell it. Are these the same?
> *Y*: I guess not.

It is essential that the all-or-nothing fear estimates be addressed, because as will be shown in the next chapter, in order to implement ERP the clinician will need some starting points. If all the estimates the child provides are at the maximum, it is not possible to begin.

Second, it is possible that the child is especially sensitive to anxiety experiences. Research has shown that many children with anxiety problems have an elevated sensitivity to interpreting physical sensations as dangerous or anxiety producing (Noel & Francis, 2011). As a result, some children will overestimate the level of anxiety they will experience for different stimuli associated with OCD symptoms. When facing such a situation, the clinician can address this by identifying ways the child may be misinterpreting the physical sensations of fear. For example:

> *C*: You mentioned that talking about poop and boogers causes you to feel a lot of fear.
> *Y*: Yes, it is really yucky, and my stomach hurts from hearing about it sometimes.
> *C*: Is the talk ever funny?
> *Y*: Sometimes.
> *C*: So if it is funny, can it also be scary?
> *Y*: No, so maybe it is not that scary.

Not Just Right Experiences/Incompleteness

It has been increasingly recognized that some symptoms of OCD are a consequence of feeling that actions are not complete or "not just right experiences" (NJRE) (Ravid, Franklin, Khanna, Storch, & Coles, 2014). This can present a conundrum for clinicians who are accustomed to viewing obsessions as fear provoking. NJRE symptoms typically do not produce fear but more a general sense of discomfort. This means that clinicians must reorient their anchor points for the hierarchy to levels of tolerability of discomfort, rather than aversive emotional consequences. We will return to NJRE in the next chapter on developing and implementing successful exposures.

Long Delay in Consequences

Developing hierarchies are most straightforward when the outcome associated with contact with the feared stimuli is brief. In the example used throughout this chapter to this point, the child reports "feeling yucky" immediately upon contact with the stimuli or situation. However, this is frequently not the case. Consider the following two examples:

Example 1: Contamination Fear of Illness

Often contamination fear is due to concerns over contracting an illness. As is well known, contact with a contamination source does not result in illness immediately after exposure. Instead, there is typically a lag, often between

36 h to several weeks, and the level of concern a child reports is dependent on several factors, including knowledge of illnesses, cognitive development, and assumptions of lethality.

Addressing this problem requires some careful planning, largely because almost every item on a putative hierarchy could lead, ultimately, to contracting the illness (according to the child) and therefore would be at the maximum level of fear provocation. On the other hand, if the clinician capitalizes on the child's likely knowledge of actual risk (as opposed to assumed, or obsessional risk), then some real headway may be made in constructing a hierarchy.

Scenario A (Extensive Illness Knowledge)

Under this scenario, the onus is on the clinician to also be familiar with the disease transmission rate of the feared illness and to also challenge the child's assumptions about risk in the local geographic setting for treatment, explanations for why others do not contract the illness despite taking risks the child is unwilling to, and what kinds of risks the child is willing to take in order to improve. This will set the stage for developing a hierarchy that can later be used for implementing treatment (see also Chapter 7, Cognitive Training Strategies).

Scenario B (Cognitive Development)

It is underappreciated that treatment is critically dependent on the child having adequate cognitive development to grapple with the requests for formulating a hierarchy. In the case of illness-related contamination fear with a long lag for onset, children who have less developed cognitive abilities can be "educated" about the risks and guided in the formulation of the hierarchy based on the knowledge the clinician imparts. This may require that the clinician engage in some brief investigation regarding the potential risks for the specific illness concern expressed by the child.

Scenario C (Assumptions of Lethality)

A fundamental question to ask is, what are the kinds of illnesses feared, and what will happen if any of them are contracted. The child may have a wide range of faulty assumptions about lethality of illness, or more generally, may hold misperceptions of harm for illnesses. As with Scenario B, in order to develop a useful hierarchy, it can be useful to educate the child about the actual risks of the various illnesses that are feared.

Example 2: Postmortem Feared Outcomes

Concerns with consequences that might occur in the afterlife are common among sufferers of OCD and can become evident in adolescents. Developing a hierarchy related to concerns such as these calls for special attention to individual cultural and religious norms (Peris & Rosenman, 2016) but also requires addressing intermediary steps since all exposure would in turn lead to the highest feared item on the hierarchy.

The following illustrates identification of intermediary outcomes associated with obsessions due to scrupulosity, in an Orthodox Jewish child age 13 who was concerned with properly completing required daily prayers. Prior to the conversation, the clinician spoke with the family's rabbi, who provided expected parameters around evening prayers.

C: So tell me, how long does it take each evening to recite the Shema?
Y: I've been taking 30 min each night, to be sure I get it right.
C: As you know, I spoke with your rabbi, who said the Shema takes about 2 min, for most kids your age.
Y: Yes, but I sometimes worry that I said one of the words incorrectly, and then God won't know I said it.
C: So I am familiar with that prayer, is there one word in the prayer that God would be less offended about being mispronounced?
Y: Huh? I thought the whole thing, each and every word, has to be said precisely.
C: I don't think so. At least according to your rabbi. You've said that prayer hundreds of times. If you think about it, is there a word or two that would not be such a big deal to mispronounce?
T: Hmm, well now that you mention it, I suppose there might be.
C: Ok, so let's start with that one, tell me how distressed would you be if you mispronounced it, and did not redo the prayer?

Distress Is Not Always Fear

The example that was used for much of this chapter, the child with contamination fear provoked by "boogers" and "poop" likely experienced fear, but also likely experienced significant disgust. It has been recognized that many individuals with OCD, particularly those with contamination fear, are motivated to avoid due to disgust (McKay & Moretz, 2009). As a result, the hierarchy should be constructed to be flexible and accommodate reports of experiencing this emotional reaction.

It should be noted that, as a result of the prominence of disgust in contamination fear and other obsessional experiences, there are some special considerations that can aid in constructing the hierarchy as well as facilitate clinician phenomenological understanding of the client. Disgust is an emotional state that can be passed on by different stimuli. Specifically, disgust follows what are known as the *laws of sympathetic magic* (Rozin & Fallon, 1987). The first one is the *law of similarity*, which is when an otherwise neutral object resembles something associated with disgust. An example of the law of similarity would be a chocolate bar that resembles "poop," in the parlance of our case example. The second is the *law of contagion*. This law operates when an otherwise neutral object comes in momentary contact with something associated with disgust. For example, if a pen were dropped into a toilet, but were later completely cleaned, the law of contagion would lead to great hesitancy in its use. If that pen came then came in contact with another pen, the second pen might be deemed dirty as well. This is the law of contagion in action.

The laws of sympathetic magic are potent in understanding how to address contamination fears and in developing hierarchies. For example, if a child struggles to articulate situations that might be tolerable while developing the hierarchy, the clinician can capitalize on the law of contagion through an exercise in "how many steps removed?" for the primary feared stimulus. Take the following example:

C: You mentioned that if you went into a bathroom where you saw someone exit after that person clearly pooped, but did not wash their hands, that it would be a 70 on our meter. Now, what would that rating be if you came in contact with a tissue that came in contact with the toilet seat?
Y: Hmm, that feels only slightly less bad, maybe 65.
C: Ok, so what if that tissue was touched by another tissue? What would your rating be for touching the second tissue?
Y: I think maybe 55.
C: Ok, so let's include that on our hierarchy.

It is at this point that the clinician need not be concerned with which emotional state is provoked by elements of the stimulus complex. These nuances will be addressed in the next chapter on implementing ERP.

Symptoms That Provoke Discomfort in Clinicians

Throughout this chapter, examples have been used that are fairly straightforward, and not likely to cause distress in clinicians as the prospects of ERP begins to loom on the horizon, with the possible exception of the complexity associated with scrupulosity. However, one symptom dimension that is commonly present in children involves unwanted thoughts, concerns with sexuality, and/or harming others. These symptoms may provoke concerns in clinicians given the sensitive nature of the content. One important consideration when developing hierarchies, particularly if there are concerns over the content of obsessions, is to consider including parents or guardians in this phase of treatment. This will necessarily require first establishing strong rapport with the child, to fully educate the parents first about the nature and scope of symptoms (see also Chapter 3), and for the clinician to also fully appreciate that the symptoms are expressions of thoughts, not intentions. Once these points are clearly established, it will be more possible for the clinician to move forward with developing the hierarchy. The following exchange illustrates how parent concerns may be addressed as the hierarchy is developed.

Parent: I just don't understand why he talks about being afraid of poop and boogers all the time. And I'm very concerned because he has also later been talking about his penis, and that he gets scared when he has an erection. He talks to me about it when its bedtime, and he gets very upset about this.
C: What does he say he fearful of happening?
P: He has heard from other kids in school about sex, and he is worried about contamination from sex. I tell him that he is not going to have sex for a long time, but then he says kids talk about how toilet seats being contaminated by sex, and the children on the playground say things about other body secretions.
C: So the children at his school talk about sex, talk about body fluids, and he finds all these things scary. Can you tell me what he knows and does not? This will be helpful in developing our treatment plan since, as you recall from our earlier discussion, we will want to set up exposure to address all the scary thoughts he is having. But to do that we need to use language he will understand.

This exchange is set up to emphasize that the therapist is sensitive to the information that the child finds distressing, addressing the level of comfort that the parent or caregiver has around these topics, and sets the stage for the material to be included in later ERP. It also gives the clinician an opportunity to discuss potentially distressing content in a calm and controlled manner.

CONCLUSIONS

Developing hierarchies is an essential component of effective treatment for childhood OCD. Given the complexity of the condition, a wide range of factors must be considered in order to effectively construct a hierarchy. Underlying the entire process is a clear need for clinicians to develop a phenomenological understanding of the specific child's symptoms, which in turn will allow for a richer and more ecologically valid hierarchy for later use in implementing ERP.

Clinicians beginning to develop hierarchies do so in the knowledge that many of the entries on the hierarchy may be sources for later exposure exercises. This means that clinicians need to be sensitive to their own values and standards for conducting exposure. This will be discussed further in the next chapter, but it is important to consider briefly here. When developing a hierarchy, recognition of the types of compassionate exercises that are about to be developed through exposure may initially provoke distress, but with the longer term outcome of significant symptom relief. Along the way, clinicians may consider evaluating their own sense of comfort with implementing specific exposure exercises based on their own biases, assumptions, and values. It is recognized that many clinicians are hesitant to conduct exposure generally, and some of the symptoms described here (i.e., scrupulosity, fears of harm, obsessions regarding sexuality) can lead to significant concerns among clinicians (see McKay & Ojserkis, 2015). Hesitancy in conducting the necessary treatment, and in the absence of adequate explanation to parents or caregivers, can be problematic in treatment planning. However, with careful planning, and with clinicians being well versed in the nature of OCD symptoms, these challenges can be ethically addressed in order to alleviate the child's symptoms.

REFERENCES

Foa, E. B., & Kozak, M. J. (1986). Emotional processing of fear: Exposure to corrective information. *Psychological Bulletin*, *99*, 20–35.

Kaufer, S., & Chemero, A. (2015). *Phenomenology: An introduction*. Cambridge: Polity.

McKay, D., & Moretz, M. W. (2009). The intersection of disgust and contamination fear. In B. O. Olatunji & D. McKay (Eds.), *Disgust and its disorders* (pp. 211–227). Washington, DC: American Psychological Association.

McKay, D., & Ojserkis, R. (2015). Exposure in experiential context. In N. C. Thoma & D. McKay (Eds.), *Working with emotion in cognitive behavioral therapy* (pp. 83–104). New York: Guilford.

McKay, D., Piacentini, J., Greisberg, S., Graae, F., Jaffer, M., & Miller, J. (2006). The structure of childhood obsessions and compulsions: Dimensions in an outpatient sample. *Behaviour Research and Therapy*, *44*, 137–146. http://dx.doi.org/10.1016/j.brat.2005.02.001.

Noel, V. A., & Francis, S. E. (2011). A meta-analytic review of the role of child anxiety sensitivity in child anxiety. *Journal of Abnormal Child Psychology*, *39*, 721–733. http://dx.doi.org/10.1007/s10802-011-9489-3.

Peris, T. S., & Rosenman, M. (2016). Treatment of scrupulosity in childhood obsessive-compulsive disorder. In E. A. Storch & A. B. Lewin (Eds.), *Clinical handbook of obsessive-compulsive and related disorders*. Cham: Springer International Publishing.

Ravid, A., Franklin, M. E., Khanna, M., Storch, E. A., & Coles, M. E. (2014). "Not just right experiences" in adolescents: Phenomenology and associated characteristics. *Child Psychiatry and Human Development*, *45*, 193–200. http://dx.doi.org/10.1007/s10578-013-0391-9.

Rozin, P., & Fallon, A. E. (1987). A perspective on disgust. *Psychological Review*, *94*, 23–41. http://dx.doi.org/10.1037/0033-295X.94.1.23.

Wolpe, J. (1990). *The practice of behavior therapy* (4th ed.). Elmsford, NY: Pergamon.

Chapter 6

Developing and Implementing Exposure Treatment in Youth Obsessive-Compulsive Symptoms

Dean McKay
Fordham University, New York, NY, United States

Exposure with response prevention (ERP) is considered the primary efficacious treatment for childhood obsessive-compulsive disorder (OCD). Numerous treatment trials have demonstrated that this approach to treatment is highly effective, with large effect sizes (Franklin et al., 2015). The premise underlying ERP is remarkably simple—identify stimuli that provoke obsessions, present those stimuli, and set the stage to block the child from engaging in the ritual. However, in actual practice there are numerous impediments to proper treatment implementation.

Before covering methods for developing and implementing ERP with youth with OCD, it is important to address some lingering difficulties that clinicians face. One challenge is that clinicians are often hesitant to implement ERP out of a concern the procedure is somehow harmful to children. Some theoretical traditions shun the approach on these grounds, citing problems such as symptom substitution as a possible outcome. As a brief reminder, the concept of symptom substitution suggests that directly alleviating a presenting symptom ignores underlying and deeper psychopathology. In hydraulic fashion, then, by alleviating the pressure from one area (presenting symptom), a new symptom will appear (see Grünbaum, 1984). Despite decades of claims that this was a hazard, and a particularly acute one for exposure-based treatments, there is virtually no support for symptom substitution (Tryon, 2008).

Another challenge in conducting ERP involves clinician fears of potential harm to clients vis-à-vis worsening of symptoms or other intervention-related damages. So great is this fear that some authors of clinical guides have emphasized that other nonexposure-based interventions could be used in the treatment of OCD successfully without ever conducting a fear-based intervention. As will

The Clinician's Guide to Cognitive-Behavioral Therapy for Childhood Obsessive-Compulsive Disorder
http://dx.doi.org/10.1016/B978-0-12-811427-8.00006-X

be shown later in this chapter, fear evocation is not an essential ingredient for symptom improvement. Further, the clinician concern over increased litigation risk is unfounded. Correctly implementing exposure-based treatments confers no greater risk for litigation than any other psychotherapeutic intervention (Richard & Gloster, 2007).

In sum, there are few risks in conducting ERP, either based on theoretical considerations or from a professional litigation perspective. Further, there is little evidence that ERP increases risk of dropout, and the only factor that could contribute to trepidation in clients is the degree that there is hesitation in the clinician (Farrell, Kemp, Blakey, Meyer, & Deacon, 2016).

AFTER THE HIERARCHY: GETTING STARTED ON ERP

In the prior chapter, a detailed framework was developed that would enable clinicians to formulate hierarchies that would be relied on for proper pacing through exposure exercises. However, in formulating the hierarchy, an important question is embedded in each item listed: *will the child be willing to participate in exposure for this item?* The answer to this question is not always so easy to obtain. Some children will simply decline to participate in even the easiest items on the hierarchy. Others will report that she or he can handle any item on the hierarchy. And yet others will exhibit inconsistency, replying that some items can be completed and others cannot, and these may not be tied logically to the anticipated distress the child provided for the item.

What this means is that engaging in ERP also means being prepared to constantly update and revise the hierarchy (see Abramowitz, Deacon, & Whiteside, 2011, pp. 112–113 for discussion). This process of ongoing behavioral assessment provides a basis for developing richer and more effective ERP exercises for the child and promote a higher likelihood of improvement in the course of treatment.

Illustrative Example 1: Over or Underestimation of Distress

One of the more common occurrences in developing the hierarchy is that the child will overestimate the level of distress she or he will experience when the time comes to actually participate in exposure. Recall the example from the last chapter of a child with fear of contamination. In that example, the child rated "talking about poop" as causing a level of distress of 60 (out of a possible 100) (see Chapter 5, Table 1). It is quite possible that once this item on the hierarchy is practiced, the child will report a far lower level of distress. If this happens, the clinician might take the opportunity to revise the hierarchy, revisiting the items to determine if the child's ratings should stay the same now that an item that evoked a high level of distress led to a lower level than anticipated. The child may find this empowering since it is common to make these overestimations, and observing that the actual experience is lower creates expectations that treatment will be less fear evoking than might be anticipated.

On the other hand, a child might underestimate the level of distress that will be experienced. In the same fashion as the overestimate, once exposure is undertaken and there is greater distress experienced than anticipated, revise the hierarchy to reflect the adjusted expectations of discomfort. There is a significant difference in this scenario, however. Should this occur, it is important that the clinician stop the exposure in order that the child can return to baseline in order that sensitization does not occur. As will be discussed in the next section, the exposure exercise was set up in collaboration with the child in expectation that it would be handled successfully. This means that the child made a prediction that the item on the hierarchy could be handled with relative ease. If greater distress is experienced, then this expectation was violated.

Illustrative Example 2: Embedded Hierarchy Items

Recall that in formulating the hierarchy, the clinician and child, with input from the parent, formulate the stimulus items and obtain anticipated ratings of distress. All of this is done through self-report and is therefore dependent on the child offering accurate retrospective report. It turns out, however, that retrospective memory is notoriously unreliable, particularly during anxiety (e.g., Patel et al., 2016). In Chapter 5, it was emphasized that constructing the hierarchy was an inherently phenomenological task, whereby the clinician had to both assess likely feared stimuli in the broader stimulus complex and appreciate the experience of the child while in the situation. This is, of course, necessarily incomplete and only after the clinician begins to conduct exposure does there become more of a shared phenomenology.

This means that exposure is also a bit of a discovery task, where the clinician uncovers situations and stimuli that are feared that were not under prior consideration. In the example earlier with the contamination fearful child, the clinician inquired about distress for "poop" and "boogers." In conducting exposure, it can easily turn out that other stimuli associated with the nose or derriere could also evoke anxiety. This means that the hierarchy might be expanded to include additional stimuli such as nostril hair, tissue boxes, tissues that appear used (i.e., wrinkled), underwear (both clean and soiled), the back pockets on pants, and other associated stimuli that were previously not considered.

Illustrative Example 3: Unfounded Bravery

Some children, particularly adolescents, might report that none of the items on the hierarchy are a problem, that avoiding is just a preference. In circumstances like these, it is best to assume that the distress ratings provided are accurate until evidence accumulates to suggest otherwise. Be prepared for some children to remain unfazed by the exposure. It is only after a session or two have passed and the child shows success both within session and between session with carrying out exposure might it be safe to proceed more aggressively up the hierarchy as guided by the predictions of the child. And even in situations like this, consultation with the parent will remain paramount to ensure that the child is successfully completing the prescribed between session therapeutic homework (discussed later).

DOES EXPOSURE NEED TO BE SCARY?

As exposure-based treatment became more well developed, the prevailing clinical theory emphasized accessing the fear structures stored in memory and, with prolonged experience in the absence of any negative outcome, and at a level the individual could tolerate, there would be corrective learning (Foa & Kozak, 1986). Since that time, research has accumulated that suggests the memory itself could be changed with treatment (Tryon & McKay, 2009) and that this might even be a suitable target for change.

Accessing the memory structure that is associated with avoidance, however, does not require evocation of fear. It is only necessary to access the memory for the behavior associated with the fear, and in turn promote new experiences. This has profound consequences for how ERP may be conceptualized.

Without the requirement that exposure necessarily evoke fear, then clinicians are free to construct situations that the client may find neutral or even amusing and still promote change. Interestingly, even before the articulation of the model that emphasized exposure where fear is activated, research existed demonstrating that fear reduction could be achieved for otherwise anxiety-provoking stimuli through exposure without the accompanying emotional experience. Foa, Blau, Prout, and Latimer (1977) showed that phobias could be successfully alleviated without fear evocation in a group of $N=36$ rat phobic individuals. Beyond this single example, a more recent model of exposure has been developed that emphasizes new learning whereby anxiety evocation may occur but is not deemed essential. The inhibitory learning model (Abramowitz, 2013; Craske, Treanor, Conway, Zbozinek, & Vervliet, 2014; Frank & McKay, in press) identified several areas that clinicians may focus upon in producing change that does not require merely waiting for habituation to take place.

Expectancy Violations

Perhaps one of the most potent aspects of ERP under the inhibitory learning model is expectancy violation. Under ordinary circumstances, the child experiences obsessive-compulsive symptoms as frightening, or at the very least, uncomfortable. However, this expectation can be challenged with the very first exposure exercise that takes place in the office. The following exchange in an early exposure for the contamination fearful example illustrates this point:

Clinician: So we are going to practice exposure for boogers. Remember you said you would feel distress at about 20 on our meter if you saw a child with their finger in their nose?
Youth: Yes, I remember that. It's so yucky!
C: Yes, it can be yucky. Here is a picture I found online of a child with his finger up his nose. Can you handle looking at it?
Y: Yes. It looks gross.
C: Really? Maybe he is looking forward to a little snack? I bet he would like something salty, and since he didn't have any money to buy chips, he decided he would see what he had in storage in his nose.
Y: Haha, that is funny.

In this illustration, the therapist is making a deliberate effort to alter the perspective that the child takes on the feared stimulus to one involving humor rather than fear. In order for this to be successful, it is necessary for the clinician to (a) have a good rapport with the child, (b) start with something fairly mild to "probe" as to whether the child has the ability to laugh at something that at the outset of treatment seemed frightening, and (c) use this approach judiciously. Excessive use of humor can be trying for clients who arrive at treatment for a problem that is distressing, but in the context of exposure early in treatment it can be refreshing and create a more engaging frame of reference for the child.

Reinforced Extinction

Exposure treatment can be challenging for the child, with or without the aforementioned expectancy violation. A constant focus for the clinician, in addition to potentially updating the hierarchy on a regular basis, is to ensure that the child is engaged in treatment. If there are inadequate reinforcements (aside from symptom alleviation), then treatment engagement will likely suffer. One important way around this is to provide reinforcement for extinction. This can be accomplished through the parent or caregiver making some prearranged reinforcement available. The following exchange illustrates the point:

Clinician: Remember that originally you said talking about poop would lead to a 60 on our distress meter? But later we found out that talking about poop was not so bad, around a 40, but talking about diarrhea, that was more like a 60? (note, in this illustration, the overestimation of distress was evident, as was the embedded hierarchy item).
Youth: Yes, I remember that. Diarrhea is so yucky!!
C: I agree, so yucky!! But, you've been doing so well with exposure and doing more and more things we had on the hierarchy. Let's practice looking at pictures I found on the internet of unflushed toilets that contain diarrhea. Ready?
Y: Um, ok.

<Clinician and youth now view pictures for about 5 min. The clinician may or may not have a running dialog now in an attempt to alter expectancies. Following is an example of the former>

> *C*: You know, sometimes when I travel and use public bathrooms I see things like this. I usually just flush the toilet then. Does that sound like something you would do if you went to a bathroom in public bathroom with your parents?
> *Y*: I … guess so. But, it is pretty yucky still.
> *C*: Oh, yes, it's not necessary to *like* it. But I think you might see this sometimes.
> *Y*: Yes, I think so.
> *C*: So look at this picture, and tell me a story about the person who made this.
> *Y*: Wait, what?
> *C*: Tell me a story? How did the person feel? How long did it take to make this? Where was the person going when they finished?
> *Y*: Can the story be funny?
> *C*: Yes, absolutely! Make it as funny as possible!
> *Y*: Okay, so here goes. This person was on the way to California. She ate a big salad, and from the looks of it, the salad was spoiled. She was really sick, and made this mess. But once she finished, she felt better and was able to get on the plane to Los Angeles.
> *C*: That was excellent! And, now that you finished your story, what is your rating on our meter?
> *Y*: It's near zero.
> *C*: That is great! Let's get your parent. I spoke with them before today and asked that they bring something special if you make it through this exercise successfully.

An important point should be raised about this example before moving on. If the child is asked to develop a story or otherwise produce imagery, be sure that it is in line with the aims of the inhibitory learning model. That is, in this case the story was not scary and had a good ending. It would be counterproductive if the story developed where there were illustrations of avoidance, excessive fear, or other maladaptive behaviors resembling those the child engages in.

Affect Labeling

It's not uncommon for physiological arousal to be identified as anxiety, when in fact it could be some other emotional reaction. In the running illustration of the contamination fearful child, the description of situations that provoked fear when developing the hierarchy (see Chapter 5) was in conditions that could just as easily been associated with happiness. The child remarked that his friends talked about the stimuli that led to distress.

Practicing in labeling emotional experiences can help children in clarifying the emotional experience associated with the stimuli that are associated with obsessive-compulsive problems. This means that during exposure exercises in the office, the clinician may state out loud the emotional experience that might also be present if the child reports distress. Again referring to the contamination fearful child is the following example:

> *Clinician*: You've been doing just great with looking at these pictures of unflushed toilets! I'm so proud of you! Now, let's look at some videos of toilets getting flushed.
> *Youth*: Are you sure that is a good idea?
> *C*: Oh, absolutely! In fact, when we started you said you would be afraid during today's session. And, were you?
> *Y*: No, I thought I would, but not really.
> *C*: No, I didn't think so either. I actually thought you were kind of happy. Does that sound right?
> *Y*: Yes, a lot of the time it was funny.

In this instance, the labeling of the experience is useful to ensure that the child can match up the physiological experience with the emotional reaction, which in this case was not fear. However, even if the emotional reaction is fear, instructing the child to label the experience accurately has been found to alleviate adverse reaction (Craske et al., 2014).

Exposure in Multiple Contexts

The goal of therapy is to promote change. This may sound obvious, but if the same exercise that is conducted in the office is not practiced in other settings, other times of day, and other conditions (i.e., while tired or hungry) then long-term improvement may be limited. While the concept of exposure in multiple contexts is consilient with the inhibitory learning model, it is also a core principle of promoting generalization of treatment from the office to the natural environment (Stokes & Baer, 1977).

In order to accomplish this aspect of exposure, several conditions must be met. First, to the extent possible, practice exposure outside the office. Second, involve the parent or caregiver in identifying different settings and contexts in which exposure might be practiced. And third, emphasize to the child that this will ensure that all the hard work in the office will "pay off."

It is on this particular point that this author's experience has shown parents and caregivers are most reluctant, or are least compliant, with the demands of treatment. Therefore one way around this is to work with the parent or caregiver to find different times that the activity will be scheduled, akin to an appointment at the office. Here is an example of the behavioral consultation that might take place.

Clinician: So far there has been great progress with alleviating fear of bathrooms, and with mucous. I'm really encouraged by the pace of within office change we've seen. To make sure that this will be most effective, some work needs to be done between sessions. As you saw, today we looked a pictures and videos of toilets that were unflushed. I'd like you to practice this after today. When would be the easiest times for you to work on this with your son?
Parent: Well, we are so busy all the time. How much time would this require? Not as much as during a full session I hope.
C: Oh, no, not at all. Just a few brief practices, probably not more than 5 min since he is doing so well so far.
P: Oh, ok. Well, maybe just before bedtime. And maybe on the weekend.
C: Ok, that is great. Bedtime is a great choice since he will be tired, and in here he is wide awake. And on the weekend, when do you think you would practice?
P: I see, you want it to be when he is *not* like he is here?
C: Exactly.
P: In that case, maybe when he first gets up on Saturday. He sleeps late typically, and once he gets up I can have him do it before breakfast.
C: Perfect.

Between Session Reinforcement

In order to increase compliance, it is desirable to provide reinforcement for engagement with treatment. Children are not necessarily enthusiastic about coming to therapy, and just because there is symptom relief does not mean the reduced daily distress will naturally motivate engagement. To promote ongoing engagement with treatment, it is often advisable to set up a reinforcement program, particularly for younger children (under age 11).

One of the most basic ways of setting up a reinforcement system is through a reinforcement chart. An effective chart has several important elements. First, the behaviors that are to be rewarded are very clearly described. Second, the chart has a manageable number of target behaviors in order to reduce caregiver burden in overseeing it. Third, the number of times the target behaviors are completed is associated with a high likelihood of success. And finally, the agreed-upon reinforcers are manageable for the caregiver to deliver and reasonable for the behaviors completed.

The following hypothetical exchange illustrates each of the pitfalls associated with a potential chart (also called a "star chart" for the stickers or "stars" that might be placed in each box when a behavior is successfully completed).

Clinician: Since you have been doing so well in the office, it seems we should make sure you continue to do well when you go home. I thought we might set up a list of things you can do each week and earn a reward for it.

Youth: Ok, what kind of things can I earn? I was hoping to get a new video game soon.
C: A new video game, hmm. So how much does the video game you want cost?
Y: It's $60.
C: I see. Well, that might require more than just one week of doing well to earn.
Y: Oh.
C: Mom, you said you would be willing to pay for a song or two on iTunes each week if the items we listed on the chart were completed. Is that right?
Parent: Oh yes, I would be happy to.
C: Ok, that is great. Now, about that video game. How many weeks might it take to earn the game?
P: I don't know. I think it may take six or eight weeks.
C: Maybe we should decide now. How many weeks?
P: How about seven?
Y: Wait, seven weeks!! I didn't want to wait that long!
C: So, mom, do you think that if six weeks, in a row, were completed, that you would be willing to get the video game?
P: I think so.
C: Ok, does that sound good to everyone?
Y: Ok. But I get iTunes each week too, right?
C: Yes, that would be part of the deal. Ok mom?
P: Yes.

In this illustration, there are several important things going on. First, the clinician is calibrating the size of the reinforcement to the rate of behavior. If the reward is too great the first week, there will be lower motivation for producing the behavior in later weeks. This is consistent with fundamental principles from the matching law, where the size of reinforcement is inversely related with the rate of behavior (McDowell, 2013). The second is negotiating a framework whereby the child might earn a larger reward, while still earning smaller intermediary rewards. If there is any chance for the child to remain motivated between sessions, the opportunity for reward must be present in an ongoing way, and not just at the point of earning the large reward at the end. In younger children, it may be necessary to set up smaller and even more frequent rewards, perhaps daily, in order to produce beneficial outcome.

Not addressed in this brief illustrative exchange is determination of the criteria for earning the reward. This is fairly arbitrary and requires a judgment call by the clinician to "guess" what will be necessary to show change in behavior but also ensure success for the child. This is most crucial in the first chart established. In this way, it may be better to err on the conservative side to guarantee success. Table 1 presents a reinforcement chart for the contamination fear example. In the table, the child has an opportunity to complete a total of

TABLE 1 Reinforcement Chart for Exposure Related to Contamination Fear—First Chart

Target Behavior	Monday	Tuesday	Wednesday	Thursday	Friday	Saturday	Sunday
Practice viewing "poop" pictures							
Practice viewing "poop" videos							
Practice not washing after blowing nose							

21 target behaviors. Assuming that the target behavior was completed easily in the office, the clinician might start the first week with a low threshold for earning the reward, say 14 of 21 target behaviors completed.

It is important to note that setting up charts like the one presented in Table 1 is most appropriate for younger children and children who are less developmentally advanced. In this author's experience, charts with children older than approximately age 12 are not as effective since the youth experiences it as infantilizing. With older children and adolescents, reinforcement should be more ad hoc, and parents are advised to provide social reward such as brief praise and greater levels of privileges.

ANATOMY OF A SESSION

The aforementioned discussion lays out the foundation for how to get oriented to the process of conducting ERP. Before starting, the clinician has one more task to undertake—estimate approximately how long it will take for the child to return to their baseline level of distress after conducting ERP during the session. This is an important consideration and it is difficult to predict. While this is not established through empirical means, this author's experience has been to judge the session duration based on two factors—severity of symptoms and complexity of symptoms. For more severe symptoms, it may be very easy to provoke distress and the return to baseline may be lengthy. In such cases, the early sessions may need to be of a longer duration. As an additional consideration, in more severe symptoms, more frequent session may be required. If a clinician's outpatient environment cannot support this, it may be necessary to refer the family to a higher level of care environment. The second factor is related to symptom complexity. It is possible that conducting exposure will be a challenge due to the degree that the stimuli might be readily available in the office, or that conditions can be replicated. If it becomes necessary to get out of the office to address the symptoms, then additional time for the session will be necessary to account for setting the occasion for symptom provocation.[1]

Setting the Agenda

Most sessions start out with questions regarding any possible changes in symptoms from the prior meeting. Conducting ERP is no different in this regard. Once it is established that the target symptoms remain effectively unchanged, make plans for what stimuli will be targeted in the session. This means taking into account all the aforementioned factors, if they have not been already.

1. Jurisdictions vary in how clinicians may bill for longer sessions, or sessions that take place outside the office. Consult local guidelines for how to best conduct sessions that deviate from the typical in office 45–50-min therapeutic hour.

Beginning Exposure

If it is the first session of ERP, sometimes it is best to introduce the stimuli gradually, with frequent checks on the distress level experienced by the child. A sample discussion from the contamination fearful child is instructive:

> *Clinician*: Let's practice some of the "talk" you said Joe and Eric have that makes you uncomfortable. Do you think I can play the role of either of them?
> *Youth*: Ok, you said you would start out easy, right?
> *C*: Yes, just like we planned. But remember, you said Joe and Eric talk a lot about boogers and poop. Who does this more?
> *Y*: They both seem to think about boogers and poop all the time. They are probably about the same.
> *C*: Ok, so I'm going to pretend to be one of them. At the end, you can tell me who I am more like.
> *Y*: Ok, I'm ready.
> *C*: Ok, here goes. You know what I had this morning for breakfast? I got it straight from the tap! A fresh, hard, booger! Oh, and it was so salty, and a little chewy!! Who did I sound like more, Joe or Eric?
> *Y*: Uh, they both say those things. You actually said something they have both said, more than once. Do they come here to see you, too?
> *C*: Haha, no, I don't know them. But I know kids your age, and so I thought it might be a good guess. Now, how upset did that make you feel, using our distress meter?

Setting the stage this way, in a nonthreatening manner, is consistent with the prior concept of violating expectancies. Here, the child is prepared for experiencing distress around the image and information associated with mucous, and given that the clinician is delivering it in the office, as an adult enacting the voice of a classmate, it is wholly inconsistent with the experience in the child's natural environment. Since the child will likely experience this as a success, it allows for more difficult exposure exercises to follow.

Ongoing Exposure During the Session

There is a critical consideration to make in this case. Should the clinician present a single stimulus, and simply wait for any distress or reaction to subside? Or is it better to engage in a succession of exposures, where distress declines somewhat, then gets provoked again, with the cycle repeating until near the end of the session? In effect, the trajectory of distress through the session would follow one of the two graphs depicted in Fig. 1.

There is no right answer to this question. Instead, the judgment should be made based on the following considerations. First, can the child tolerate multiple stimuli within a single session? This may be established when first introducing exposure, if it appears that the child has difficulty returning to

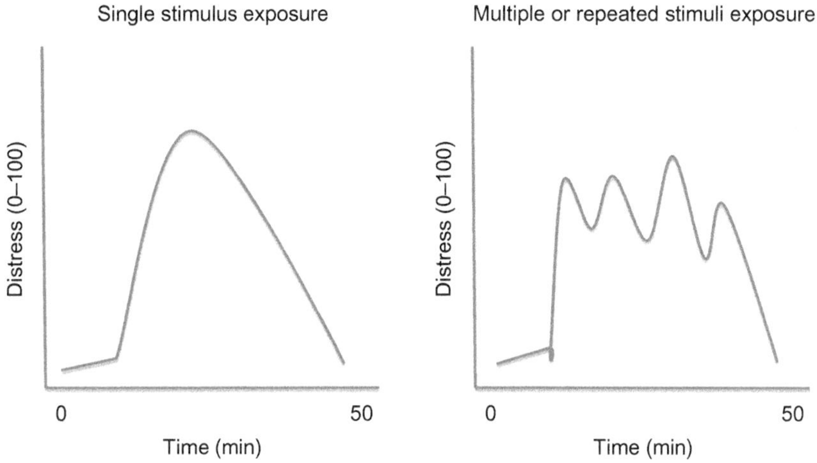

FIG. 1 Within session trajectories of evoked distress during exposure with response prevention.

baseline. In such a case, reliance on a single stimulus exposure may be the best strategy to ensure that the child leaves the office feeling less distress than when the session began. If, on the other hand, there is a surfeit of symptoms and stimuli, and the child can tolerate exposure well, then introducing multiple stimuli during a session may be desirable. The other way consideration that can accentuate efficacy is to repeatedly present, with slight variations, the core stimuli, which will produce the variable distress rate within session. Here is a sample discussion, following from the earlier transcript where exposure was introduced.

Clinician: You've been doing great handling my acting like Joe and Eric! Are you ready to go further?
Youth: Yes, it's been really funny actually.
C: Ok, here goes. So you know what happened after I ate my booger breakfast? I went to the bathroom! And wow, what a poop came out!! It was really impressive. My mom ran in because the noise was so loud.
Y: Haha, I could see Eric saying that.
C: Ok. I'm going to continue. My mom was so shocked, she asked if I needed to go to the doctor it was so loud. Then she smelled it, and I think it was so bad she began to cry a little.
Y: Heehee, that sounds like Joe.
C: It was so big, the toilet overflowed a little. I think some got on the floor and my shoes.
Y: Uh, that seems a little scary.
C: Picture that you are in school for a minute, and either Joe or Eric said something like this. Can you be brave and stick with this?

Y: Yeah, it's been mostly funny.

C: Good. Remember, you called this funny. That means even if it feels a little scary, what emotion did you feel?

Y: Probably happy.

In this brief transcript, several concepts are being illustrated concurrently. First, clearly the child's expectations are being violated around the danger of exposure to scatological talk. Second, the stimulus is being repeatedly presented. And third, when the child reported feeling distressed, the focus shifted slightly to reinforcement for "being brave" and to affect labeling to ensure that the correct attribution is made regarding the experience.

Running Dialog During ERP

What makes exposure engaging for the clinician and child is the degree of ongoing involvement by the clinician aimed at maintaining focus on the stimuli. As the prior transcripts have illustrated, the onus on the clinician is to creatively produce additional material that would make the stimuli for exposure more closely resemble what happens outside the office. It is also part of the effort to produce some measure of imagery. With the emphasis on a phenomenological perspective on understanding the stimuli, the imagery should also represent a provocation of the real-world experience the child has for the feared or avoided stimuli.

Research has demonstrated that the most effective ERP sessions contain both live (in vivo) exposure with imagery (Abramowitz, Whiteside, & Deacon, 2005). That means the clinician should consider a "running dialog" that aims to maintain focus on the stimuli that is the source for exposure, as well as include information germane to the feared outcomes resulting from contact with the stimuli. It is here that the clinician must be facile with the stimulus complex described in the hierarchies chapter, and all the associated elements. This may include, when necessary, drawing on imagery for not only the sights, but also the smells, sounds, and tactile experiences that might be expected for the stimuli.

Ending the Session

The clinician should be mindful of time constraints in order to start wrapping up exposure and begin thinking about between session homework. In order to ensure generalization and promote the greatest change, homework is essential. In adult treatment trials for OCD, it has been shown to be the single best predictor of improvement (Simpson, Marcus, Zuckoff, Franklin, & Foa, 2012). Accordingly, the exposure exercises practiced during the session should form the basis for the between session exercises. As a general rule of thumb, the homework should be practiced regularly, typically daily. However, attention should be paid to feasibility and caregiver burden in conducting these exercises.

Recall the discussion in the hierarchies chapter. There, it was emphasized that the task for the clinician is to adopt a phenomenological perspective on the child's environment and daily life. This extends to the crafting of behavioral homework for exposure. Here, the clinician needs to answer questions such as: How will the child practice this assignment in my absence? How will the parent or caregiver assist in the homework? How much instruction on how to conduct ERP outside the office and without my presence will be necessary? Answering these questions will aid in crafting homework that the child will be able to execute, with or without the caregiver's assistance, and increase the likelihood of treatment success.

CONCLUDING REMARKS

The chapter opened by emphasizing that exposure is a seemingly easy concept that is inherently challenging to execute. As illustrated in this chapter, there is a wide range of factors that clinicians must take into consideration when first implementing ERP with children. Many of these factors must be considered concurrently, as was shown in the last illustrative treatment transcript. What this requires then is flexibility on the part of the clinician, and a frank acknowledgment that each session is filled with unexpected events, new discoveries (such as the aforementioned additional features of the hierarchy that might be uncovered in the course of exposure), and possibly entire domains of feared stimuli that were not previously described.

Effective clinicians often operate, at least implicitly, from a postmodernist perspective. That is, if the clinician assumes that there will always be limited orderliness to the sessions, and that any advanced planning may be subject to adjustments, it allows for a readiness to engage in exposure as the situation demands rather than as preplanned based on assumptions the clinician brings to the session. All that is necessary for the session is a fundamental understanding of the principles of exposure and how to carry it out, with a context driven by the presenting symptoms of the child. Once this is accepted, the clinician is more likely to engage fluidly with practicing exposure, and it will be a pleasant experience for both clinician and child. From the clinician's perspective, viewing ERP as an opportunity for creative expression by identifying novel situations that resemble the child's environment sets the tone for what Csikszentmihalyi (1996) refers to as *flow*. Under such conditions, the clinician may find exposure to be a liberating and truly compassionate intervention, and provide real meaning in the work of providing ERP for children with OCD.

REFERENCES

Abramowitz, J. S. (2013). The practice of exposure therapy: Relevance of cognitive-behavioral theory and extinction theory. *Behavior Therapy*, *44*, 548–558.

Abramowitz, J. S., Deacon, B. J., & Whiteside, S. P. H. (2011). *Exposure therapy for anxiety: Principles and practice*. New York, NY: Guilford.

Abramowitz, J. S., Whiteside, S. P., & Deacon, B. J. (2005). The effectiveness of treatment for pediatric obsessive-compulsive disorder: A meta-analysis. *Behavior Therapy*, *36*, 55–63.

Craske, M. G., Treanor, M., Conway, C. C., Zbozinek, T., & Vervliet, B. (2014). Maximizing exposure therapy: An inhibitory learning approach. *Behaviour Research and Therapy*, *58*, 10–23.

Csikszentmihalyi, M. (1996). *Creativity: Flow and the psychology of discovery and invention*. New York: Harper.

Farrell, N. R., Kemp, J. J., Blakey, S. M., Meyer, J. M., & Deacon, B. J. (2016). Targeting clinician concerns about exposure therapy: A pilot study comparing standard vs. enhanced training. *Behaviour Research and Therapy*, *85*, 53–59.

Foa, E. B., Blau, J. S., Prout, M., & Latimer, P. (1977). Is horror a necessary component of flooding (implosion)? *Behaviour Research and Therapy*, *15*, 397–402.

Foa, E. B., & Kozak, M. J. (1986). Emotional processing of fear: Exposure to corrective information. *Psychological Bulletin*, *99*, 20–35.

Frank, B., & McKay, D. (in press). The suitability of an inhibitory learning approach in exposure: When habituation fails. *Cognitive and Behavioral Practice*.

Franklin, M. S., Dingfelder, H. E., Freeman, J. B., Ivarsson, T., Heyman, I., Sookman, D., et al. (2015). Cognitive behavioral therapy for pediatric obsessive-compulsive disorder: Empirical review and clinical recommendations. *Psychiatry Research*, *227*, 78–92.

Grünbaum, A. (1984). *The foundations of psychoanalysis: A philosophical critique*. Berkeley, CA: University of California Press.

McDowell, J. J. (2013). On the theoretical and empirical status of the matching law and matching theory. *Psychological Bulletin*, *139*, 1000–1028.

Patel, N., Vytal, K., Pavletic, N., Stoodley, C., Pine, D. S., Grillon, C., et al. (2016). Interaction of threat and verbal working memory in adolescents. *Psychophysiology*, *53*, 518–526.

Richard, D. C. S., & Gloster, A. T. (2007). Exposure therapy has a public relations problem: A dearth of litigation amid a wealth of concern. In D. C. S. Richard & D. Lauterbach (Eds.), *Handbook of exposure therapies* (pp. 409–429). Amsterdam: Elsevier.

Simpson, H. B., Marcus, S. M., Zuckoff, A., Franklin, M., & Foa, E. B. (2012). Patient adherence to cognitive-behavioral therapy predicts long-term outcome in obsessive–compulsive disorder. *Journal of Clinical Psychiatry*, *73*, 1265–1266.

Stokes, T. F., & Baer, D. M. (1977). An implicit technology of generalization. *Journal of Applied Behavior Analysis*, *10*, 349–367.

Tryon, W. W. (2008). Whatever happened to symptom substitution? *Clinical Psychology Review*, *28*, 963–968.

Tryon, W. W., & McKay, D. (2009). Memory modification as an outcome variable in anxiety disorder treatment. *Journal of Anxiety Disorders*, *23*, 546–556.

Chapter 7

Modifying Cognitions in the Treatment of OCD in Young People

Tim I. Williams
University of Reading, Reading, United Kingdom

INTRODUCTION

Cognitive theories of psychopathology have become increasingly influential since the 1970s. In its broadest sense, the cognitive model states that psychopathology is due to dysfunctional thinking or cognitions about events that drive both affective and behavioral responses. These events may be external such as the appearance of a spider, or they may be internal events like the thought that "my hands are dirty." In OCD, the events are internal and may consist of thoughts, urges, and/or images, which will be described in this chapter under the umbrella term of "intrusive thoughts." The intrusive thoughts are believed by the patient to indicate that serious harm will occur either to the patient or to others. Young people do not always describe the affect produced by the intrusive thoughts as anxiety, but may prefer terms such as "distress" or "disgust." This raises the issue of the language used when talking with young people and their families. The young person will understand more of the process of change if their language is used, rather than the more technical language used by clinicians. For instance, DSM5 describes intrusive thoughts as obsessions and repetitive behaviors as compulsions (APA, 2015). A young person might describe them as "horrible thoughts" and "rituals," respectively. Use of these terms will demonstrate that the therapist has listened to the patient and will help in establishing rapport.

The cognitive theory of OCD states that misinterpretation of the intrusive thoughts leads to unpleasant affective changes and repetitive behaviors. Rachman and de Silva (1978) showed that the types of intrusive thoughts experienced by people with OCD are no different from those experienced by people without OCD. The implication that follows is that it is straightforward to demonstrate that the thoughts and behaviors in OCD are seen in people

The Clinician's Guide to Cognitive-Behavioral Therapy for Childhood Obsessive-Compulsive Disorder
http://dx.doi.org/10.1016/B978-0-12-811427-8.00007-1

without OCD. For instance, parents can be asked then to consider whether they ever check the locks of their cars or houses when leaving them. It is rare indeed to find parents who do not recognize this behavior, although because it is neither upsetting nor interfering with their lives, it is not considered as OCD. Demonstrating that their behaviors are seen in other people often helps young people realize that they are not abnormal or going mad. (Note that this is a cognitive appraisal of the illness itself and can be considered a possible therapy target.)

The methods described in this chapter are based on those developed since the late 1990s by a group of clinicians working in the United Kingdom (largely summarized in Waite & Williams, 2009). The treatment is focused on the appraisals of the intrusive thoughts present in young people with OCD. The protocol is flexible and does not prescribe which activities should take place in which sessions. The model of OCD can be seen in Fig. 1. Intrusive thoughts lead to appraisals which lead variously to behavioral (avoidance, hypervigilance, repetitive behaviors) and affective changes. Cognitive behavioral theory goes on to state that the behavioral parts of the process are reinforced by the reduction in unpleasant affect that accompanies the behavior.

This diagram or something like it is used to develop a personalized formulation. To do this the therapist starts by a evoking a recent occasion when the ritual had to be performed or when the OCD was troublesome. In the course of working through that occasion in great detail, the therapist needs to be alert to cognitions related to OCD which might be helping to maintain it. At least 10 different appraisals or cognitive distortions have been proposed as critical in the maintenance of OCD. Proponents of each type of appraisal tend to consider that one as the primary one, but the evidence so far does not support any of them exclusively (Cougle & Lee, 2014). The Obsessive Compulsive Cognitions Working Group (1997) proposed that the following were prime candidates:

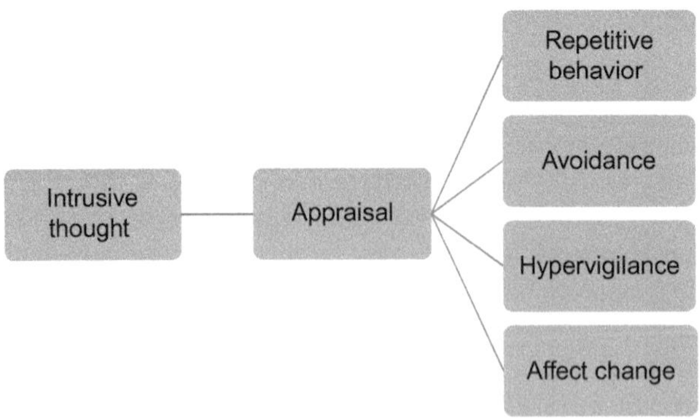

FIG. 1 Model showing link between intrusive thoughts, cognitions (appraisals) and behaviors, and affect in OCD. This diagram is used as the basis for a formulation diagram which is revised repeatedly through treatment.

1. Beliefs about the controllability of thoughts
2. Thought-action fusion (TAF)
3. Inflated responsibility
4. Perfectionism
5. Overestimation of threat
6. Intolerance of uncertainty
   A more recent review (Hezel & McNally, 2015) added
7. Metacognition
8. Memory problems
9. Attention problems
10. Diminished access to internal states

In the sections that follow, each of the appraisals outlined earlier will be briefly described with supporting evidence before considering examples of interventions designed to combat the appraisal. Although the order in which the appraisals are addressed is quite flexible, therapists find it easier to consider potential misunderstandings of the nature of thoughts and thinking (i.e., beliefs about the controllability of thoughts), before moving on to consider other types of cognitive distortion. During treatment, a cognitive therapist will use the working formulation to select the types of appraisal which need to be addressed on a case-by-case basis. Methods such as experiments and discussion are used to address the 10 appraisals listed earlier. They are based on those used in the two randomized controlled trials (Bolton et al., 2011; Williams et al., 2010) which used treatment manuals based on those of Salkovskis (1985, 1999). Further examples may be found in Waite and Williams (2009) description of the protocol, which also includes suggestions for how modifications can include younger and older children.

CHANGING COGNITIONS

Controllability of Thoughts

Young people often believe that they should be able to control their thoughts. The research evidence suggests otherwise. Najmi, Riemann, and Wegner (2009) studied the effects of three techniques for managing intrusive thoughts: suppression, focused distraction, and acceptance on distress ratings and frequency of obsessions. They found that thought suppression did not increase frequency, but did increase distress associated with the obsessions. Focused distraction was most effective at decreasing distress, whereas acceptance reduced distress and frequency during and post experiment.

Earworms (music that pops in to your head and then repeats—Williams, 2015) are a useful everyday example of an intrusive thought. Nearly everyone has the experience of earworms (Beaman & Williams, 2010), which are generally unthreatening and hence easy to discuss. The control of earworms can be discussed within the therapeutic team (child, family, and/or therapist) by finding out what methods people use to get rid of them. A surprising variety of techniques may be revealed such as singing the song to its conclusion, singing another song, or even just ignoring them. In later sessions the therapist might return to the methods used for getting rid of earworms when discussing intrusive thoughts (obsessions) in OCD. Presented here are three examples on how to challenge the controllability of thoughts.

The Persistent Pink Giraffe

The therapist introduces this topic by asking the people in the room to say how much they believe that thoughts (other than earworms) can be controlled. Many people believe that they should be able to control their thoughts so we use several types of experience to show them that control of thoughts is not easy and that it may be undesirable.

> *T*: Okay, so now we are going to talk about thoughts. How much do you think you should be able to control your thoughts?
> *YP*: A lot … most of the time … yeah
> *T*: So if I was to put your belief in the controllability of thoughts on this line (therapist produces a line with endpoints marked as 0 and 100%) you would say what?
> *YP*: 90%
> *T*: Okay, so let me try an experiment. You believe that you can control your thoughts right?
> *YP*: Yeah
> *T*: We'll call that Theory A. I believe that you cannot control your thoughts, so we'll call that Theory B. Now I'm going to give you a thought and I want you to try and get rid of it. Imagine that there's a giraffe outside, a pink giraffe. He's a very friendly animal and he comes over to the therapy room windows and tries to see what's happening inside. Can you see him looking through the window now, see how he is chewing leaves from that tree over there …
> YP (doubtfully): Yeah
> *T*: Imagine the giraffe walking around slowly. Picking leaves off the tops of the trees, and chewing ever so slowly … now I want you to stop thinking about it, and if you do put your hand up. (T looks ostentatiously at their watch).

Within about 20 s most young people will have put their hands up (as will their parents). The therapist might conclude like this:

> *T*: So what did you learn about thinking and thoughts?
> *YP*: Er … not sure
> *T*: Well, could you stop thinking of the pink giraffe?
> *YP*: Aargh … no, not really (smiles)

T: So Theory A (that you can control your thoughts) did not make the right predictions, whereas Theory B (you cannot control your thoughts) did. So maybe when it comes to the horrible thoughts that you get from your OCD, you may not be able to control them, so perhaps we need to try to do something else instead …

The point being that a failure to control thoughts is natural. It is usual to provide further information to young people such as: "We know that more than 80% of young people experience unwanted intrusive thoughts" (based on Allsopp & Williams, 1996) and for thoughts like earworms very few people can honestly say that they have never had them. Finally, the therapist would ask the young person to rate the controllability of their thoughts using the same measure as before.

Total Control—The Robot Brain

Often in one of the first few session therapists will find that a young person believes that they should not have OCD thoughts and therefore thinks that having the thoughts indicates that in some way they are a bad person. We find that is it useful to get the young person to do a thought experiment. The conversation might run like this:

T: You said in the assessment that your thoughts meant that you were a bad person. Is that right?
YP: Yes, no good person would imagine their younger brother squashed beneath them, would they?
T: So you are saying that you should be able to decide what thoughts come into your mind?
YP: Yes, of course.
T: Okay, let's try a thought experiment. Suppose you could only have thoughts if you asked for them. What would life be like then?
YP: Oh, I guess that it might be pretty boring.
T: Yeah, that's right. If you only had thoughts when you needed them, you would not be able to do lots of things like have those sudden good thoughts, like what to get your Mom for Mother's Day. Do you ever get tunes stuck in your head?
YP: Yes, they're really annoying.
T: Well, they are thoughts too just like your OCD thoughts or those funny inspirations that pop in to your mind at any time. As a matter of interest, what do you do to get rid of those tunes that get stuck (could also use the word earworms)?
YP: Well, nothing really, they kind of go away on their own.
T: Yes, and may be that would happen to your OCD thoughts as well if you did not try to get rid of them. What do you think? Is that possible?

At this point the therapist might go on to explain that research has shown that the thoughts in OCD are the same as the thoughts that everyone else gets. The only difference is that people with OCD do something about the thoughts, whereas most people do not.

Here the therapist can insert one of the beliefs that are common in young people such as "having bad thoughts means that I am a bad person" or "having these thoughts means I am going mad."

Belief That They Are Going Mad

Commonly, young people believe that the fact they are having thoughts means that they are going mad (or "crazy"). In initial assessments therapists might well tell the young person that the thoughts in OCD are not the same as those in true "madness" but are the same as those that everyone experiences. This can be further confirmed by doing a survey of people to find out what they believe. For instance, if someone is worried about offending God by thinking the wrong things in a place of worship, we might do a survey of regular worshippers to find out whether their minds ever wander during the service or prayers. It is highly likely that the majority of respondents to a survey will confess that they do daydream sometimes during services or prayers. A follow-up question would be to ask worshippers how they felt about themselves if they did daydream during the service. Another example that is helpful is to survey parents about whether they have ever worried about dropping their babies on a hard floor. If the topic is particularly sensitive (e.g., incestuous or pedophilic thoughts) the therapist might survey clinical colleagues who work with people with OCD about whether they have ever experienced such thoughts. Once it has been established that having intrusive thoughts (especially unpleasant intrusive thoughts) is normal or common, the young person can be helped through discussion to understand that intrusive thoughts are not themselves abnormal, it is only what is done with the intrusions that leads to trouble and distress.

Thought-Action Fusion

TAF has often been considered an important component of OCD. Broadly TAF refers to the belief that thinking something is the same as that thing happening in the real world. Following Shafran and Rachman (2004) it is helpful to distinguish different types of TAF:

- TAF moral, i.e., thinking about doing something bad is the moral equivalent of doing it (e.g., thinking about hurting my baby brother is the moral equivalent of harming him).
- TAF-likelihood, i.e., the belief that thinking about a negative outcome occurring increases its likelihood (e.g., thinking about a plane crashing

increases the chances of its occurrence; Rachman, 1993; Rachman & Shafran, 1999; Shafran, Thordarson, & Rachman, 1996) TAF-likelihood can be subdivided in to

- "likelihood self," the belief that thoughts will result in harm for oneself, or
- "likelihood-other," the belief that thoughts will result in harm to others.

Shafran et al. (1996) have published the Thought-Action Fusion Scale which can be used to identify the presence of TAF in young people with OCD. Amir, Freshman, Ramsey, Neary, and Brigidi (2001) found that TAF includes beliefs about the power of thoughts to prevent harm (this can also be managed under the rubric of responsibility cognitions). Evans, Hersperger, and Capaldi (2011) found that TAF scores changed with age. Older children reported less TAF than younger children.

Thoughts Leading to Action

The therapist identifies an action that the young person might not want to act upon.

T: Can you stick your tongue out at me?
YP: Yes, but I wouldn't
T: Okay, I would like you to think about sticking your tongue out at me. If thoughts make you do something, then if you think about it enough you should do it right? This is the OCD theory (Theory A). How much do you believe that thinking something can make something happen? I believe that if you think about something nothing happens unless you choose to do it (non-OCD theory or Theory B). Okay, now start thinking about sticking your tongue out at me.
[after 30 s or so]
Nothing has happened, are you thinking about sticking your tongue out at me? .... So why doesn't it happen?

The therapist explains that this experiment proves that thinking something is not enough to make a person do it. They also have to choose how to do it, when to do it and so on.

Thoughts Causing Events to Happen

Some young people believe that thoughts make events happen. Again the therapist might start with an experiment where the consequences are unimportant. As a footnote one might also explain that there are benefits to positive thinking (Friedman & Kern, 2014), in particular for feeling better about oneself, but there is a still a considerable effort involved in maintaining a positive outlook. One common example is to make something fall down and break just by thinking (a likelihood self-thought). In the therapy room, this is often making a book fall off a shelf. At home, the homework might be to make your mother drop a cup (a likelihood other thought). The experiment should be set up with belief ratings before doing the experiment and afterward so that the young person can see that their beliefs are weakening. Having done this experiment, the therapist would move on to considering experiments where the harm rather than being to something, would be to someone. For instance, the patients might be asked to think about the therapist falling over as they walk around. In one case, a 12-year-old boy believed that turning off the television when it was on an odd numbered channel would lead to other people in the room becoming ill.

T: Shall we try an experiment about the television?
YP: Okay
T: Let me see if I have understood this correctly. You believe that if you turn off the television on channel 3, and I am in the room, I will get ill?
YP: That's it.
T: How ill would I get?
YP: A bit ill
T: What, like a sore throat or something?
YP: Yes
T: So would that be quickly? Even straightaway?
YP: Yes.
T: Let's try it then. How anxious do you feel (using a 0–10 scale)?
YP: 7 (switches TV off on channel 7)

After a minute the therapist can then ask the anxiety rating again and talk about whether the prediction of imminent ill health is coming true. The young person sees that the therapist does not look ill, and the anxiety ratings reduce markedly. Sometimes however, the young person's obsession relates to some event that is very distant in time, such as dying of a cancer in one's 70s. In this case it is important to consider a number of aspects of the belief such as how the cancer is caused (the chain of causation), what it is that makes them believe that they are going to get cancer, and how they know it is more than just a feeling. The chances are that the chain of causation is testable in some way (sometimes by referring to scientific evidence). If they are relying on feelings to make their judgments about future risk, an experiment could be devised in session to test whether it is a feeling or a reality. In practice this relies on the young person having knowledge of the anxiety curve described elsewhere in this chapter.

Inflated Responsibility

Salkovskis (1985) proposed that an increased sense of personal responsibility for negative events lay at the root of OCD. The most recent definition of this is that "one has power which is pivotal to bring about or prevent subjectively crucial negative outcomes." There is debate about the relative contribution of responsibility appraisals to OCD. What is clear though is that young people with OCD do report high levels of responsibility appraisals (Libby, Reynolds, Derisley, & Clark, 2004). There is also some evidence that events that have occurred in the past are seen as being due to the young person. In other words, they report feeling responsible for negative life events (Lawrence & Williams, 2011). In young people without OCD, increasing responsibility for preventing a negative consequence was found to increase checking in a similar way to the behavior seen in OCD (Reeves, Reynolds, Coker, & Wilson, 2010). Finally, there is evidence that responsibility appraisals decrease during the course of cognitive behavior therapy (CBT) in line with the reduction in symptoms of OCD (Bolton et al., 2011; Williams, Salkovksis, Forrester, & Allsopp, 2002).

Responsibility appraisals can be measured using the Responsibility Attitudes Scale and the Responsibility Intrusions Questionnaire (Salkovskis et al., 2000—freely available at http://www.kcl.ac.uk/ioppn/depts/psychology/research/ResearchGroupings/CADAT/Research/OCD-Questionnaires.aspx).

One of the most useful methods to alter appraisals of responsibility for events is to use a responsibility pie chart. The therapist sets up the experiment as follows.

> *T*: Now today, I would like to explore with you your feelings of responsibility for that car accident that you were in with your mom. So, if I remember right, you were in the back of your mum's car when it crashed. It was hit from behind and it hit the car in front. Is that right?
> *YP*: Yes and I screamed.
> *T*: Okay, so let's start with listing all the possible reasons that might have led to the crash.
> *YP*: The driver behind us was going too fast … the road was very wet and it was snowing … the car in front switched lanes on the highway suddenly … I was making too much noise …
> *T*: Right so let's start with the most important cause of the crash—what do you think that was?
> *YP*: The snow?
> *T*: Okay, so what percentage was the snow responsible for the crash?
> *YP*: Maybe fifty percent?

The therapist then goes through all the causes for the accident, leaving the responsibility of the young person to last. While doing this, they draw a responsibility pie diagram (see Fig. 2):

Finally the therapist asks the young person if there is anything that they could learn from this way of looking at the car crash. The most common response is to express surprise that their responsibility seems so much less than they had thought. In setting up responsibility pie charts, it is important to choose events in the past and end with the young person's own contribution to the event. The danger with identifying the young person's contribution first is that they will choose a high level of responsibility, which will defeat the point of the experiment.

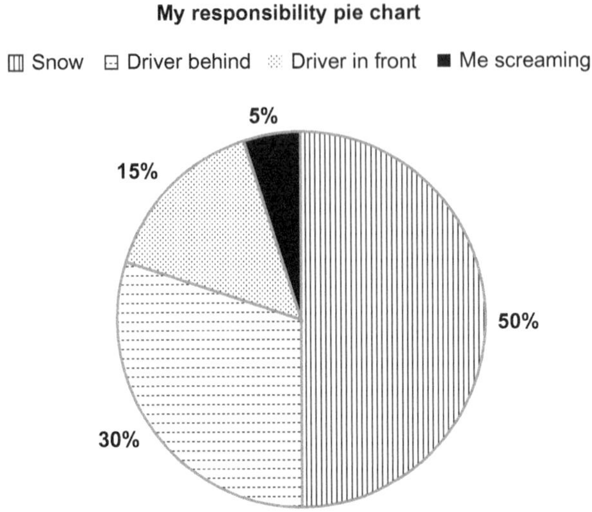

FIG. 2 Shows the responsibility attributions of a young person for a car crash that they were in.

Perfectionism

Perfectionism in young people is associated with severity of OCD (Soreni et al., 2014; Ye, Rice, & Storch, 2008) just as it is in adults. Perfectionism is often considered to have multiple facets, although there is uncertainty about the best subdivision. One possible classification differentiates self-oriented perfectionism from socially prescribed perfectionism (Flett, Hewitt, & Dyck, 1989). An alternative approach is to use four dimensions: sensitivity to mistakes, contingent self-esteem, compulsiveness (preference for ordering), and need for admiration (Rice & Preusser, 2002).

Perfectionism can be measured using the Child and Adolescent Perfectionism Scale (Flett, Hewitt, Boucher, Davidson, & Munro, 1997) and/or the Adaptive/Maladaptive Perfectionism Scale (Rice & Preusser, 2002). A number of other perfectionism scales have been developed for young people, although there is little agreement on which works best. A recent paper (Sironic & Reeve, 2015) suggests that the different questionnaires may measure different constructs and therefore should be combined. Therapists wishing to measure perfectionism should consider the burden of filling in multiple questionnaires and the clinical utility of each one before deciding on their use in treatment. In practice, it may be more useful to employ experiments designed pragmatically to manage particular situations than to consider which possible type of perfectionism is at the root of the problem.

Many young people believe that they should be doing things perfectly so that bad things do not occur. Conversely, they believe that if they make mistakes the consequences can be terrible. For instance, one young person we worked with believed that if he spelt words incorrectly, he would get in to terrible trouble with his teachers and parents. We set up a series of experiments to test this. We started with writing words on pieces of paper that would be destroyed by the therapist. In this case, the therapist set the experiment up as one of testing what happens to anxiety or distress. So the young person would be asked to rate on a 10-point scale what they thought their anxiety would be immediately after misspelling a word, then what it was immediately after misspelling and then at frequent intervals thereafter until the anxiety is at low levels. The first experiment in the session demonstrated that the anxiety dissipated very rapidly, so the therapist moved on to keeping the misspelling until the next week, and then they agreed what piece of school-related work would be used to test whether the dire predictions would come true. The young person rated the probability that he would be singled out for his spelling mistake as nearly 90% beforehand. When the experiment was repeated the following week, his rating was 20% probability that he would be singled out by the teacher.

A possible discussion topic is that of how other people do things. For instance, the therapist might ask how a young person knows that their hands are clean. People with contamination obsessions and washing compulsions as part of their OCD will often respond that their hands are clean if they feel clean. People without such concerns respond that they have clean hands when they look clean. Health systems such as hospitals have rules about hand washing, but none of them extend to tens of minutes unlike people with OCD. A similar issue can be dealt with by considering what construction workers do when they want to eat their sandwiches. Do they clean their hands carefully?

Overestimation of Threat

Hezel and McNally (2015) considered that overestimation of threat was strongly linked to the feelings of responsibility in OCD. In particular, people with OCD have been found not to overestimate the occurrence of threat, but rather they fail to show the characteristic overoptimism of other people (Moritz & Pohl, 2009). In practical terms, this means that people with OCD are more likely to perceive the consequences of a threat as more dangerous than other people do.

A young boy aged about 10 years old believed that he had to wash his hands for 30 min at a time in order to prevent himself getting a dangerous stomach bug which could kill him or at least land him in hospital for a long time. This is a clear example of overestimation of the danger of not washing his hands before eating. We introduced the topic of whether he always needed to wash his hands so thoroughly by asking him to consider what happened when he had a picnic or a school friend offered him sweets in the playground. When he discussed this with the therapist he realized that he did not always wash his hands before eating something. They agreed that he would come in with his favorite snack to the next session. The therapist then gave him the snack without washing her hands and without letting him wash his hands and encouraged him to take a bite.

Ratings of anxiety and belief in the reality of contamination were used before and during the experiment to find out what happened. To his surprise he found that his anxiety and belief in contamination reduced very rapidly (within 10 min, he was rating his anxiety as 1—on a scale of 0–10). For homework, he agreed to eat his snacks without washing his hands. He rated his anxiety before and after the home-based experiments and over the week until the next session found that his feelings of anxiety about the threat posed by eating food without washing his hands first were diminishing.

For many young people, it is important to understand that the terrible consequences of not doing the rituals are a worry and not a realistic appraisal of the situation. In other words, it is a misinterpretation of the perception of threat. To some extent therapists can manage this by demonstrating that anxiety decreases even if nothing is done about it (see later section on Nature of Anxiety). It is more difficult to manage if the consequence is very remote such as the possibility that offending God will cause the patient to go to Hell when they die. A possible way of helping the young person understand that their thoughts are not widely held is to survey members of their faith community about the consequences of sinning. However, the therapist has to be sure that they have a good understanding of the likely answers. It is often helpful to see that there are differences between committing the sin itself and thinking of it. This approach has also been used for thoughts such as worries about pedophilia or sexuality.

Intolerance of Uncertainty

People with OCD who check often want to be absolutely certain that something is safe. The inability to manage uncertainty is present in many forms of psychopathology (McEvoy & Mahoney, 2012). It is thought to be driven by a sensitivity to anxiety separately from depression or other forms of anxiety. There is a scale for measuring the intolerance of uncertainty in children which has not yet been widely researched (Read, Comer, & Kendall, 2013). Methods for combatting intolerance of uncertainty could include hierarchies of exposure to increasingly uncertain situations, or it may be reduced if people can see that their behavior may act in a counterintuitive way to increase uncertainty rather increase certainty. For instance, someone who is concerned about the possibility of burglary at their home might check that the front door is locked shut multiple times when they leave the house. To demonstrate that this behavior is decreasing certainty, the therapist might engage the young person in an experiment to see what happens when something is checked multiple times.

T: Now, it seems to me that you do a lot of checking things at home. Is that right?
YP: Yes …
T: So why are you checking?

YP: To make certain that it is right. So when I leave the house, I have to check to make sure that the front door is locked shut.
T: And how do you do that?
YP: Well I go back and try to open the door.
T: Do you just do this once?
YP: Well, it can take me twenty minutes to get out of the front garden.
T: so it might be quite a few times of checking?
YP: Yes.
T: Okay, so let's see what happens when you check the door of this room. But before you do, tell me how certain are you that the door is closed.
YP: 99.9%
T: Well, let's just make sure – would you mind trying the door?

This is repeated with ratings of certainty on each occasion. The ratings of certainty will be seen to reduce. This is then drawn to the attention of the young person. Through discussion they can see that repeated checking does not increase certainty, but instead increases uncertainty.

Inappropriate Criteria

A young woman was worried that she might not be good enough to get in to heaven when she died. Her family was religious and went to church every Sunday and took part in several other church activities. She came to believe that God would only help her if she talked to Him in the correct way. If she had any bad thoughts when she was praying or if she thought she had not completed her prayers correctly she was convinced that she would go to hell. I discussed with her what a correct prayer would be. She said that she had said all the words perfectly and always finish a prayer with the word "Amen." We explored the effect of this thinking on her life as follows:

T: Let me see if I have understood this correctly. You have to say a prayer correctly before you can eat or do your homework. Is that right?
YP: Yes, that's right.
T: How do you know if the prayer has been said correctly?
YP: By saying "Amen" at the end.
T: So what would happen if you did not say "Amen"?
YP: God would be angry with me, and I would go to hell when I die.
T: Can I just check how you know that God is angry with you? Does he talk to you?
YP: No …
T: So what tells you that he is angry with you? Is it may be a feeling inside you?
YP: Maybe …
T: Okay, let's think about another possibility. Could you do your homework in the middle of a prayer? So, you could say the first few lines of the Lord's

Prayer. Stop, do your homework and then return to the Lord's Prayer where you left off, and finish with Amen?
YP: I could try
T: Okay, I would like you to try and I would like you to rate your anxiety at the beginning of your homework and at the end. And then again at the end of the prayer.

Rather to this young woman's surprise, when she tried it, she found that although she felt really anxious to start with, once she had tried the exercise a few times, she was able to feel at ease with her religious beliefs. As a result she felt more comfortable about trying out different ways of praying to God, and she no longer felt the fear that she would go to hell if she missaid a prayer.

Metacognition

Wells and Matthews (1996) proposed that cognitive appraisals about the world should be distinguished from beliefs and processes used to appraise, regulate, and monitor thoughts and internal states, which they termed metacognitions. They considered that there were two types of metacognition: beliefs about the meaning and power of thoughts, and beliefs about rituals. Myers, Fisher, and Wells (2009) proposed that metacognitions were central to the development and maintenance of OCD, and that they gave rise to the belief in personal responsibility. In particular, they considered that the "stop" signals used by patients with OCD to tell them when to stop rituals were a type of metacognition. Internal stop signals are harder to achieve than external ones. From the point of view of the practicing clinician, there is probably little value in distinguishing metacognitions from other types of faulty cognitions in OCD because what is required is change in any or all of the cognitions maintaining the OCD.

There is value in considering whether an experiment should be used to modify unusual stop signals being used by people with OCD. For instance, one might alter the significance of a particular number of repeats as follows (based on the case of a 15-year-old girl). The history is that she has gradually been increasing the length of her hair washing ritual, but friends and parents have been warning her that she has damaging her hair in the process.

T: So, let me see if I have understood you correctly. You have to wash your hair eleven times, every time you wash it, is that correct? In other words, you put shampoo on eleven times and wash it off eleven times, yes?
YP: Yes.
T: Why does it have to be eleven times?
YP: Because it feels right.
T: Okay, so it should feel even better if you washed your hair twelve times right? Because if eleven times makes your hair sure to be clean, then twelve times would be even better.
YP: I suppose so.

T: Could you do that for me for a week as homework? So we can see how you feel about doing it more. What do you predict will happen?
YP: The OCD might say that it will be better than eleven times.
T: Okay, so we need to measure what happens with eleven times and twelve times, right?
YP: Yes.
T: Okay so let me suggest that you toss a coin to see whether you wash your hair eleven or twelve times. How about that?

The following week she came back rather shamefaced to say that she could not do the homework. In discussion it transpired that she found that the OCD thinking made her stop at 11 times. We discussed what that meant about her stop rule for washing her hair, and she agreed to try washing her hair 10 times and then leaving it, while she did something interesting like chat to other people on Facebook. Following this suggestion she found that she could reduce her hair washing more than she expected and by the next week she was down to seven times, and after 3 more weeks of trying she was back to only twice, at which point we agreed to stop. This example illustrates that increasing the rituals can be as difficult as reducing them for people with OCD, because it breaks the OCD rules. The effect of not following the OCD rules is that the belief in the power of the ritual is diminished and the young person feels less compelled to perform compulsions.

Stop rules can also be the subject of surveys. For instance, someone who washes their hands until they feel right could be asked to survey staff in the clinic to find out what their stop rules are for hand washing. In the United Kingdom, there are NHS guidelines for hand washing (http://www.nhsprofessionals.nhs.uk/download/comms/cg1%20standard%20infection%20prevention%20and%20control%20guidelines%20v4%20march%202013.pdf) which state that "Hand washing should take at least 15 s, but no longer than 3 min." On its own this is unlikely to bring about change in behavior, but it may be helpful to start the conversation about what sort of behavioral experiment might be tried.

Memory Problems

There is a long tradition of research on memory problems in OCD. As Hezel and McNally (2015) have noted, the results have been mixed, although it is possible that patients with OCD have more problems with nonverbal memories than the general population. However, it is clear that people with OCD do have problems with self-monitoring particularly of memory. The process of self-monitoring consumes cognitive resources so itself will impede certainty of recall processes (Exner, Martin, & Rief, 2009). Some authors (e.g., Radomsky & Alcolado, 2010) have considered memory monitoring to be a form of checking and have demonstrated that it has significantly detrimental effects on memory confidence. In order to help young people with OCD, we can use similar experiments as described earlier for closing the front door.

T: I would like to see what happens if you keep thinking about whether something has happened. What did you have for breakfast?
YP: Rice pops
T: How many spoons?
YP: Six
T: How sure are you that you took six spoons?
YP: 100%
T: Just think about that, when you were in the kitchen getting the cereal did you count the spoons?
YP: No ...
T: So just take me through the situation. You went in to the kitchen what did you see or do first?
YP: I picked up the bowl for my cereal and went to the cupboard, got the cereal out and then put the cereal in my bowl
T: Did you count the spoons?
YP: No
T: So how sure are you that it was six and not five or seven? Can you think about what happened really carefully? ....
Now how sure are you that you took six spoons?
YP: 80%

The conversation continues until the young person's rating has declined significantly and the therapist can say something like: "At first before we started thinking about what you remembered you said you were 100% sure, but then it became less and less so that now you are not really sure at all. What does that tell us about checking our memories?" Young people rapidly realize that checking memories is as useful as checking actions in increasing certainty. In fact repeated checking of memories or actions reduces certainty. Interestingly, Radomsky and Alcolado's (2010) study shows that the checking is domain specific. So, when working with patients with OCD it is important to make sure that they work on checking across both cognitions and actions.

Biased Attention or Hypervigilance

Biased attention in OCD is a well-established feature (Hezel & McNally, 2015). For instance, people with contamination obsessions will often notice the slightest changes in the skin on their hands and immediately inspect it to ascertain whether it is a sign of contamination. Interestingly, Bradley et al. (2016) using eye tracking demonstrated that the attentional bias to OCD-related stimuli is not restricted to people with a diagnosis of OCD, but can also be found in people with higher levels of self-rated OCD symptoms. A therapist can introduce this topic by discussing how people with phobias see things that other people miss out on. It is common to use fear of dogs as an example. The therapist would explain that people with dog phobia are constantly looking for dogs when they are outside, especially in areas where people walk their dogs. The therapist would explain that because they are frightened of dogs, the dog phobic sees more dogs more quickly than someone is not afraid. Most young people can understand this idea without persuasion. The therapist can then introduce the focus of the young person's OCD and explain how they might be constantly looking out for signs that something bad is going to happen. For instance to demonstrate that this is a problem, the therapist might ask a young person with contamination fears to do a sensory experiment. For one young person with a fear of contamination with blood, the therapist and the patient first walked 50 paces along a path in the clinic grounds and the patient pointed out all the spots which could have been blood. Her anxiety was rated at the beginning and end of the walk, and she found that it did not decrease. Then the therapist and the patient walked along the path and kept their eyes on the top of a building, to her surprise she found that she felt better for achieving this goal (her anxiety ratings decreased). For homework she agreed to try to do some short walks without looking at the ground the whole time and report back how she felt the next week. It is important that it is explained to the young person that what they are doing is not avoiding the triggers for obsessions, but instead looking at other things. In practice it is almost impossible to walk along a path without looking where your feet will be. So the next stage in this progression of experiments might be to look at the floor but not avoid whatever is seen on the ground.

Diminished Access to Internal States

Lazarov, Dar, Oded, and Liberman (2010) suggested that people with OCD lacked access to the inner states of feelings, preferences, and comprehension. As a result they may ask repeatedly for reassurance, check things repeatedly, or carry out other compulsions to improve the subjective feeling of certainty. They supported their argument by a study of students who scored either high or low on measures of OCD symptoms. Those students who scored high were found to be less able to relax, as measured by galvanic skin response. More importantly when provided with objective feedback from the GSR machine those students with high OCD symptom scores relaxed more than those with low symptom scores. This theory can also be seen as a variant on the memory problem or of the intolerance to uncertainty. In any of these cases, it is likely to be useful to consider how checking one's internal state is not helpful. Surveying how other people monitor internal states could also be instructive. For instance, if you survey how people decide when to stop washing their hands, it is rare to find people using internal states (they feel clean) although some people will use visual evidence of clean hands as an indicator. Some internal cues are more difficult to manage with surveys, so it can be helpful to discuss with patients whether or not to use internal cues. For instance, how does one decide which sock to put on first in the morning? Yet if you try to put the nonhabitual sock on first it might feel peculiar initially, but one soon habituates to it. The therapist would then encourage experiments to see what happens if the decision to stop a ritual is determined by, for instance, a kitchen alarm set at a predetermined interval. There would be some discomfort initially, but the experiment would demonstrate that it would dissipate as predicted by knowledge of the anxiety curve.

OUTLINE OF APPROACH

In the first session, the therapist provides information about CBT. It is explained that the young person will be a detective or scientist discovering more about their own OCD and how it works. The young person is treated as the expert on their own OCD, while the therapist is there to help make changes in behavior and thinking by acting as a guide to achieving the young person's own goals. Often times a parent will sit in on sessions, so the therapist describes the group (young person, parent, therapist) as a team which needs to work together to solve the problems of OCD. The implication of taking this approach is that the young person is an active collaborator in the design of their treatment, and as such can determine the pace and direction of treatment within broad parameters. Thus the young person and their parents are encouraged to take part in setting the agenda for each session, designing experiments, and then carrying them out both in and out of the sessions. To understand that CBT is an active treatment it is helpful to ask the young person what would happen if they and the therapist just talked about the OCD rather than actively trying out new ways of doing things. These points are worth remembering if the young person is having difficulty completing homework tasks.

Some young people may not see that advice from another person like the therapist could be helpful. One way of tackling this initial lack of engagement is to discuss with them what happens if you break a leg. This can be done in the form of a story or in a discussion. To start the story, the therapist would ask the young person to recall someone who had broken an arm or leg. One can then ask what helped them get better. Often a plaster cast or a sling will be described. If asked the young person will readily admit that with a broken bone, they would need to have helped to get better, so the therapist then says that with OCD it is the same. In order to get better, the young person will need a bit of help at first, but they will get better through their own efforts.

The Nature of Experiments

Experiments should be designed so that they start with easily attainable goals, before moving on to more difficult topics. For this reason experiments about the controllability of thoughts are used in the first sessions. In general too, the therapist should be willing to carry out the experiments on themselves, so as to enable the young person to see that the experiment is possible. So it is likely that the therapist will have to model the experiment in front of the young person. Experiments that the therapist models should be designed to produce anxiety or discomfort in anyone but focused on the obsessions of the young person. The therapist should feel some discomfort that is clear to the young person. The therapist can also model how the discomfort decreases over time. Thus the experiment might be thinking about a loved one dying or rubbing the palm of the hand on the bottom of their shoe before licking it.

It is important for young people to develop skills that will protect them against a return of the OCD. However, throughout the intervention we encourage the young people to design their own experiments. This is advantageous because it also helps to protect against the danger of obtaining reassurance from the therapist by shifting responsibility for danger away from themselves (e.g., if something goes wrong it is not my fault because my therapist told me to do it). It has been found helpful to have a hierarchy of increasing responsibility for designing and evaluating experiments as follows:

1. The therapist provides the idea and carries it out (modeling). The young person then does the experiment as well.
2. The therapist provides the idea and then asks the young person to do the experiment.
3. The young person provides the idea and does the experiment in front of the therapist.
4. The young person provides the idea, does not tell the therapist, and does the experiment. The therapist and young person then discuss the results.
5. The young person provides the idea, does not tell the therapist about the experiment, and only discusses the results with the therapist in terms of what they might mean.

Differentiating Experiments and Exposure and Response Prevention

Most guidelines that have been published for the treatment of OCD (Koran & Simpson, 2013; NICE, 2005) describe psychological therapies as consisting of exposure and response prevention (E/RP) as the main intervention. Although it is based on learning theories like CBT, E/RP can be challenging for many people because it requires exposing themselves to very unpleasant situations until the unpleasant feeling reduces. It is based on the purely behavioral idea that breaking the link between a stimulus (obsession) and a response (compulsion) through the process of extinction is required. The cognitive approaches described here do not use E/RP as a major aspect of treatment. Instead the aim of therapy is to reduce the importance and misinterpretation of intrusive thoughts (obsessions) to such an extent that the patient no longer sees the necessity of performing compulsions to reduce their anxiety. More recent work on extinction has found that extinction is not simply habituation to not responding but also requires the learning of an inhibitory response (Craske, Treanor, Conway, Zbozinek, & Vervliet, 2014). Table 1 summarizes the differences between behavioral experiments and E/RP.

TABLE 1 Shows a Summary of the Features Differentiating Behavioral Experiments From Exposure and Response Prevention (E/RP) and Inhibitory Learning Exposure and Response Prevention

Differences Between Behavioral Experiments and Exposure and Response Prevention	Behavioral Experiments	Classic Exposure and Response Prevention	Inhibitory Learning Exposure and Response Prevention
Primary purpose	To test the validity of a specific belief/s	To facilitate habituation—becoming accustomed to the fear stimuli	Violation of expectancies
Frequency	Usually once is sufficient	Exposures repeated multiple times	As many times as needed, often multiple times
Systematically graded	No	Yes, generally from least frightening to most frightening; a fear hierarchy	Initial exposures are graded, but then variability is introduced
Fear hierarchy	Not necessary to construct a fear hierarchy	Fear hierarchy is constructed	Hierarchy developed to guide initial exposures and monitor progress
Duration	Brief	Prolonged exposures	Until expectation is violated
Evokes anxiety	Not necessary	Essential	Important
Response prevention	Irrelevant	Essential	Essential
Aim	Change cognitions	Change anxiety response—strictly speaking to decouple emotional and behavioral response from stimulus	Strengthen inhibitory extinction learning

Modified from Williams, T. I., & Shafran, R. (2015). Obsessive–compulsive disorder in young people. *BJPsych Advances, 21*(3), 196–205. http://dx.doi.org/10.1192/apt.bp.113.011759.

The literature does not yet provide clear evidence for the superiority of either approach. Studies comparing E/RP with CBT directly have been equivocal (e.g., Whittal, Thordarson, & McLean, 2005) and literature reviews have concluded that both in adults (Öst, Havnen, Hansen, & Kvale, 2015) and young people (Skarphedinsson et al., 2015) there are no statistically significant differences between methods. The British approach has been based largely on using cognitive modification primarily as the means for resolving symptoms of OCD, and the results have demonstrated very similar effect sizes across different teams (Bolton et al., 2011, Reynolds et al., 2013; Turner et al., 2014; Williams et al., 2010).

Young people usually need some encouragement to carry out experiments outside sessions at home or in the community. Partly this is because therapists are seen as similar to teachers, and the requests to do work outside sessions are viewed as homework, which is received unenthusiastically. It is helpful to persuade the young person to consider why the tasks might be important. From the point of view of the therapist it is about building skills and helping the young person feel that they "own" the tasks. One might discuss how all skills need practice—hockey players don't improve by sitting in front of a screen playing computer games. If they did do that, when they got on the ice as the match started, they would be unable to match the skills of their opponents. Equally, it is not always possible to try out all exercises during the clinic sessions so some tasks that are done between sessions enable extra information to be gained or offer opportunities for family members to model coping with and tackling OCD type problems.

NON-OCD COGNITIVE ISSUES

Establishing and Maintaining Motivation

A common problem when working with young people is that they have come because someone else has told them to, but they themselves are reluctant to change and suspect that the therapist is going to change them in some fundamental way. It is therefore important to gain their trust and develop their motivation to change. We can view some of their lack of motivation as resulting from misconceptions about whether or not they need to change the way that they manage their OCD. Waite, Gallop, and Atkinson (2009) suggest that starting from the following questions the therapist can begin to identify misconceptions around OCD:

- "Have there been times when you did not carry out a ritual and nothing happened?
- Have you ever had a thought about harm followed by nothing happening?
- Has your worry become better or worse since carrying out rituals?
- What was your worry like before you had OCD?

- Have you ever noticed that in the long-term the OCD gets worse when you do the things it wants?
- Have you ever carried out a ritual and it did not work?"

The first two questions allow the therapist to start asking about the beliefs that the young person has about their OCD. Do they believe that they must always do their rituals?

Alligator and Salt to Weaken Motivation for Going on With OCD

Young people often have a degree of ambivalence about starting or carrying on with treatment. It is therefore useful to have some thought experiments, to explain why it might be helpful to change how the young person manages their behavior and thinking. For instance, we might explain the need for changing the way that the problem of OCD is approached by telling the following story:

T: Do you know the story about the man throwing salt in Times Square?
YP: No
T: Do you know Times Square? (The therapist can substitute a more relevant place here)
YP: Yeah
T: If you go down there you will see someone walking round throwing salt all over. How would we find out why he is doing it?
YP: Dunno ... maybe go up and ask him?
T: Okay, and what might he say?
YP: I dunno
T: Then he tells you that he is keeping the alligators away. So how could he find out if throwing salt is really keeping alligators away?
YP: Oh ... he might have to stop throwing salt for a while.
T: And then if the alligators did not come back, what would that mean?
YP: That the salt was not keeping alligators away?
T: Could that be like your OCD? That you keep doing rituals to stop bad things happening?
YP: Maybe ...
T: So what might you do differently, so that you could find out?
YP: Stop my rituals? But that might cause something awful to happen, I can't do that.
T: Perhaps stopping the rituals is a bit much to start with, but we could try other things first, like doing the rituals in a different way and finding out how you feel.

Meaning of Thoughts

It is important that a young person can understand that there are often several explanations of events. For instance:

T: What do you think if you hear a banging noise at night?
YP: It could be burglars?
T: Yes, or in our house it might well be the cat jumping off one of the kitchen stools and knocking it over. Or even the wind slamming a door. The point is that you wake up frightened, but calm down as soon as you know what it is, having worked through a series of ideas of what it might be.

This particular example might not work so well if the OCD involves checking locks and window at night, but other examples can be chosen to illustrate that events may have alternative explanations to the worst one.

When intrusive thoughts are interpreted as meaning that one is a bad person, further work may be necessary to identify that this is not the case. The continuum method can be used to identify what sort of thoughts different people might have. In this method, the therapist draws a straight line on a sheet of paper (see Fig. 3). First the young person is encouraged to choose an evil person to place at one end of the line and a wonderful person at the other end. In this example the young person has chosen Hitler at the worst end and Mother Teresa at the other end. Then people that the young person knows well (friends, family, school bully, teachers) are placed on the line, until finally the therapist asks the young person to place themselves on the line.

Then the young person identifies the types of thinking that different people might have. It can be helpful to think about how a professional assassin might think about killing people and then contrast it with what Mother Teresa would think. Then the therapist would reintroduce the idea that thoughts are not controllable, and might for example say that the therapist has thoughts about killing their manager from time to time. Does that make the therapist a bad person? The young person is then encouraged to identify what thoughts (bad or good) the people on his continuum have. As a result they will find out that although everyone has bad thoughts, they do not mean anything about the person having them.

Nature of Anxiety

T: Suppose a balloon bursts suddenly behind you, what happens?
YP: I jump, my heart races …
T: Yes and how quickly do you calm down again?

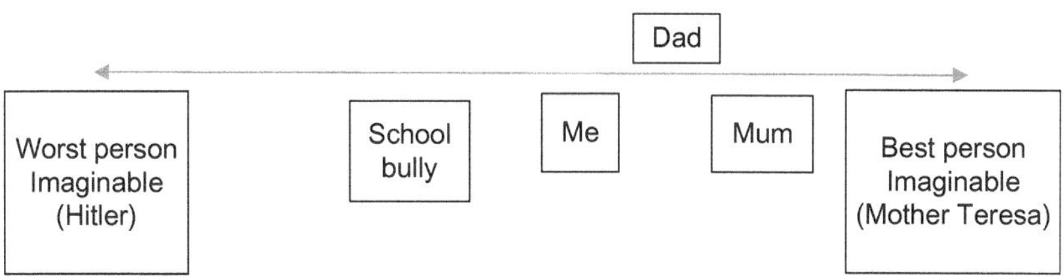

FIG. 3 Continuum diagram to illustrate a way of modifying cognitions about obsessions.

YP: A few minutes, I suppose.

T: Yes, that's right, when something frightening happens, we react very fast to it, but we do also calm down in time.

This can be a useful way of introducing how the body reacts when a person becomes anxious. The therapist explains how adrenaline is released in the body when we are frightened, and that it does not get released continuously and that it goes away after a while anyway. Therapists often go on to explain how adrenaline is a hangover from our evolutionary past in that it enables the "fight-flight" response. This is accompanied by asking the young person to draw the anxiety curve (Fig. 4):

Once the young person understands how anxiety works in general terms, the therapist can go on to explain how anxiety works in OCD (Fig. 5). "OCD works by teaching you that if you do your compulsion, you get to feel better really quickly." The therapist would then go on to explain that even if you did nothing your anxiety would decrease anyway (Fig. 6).

The conversation could go on like this:

T: Do you think your OCD could be like this? Have you ever gone against what OCD has told you to do?

YP: I don't know. I can't remember any times when I haven't done what OCD says.

T: May be there have been times when you have felt nervous or worried, like before an exam?

YP: Oh yes, I was really scared when I went to secondary school.

T: And what happened? Did you go on feeling anxious and scared?

YP: After I started lessons, they got better, but they did come back at break time.

T: So which of these pictures did it look like?

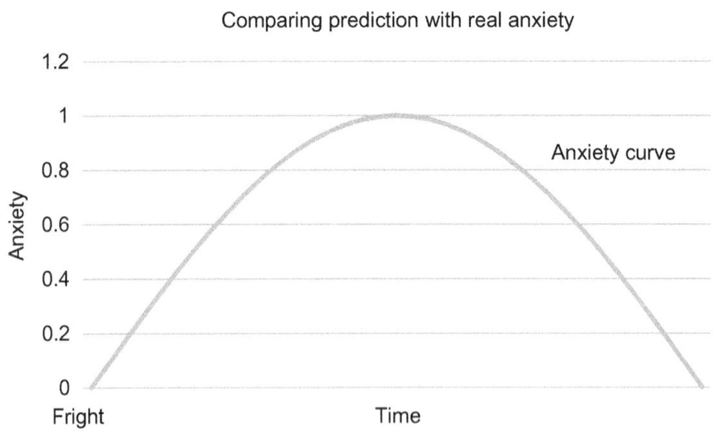

FIG. 4 Showing how anxiety waxes and wanes when something frightening happens.

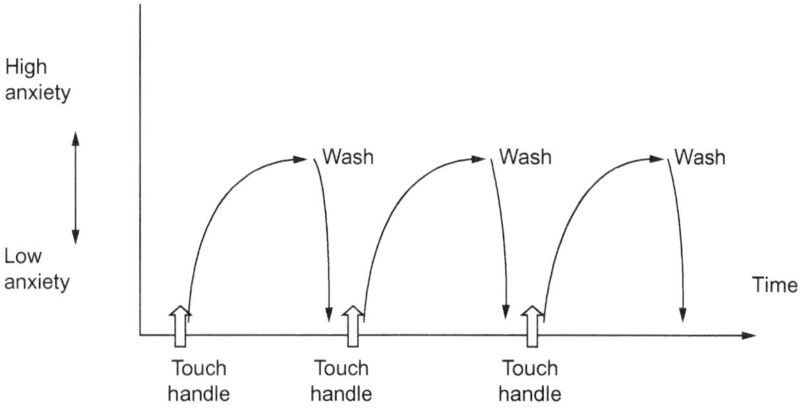

FIG. 5 Diagram to show how OCD works. Repeated washing teaches the young person that if they wash when they have a contamination obsession they feel better and so do it again. *(Modified from figure 4.5 on page 66 in Waite, P., & Williams, T. (2009).* Obsessive compulsive disorder. CBT with children, adolescents and families. *London: Taylor & Francis, with permission from Taylor & Francis.)*

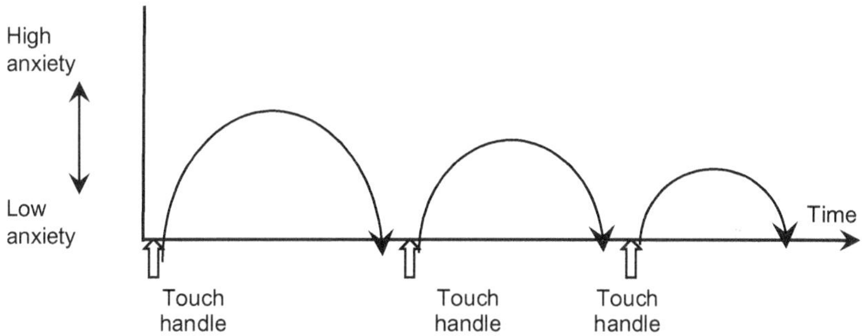

FIG. 6 Diagram to show what would happen if someone did not wash following each contamination obsession. *(Modified from figure 4.4 on page 66 from Waite, P., & Williams, T. (2009).* Obsessive compulsive disorder. CBT with children, adolescents and families. *London: Taylor & Francis, with permission from Taylor & Francis.)*

YP: This one (points to Fig. 4).
T: Do you think that might be true for OCD as well?
YP: Maybe.
T: Okay, let's say it is the same. If the next time you got an OCD thought what do you imagine would happen if you went against what the OCD said?
YP: I guess it could get easier
T: How would that work?
YP: Well I've done it before so I know it's going to be okay.
T: And if you did it more times?
YP: If I did it enough times and nothing bad happened then I would get less worried.

T: So, how will we find out if it works like this for you?
YP: I could try not to do the OCD thing a few times?
T: And what would you think would happen?
YP: OCD would tell me that I would feel worse and worse forever. But it might be like starting secondary school. It got easier after a time.
The therapist can use this discussion to show that anxiety is not something that stays with someone forever. In fact anxiety diminishes quite quickly once the initial shock is over.

CONCLUSIONS

Cognitive change can be achieved through discussion, surveys, and experiments among other techniques. Therapists using cognitive methods should not restrict themselves to those prescribed by any one cognitive theory of OCD, but instead should use the case formulation as the means of describing the particular cognitive issues relevant to their patients. The formulation is not a static statement of the problem, but rather is a working document that undergoes changes as more information comes to light in the course of therapy. Where an obsession is particularly troubling (e.g., the worry that one is a pedophile), it may take many sessions of treatment to discuss it overtly, but the experiments outlined earlier can help to change the understanding of intrusive thoughts (obsessions), and hence enable beneficial change. At the same time therapists should be aware of other issues like motivation or family accommodation and beliefs that may impede progress during treatment.

Each of the cognitive problems outlined earlier can be important to one of the young people with OCD that are seen on a daily basis in clinics. There is no evidence to suggest that only one approach or one cognitive appraisal is fundamental to OCD or its treatment. Therapists therefore have to use the information provided by the young person and their family to identify thinking/cognitive problems and be creative and flexible in devising experiments, surveys, or discussions to reduce their significance so that young people are able to live their lives without being handicapped by OCD.

REFERENCES

Allsopp, M., & Williams, T. (1996). Intrusive thoughts in a non-clinical adolescent population. *European Child & Adolescent Psychiatry*, *5*(1), 25–32. http://doi.dx.org/10.1007/BF00708211.

American Psychiatric Association. (2013). *Diagnostic and statistical manual of mental disorders (DSM-5®)*. Arlington, VA: American Psychiatric Publishing.

Amir, N., Freshman, M., Ramsey, B., Neary, E., & Brigidi, B. (2001). Thought–action fusion in individuals with OCD symptoms. *Behaviour Research and Therapy*, *39*(7), 765–776.

Beaman, C. P., & Williams, T. I. (2010). Earworms ('stuck song syndrome'): Towards a natural history of intrusive thoughts. *British Journal of Psychology*, *101*, 637–653. http://dx.doi.org/10.1348/000712609x479636.

Bolton, D., Williams, T., Perrin, S., Atkinson, L., Gallop, C., Waite, P., et al. (2011). Randomized controlled trial of full and brief cognitive-behaviour therapy and wait-list for paediatric obsessive-compulsive disorder. *Journal of Child Psychology and Psychiatry*, *52*, 1269–1278. http://dx.doi.org/10.1111/j.1469-7610.2011.02419.x.

Bradley, M. C., Hanna, D., Wilson, P., Scott, G., Quinn, P., & Dyer, K. F. (2016). Obsessive–compulsive symptoms and attentional bias: An eye-tracking methodology. *Journal of Behavior Therapy and Experimental Psychiatry*, *50*, 303–308.

Cougle, J. R., & Lee, H. -J. (2014). Pathological and non-pathological features of obsessive-compulsive disorder: Revisiting basic assumptions of cognitive models. *Journal of Obsessive-Compulsive and Related Disorders*, *3*(1), 12–20.

Craske, M. G., Treanor, M., Conway, C. C., Zbozinek, T., & Vervliet, B. (2014). Maximizing exposure therapy: An inhibitory learning approach. *Behaviour Research and Therapy*, *58*, 10–23. http://dx.doi.org/10.1016/j.brat.2014.04.006.

Evans, D. W., Hersperger, C., & Capaldi, P. A. (2011). Thought-action fusion in childhood: Measurement, development, and association with anxiety, rituals and other compulsive-like behaviors. *Child Psychiatry & Human Development*, *42*(1), 12–23.

Exner, C., Martin, V., & Rief, W. (2009). Self-focused ruminations and memory deficits in obsessive–compulsive disorder. *Cognitive Therapy and Research*, *33*(2), 163–174.

Flett, G., Hewitt, P., Boucher, D., Davidson, L., & Munro, Y. (1997). *The child-adolescent perfectionism scale: Development, validation, and association with adjustment.* Unpublished manuscript.

Flett, G. L., Hewitt, P. L., & Dyck, D. G. (1989). Self-oriented perfectionism, neuroticism and anxiety. *Personality and Individual Differences*, *10*(7), 731–735. http://dx.doi.org/10.1016/0191-8869(89)90119-0.

Friedman, H. S., & Kern, M. L. (2014). Personality, well-being, and health. *Annual Review of Psychology*, *65*(1), 719–742. http://dx.doi.org/10.1146/annurev-psych-010213-115123.

Hezel, D. M., & McNally, R. J. (2015). A theoretical review of cognitive biases and deficits in obsessive–compulsive disorder. *Biological Psychology*, *121*, 221–232. http://dx.doi.org/10.1016/j.biopsycho.2015.10.012.

Koran, L. M., & Simpson, H. B. (2013). *Guideline watch (March 2013): Practice guideline for the treatment of patients with obsessive-compulsive disorder.* Arlington: American Psychiatric Association.

Lawrence, P. J., & Williams, T. I. (2011). Pathways to inflated responsibility beliefs in adolescent obsessive-compulsive disorder: A preliminary investigation. *Behavioural and Cognitive Psychotherapy*, *39*(2), 229–234. http://dx.doi.org/10.1017/s1352465810000810.

Lazarov, A., Dar, R., Oded, Y., & Liberman, N. (2010). Are obsessive–compulsive tendencies related to reliance on external proxies for internal states? Evidence from biofeedback-aided relaxation studies. *Behaviour Research and Therapy*, *48*(6), 516–523.

Libby, S., Reynolds, S., Derisley, J., & Clark, S. (2004). Cognitive appraisals in young people with obsessive-compulsive disorder. *Journal of Child Psychology and Psychiatry*, *45*(6), 1076–1084.

McEvoy, P. M., & Mahoney, A. E. (2012). To be sure, to be sure: Intolerance of uncertainty mediates symptoms of various anxiety disorders and depression. *Behavior Therapy*, *43*(3), 533–545.

Moritz, S., & Pohl, R. F. (2009). Biased processing of threat-related information rather than knowledge deficits contributes to overestimation of threat in obsessive-compulsive disorder. *Behavior Modification*, *33*(6), 763–777. http://dx.doi.org/10.1177/0145445509344217.

Myers, S. G., Fisher, P. L., & Wells, A. (2009). An empirical test of the metacognitive model of obsessive-compulsive symptoms: Fusion beliefs, beliefs about rituals, and stop signals. *Journal of Anxiety Disorders*, *23*(4), 436–442.

Najmi, S., Riemann, B. C., & Wegner, D. M. (2009). Managing unwanted intrusive thoughts in obsessive–compulsive disorder: Relative effectiveness of suppression, focused distraction, and acceptance. *Behaviour Research and Therapy*, *47*(6), 494–503.

NICE. (2005). *Obsessive-compulsive disorder: Core interventions in the treatment of obsessive-compulsive disorder and body dysmorphic disorder*. London: National Institute for Health and Clinical Excellence.

Obsessive Compulsive Cognitions Working Group. (1997). Cognitive assessment of obsessive-compulsive disorder. Obsessive Compulsive Cognitions Working Group. *Behaviour Research and Therapy*, *35*(7), 667–681.

Öst, L. -G., Havnen, A., Hansen, B., & Kvale, G. (2015). Cognitive behavioral treatments of obsessive–compulsive disorder. A systematic review and meta-analysis of studies published 1993–2014. *Clinical Psychology Review*, *40*, 156–169.

Rachman, S. J. (1993). Obsessions, responsibility and guilt. *Behaviour Research and Therapy*, *31*, 149–154.

Rachman, S., & de Silva, P. (1978). Abnormal and normal obsessions. *Behaviour Research and Therapy*, *16*(4), 233–248.

Rachman, S., & Shafran, R. (1999). Cognitive distortions: Thought-action fusion. *Clinical Psychology & Psychotherapy*, *6*(2), 80–85.

Radomsky, A. S., & Alcolado, G. M. (2010). Don't even think about checking: Mental checking causes memory distrust. *Journal of Behavior Therapy and Experimental Psychiatry*, *41*(4), 345–351. http://dx.doi.org/10.1016/j.jbtep.2010.03.005.

Read, K. L., Comer, J. S., & Kendall, P. C. (2013). The intolerance of uncertainty scale for children (IUSC): Discriminating principal anxiety diagnoses and severity. *Psychological Assessment*, *25*(3), 722.

Reeves, J., Reynolds, S., Coker, S., & Wilson, C. (2010). An experimental manipulation of responsibility in children: A test of the inflated responsibility model of obsessive-compulsive disorder. *Journal of Behavior Therapy and Experimental Psychiatry*, *41*(3), 228–233. http://dx.doi.org/10.1016/j.jbtep.2010.01.007.

Reynolds, S. A., Clark, S., Smith, H., Langdon, P. E., Payne, R., Bowers, G., et al. (2013). Randomized controlled trial of parent-enhanced CBT compared with individual CBT for obsessive-compulsive disorder in young people. *Journal of Consulting and Clinical Psychology*, *81*(6), 1021–1026. http://psycnet.apa.org/doi/10.1037/a0034429.

Rice, K. G., & Preusser, K. J. (2002). The adaptive/maladaptive perfectionism scale. *Measurement and Evaluation in Counseling and Development*, *34*(4), 210.

Salkovskis, P. M. (1985). Obsessional-compulsive problems: A cognitive-behavioural analysis. *Behaviour Research and Therapy*, *23*, 571–583.

Salkovskis, P. M. (1999). Understanding and treating obsessive-Compulsive disorder. *Behaviour Research and Therapy*, *37*, S29–S52.

Salkovskis, P. M., Wroe, A., Gledhill, A., Morrison, N., Forrester, E., Richards, C., et al. (2000). Responsibility attitudes and interpretations are characteristic of obsessive compulsive disorder. *Behaviour Research and Therapy*, *38*(4), 347–372.

Shafran, R., & Rachman, S. (2004). Thought-action fusion: A review. *Journal of Behavior Therapy and Experimental Psychiatry*, *35*(2), 87–107. http://dx.doi.org/10.1016/j.jbtep.2004.04.002.

Shafran, R., Thordarson, D. S., & Rachman, S. (1996). Thought-action fusion in obsessive compulsive disorder. *Journal of Anxiety Disorders*, *10*(5), 379–391.

Sironic, A., & Reeve, R. A. (2015). A combined analysis of the Frost Multidimensional Perfectionism Scale (FMPS), Child and Adolescent Perfectionism Scale (CAPS), and Almost Perfect Scale—Revised (APS-R): Different perfectionist profiles in adolescent high school students. *Psychological Assessment*, *27*(4), 1471–1483.

Skarphedinsson, G., Hanssen-Bauer, K., Kornør, H., Heiervang, E. R., Landrø, N. I., Axelsdottir, B., et al. (2015). Standard individual cognitive behaviour therapy for paediatric obsessive-compulsive disorder: A systematic review of effect estimates across comparisons. *Nordic Journal of Psychiatry*, *69*(2), 81–92. http://dx.doi.org/10.3109/08039488.2014.941395.

Soreni, N., Streiner, D., McCabe, R., Bullard, C., Swinson, R., Greco, A., et al. (2014). Dimensions of perfectionism in children and adolescents with obsessive-compulsive disorder. *Journal of the Canadian Academy of Child and Adolescent Psychiatry*, *23*(2), 136.

Turner, C. M., Mataix-Cols, D., Lovell, K., Krebs, G., Lang, K., Byford, S., et al. (2014). Telephone cognitive-behavioral therapy for adolescents with obsessive-compulsive disorder: A randomized controlled non-inferiority trial. *Journal of the American Academy of Child and Adolescent Psychiatry*, *53*(12), 1298–1307.

Waite, P., Gallop, C., & Atkinson, L. (2009). Planning and carrying out treatment. In P. Waite & T. I. Williams (Eds.), *Obsessive compulsive disorder: Cognitive behaviour therapy with children and young people* (1st ed., pp. 51–66). London: Routledge.

Waite, P., & Williams, T. (2009). *Obsessive compulsive disorder. CBT with children, adolescents and families*. London: Taylor & Francis.

Wells, A., & Matthews, G. (1996). Modelling cognition in emotional disorder: The S-REF model. *Behaviour Research and Therapy*, *34*(11), 881–888. http://dx.doi.org/10.1016/S0005-7967(96)00050-2.

Whittal, M. L., Thordarson, D. S., & McLean, P. D. (2005). Treatment of obsessive–compulsive disorder: Cognitive behavior therapy vs. exposure and response prevention. *Behaviour Research and Therapy*, *43*(12), 1559–1576.

Williams, T. I. (2015). The classification of involuntary musical imagery: The case for earworms. *Psychomusicology: Music, Mind, and Brain*, *25*(1), 5–13. http://dx.doi.org/10.1037/pmu0000082.

Williams, T., Salkovksis, P., Forrester, E. A., & Allsopp, M. A. (2002). Changes in symptoms of OCD and appraisal of responsibility during cognitive behavioural treatment: A pilot study. *Behavioural and Cognitive Psychotherapy*, *30*(1), 69–78.

Williams, T. I., Salkovskis, P. M., Forrester, L., Turner, S., White, H., & Allsopp, M. A. (2010). A randomised controlled trial of cognitive behavioural treatment for obsessive compulsive disorder in children and adolescents. *European Child & Adolescent Psychiatry*, *19*(5), 449–456. http://dx.doi.org/10.1007/s00787-009-0077-9.

Ye, H. J., Rice, K. G., & Storch, E. A. (2008). Perfectionism and peer relations among children with obsessive-compulsive disorder. *Child Psychiatry and Human Development*, *39*(4), 415–426. http://dx.doi.org/10.1007/s10578-008-0098-5.

FURTHER READING

Magee, J. C., Harden, K. P., & Teachman, B. A. (2012). Psychopathology and thought suppression: A quantitative review. *Clinical Psychology Review*, *32*(3), 189–201.

Öst, L. -G., Riise, E. N., Wergeland, G. J., Hansen, B., & Kvale, G. (2016). Cognitive behavioral and pharmacological treatments of OCD in children: A systematic review and meta-analysis. *Journal of Anxiety Disorders*, *43*, 58–69. http://dx.doi.org/10.1016/j.janxdis.2016.08.003.

van den Hout, M., & Kindt, M. (2003). Repeated checking causes memory distrust. *Behaviour Research and Therapy*, *41*(3), 301–316.

Chapter 8

Involving Family Members of Children With OCD in CBT

Allison Vreeland* and Tara S. Peris†
*Vanderbilt University, Nashville, TN, United States, †University of California, Los Angeles, Los Angeles, CA, United States

The number of treatments for child and adolescent obsessive-compulsive disorder (OCD) has increased rapidly over the past two decades, with consistent evidence emerging in support of cognitive-behavior therapy (CBT) as a front-line intervention for children and adolescents (see Freeman et al., 2014, for review). Mild to moderate cases of the disorder may fully remit with CBT, while more severe cases may be better managed with combined treatment (POTS, 2004). Whether administered alone or in combination with medication—or in a child or "family-focused" format—virtually every CBT protocol for child and adolescent OCD involves some degree of family involvement in treatment (Barrett, Healy-Farrell, & March, 2004; Grunes, Neziroglu, & McKay, 2001; POTS, 2004). Family involvement in treatment stems both from developmental considerations inherent in treating children and adolescents and from a well-established body of literature documenting the role of the family system in shaping outcomes for youth with OCD (Merlo, Lehmkuhl, Geffken, & Storch, 2009; Peris, Benazon, Langley, Roblek, & Piacentini, 2008; Peris, Bergman, et al., 2008; Peris et al., 2012; Storch et al., 2007). In this chapter, we provide a brief overview of specific family factors that are associated with child and adolescent OCD, and we document their links to CBT outcome. We then describe evidence-based strategies aimed at harnessing family involvement in treatment to optimize outcomes for this complex and challenging condition.

FAMILY FACTORS AND CHILD AND ADOLESCENT OCD

Child and adolescent OCD is characterized by a number of family features that commonly influence the course of the disorder and how it responds to treatment (Garcia et al., 2010, Ginsburg, Kingery, Drake, & Grados, 2008; Peris et al., 2012; Torp et al., 2015). Accommodation is perhaps the most widely studied

The Clinician's Guide to Cognitive-Behavioral Therapy for Childhood Obsessive-Compulsive Disorder
http://dx.doi.org/10.1016/B978-0-12-811427-8.00008-3

family correlate, and it refers to a process wherein family members become involved directly in the child's OCD symptoms. Accommodation occurs in many forms and may include behaviors such as providing verbal reassurance, participating in complex rituals, purchasing items for use in rituals (e.g., soap, laundry detergent, toilet paper), or enabling avoidance behaviors. It is present in the overwhelming majority of families of youth with OCD, and, for many, it is a part of everyday life (Garcia et al., 2010; Lebowitz, Panza, Su, & Bloch, 2012; Peris, Benazon, et al., 2008; Peris, Bergman, et al., 2008; Storch et al., 2007; Wu, Lewin, Murphy, Geffken, & Storch, 2014; Wu et al., 2016).

In some cases, accommodation can stem from an active attempt to soothe the child's distress or to minimize the disruption caused by symptoms. In others, it may evolve gradually over time in a manner that is difficult to detect. Parents may provide reassurance about a child's worries for some time before recognizing that they are participating in ritualistic behavior. Unfortunately this means that many families are already deeply entrenched in pervasive patterns of accommodation by the time they seek treatment. These patterns take a toll on children and parents alike, and are often accompanied by parental anxiety, depression, and distress, as well as high levels of family conflict (Amir, Freshman, Ramsey, Neary, & Brigidi, 2001; Peris & Piacentini, 2014).

To this end, several broader family dynamics are also important to consider when beginning treatment. Parental distress is common in childhood OCD, and it tends to worsen alongside the severity of the child's illness (Storch et al., 2009). This in turn can lead to higher levels of symptom accommodation, perpetuating the illness over time. Indeed, many parents find themselves in a double bind wherein accommodating their child leaves them feeling depressed and drained but refraining from accommodation leaves them feeling anxious and overwhelmed (Amir et al., 2001).

In addition to these challenges, many families are perplexed by symptoms and/or have a difficult time differentiating them from other developmentally normative behavioral difficulties (e.g., noncompliance). Many feel that symptoms fall within the child's control or that they represent an act of defiance. As a result, it is common for families to report high levels of distress as well as high levels of conflict, blame, and hostility (Hibbs, Zahn, Hamburger, Kruesi, & Rapoport, 1992; Peris et al., 2012; Renshaw, Steketee, & Chambless, 2005). Research also suggests that families of youth with OCD are characterized by more negative parent-child interactions, poorer problem solving, less warmth, and lower levels of support or cohesion compared to youth without the disorder (Barrett, Shortt, & Healy, 2002; Chambless, Bryan, Aiken, Steketee, & Hooley, 2001; Peris et al., 2012; Valleni-Basile et al., 1995). Many of these features are found in other forms of child psychological problems as well (Lim, Wood, & Miller, 2008, Lim, Wood, Miller, & Simmens, 2011; Lovejoy, Graczyk, O'Hare, & Neuman, 2000); however, they are particularly important for youth with OCD inasmuch as they have the potential to interfere with a family's ability to engage in core tasks of evidence-based treatment (e.g., practicing exposures; disengaging from symptom accommodation; Peris & Piacentini, 2014).

PREDICTORS OF TREATMENT OUTCOME

Beyond being well-established family correlates of OCD (see Renshaw et al., 2005 for review), several of these features have been linked directly to CBT outcomes for youth. In particular, research has found that higher levels of parental distress are associated with poorer response to evidence-based OCD treatments (Storch et al., 2008). Research indicates that high levels of family conflict, high levels of blame, and low levels of family cohesion or supportiveness each predict poorer response to CBT, even when the child's level of baseline symptom severity is taken into account. Indeed, these features tend to cooccur, and as the level of family dysfunction increases, there are corresponding decreases in CBT outcome (Peris et al., 2012). With respect to symptom accommodation, there is evidence that levels of family accommodation at the beginning of treatment predict how youth fare at the end (Garcia et al., 2010). Importantly—particularly for those clinicians working holistically with the family—research also suggests that reductions in family accommodation precede improvements in OCD symptomatology (Piacentini et al., 2011), and that they may mediate the link between level of impairment and treatment outcome (Caporino et al., 2012; Merlo et al., 2009; Wu et al., 2014).

INVOLVING THE FAMILY IN TREATMENT

In light of this picture, how should families be involved in treatment for child and adolescent OCD? Although family involvement in treatment is recommended in both professional practice parameters and expert reviews of the literature (Freeman et al., 2014; Geller & March, 2012), to date, no study has tested the incremental efficacy of adding family therapy to individual child CBT. Moreover, current recommendations remain open ended and loosely defined. In the following sections, we offer evidence-based strategies, recognizing that, while they show clinical utility, they do not address these larger questions for the field (Peris & Piacentini, 2016; Piacentini, Langley, & Roblek, 2007). The strategies we outline are aimed at educating families more fully about their role in the treatment process, helping them learn to monitor and regulate the emotions that OCD elicits, and to problem solve constructively around difficult episodes that invariably come up. These skills are viewed as necessary precursors for helping families to decrease symptom accommodation, support exposure therapy, and optimize CBT outcomes (Peris & Piacentini, 2013, 2016).

In general, we recommend including family members in treatment as much as possible. This may mean having them shadow child-focused ERP sessions in addition to attending separate "family-focused" sessions. In cases where that is not possible (or, where family conflict and/or parental anxiety are so severe that weekly involvement is contraindicated in the early stages of treatment), staggering separate family sessions at regular intervals throughout the child's individual treatment may also be useful. Similarly, to promote generalization of treatment skills, we encourage participation from as many family members as possible including siblings, grandparents, and other caregivers as appropriate.

PSYCHOEDUCATION AND INTRODUCING TREATMENT

CBT for child and adolescent OCD typically begins with psychoeducation about the disorder, including its causes and prevalence and its maintenance over time via negative reinforcement cycles. This information provides a springboard for explaining how exposure-based treatment will "break" the OCD cycle. For readers who are less familiar with this content, established protocols can provide detailed scripts for use in clinical practice (e.g., March & Mulle, 1998; Piacentini et al., 2007; see also Chapter 3).

Although some version of this basic psychoeducation is standard in all child and adolescent OCD treatment, specific focus on the role of the family in the OCD cycle can help families to better understand their roles in the treatment process. When incorporating families in treatment, it is often helpful to begin by explaining that OCD does not affect a single person; rather, it can and does affect the entire family. Thus a family approach to responding to symptoms enables everyone to work as a team to break the cycle of OCD and minimize its impact. First, provide an enhanced version of psychoeducation by including the following topics:

1. Accommodation and its role in the OCD cycle.
2. Reduction of accommodation as a primary family treatment goal.
3. Barriers to reducing accommodation (e.g., family conflict, parental anxiety, poor family cohesion).
4. The role of the family in supporting exposure-based treatment.

To address these topics, begin by describing what accommodation is and how it can occur in many forms (e.g., providing soap for hand washing, excusing the child from chores). Normalize it as a common feature for all families where someone has OCD, and then describe that a central goal of family treatment is to *learn a new way to respond to symptoms*. Just as the child learns in individual therapy to resist OCD urges, family members will learn to recognize patterns of accommodation and to change them gradually over time (Peris & Piacentini, 2016).

> *Accommodation happens in almost every family where someone has OCD. Many times it begins innocently by someone trying to be helpful. Maybe mom or dad wants to soothe the distress caused by OCD. But just like with other OCD compulsions, what works in the beginning does not work for long, and family members often have to do more and more to make it feel okay.*

To help families understand the importance of reducing accommodation, it is helpful to also describe it as part of the OCD cycle. Ask the child to begin by identifying a compulsion that he completes by himself (e.g., washing his/her hands). Then explain that in many cases, compulsive behavior shifts to involve family members (e.g., asking parents to avoid touching dirty objects or asking parents to wash their hands). Both patterns of responding bring the same short-term relief, and thus both form part of the same central cycle. They can be visualized via the example and simple graphic (see Fig. 1).

> *Earlier we talked about how when OCD makes you think you're dirty, you go to the bathroom and wash your hands. So you have a thought that makes you feel anxious, and to feel better, you do your compulsion. That's the basic OCD cycle we've already described. But sometimes, OCD can be sneaky and rope other people in, too. You also mentioned that sometimes you ask your mom if your hands are really clean or if you did a good job. What happens when she answers? You feel better. It's the same effect, right? You feel worried or anxious and to feel better, you do a compulsion that involves other people. We can see how accommodation works in this picture here.*

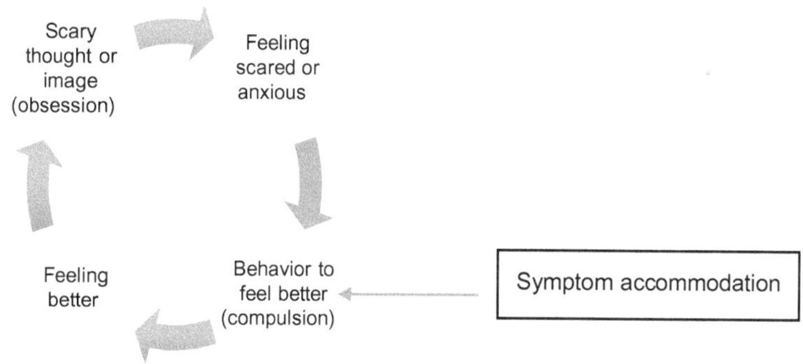

FIG. 1 Family involvement in the OCD cycle: accommodation negatively reinforces compulsions by providing short-term relief.

The goal of this discussion is to help parents understand that accommodation is problematic for exposure-based treatment because it reinforces the child's fear and avoidance behaviors and maintains symptoms over time. Thus the primary goal of family treatment is to learn to respond to symptoms without accommodating (i.e., reinforcing) them.

Although this goal may seem straightforward, it is important to recognize that some families have an easier time than others when it comes to reducing symptom accommodation. Families characterized by high levels of anxiety or high levels of family conflict may have a much more difficult time resisting accommodation. Indeed, they report more distress and worse responses from the child when they attempt to do so (Peris, Bergman, et al., 2008). By contrast, families who describe themselves as high in cohesion—that is, high in warmth and supportiveness—report much more favorable outcomes. With this in mind, use psychoeducation as an opportunity to explain that additional family goals center around learning to manage the heated emotions that come up around OCD and to build positivity and supportiveness in the home environment. As detailed later, both of these goals are achieved through structured skills training in emotion regulation.

INITIAL RESPONDING TO OCD

Armed with a better understanding of symptom accommodation and its role in maintaining OCD over time, families are well positioned to begin practicing new skills related to managing OCD. However, disengaging from accommodation is a long-term process and families often need a more immediate set of instructions for what to say and do when their child pulls for their involvement in symptoms. Although the ultimate goal is to resist accommodation altogether, a shaping procedure is often needed. This can be introduced to families by coaching them using the following simple sequence.

1. *"Do you think that's your OCD talking right now?"*
2. *"Is there a skill you can use?" (if yes, praise effort)*
3. *If no, "Do you really need me to do that?" (Look for smallest form of accommodation the child can tolerate).*

This approach is meant to provide gentle prompts for the child to resist OCD urges and to provide an initial step toward delaying and reducing accommodation. It can be introduced early in family treatment as a short-term strategy that will be modified over time as the child progresses in ERP and becomes more ready for parents to disengage from accommodation altogether. Because there is potential for confusion ("*Hey! Didn't you tell me not to accommodate this stuff?*"), it is okay to be up front with parents and acknowledge that they are, in fact, still accommodating while using this sequence of steps. However, they are prompting the use of a skill first, and, in cases where the child is unable to draw on useful coping skills, they are delaying the process of "giving in" to requests and looking for smaller forms of accommodation. In the initial stages of treatment, these are all steps in the right direction.

DEVELOPING A LONG-TERM PLAN FOR ACCOMMODATION

In order to keep the process of reducing accommodation moving, lay out a game plan for how symptom involvement will be addressed more fully over time. As a first step, work with the family to gain greater awareness of how they respond symptoms. Even with targeted psychoeducation, families can vary in their level of insight into their patterns of accommodation, and it can be helpful to use structured exercises to direct their attention to their involvement in symptoms. To this end, have each family member make a list of the ways in which they accommodate their child's OCD symptoms. This list can be modified over time as they identify new behaviors or learn to disengage from others. Beside each form of accommodation, the parent can use a 0–10 Likert scale to indicate how hard it would be for them if they refrained from that specific act of accommodation. In a separate column, they can indicate how hard they think it would be for their child. Separately, have the child provide their own ratings for how challenging it would be if their family members refrained from accommodating in each situation. Including each family member's difficulty rating allows you to process differences in what each family member is ready for. For example, parents often report higher levels of anxiety about refraining from a given form of accommodation than their children do. Alternatively, parents may assign a high rating to how hard they believe a given task will be for their child, only to have their child report a much lower rating (or vice versa). Including these subjective ratings of difficulty can be used to highlight the challenges of changing accommodation, particularly as they relate to parental anxiety and family distress (i.e., everyone must be ready). As appropriate, it can also be used to note that sometimes youth can take on more than we think they can. This exercise is completed early in family treatment with two specific goals: (1) increasing family awareness of patterns of symptom accommodation; (2) developing a hierarchy of family treatment targets. That is, the ratings family members assign to each form of accommodation can be used to identify easier and more difficult situations to target and to organize a plan for where to begin changing family responses to OCD.

A word of caution is often helpful as families learn more about accommodation and its role in OCD. Often, once parents learn that symptom accommodation fuels their child's OCD, they are eager to change their behavior all at once, resisting the child's requests altogether. Although this is a desirable long-term goal, it is typically ill advised to take such a dramatic approach. Instead, inform families that it takes time to practice and master new skills. The child must develop proficiency with exposure-based techniques in individual sessions, and the family must have an organized plan for making gradual changes that map to where the child is at in treatment.

EMOTION REGULATION

Having created a hierarchy for family accommodation, it is tempting to jump right in to tackling the items on the list. However, before addressing items on this list, pivot briefly to focus on a different skill set for families: emotion regulation. Anxious children frequently have parents who are also anxious.

Even if they are not worriers by nature, the process of observing a child in severe distress can be activating and unsettling for parents. Indeed, many parents experience a range of difficult feelings that may complicate their ability to respond to OCD effectively (e.g., anxiety, frustration, anger, sadness). These feelings are natural and expected, and it is important to give parents an opportunity to voice them. This can be accomplished by carving out a separate session (or portion of a session) to ask parents directly, "*What has this been like for you?*" and "*How are you coping*?" The following can also be helpful when meeting individually with parents:

> *Many parents describe a wide range of reactions to their child's OCD. Some tell me that they're sad, some react in frustration and anger, and some tell us they're worried. Please let me know if you have experienced any of the following reactions to your child's OCD:*

1. *Feeling angry that your child won't "just stop"?*
2. *Feeling guilty because you cannot stop your child's suffering?*
3. *Feeling resentful of how your child's symptoms negatively affect the family?*

Work in session to normalize all of these emotional responses to OCD—including anger, frustration, and resentment, which are quite common (Peris, Benazon, et al., 2008; Renshaw et al., 2005), while at the same time conveying that it is difficult to respond effectively to challenging OCD situations when emotions become too heated. Thus an important goal for family members is to learn to recognize and monitor their own emotional responses to OCD and to work on *managing them effectively*. Address this need by teaching family members to monitor and track their emotions in the service of keeping them in check. To do this, have them use a "feelings thermometer" akin to those used in evidence-based assessment (see ADIS-IV; Silverman & Albano, 1996) and treatment protocols (see Coping Cat, Kendall & Hedtke, 2006; Piacentini et al., 2007). Family members can use this visual aide to identify what they are feeling (e.g., angry) and how intense the reaction is on a 0–10 scale. Present the rationale for this approach as follows:

> *Even though it's normal to have big reactions in difficult or unexpected OCD situations, it becomes harder to make good decisions when we're overwhelmed by our feelings. The goal of emotion monitoring is to keep track of what you are feeling and how much of it you are feeling so that you can prevent yourself from making poor or impulsive decisions in the midst of an OCD episode. As you notice your feelings rising, it's an opportunity to intervene before your emotions get the better of you. Each of us has a tipping point for when our feelings begin to overwhelm us, and with practice, we can get a sense of where that point generally is. If you can see it coming, you can act strategically before it's too late.*

To further illustrate how this works, prompt families to think about a recent time they confronted a difficult situation related to OCD. Ask them to walk through what happened step by step, tracing what they were feeling and how intense their reaction was at each juncture. From there, ask them to identify the point at which they felt overwhelmed or unable to be constructive (this can also be called the "point of no return"). Explain that the goal is to track our emotions so that we can intervene before we reach a tipping point.

DISENGAGING FROM DIFFICULT OCD EPISODES

What does it mean to intervene with feelings before it's too late? For many family members, this means removing themselves from a quickly deteriorating situation. Accordingly, encourage family members to use the thermometer to track their emotions and to take breaks before they spiral out of control. This can prevent family conflict from escalating in a challenging OCD situations and it can prevent parents from entering into coercive exchanges or no-win situations where everyone ends up more upset. Taking a break from the situation also allows children to practice self-soothing skills and to observe their parents modeling their own adaptive coping skills (i.e., "*I'm feeling upset and I need to take a break to calm down.*"). When describing the value of disengaging from difficult OCD episodes by walking away, it may be helpful to provide the following additional rationale:

- When a child is anxious and activated, they are often not able to process information clearly. These are not teachable moments.
- Emotions can be contagious and continuing to engage in a heated exchange will likely cause both parties to become increasingly upset.
- Walking away does not condone inappropriate behavior during tantrums; instead, it communicates that those behaviors are not an effective strategy for handling distress.
- Taking a break or a "time out" shows that the parent has confidence in the child's ability to manage their emotions. As noted, it also provides time and space for the child to practice his or her self-soothing skills.

Although this approach helps parents to disengage from heightened emotional situations before they escalate, when first implementing this new strategy, children may try intensified tactics to engage their parents. Demonstrate how the parents should not attend to these behaviors through brief role plays.

> *When parents first begin walking away from difficult OCD symptoms, it's common for kids to try and engage them further by protesting, using foul language, slamming doors, or trying out other inappropriate behaviors. The child's goal in these settings is to keep you engaged, which we know is rarely productive. If your child does display any of these inappropriate behaviors, we are going to work on not attending to them by keeping a calm and neutral expression and not making eye contact.*

It is important to not only prepare the parents for these situations, but to inform the child of the new way that their parents have learned to respond to OCD symptoms. That is, tell children the goal is for everyone to stay calm in difficult OCD situations and that everyone—even parents—should take breaks when they feel themselves getting too upset to be a good problem-solver. The child, in turn, can be encouraged to use these situations as an opportunity to practice skills used in session.

SELF-SOOTHING SKILLS

What should parents and siblings do when they manage to successfully walk away from a difficult OCD episode? Encourage them to use a self-soothing skill to help them bring emotions into check. Accordingly, it may be helpful to carve out time in session to introduce relaxation skills such as diaphragmatic breathing, progressive muscle relaxation, or guided imagery. Brief mindfulness meditation exercises may also serve the same purpose, and they are readily available online. Incorporating a new skill into each family therapy session allows family members to practice together in a brief exercise either at the start or end of the session. Where appropriate, encourage them to practice together at home. This provides a positive family activity in which to engage, and it provides both parents and children with strategies for soothing themselves when upset. Importantly, it also cues parents into additional skills beyond exposure which may be helpful in managing unexpected or challenging situations that arise with OCD. Although self-soothing skills are not the ideal strategy to use when managing the distress caused by exposure (instead distress tolerance should ideally be used), they can be helpful adjunctive coping skills when youth feel overwhelmed or upset.

FAMILY PROBLEM SOLVING

Having practiced some initial emotion regulation skills (i.e., labeling, monitoring, intervening early), families are often ready to begin more active problem-solving exercises. This topic is broad and can encompass an array of issues. Two interrelated categories to focus upon are issues related to accommodation and broader family dynamics (e.g., difficulty with bedtime or homework, disagreements about parenting, or pervasive family conflict). These are potentially interrelated because families with poor instructional control are unlikely to have success with getting their children to practice challenging exposure homework outside of session. Likewise, inconsistent parenting and family conflict will complicate efforts to follow through with basic treatment requirements. We address strategies for problem solving in each of these arenas later.

SCAFFOLDING TECHNIQUES TO GUIDE DISENGAGEMENT FROM ACCOMMODATION

Teaching families how to gradually disengage from symptom accommodation is similar to teaching them about exposure: After the rationale has been presented, use the feelings thermometer or other rating of subjective units of distress (SUDS) to talk about scaffolding. This principle derives from the child development literature, and it focuses on identifying tasks that are neither too easy not too difficult. This sweet spot is meant to allow the child to grapple with the right amount of challenge in the service of learning something new. If tasks are too easy, no learning takes place. Conversely, if they are too difficult, youth may feel overwhelmed or helpless and simply give up. To use scaffolding, parents need to be able to work with the child to pick the right task (i.e., "0–10, how difficult is this for you?") and to provide the right amount of support for exposure without accommodating ("How can we modify the task to make it more manageable? What can we do to make it a 6 rather than a 10?"). At a broad level, this approach involves teaching parents to guide or prompt their child's use of tools learned in treatment, while gradually providing the child less and less help to promote self-regulation (Freeman et al., 2014).

Once the family understands how scaffolding allows us to choose the right exercises on which to work, apply the concept to disengaging from accommodation. Families can begin to use the feelings thermometer to gauge how difficult a given task is and, if necessary, modify it to fall within the target range with respect to challenge. This process is often facilitated by in vivo practice in session, where parents increasingly take the lead in working with their children to pick tasks and/or modify them as needed. Indeed, parents can sometimes be discouraged if it seems like their children are working on tasks that are too easy or low on the hierarchy. In these situations, it is easy for them to rush or push too hard. Remind them that all skills take practice, from riding a bike ("*You used training wheels, right?*") to competitive sports (e.g., pick your athlete story of choice) to learning to play an instrument (e.g., rote practice of scales). In vivo practice in session allows us to coach parents as needed to meet children where they are at. It also allows parents to see how we can incrementally adjust tasks to be more difficult and how we support children when they struggle without reinforcing symptoms. Throughout this practice, the feelings thermometer creates a shared language and a tool for working collaboratively to find the right difficulty level, and it might go something like this:

> Child at a restaurant: "*Will you hold the menu for me? It's dirty.*"
> Parent: "*Hmm, is that your OCD talking? Is there a skill you can use right now?*"
> Child: "*Yes it's my OCD, but it's too hard and I can't do it, so can you please just hold the menu for me while I look?*"
> Parent: "*I know that seems easier, but let's see if we can find a way to fight OCD together rather than just giving in. Zero to ten, how hard would it be for you to touch the menu?*"
> Child: "*At LEAST a 10!*"
> Parent: "*Can we find something that feels more like a 6 or 7? You've been doing that in session, no problem. What about if you hold the menu at the very edges with both hands?*"

Child: "*That's still an 8.*"
Parent: "*What would make it more of a 6–7?*"
Child: "*Holding the very edge of the menu with just one hand on just one side.*"
Parent: "*Deal! Nice job with that!*"

As families gain proficiency using this approach to choose and modify exercises, revisit the initial strategy they were given to respond to symptoms (see earlier). As seen in this vignette, the original sequence of steps for responding to OCD can be modified to include more on-the-spot problem solving, with a specific focus on persisting in tough situations (rather than giving up or giving in) and working to find the best response to fighting OCD (even if it is incremental). Use the family's accommodation hierarchy to pick an item that aligns (at least in difficulty level) with the child's progress in individual exposure and response prevention (ERP) treatment, and guide them through the following steps:

- As before, have the parents ask "*Do you think that's your OCD?*"—There are some children who do not like to be asked this, especially when the answer is obvious. In these cases, work with the family to identify an alternative phrasing or "code word" that can cue the child to use ERP skills. Some alternatives are: "*That sounds like OCD, and we don't listen to OCD,*" or in response to a request for reassurance and/or accommodation, "*I know this is hard, but you know that I can't do that for you.*"
- "*Is there a skill that you can use right now?*"
- If the child appears to struggle, give a reminder: "*What's our goal? What are our tools?*"
- "*0–10, how difficult does this task feel?*"
- Use scaffolding concepts to identify small steps in the right direction.

BROADER FAMILY DYNAMICS

For issues that extend beyond accommodation, it can be helpful to teach families a specific sequence of steps for working collaboratively to identify problems and their corresponding solutions.

IDENTIFY FAMILY PROBLEMS

As a first step, ask each family member to create a list of "problems" they would like to see addressed. This can be phrased as, "*Tell me about things you would like to see us work on in family treatment*" or "*What are some family issues we can work on together while we're here*?" When creating the list of family problems, encourage them to keep a broad focus. The list does not have to focus squarely on OCD, and it can include both issues related to accommodation and other challenges the family is facing. It helps to prompt them to be as specific as possible. For example, instead of listing "We fight a lot," have them identify what it is they fight about (e.g., "We argue a lot when we don't agree on how to respond to our child's misbehavior"). If a family is having a hard time producing examples on the spot, it may be helpful to provide the following prompts:

- *Write down as much as you want.*
- *If you are having difficulty identifying specific problems, write down whatever comes to you and we can narrow it down later.*

After each family member has produced their own list of "problems," open up the discussion to the whole family and create a master list using problems contributed by everyone. Have each family member identify how upsetting each problem is to them on a 0–10 scale and include this information on the list. When guiding where to start, it can be helpful to avoid particularly hot topics early in treatment.

PRACTICE STEPS FOR FAMILY PROBLEM SOLVING

Once the list is created, work together to identify an item that is low to moderately emotionally charged for everyone. Just like the small steps taken in exposure-based treatments, it is important to proceed gradually when tackling tough family issues; it is most important to give the family practice working together collaboratively and managing emotions during this process. The goal is for them to feel successful so that they persist with their problem-solving efforts. To that end, try to work with the family during these problem-solving exercises with a specific eye toward building skills to encourage and support each other while identifying problems and searching for solutions. This concept might be introduced in the following manner:

> *Change is hard, and one of the most important things you can do is be patient with each other. As you each try new things, you'll see how hard it is to break old habits. This is why we will be proceeding very slowly. It may be tempting to start with an item that is causing extreme distress in your family, but it may be too difficult for now. Let's start with something a bit lower on everyone's list. If we come up with a quick and workable solution, we can try it out and move on to something different next week*

After working with the family to identify their target difficulty/conflict, problem solving this topic begins with a functional analysis of features that may reinforce or shape the target problem. It is helpful to introduce the family to the ABC model (Antecedent-Behavior-Consequence). Ask the family what is happening when challenges arise. What happens before and after? Can the family identify smaller difficulties that lead up to the bigger problem?

The more detail collected through this analysis, the more it will facilitate possible solutions. Ask each of the family members:

- *Why do you think the problem is occurring?*
- *What do you think you can do to prevent the problem or improve the problem?*
- *What's hindering you from taking steps to resolve the problem?*
- *What are possible solutions?*

Encourage the family to generate a list of potential solutions to their problem. This should be open ended and flexible, and family members should refrain from censoring themselves or someone else as they come up with ideas. Once a list has been created, the family can talk through the pros and cons of each idea and rank order their preferences.

Systematically progress through these steps with the family, tackling their family problem using the appropriate sequence of steps and developing an effective plan to respond. The most important thing is that they land on a solution that everyone is *willing to try*. Collaborative problem solving is an important skill that families should continue to work on throughout the remainder of treatment. Introduce these skills at the midpoint of treatment and then check in with families regularly each week to monitor progress and to identify new problems on which to work. Throughout this process, look for opportunities to reinforce earlier skills (e.g., "*You did a really good job knowing that you needed a break*").

As treatment progresses, work to let the family take a more active the lead in generating potential solutions. Assist as needed in generating a course of action, clarifying and emphasizing common goals, gaining information from the functional analysis, and reframing disagreements. Make sure to observe the process with an awareness of family roles that often emerge from these discussions. Who is the leader and who is more passive? Do any family members gang up on another? Is anyone scapegoated as the problem is analyzed? Are the parents united in their approach? It can be helpful to use these observations to help create a balance and support the family through the intervention.

INVOLVING PARENTS IN EXPOSURES

It is crucial that parents witness and participate in exposure tasks so that they learn the language and techniques involved. In some cases, as with younger children, parents may be present for virtually all of the treatment sessions. In these situations, parents should increasingly take the lead in choosing, coaching, and rewarding exposure tasks as treatment progresses. If parents are not present for all treatment sessions, choose exercises that the child has practiced in individual ERP sessions to try again during family meetings, allowing parents to observe the process of identifying the right task and modifying it as needed throughout practice. This allows the child to show off her progress; allows family members to stay abreast of where she is at in treatment in more concrete, real-world terms; and to see how the therapist coaches the child and adjusts the task over repeated practice trials. As noted earlier, it can often be helpful to choose an exercise that is related to one of the identified family problems (i.e., an area of accommodation). For example, if a family has identified that it is difficult to go out to dinner because the child believes many restaurants are contaminated, practice scaffolding exposures around this difficulty. Have the child look at pictures of the restaurant online. If this is too easy, have the family bring in a menu from the restaurant and have the child practice holding it. As the child gain momentum, the family may practice driving by the restaurant or even going inside. Involving parents in exposure practice helps them get a feel for the approach that is used and will aid them in negotiating stages of practice.

MODELING AND MANAGING EMOTIONS

An important aspect of exposure treatment involves helping parents to manage their own anxiety while modeling calm responses to OCD symptoms. It can be very distressing to watch a child struggling with OCD symptoms and the distress they cause. For many parents, participating in exposure practice is additionally difficult, either because they are witnessing heightened anxiety in their child or because they themselves find the practice task unpleasant (e.g., picking up cigarette butts in a parking lot, conversing with homeless people). It is not uncommon for parents to do or say things that are directly at odds with the goal of the exposure ("*That was pretty gross!*"), and it is important to educate them about the role of parental modeling in OCD and anxiety (Burstein & Ginsburg, 2010; Lebowitz, Shic, Campbell, MacLeod, & Silverman, 2015). With this in mind, parents may need specific help with learning to tolerate distress related to OCD and ERP treatment. There are many strategies for teaching distress tolerance, but in general, the first step rests with helping parents to be aware of their own behavior and the example they set during exposures. Understanding the role of parental modeling sets the stage for further work on emotion regulation. Present the rationale for this skill in the following way:

> *Children can learn from us, even if we are not thinking much about it. When it comes to OCD, parents can unknowingly contribute to their child's OCD symptoms by modeling anxious behaviors. These behaviors may be inconsequential for children who are not already anxious, however they may send powerful messages to anxious kids who are more sensitive to them. They signal that the world is indeed a dangerous place, and that they do need to take measures to stay safe. Our goal is not to have you avoid anxiety altogether—that's not possible. Instead, we want to model healthy, positive ways of confronting it and managing it. This "coping model" allows kids to see adaptive strategies for handling routine worries like being stuck in traffic as well as those that relate directly to their OCD symptoms.*

Provide examples of how modeling might work to reinforce OCD symptoms. Some common examples include a parent who uses his foot to flush the toilet, a parent who uses paper towels to open doors, a parent who constantly is using disinfectant, a parent who will not share cups or water bottles, a parent who displays discomfort or disgust during exposure exercises, and a parent who expresses doubt or judgment in exposures (e.g., "I would never do that," "Do you really think you can do that?").

Sometimes exposures require behaviors that are not particularly enjoyable for anyone (e.g., touching cockroaches, inhaling secondhand smoke, taking things out of the trash). In these cases, it is important for parents (and therapists, for that matter) to "fake it," presenting a calm, neutral demeanor even if it does not correspond to how they really feel inside. Over time, it will become easier for parents. Practice with the parents on presenting the most neutral, supportive reaction possible, regardless of how much anxiety or uncertainty they may be feeling. It can be helpful to provide a personal experience when you had to "fake it." Remind parents that their work in managing their emotions and modeling calm responses helps support their child's treatment.

CONCLUDING TREATMENT

When treatment enters its final stages, begin to discuss termination by exploring several themes, including where the family began in treatment and where they are at now; how well they feel they can identify and respond to OCD symptoms (i.e., their sense of self-efficacy); and how they feel about termination. Some family members are relieved to be concluding treatment as it means no longer coordinating multiple schedules and transportation to and from treatment. They may crave the return to normal family life that termination represents. For other families, there is a sense of anxiety about stepping away from an ongoing source of support in their fight against OCD. Use the final stages of treatment to explore each family member's thoughts and feelings about concluding treatment. Ask each family member some or all of the following questions:

- *How well do you feel you understand your child's OCD?*
- *How confident are you in your ability to manage it?*
- *How well do you think you manage your child's OCD?*

Normalize the full spectrum of emotional responses and remind anxious families that they will grow more confident as each week passes and they continue to manage OCD successfully together. Termination is, in effect, just another exposure.

RELAPSE PREVENTION

The final stages of treatment are also an important time to focus on relapse prevention and to help the family to develop a plan for monitoring symptoms on their own (see also Chapter 10). Remind families that although exposure-based CBT demonstrates favorable long-term outcomes for many youth (Mancebo et al., 2014), it is not uncommon for symptoms to return especially with stress or change. This does not mean that they are back to square one with the illness. Similarly, it does not necessarily signal a relapse. However, it does mean that it is important to have a strategy in place for monitoring symptoms over time. With this in mind, work with the family to develop a plan for how symptoms will be tracked and how they will discuss concerns that arise. This plan is tailored based on the child's age and clinical picture. Younger children may require more ongoing parental involvement in monitoring and practice. Older children benefit from autonomy balanced with parental support. In both cases, broker discussions about how parents can inquire about how things are going without seeming intrusive or overbearing, and discuss initial strategies for responding to new symptoms (i.e., "Can you think of an exposure for that?"). Encourage them to return to regular exposure practice should new symptoms emerge and to reach out to the therapist should they feel they need more ongoing assistance.

CONCLUSION

The last decade has witnessed enormous gains in evidence-based family treatment for youth with OCD. Numerous clinical trials have established the efficacy of family-based CBT approaches (Freeman et al., 2014) and there is growing appreciation of broader family dynamics that may merit consideration in treatment (Peris & Piacentini, 2016). Clinicians committed to evidence-based practice are thus encouraged to assess families at the outset of treatment carefully and to consider specific family dynamics likely to interfere with exposure-based techniques. Family accommodation, emotion regulation, and problem solving are all worthy targets for family intervention and they have the potential to optimize outcomes for youth with OCD.

REFERENCES

Amir, N., Freshman, M., Ramsey, B., Neary, E., & Brigidi, B. (2001). Thought-action fusion in individuals with OCD symptoms. *Behaviour Research and Therapy*, *39*(7), 265–776.

Barrett, P., Healy-Farrell, L., & March, J. S. (2004). Cognitive-behavioral family treatment of childhood obsessive-compulsive disorder: A controlled trial. *Journal of the American Academy of Child and Adolescent Psychiatry*, *43*(1), 46–62.

Barrett, P., Shortt, A., & Healy, L. (2002). Do parent and child behaviours differentiate families whose children have obsessive-compulsive disorder from other clinic and non-clinic families? *Journal of Child Psychology and Psychiatry*, *43*(5), 597–607.

Burstein, M., & Ginsburg, G. S. (2010). The effect of parental modeling of anxious behaviors and cognitions in school-aged children: An experimental pilot study. *Behaviour Research and Therapy*, *48*(6), 506–515.

Caporino, N. E., Morgan, J., Beckstead, J., Phares, V., Murphy, T. K., & Storch, E. A. (2012). A structural equation analysis of family accommodation in pediatric obsessive-compulsive disorder. *Journal of Abnormal Child Psychology*, *40*(1), 133–143.

Chambless, D. L., Bryan, A. D., Aiken, L. S., Steketee, G., & Hooley, J. M. (2001). Predicting expressed emotion: A study with families of obsessive-compulsive and agoraphobic outpatients. *Journal of Family Psychology*, *15*(2), 225–240.

Freeman, J., Sapyta, J., Garcia, A., Compton, S., Khanna, M., Flessner, C., et al. (2014). Family-based treatment of early childhood obsessive-compulsive disorder: The pediatric obsessive-compulsive disorder treatment study for young children (POTS Jr)—A randomized clinical trial. *JAMA Psychiatry*, *71*(6), 689–698.

Garcia, A. M., Sapyta, J. J., Moore, P. S., Freeman, J. B., Franklin, M. E., March, J. S., et al. (2010). Predictors and moderators of treatment outcome in the pediatric obsessive compulsive treatment study (POTS I). *Journal of the American Academy of Child and Adolescent Psychiatry*, *49*(10), 1024–1033.

Geller, D. A., & March, J. (2012). Practice parameter for the assessment and treatment of children and adolescents with obsessive-compulsive disorder. *Focus*, *10*(3), 360–373.

Ginsburg, G. S., Kingery, J. N., Drake, K. L., & Grados, M. A. (2008). Predictors of treatment response in pediatric obsessive-compulsive disorder. *Journal of the American Academy of Child and Adolescent Psychiatry*, *47*(8), 868–878.

Grunes, M. S., Neziroglu, F., & McKay, D. (2001). Family involvement in the behavioral treatment of obsessive-compulsive disorder: A preliminary investigation. *Behavior Therapy*, *32*(4), 803–820.

Hibbs, E. D., Zahn, T. P., Hamburger, S. D., Kruesi, M. M., & Rapoport, J. L. (1992). Parental expressed emotion and psychophysiological reactivity in disturbed and normal children. *The British Journal of Psychiatry*, *160*, 504–510.

Kendall, P. C., & Hedtke, K. A. (2006). *Cognitive-behavioral therapy for anxious children: Therapist manual*. Ardmore, PA: Workbook Publishing.

Lebowitz, E. R., Panza, K. E., Su, J., & Bloch, M. H. (2012). Family accommodation in obsessive–compulsive disorder. *Expert Review of Neurotherapeutics*, *12*(2), 229–238.

Lebowitz, E. R., Shic, F., Campbell, D., MacLeod, J., & Silverman, W. K. (2015). Avoidance moderates the association between mothers' and children's fears: Findings from a novel motion-tracking behavioral assessment. *Depression and Anxiety*, *32*(2), 91–98.

Lim, J., Wood, B. L., & Miller, B. D. (2008). Maternal depression and parenting in relation to child internalizing symptoms and asthma disease activity. *Journal of Family Psychology*, *22*(2), 264.

Lim, J., Wood, B. L., Miller, B. D., & Simmens, S. J. (2011). Effects of paternal and maternal depressive symptoms on child internalizing and externalizing symptoms and asthma disease activity: Mediation by interparental negativity and parenting. *Journal of Family Psychology*, *25*, 137–146.

Lovejoy, M. C., Graczyk, P. A., O'Hare, E., & Neuman, G. (2000). Maternal depression and parenting behavior: A meta-analytic review. *Clinical Psychology Review*, *20*, 561–592.

Mancebo, M. C., Boisseau, C. L., Garnaat, S. L., Eisen, J. L., Greenberg, B. D., Sibrava, N. J., et al. (2014). Long-term course of pediatric obsessive–compulsive disorder: 3 Years of prospective follow-up. *Comprehensive Psychiatry*, *55*(7), 1498–1504.

March, J. S., & Mulle, K. (1998). *OCD in children and adolescents: A cognitive-behavioral treatment manual*. New York, NY: Guilford Press.

Merlo, L. J., Lehmkuhl, H. D., Geffken, G. R., & Storch, E. A. (2009). Decreased family accommodation associated with improved therapy outcome in pediatric obsessive-compulsive disorder. *Journal of Consulting and Clinical Psychology*, *77*(2), 355–360.

Pediatric OCD Treatment Study [POTS] Team. (2004). Cognitive-behavior therapy, sertraline, and their combination for children and adolescents with obsessive-compulsive disorder: the Pediatric OCD Treatment Study randomized controlled trial. *Journal of the American Medical Association*, *292*, 1969–1976.

Peris, T. S., Benazon, N., Langley, A., Roblek, T., & Piacentini, J. (2008). Parental attitudes, beliefs, and responses to childhood obsessive compulsive disorder: The Parental Attitudes and Behaviors Scale. *Child & Family Behavior Therapy*, *30*(3), 199–214.

Peris, T. S., Bergman, R. L., Langley, A., Chang, S., McCracken, J. T., & Piacentini, J. (2008). Correlates of accommodation of pediatric obsessive compulsive disorder: Parent, child and family characteristics. *Journal of the American Academy of Child and Adolescent Psychiatry*, *47*(10), 1173–1181.

Peris, T. S., & Piacentini, J. (2013). Optimizing treatment for complex cases of childhood obsessive compulsive disorder: A preliminary trial. *Journal of Clinical Child & Adolescent Psychology*, *42*(1), 1–8.

Peris, T. S., & Piacentini, J. (2014). Addressing barriers to change in the treatment of childhood obsessive compulsive disorder. *Journal of Rational-Emotive & Cognitive-Behavior Therapy*, *32*(1), 31–43.

Peris, T. S., & Piacentini, J. (2016). *Helping families manage childhood OCD: Decreasing conflict and increasing positive interaction, Therapist guide*. New York, NY: Oxford University Press.

Peris, T. S., Sugar, C. A., Bergman, R. L., Chang, S., Langley, A., & Piacentini, J. (2012). Family factors predict treatment outcome for pediatric obsessive-compulsive disorder. *Journal of Consulting and Clinical Psychology*, *80*(2), 255–263.

Piacentini, J., Bergman, R. L., Chang, S., Langley, A., Peris, T., Wood, J. J., et al. (2011). Controlled comparison of family cognitive behavioral therapy and psychoeducation/relaxation training for child obsessive-compulsive disorder. *Journal of the American Academy of Child and Adolescent Psychiatry*, *50*(11), 1149–1161.

Piacentini, J., Langley, A., & Roblek, T. (2007). *Cognitive behavioral treatment of childhood OCD: It's only a false alarm therapist guide*. New York, NY: Oxford University Press.

Renshaw, K. D., Steketee, G., & Chambless, D. L. (2005). Involving family members in the treatment of OCD. *Cognitive Behaviour Therapy*, *34*(3), 164–175.

Silverman, W. K., & Albano, A. M. (1996). *Anxiety disorders interview schedule for DSM-IV.: Child interview schedule*. San Antonio, TX: Graywind Publications Incorporated.

Storch, E. A., Geffken, G. R., Merlo, L. J., Jacob, M. L., Murphy, T. K., Goodman, W. K., et al. (2007). Family accommodation in pediatric obsessive-compulsive disorder. *Journal of Clinical Child and Adolescent Psychology*, *36*(2), 207–216.

Storch, E. A., Lehmkuhl, H., Pence, S. L., Jr., Geffken, G. R., Ricketts, E., Storch, J. F., et al. (2009). Parental experiences of having a child with obsessive-compulsive disorder: Associations with clinical characteristics and caregiver adjustment. *Journal of Child and Family Studies*, *18*(3), 249–258.

Storch, E. A., Merlo, L. J., Larson, M. J., Marien, W. E., Geffken, G. R., Jacon, M. L., et al. (2008). Clinical features associated with treatment-resistant pediatric obsessive-compulsive disorder. *Comprehensive Psychiatry*, *49*(1), 35–42.

Torp, N. C., Dahl, K., Skarphedinsson, G., Thomsen, P. H., Valderhaug, R., Weidle, B., et al. (2015). Effectiveness of cognitive behavior treatment for pediatric obsessive-compulsive disorder: Acute outcomes from the Nordic long-term OCD treatment study (NordLOTS). *Behaviour Research and Therapy*, *64*, 15–23.

Valleni-Basile, L., Garrison, C. Z., Jackson, K., Waller, J. L., McKeown, R. E., Addy, C. L., et al. (1995). Family and psychosocial predictors of obsessive-compulsive disorder in a community sample of young adolescents. *Journal of Child and Family Studies*, *4*(2), 193–206.

Wu, M. S., Lewin, A. B., Murphy, T. K., Geffken, G. R., & Storch, E. A. (2014). Phenomenological considerations of family accommodation: Related clinical characteristics and family factors in pediatric obsessive–compulsive disorder. *Journal of Obsessive-Compulsive and Related Disorders*, *3*(3), 228–235.

Wu, M. S., McGuire, J. F., Martino, C., Phares, V., Selles, R. R., & Storch, E. A. (2016). A meta-analysis of family accommodation and OCD symptom severity. *Clinical Psychology Review*, *45*, 34–44.

Chapter 9

Medication Management of Childhood OCD

Tord Ivarsson*, Gudmundur Skarphedinsson†, and Bernhard Weidle‡,§
*Center for Child and Adolescent Mental Health, Eastern and Southern Norway, Oslo, Norway, †Sorlandet Hospital, Kristiansand, Norway, ‡Norwegian University of Science and Technology, Trondheim, Norway, §St. Olavs University Hospital, Trondheim, Norway

INTRODUCTION AND A SHORT HISTORY OF PSYCHOPHARMACOLOGY IN PEDIATRIC OCD

Before considering the evidence for psychopharmacology in pediatric OCD, it is of importance to take into account the context in which such treatment should be used, based on the evidence for these treatments which is summarized in this chapter. We argue that psychopharmacology always should be part of a multimodal approach including cognitive-behavior therapy (CBT) and family support. Thus the psychopharmacologist should act as a part of a child treatment team. The implication is that s/he, if being in private practice, needs to cooperate with a competent CBT therapist, which, while may not be easy everywhere, is important in all cases. The reason is that all children with OCD need to learn better ways to handle themselves in OCD-relevant situations, and that it is not realistic for the psychopharmacologist in most cases to both be a good doctor and intervene psychologically.

Psychopharmacological treatment in OCD (in adults) started more than 50 years ago when Fernandez and Lopez-Ibor (1967), in a mixed case report, suggested that clomipramine may relieve obsessive-compulsive symptoms. Later, a Swedish group put these findings to an empirical test in a randomized controlled trial and showed that clomipramine indeed showed efficacy in adult OCD (Thoren, Asberg, Cronholm, Jornestedt, & Traskman, 1980). Another Swede, the Nobel laureate Arvid Carlsson (1969) showed that the antidepressant effect of clomipramine depended upon its acting on serotonin. The hypothesis that clomipramine inhibited the reuptake of serotonin in the neurons' synapses has since been confirmed (Asberg et al., 1977). While clomipramine was a nonspecific serotonin reuptake inhibitor (SRI), drugs developed later have been more specific and hence called SSRI. Following these seminal

The Clinician's Guide to Cognitive-Behavioral Therapy for Childhood Obsessive-Compulsive Disorder
http://dx.doi.org/10.1016/B978-0-12-811427-8.00009-5

reports, Rapoport, Elkins, and Mikkelsen (1980) showed that clomipramine was effective in adolescent OCD. Another landmark study from Rapoport's group showed that the clomipramine efficacy in pediatric OCD was specific and based on its serotonin actions rather than on its antidepressant properties (Leonard, Swedo, Rapoport, Coffey, & Cheslow, 1988). They used a cross-over design with another drug that inhibited the reuptake of noradrenalin (desipramine) rather than serotonin.

For the last several decades, serotonin-activating drugs have been the main pharmacological intervention in pediatric OCD, and the evidence that has been assembled is substantial although not large showing that most SSRI are superior to placebo in randomized controlled trials (Geller, Biederman, Stewart, Mullin, Martin, et al., 2003; Watson & Rees, 2008). In addition, other drugs have been used to augment treatment when SSRI response is incomplete (Skarphedinsson & Ivarsson, 2015). These will be described later in the section on resistance to evidence-based treatments.

SRI EFFECTS/ PHARMACODYNAMICS

SRI given in adequate doses inhibit the reuptake of serotonin in the neurons' synapses, thereby starting a cascade of events where the neurons adapt to increased serotonin levels postsynaptically, but as well through auto-receptors presynaptically [see (Stahl, 2013) for a description]. However, the actions of a drug is not only on a synaptic and cellular level. Serotonin neurons and synapses are part of neuronal circuits [first described by (Alexander & Crutcher, 1990)] that perform complex executive and computational tasks [see (Shipp, 2016) and (Carli & Invernizzi, 2014) for reviews] so that the effects and side effects of these drugs need to be put in a wider context. The circuits involving the prefrontal *c*ortex, the *s*triatum and thalamus (i.e., the executive *CSTC* circuits) are modulated not only by the serotonergic system, but also by dopamine and acetylcholine, each affecting the glutamate drive in the circuit. Moreover, each receptor family has subreceptor types that have different actions (e.g., stimulation or inhibition) and locations (Carli & Invernizzi, 2014) so that the influence on the CSTC circuits' functions of serotonin activation using a serotonin reuptake inhibitor is not well understood. Thus the net effect of a SSRI may vary due to many individual differences across patients, as the neurobiological heterogeneity across studies and patient groups is common in OCD (Piras et al., 2015). SSRIs have, moreover, different profiles with regard to their patterns of 5-HT receptor subtype actions, which increase individual differences with regard to SSRI response even further.

OCD is a complex disorder from the neurobiological perspective. It is now clear that in addition to involvement of the "classical" ventral/affective OCD circuit, the dorsal executive functioning (EF) circuit (most known for contributing to ADHD), and the error/monitoring circuit have key roles in OCD pathogenesis. These circuits fulfill different roles in goal-directed behaviors, which characterize OCD to the greater part. The circuits have important roles in all humans, dealing with both complex "life"-oriented goals and behaviors as well as more modest behaviors like doing your homework and making a cup of coffee. In OCD, the ventral/affective circuits and error/monitoring circuits are presumed to be overactive (leading to obsessions, i.e., goals of compulsions, and to a persistent signal that the behavior has not reached its set goal). Furthermore, the dorsal/executive circuit is presumed to be underactive (contributing to disinhibition of compulsive behaviors although the patient see they are irrational) (Pauls, Abramovitch, Rauch, & Geller, 2014; Piras et al., 2015). Thus given these circuits' vital roles in human life, SSRI may have effects that vary from beneficial in many (relief of OCD) to detrimental, e.g., psychiatric side effect called "demotivation" and to general behavioral activation, seen mostly in adolescents, respectively, children (Murphy, Segarra, Storch, & Goodman, 2008). Moreover, insular circuits that are believed to be the basis for the effect of disgust which plays a vital role in OCD (see (Nieuwenhuys, 2012) for the role of Insula in general) are involved in OCD (Piras et al., 2015) and affected by SSRI in ways that are not well known.

In summary, there may be great individual differences across patients and drugs with regard to response on OCD symptoms and the kind and severity of side effects. Such differences are averaged out in RCTs but may explain why some patients respond and some do not to one particular SSRI and why it may be worthwhile to switch to another SSRI if one fails.

EVIDENCE BASE FOR SSRI AS FIRST TREATMENT

As mentioned previously, serotonin activation using a SSRI is the main pharmacological intervention in pediatric OCD, and metaanalyses have shown that most SSRI are superior to placebo in randomized controlled trials and that they have a moderate effect size (ES) corresponding to about 3 points on the CY-BOCS OCD measure across 3 months (Geller, Biederman, Stewart, Mullin, Martin, et al., 2003; Ivarsson et al., 2015; Watson & Rees, 2008). Furthermore, it seems like no SSRI is markedly more efficient than another. The data for sertraline and fluoxetine and to some extent fluvoxamine seem more robust than those for the other SSRI (e.g., paroxetine, citalopram, and escitalopram), so based on current evidence sertraline or fluoxetine should be the drug of choice, and following them there is a place for fluvoxamine (see Table 1). Data from the trials indicate that these drugs are tolerated well (Ivarsson et al., 2015). The nonspecific SRI clomipramine has as well an evidence base that is acceptable and has a greater effect size than the SSRI group in indirect comparisons using metaanalytic methods (Geller, Biederman, Stewart, Mullin, Martin, et al., 2003; Ivarsson et al., 2015; Watson & Rees, 2008). However, the difference is not statistically significant across all studies (McGuire et al.,

TABLE 1 (S)SRI in OCD and Their Effects on Brain Systems and Receptors, Kinetics and Evidence Summary

Generic Name	Serotonin Re-uptake Inhibition	Noradrenaline Effects	Dopamine Re-uptake Inhibition	Acetylcholine	Sigma 1	Half-Time[a]	Start Dose (mg)	Max Dose (mg)	Evidence Base[b]
Sertraline	Yes	No	Weak DA activation	No	Yes, weak effect	26 h	25	200	1a
Fluvoxamine	Yes	Very weak	No	No	Yes, may have importance for effects on depression-, anxiety and cognitive symptoms	16 h	25	200	1a
Fluoxetine	Yes, and antagonism against one serotonin receptor ($5HT_{2C}$)	No	No	No	Yes, unclear if it is of importance	4–6 days, 4 weeks to steady state	10	80	1a
Citalopram	Yes, the molecules' two forms (enantiomers) may have antagonistic effects	No	No	No	No	35 h	10 mg	40 mg	3b
Clomipramine has a pharmacologically very active metabolite desmethylclomipramine	Yes, the mother substance clomipramine	Yes, through the metabolite desmethylclomipramine that has a strong NA-effect	Yes	Yes, anticholin-ergic effects give problematic side effects	No	35 h 50 h for metabolite desmethylclomipramine	10–25	200	1a

[a] *At an average as published in Wikipedia.*
[b] *According to the Centre for Evidence-Based Medicine at the University of Oxford.*

2015). Moreover, due to troublesome side effects clomipramine is not to be used as a first drug.

It is important to consider that a placebo-controlled trial does not inform us about which place a drug such as an SSRI should have as compared with other evidence-based treatments. A trend in treatment research, in general, is to do comparisons with other proven treatments. Haynes, Sackett, Guyatt, and Tugwell (2006) have, for example, discussed the pros and cons of controls using other treatments besides placebo in medicine, and for which situations placebo-controlled trials should be used. Shortly, comparisons with placebo show whether a drug has an effect at all on symptoms as compared with nonspecific therapeutic effects and are appropriate when the condition has no proven treatment. However, a comparison with another proven treatment may show which role is appropriate for a treatment, given the relative effect sizes, side effects but also other factors like acceptance, cost, and other benefits to the patient than symptom relief (Basham, 1986; Haynes et al., 2006). Using this approach to the extant studies, it is clear that in direct comparisons, CBT is significantly more effective than SSRI and has fewer side effects (Ivarsson et al., 2015; Rynn et al., 2015). If adult head-to-head CBT and SSRI trials are added, the pooled effect for CBT compared with SSRI is clearly superior (Romanelli, Wu, Gamba, Mojtabai, & Segal, 2014). Moreover, while an SSRI does not enhance CBT efficacy relative to CBT alone (Storch et al., 2013), CBT does augment incomplete response in SSRI treatment (Franklin et al., 2011), and sertraline and continued CBT do as well following nonresponse to CBT (Skarphedinsson, Weidle, Thomsen, et al., 2015). We regard these data as an indication that CBT is not only more effective but also more robust than SRI as a treatment for pediatric OCD. In addition, both the child and the parents learn actively from CBT in ways which we believe is beneficial across development.

A weakness in the SSRI evidence base for effectiveness is the lack of long-term follow-up studies. However, a 3-month RCT showing sertraline efficacy (average dose at 3 months was 161.6 mg/day) (March et al., 1998) was followed by two reports that give some insight into the 1-year outcome (Cook et al., 2001; Wagner, Cook, Chung, & Messig, 2003). At the end of the follow-up, the mean daily sertraline dose was 120 mg, slightly less (108 mg) in children versus adolescents (132 mg). Through this regime, continued improvement took place so that mean scores were ~10 points or less on the CY-BOCS, a score which is often viewed as an indication of remission (Cook et al., 2001). However, at end-point more than half of the original sample had dropped out due to lack of efficacy or side effects.

In summary, we argue that SSRI treatment in pediatric OCD should be used only in those cases who do not benefit from CBT, or when informed patient preference suggests its use as the first treatment (Ivarsson et al., 2015). Paradoxically, in this situation (namely as a second-line treatment) the evidence base is meager (see later).

COMBINATION TREATMENT

To increase the likelihood of effective treatment in severe cases, some have recommended CBT and SSRI treatment used conjointly (Geller, March, & CQI, 2012). However, neither child- and adolescent-, nor adult studies have shown that combined treatment provides an incremental benefit to CBT alone (Romanelli et al., 2014). Examining the pediatric literature of combined treatment as compared with CBT alone (POTS Treatment Study Team, 2004; Storch et al., 2013), their combined effect size does not show that the combination is superior ($g = -0.13$) (Ivarsson et al., 2015). We have concluded that the extant data support the NICE European guidelines (NICE, 2005), rather than the US practice parameter (Geller et al., 2012). This is supported in the POTS predictor study, which shows that baseline OCD severity was not a moderator of treatment outcomes, indicating that all treatments (CBT alone, an SSRI alone, and the combined treatment) were effective regardless of OCD severity at baseline (Garcia et al., 2010). One could speculate, based on the POTS study (2004), that with a high level of CBT expertise, the addition of an SSRI does not necessarily confer any greater benefit. However, with lower CBT efficiency, the addition of an SSRI may be required to obtain the same symptom relief as when high CBT expertise is available. However, in individual patients with very severe OCD and marked avoidance (when the CY-BOCS score is not always so high due to less need for rituals) the question is a difficult one and based on clinical judgment.

The case is different in patients coming to the clinic already with an SSRI, usually with an incomplete response; in these instances research shows that combined treatment is significantly more effective than an SSRI alone (Franklin et al., 2011; Neziroglu, Yaryura-Tobias, Walz, & McKay, 2000) with a pooled effect size of $g = -0.59$ (Ivarsson et al., 2015). The pooled results from a recent metaanalysis of pediatric and adult OCD trials also showed the superiority of the combined treatment over SRI alone (Romanelli et al., 2014).

SSRI TREATMENT IN PRACTICE

In starting treatment with a SSRI, it is essential to start low and increase slowly due to the relatively long period it takes the beneficial effects to develop, and the prompt onset of side effects (see Stahl for a discussion (2013)). Using sertraline as an example, 25 or 50 mg (in adolescents and heavier children) is a usual start dose (see Table 1) that may be increased every 3–7 days, up to a level when 75–125 mg/day has been reached (lower range for smaller children and upper range for a heavier adolescent), which is the level where some effect on symptoms can be expected and some additional time is needed (usually 2–3 weeks) to observe the balance between effect on symptoms and the presence of side effects. In our clinical experience, the psychopharmacologist needs to consider the patient at hand, is s/he a hardy child that easily tolerates unpleasant sensations and feelings (if applicable) or is s/he sensitive and easily overcome? In negotiating the forms the drug treatment will take, one must also consider if the child prefers faster, rather than later response? So, in "resilient" children, you may increase doses every 3–4 day, but in a sensitive child you may need up to a week or even more per dose increase, because side effects will dominate the child's experience and compliance is jeopardized. Moreover, the parent's ability to handle the child's reaction as well as their own tendencies for worry needs to be considered. We recommend that things are discussed with the child and the parent and that these themes are talked about openly. It is advisable to let the parent confirm the child's self-image with regard to his/her "resilience." Anyway, the consequences of fast versus slow titration need to be talked about openly.

It follows from these concerns that the onset of effect from a SSRI may vary, sometimes taking 5 weeks or more before a noticeable effect may be expected, and the balance between effect and side effects can be assessed. It is the task of the psychopharmacologist to give the reasons for the delay, and a rationale for tolerating the period when mostly side effects are experienced to when the benefits are expected.

From the period when the effect sets in, the task of the psychopharmacologist is to push the child toward the maximum effect that can be obtained while the side effects experienced are still tolerable. The principle, "start low, go slow, but go" has been used in most trials (e.g., the POTS trial (2004)), so that most patients have tried the maximum dose (200 mg for sertraline) at some point. Moreover, the average endpoint dose in the POTS was 170 mg/day, showing that higher doses are needed to obtain adequate effect. The same attitude needs to be used in clinical practice if the benefit showed in the trials is to be reached. Even so, due to individual differences in psychopharmacodynamics and pharmacokinetics, response may vary greatly across patients, and in children who respond weakly, maximum doses must be tested, otherwise the drug trial with an SSRI for the child was not appropriate. In patients with fast metabolization of the SSRI, even higher doses than the maximum dose may be needed if the benefits are to match that of patients with an average metabolization. For most SSRI, serum concentration tests are available and can be measured in such situations. See Table 1 for doses, half-life, and evidence base.

The period using maximum doses that are tolerated has a variable length due to what other resources are used, but has as its goal that remission should be in place. Recently, based on the Nordic Long-term OCD Treatment Study (NordLOTS), a CY-BOCS raw cutoff score of $\leq$11 was the best sign of remission following CBT (Skarphedinsson, De Nadai, Storch, Lewin, & Ivarsson, 2017), while a corresponding North American study found a raw score of $\leq$14 as most appropriate (Storch, Lewin, De Nadai, & Murphy, 2010). If the child has CBT with ERP following the initial failure (presuming that SRI is used according to clinical guidelines), the time needed for remission, plus some months for showing stability of remission, may be about half a year. If just SRI treatment is used, the time frame to reach remission commonly is a year or longer.

Following the full dose period and when the goal of remission is reached, a lower maintenance dose may be used. This dose is not based on research but rather on clinical experience and may vary depending on weight and dose needed to get response and remission. The length of the period on maintenance is dependent on several aspects. The clinician needs to see that the child can handle the stress surrounding the school year and the vicissitudes of peer relations in school without getting relapsing symptoms (even if not a clinical level relapse). On the positive side, the psychopharmacologist wants to see reestablished peer- and friendship relations, restored family relations, as well as a capacity to work in school, and to do homework, etc. Moreover, the fatigue and mood associated with the darker half of the year may not be a good period to start the final termination, particularly in the arctic/subarctic region this can be a real problem.

Termination is discussed later.

PSYCHOEDUCATION IN DRUG TREATMENT

When starting up a psychopharmacology trial it is also important to consider what messages the psychopharmacologist gives with regard to the OCD symptoms. Based on clinical experience, as well as research in adults, the child and parent need to understand the importance of actively combating the symptoms by doing things that provoke anxiety and accordingly expand the experience base in the child's life. Presumably, this must include some degree of self-guided exposure at home and in school (Marks et al., 1988). Avoidance of anxiety-provoking situations is as detrimental to drug treatment as to CBT. In children and adolescents that had adequate CBT before the SSRI trial, this is usually understood, even though it may need to be emphasized in the new situation with drug treatment. However, if the failure to respond to CBT was due to too much avoidance and/or a high degree of family accommodation, which often has the function to mask for child avoidance, an intervention by the psychopharmacologist is needed so that both the patient and the parent understand that there is no magic involved. (S)SRI treatment works best if the child and parents do their best to comply with the demands of daily life, irrespective of mild-moderate anxiety. This part of the psychoeducation must be allowed to take some time and may need to include queries about the child's and parents' beliefs around drug treatment, and the attitude to psychiatric treatment. A special problem is anxious parenting that tries to reduce the child's anxiety. In these cases, deep-seated attitudes about anxiety may need to be dealt with, attitudes bordering on existential questions that may take time to sort out. The need to feel and accept anxiety or other difficult affects such as disgust may border on those underlying "Acceptance and Commitment Therapy"

(Twohig et al., 2010). The discussion should include parental views of what the treatment should accomplish. It is true that the medical paradigm has mostly, but not exclusively, seen symptom relief as a primary goal, but in pediatric OCD, relief of anxiety and disgust must be subordinate and secondary to a CBT-like attitude of obtaining mastery, tolerance, and acceptance which eventually will include less anxiety.

Psychoeducation must consequently be broad, incisive, and consistent. Dysfunctional beliefs need to be addressed whatever their kind and tenacity and with respect for views which may be prevalent in that subculture.

Giving realistic information about what can be expected from a drug treatment with a SSRI is as well important. As described previously, a moderate effect with about 3-point symptom reduction on the CY-BOCS is the average response over a 3-month period (as compared with placebo), and that through a prolonged treatment up to 1 year further symptom reduction is to be expected, but half of the group will still have a clinical level of symptoms (Cook et al., 2001). The implication is that even in the face of CBT nonresponse prior to SSRI treatment, it is advisable to continue with CBT work as soon as feasible given the reason for the failure.

The data cited previously show as well that SSRI treatment should not be a stand-alone treatment in pediatric OCD. In cultures where beliefs that drug treatment could "cure" the patient, and where a psychological approach to mental health is uncommon, realistic information must be given showing the need for including CBT at some point if not at first.

Another important point is the time frame needed to reach the level of improvement that is realistic. As follows from the Cook study (2001) one full year of treatment is needed in most cases, and the treatment for many patients needs to be appreciably longer, often many years. It is clear at least from a crossover study that the risk of relapse is great even following at an average 1½ year clomipramine treatment: Eight out of nine patients relapsed when changed to a drug which has mainly noradrenergic and antidepressant properties (Leonard et al., 1991).

No psychoeducation before starting SSRI treatment is adequate without information on side effects. Initially, information about what kind of side effects may occur, and which ones are most common is needed. Among them it is mandatory as well to include increased levels of anxiety (particularly in severely anxious kids) some weeks into treatment, often preceding the first signs of improvement of symptoms with some days up to a week. Children and parents who are aware of this do not react with increased anxiety, but rather with a kind of welcoming attitude, that relief is coming soon. If unprepared, you may instead see interpretations that the drug is making the OCD worse, and fast termination may be embarked upon through the patient or parents. As side effects are many and varied, the psychopharmacologist needs to repeat the information and be more specific as side effects are manifesting.

HANDLING SIDE EFFECTS

Assessing side effects should be done in a systematic manner. No assessment is adequate unless the child and the parent(s) have had a possibility to rate symptoms and signs, and unless a physical examination is made and a doctor or psychiatric nurse with training has evaluated the ratings. Useful scales are, for example, the Pediatric Adverse Event Rating Scale, which is available commercially, but other noncommercial scales, e.g., the Treatment Emergent Adverse Symptom Profile (TEASAP) are available too (Bussing et al., 2013; Reid et al., 2010). Child and parental ratings should be carefully evaluated because, although the phenomena leading to the ratings are truly experienced, their interpretation is not easy, and judgments of causality are challenging. It is not enough to ask in general "did you have any side effects," specific areas need to be covered so that both physical and psychiatric side effects can be detected. The largest and best designed study where side effects can be compared across multiple treatment contingencies is the CAMS study of child and adolescent anxiety disorders (Rynn et al., 2015) with a double blind sertraline vs pill placebo comparison and as well open comparisons of CBT + sertraline and CBT only. Overall, the study showed a good tolerance of sertraline and good benefit versus side effects ratio, using doses that were somewhat lower than the POTS trial, but still of a magnitude that is close to what is needed in OCD. Psychiatric side effects (disinhibition, increased motor activity, disobedience/defiance, restlessness, and aggression) was more common in those treated with sertraline (twice or more than twice as common) as in the CBT only and placebo groups. In such cases it is essential to evaluate the benefit vs harm of the side effect in question, and to reduce the dose in a way that retains a beneficial ratio. Among the psychiatric side effects, harm-related thoughts, impulses, and acts as well play an important role. In the CAMS these side effects were each quite uncommon, except aggression (more common in the CBT + sertraline group than in all other groups) showing that SSRI emergent harm-related side effects need to be taken seriously but is not usually a big problem. In the situation with OCD with depression the harm/suicidality-related side effects need to be considered in particular. The CAMS findings are compatible with those of the POTS study, which, however, did not have as comprehensive a report of psychiatric side effects (POTS Treatment Study Team, 2004). Another side effect called demotivation, a pervasive lack of motivation that looks very much like apathy in depression without the associated mood and cognitive symptoms was first described in case reports by Garland and Baerg (2001) and has not been included in the big RCTs, because of assessment problems. Thus we do not know how common it is relative to similar problems in OCD in general. However, it needs to be considered and dealt with appropriately. For an insightful discussion on how to monitor and manage side effects, see a review by Murphy et al. (2008).

Physical side effects are common in SSRI treatment, and the CAMS study showed symptoms and signs more often in the sertraline groups than in the other groups, similar to findings from other studies (POTS Treatment Study Team, 2004; Skarphedinsson, Weidle, Thomsen, et al., 2015). Particular problems seem to be insomnia, fatigue, but also stomach problems and pains. Neurological symptoms (tremor and akathisia) are common, and the latter may as well spill over into a sense of restlessness (Skarphedinsson, Weidle, Thomsen, et al., 2015). The review by Murphy et al. (2008) provides a comprehensive description of these side effects and their clinical management.

HOW TO EVALUATE DRUG EFFICACY

The treatment effect must for each child and adolescent be assessed with a reliable and valid measure like the CY-BOCS, in addition to the psychopharmacologist's clinical impression in a structured way, for example, using the Clinical Global Impression (CGI) scale. Vague probes like "how do you feel" and "do you feel better" are nice greeting phrases but provide little information. As the treatment unfolds, current "feelings" may vary because the child does things that may be anxiety provoking and may be involved in battles with the parents because accommodation is reduced but also because of inhibitions that are released, including the general side effect "activation." These must be distinguished from the anxiety symptoms that are targeted, so we need both to measure side effects and symptoms objectively and reliably (as suggested previously) as well as gauging the degree of impairment (Piacentini, Peris, Bergman, Chang, & Jaffer, 2007). Using good measures for the clinical effect and for side effects across time is a prerequisite for assessing the ratio of benefit versus side effects. A series of visits where the psychiatrist and, for example, a psychiatric nurse cooperate and alternate is optimal (e.g., frequent visits the first month, and regular but less often the second-third month and at least quarterly for as long as the treatment lasts).

TERMINATION OF SRI TREATMENT

Planning the termination ahead should include that the psychopharmacologist from the start makes clear what criteria need to be fulfilled for termination. Little empirical evidence is at hand to guide the practitioner, but clinical experience suggests that (1) the patient should be in remission; (2) so much time must have been spent in remission that the patient regained earlier lost functioning (friends/peers and school are especially important), and started to think of him/herself as s/he used to before OCD onset; (3) family accommodation is no longer occurring at significant levels; and (4) no secondary illness gains are left. It is unusual for a SRI treatment to last less than 1 year; 2–3 years could be seen as an average before termination is embarked upon. However, the evidences for this last claim are still missing.

Termination should be done in a gradual way, stepwise lowering the dose to nil during a 3-month period. During this period and the 3 months following termination, informing about and monitoring for discontinuation reactions are needed. Such reactions are worst (although in most children relatively mild) during the first 1–2 weeks and usually analogous to the side effects, but unusual ones may be encountered such as a sudden "shock sensation," or as an adolescent described it, a sense of depersonalization (which lasted 2 days). Common discontinuation reactions are dizziness, slight coordination problems, and transient headaches. For a description of discontinuation reactions, see Black, Shea, Dursun, and Kutcher (2000). Appropriate communication about these potential reactions with the child or adolescent may reduce the fear felt in experiencing such symptoms as well as the need to reinstate a SSRI.

FOLLOW-UP FOLLOWING TERMINATION

Clinical experience shows that commonly some OCD symptoms might come back during the first 3–6 months following termination. Cooperating with a CBT therapist delivering a few booster sessions to remind the child of previously learned techniques (i.e., applying ERP) is useful if the psychopharmacologist him/herself cannot provide this kind of intervention. There are currently no data available concerning the risk of relapse following a long enough time frame for the SRI treatment. For short treatment periods, the relapse rate is around 50% (Asbahr et al., 2005; Leonard et al., 1988), but even higher relapse rates have been described (Leonard et al., 1991). It is unknown, but to be presumed that providing CBT interventions following termination decreases this risk. The risk of relapse requires a follow-up scheme including a visit every month the first 2–3 months and then quarterly planned visits for a year or more. Moreover, quick access to assessment and CBT interventions should be available, if relapsing symptoms come back between visits, i.e., applying ERP, rather than routinely reinstate SSRI treatment.

EVIDENCE BASE FOR SSRI IN CBT NONRESPONSE

When should CBT be considered unsuccessful? The evidence for CBT efficacy comes from trials with a duration of 3–4 months (Skarphedinsson, Hanssen-Bauer, et al., 2015). If standard CBT is unsuccessful after 3–4 months we believe that the clinician may choose from three different strategies: First, continue with CBT. The necessary requirement would be to identify barriers which might have interfered with the previous CBT trial. Common barriers might be, for instance, too long time for the child to engage and start exposure exercises, family factors, no-optimal relationship between the child/family and the therapist, OCD appearing predominantly at home or other settings, and in-office exposures not generating high enough anxiety levels to be helpful. In these instances formulating a new case conceptualization might be necessary. The second option might be to continue with CBT (but formulate a new case conceptualization) and augment with an SSRI. The third option is to terminate CBT and switch to an SSRI. Expert guidelines recommend that SSRIs should be added to unsuccessful CBT (Geller et al., 2012; NICE, 2005). However, the sequence of treatment (i.e., start with CBT and if the patient does not respond, augment with an SSRI) is only based on expert consensus, not empirical evidence. Only one study has compared different strategies for CBT nonresponders. Children and adolescents that still had moderate-to-severe OCD (CY-BOCS > 15) after 14 weekly sessions of CBT were randomized to continue with CBT for 10 sessions or switched to an SSRI (sertraline) for 16 weeks. No significant differences between the groups were found for the primary outcomes. However, both groups seemed to benefit from the treatment (Skarphedinsson, Weidle, Thomsen, et al., 2015). So, we do have the paradoxical situation that in the situation where a SSRI is recommended, the evidence base is unsatisfactory.

In clinical practice many patients get extended CBT after limited response; however, could SSRI still be beneficial even then? A recent observational study shows that a minority of patient not responding to CBT (22% that were nonresponders after two CBT trials) did respond to sertraline (Skarphedinsson, Weidle, & Ivarsson, 2015), showing that SSRI may be useful even in such situations.

SWITCHING TO ANOTHER SSRI OR CLOMIPRAMINE

If a child does not respond to one SSRI, the next step could be to switch to another SSRI (NICE, 2005). However, minimal data exist that can direct the choice (Geller et al., 2012). By analogy, switching fluvoxamine nonresponders to fluoxetine was effective for anxious children in the Research Unit on Pediatric Psychopharmacology Anxiety study (Walkup et al., 2002). As shown previously (Table 1) the profiles of the different SRI differ, so it may be worthwhile given the clinical need. In switching, the psychopharmacologist needs to consider the half-life of the two compounds. For example, following fluoxetine treatment, a longer washout period and a lower start dose of the second drug with shorter half-life is needed. When switching from a compound with shorter half-life (e.g., sertraline) to that with a longer half-life (e.g., fluoxetine) the risk of a "dip" in serotonergic action is present, because using fluoxetine the time to reach steady state is several weeks. In these cases, it may be best to start with fluoxetine before sertraline is terminated.

Another strategy recommended by expert guidelines is to add clomipramine to an SSRI (Geller et al., 2012). The rationale is to combine the serotonergic effects of each medication but to minimize adverse events across different drug classes. Fluvoxamine may then be the best SSRI choice, offering the greatest synergistic effect when added to clomipramine because it inhibits the conversion of clomipramine to desmethyl-clomipramine increasing it to a ratio that is in favor of the serotonergic compound. However, the psychopharmacologist needs to monitor the EKG indices when clomipramine is used when combined with an SSRI, and a cautious attitude is recommended. Additionally, if clomipramine is combined with a CYP-450 2D6 inhibitor, such as fluoxetine or paroxetine, serum clomipramine levels need to be monitored because of the potentially toxic increases. However, the risk should be weighed against the harm to the patient from the OCD (Arumugham & Reddy, 2013; Geller et al., 2012).

Higher dose of clomipramine and lower dose of fluvoxamine (as a metabolic blocker mainly) may work best. The evidence for this combination is limited. Only two case series exist in pediatric OCD showing beneficial effects on OCD symptoms as well as adverse events particularly cardiovascular ones showing the need for close monitoring (Figueroa, Rosenberg, Birmaher, & Keshavan, 1998; Simeon, Thatte, & Wiggins, 1990). Data from adult OCD gives some, albeit tenuous support for these combinations (Diniz et al., 2011).

ATYPICAL ANTIPSYCHOTICS (NEUROLEPTICS)

In cases of pediatric OCD where the SRI class of drugs fail, the most prominent augmentation strategy is the use of atypical antipsychotics, also called second-generation antipsychotics (SGAs). These work mainly by blocking the dopamine pathways within the cortex. In adults with OCD, randomized controlled trials (RCTs) have been conducted to show the effects of risperidone, aripiprazole, quetiapine, olanzapine, and haloperidol, the latter a typical or first-generation antipsychotic (Bloch et al., 2006; Dold, Aigner, Lanzenberger, & Kasper, 2013). The effect seems to be greater in patients with comorbid OCD and tic disorder (Bloch et al., 2006). However, no RCT exists in pediatric OCD, and inferring that children and adolescents should benefit in the same way as adults is fraught with difficulties and depends on the presupposition that adult and pediatric OCD are equivalent, even though the transmitter systems in young people are not mature as those in adults (Bylund & Reed, 2007). However, naturalistic open trials using risperidone and aripiprazole as an augmentation to an SSRI in pediatric OCD indicate that the combination may be beneficial (Masi et al., 2005, 2009; Masi, Pfanner, & Brovedani, 2013). In a naturalistic comparative study, children with tic-related OCD that were nonresponders after an SSRI trial ($N=69$) showed equal benefits from risperidone and aripiprazole. However, risperidone was associated with serious metabolic adverse events such as weight gain and sedation and aripiprazole to mild-moderate agitation (Masi et al., 2013). Moreover, if aripiprazole is combined with a SSRI, it has to be taken into consideration that SSRIs are potent inhibitors of the enzyme system CYP 2D6, which is important for the elimination of aripiprazole. Therefore elevated plasma concentration of aripiprazole is possible and dose reduction has to be considered. The use of risperidone is supported by case studies showing that it might be beneficial (Fitzgerald, Stewart, Tawile, & Rosenberg, 1999; Lombroso et al., 1995; Thomsen, 2004). However, many of the patients included were CBT naïve before using SGAs and have, as stated previously, problematic metabolic side effects and hence SGA should be used with great caution. A study of adult OCD shows that SSRI nonresponders that have not received CBT previously fare better if randomized to CBT in contrast to risperidone (Simpson et al., 2013). Thus by taking the effects and adverse events into account, we argue that using SGAs is not a viable option unless adequate trials of CBT and SSRI have been conducted. The risk of untreated OCD should be compared with potential SGA adverse events and the pharmacotherapist should follow the advice of Maayan and Correll (2010) in monitoring for and managing these side effects.

NEW AND PROMISING PSYCHOPHARMACOLOGICAL INTERVENTIONS FOR PEDIATRIC OCD

D-Cycloserine and CBT

D-Cycloserine is believed to enhance the extinction of learned fear (Norberg, Krystal, & Tolin, 2008). The theoretical mechanism is that the *N*-methyl-D-aspartate (NMDA) receptor is involved in fear extinction and that D-cycloserine as an NMDA partial agonist is able to enhance this extinction. As the mechanism of CBT for OCD is to extinguish the relationship between an anxiety-producing stimulus and obsessive fear by exposing patients to these stimuli, one could potentially enhance this extinction by taking D-cycloserine approximately 1 h before CBT sessions. A metaanalysis (Norberg et al., 2008) and two recent RCTs have confirmed that D-cycloserine has an additive effect when combined with CBT, as it was demonstrated to be superior to CBT + pill placebo (Farrell et al., 2013; Storch, Murphy, et al., 2010). In line with this synthesized theory, D-cycloserine does not seem to work when administered after E/RP sessions (Mataix-Cols et al., 2014). However, in a placebo-controlled randomized clinical trial with 142 children and adolescents, D-cycloserine augmentation of CBT did not confer additional benefit relative to placebo among youth with OCD (Storch et al., 2016). Pending further studies, the augmentation of D-cycloserine seemed to be an option to reduce OCD symptoms in adult populations, but the initial results in children and adolescent are rather discouraging and other augmentation approaches should be explored.

N-Acetylcysteine

N-Acetylcysteine (NAC), a natural occurring amino acid, is also a glutamate-modulating drug with a very beneficial safety profile that may be a good alternative to children that have failed both CBT and SSRI trials. Currently there are ongoing randomized controlled trials using NAC for OCD in both adult and pediatric OCD. The preliminary results are encouraging; NAC seems to reduce the severity of OCD symptoms at least in a subgroup of patients, with minimal adverse effects, mainly mild gastrointestinal symptoms (Oliver et al., 2015; Pittenger, 2015).

Benzodiazepines

Using benzodiazepines such as clonazepam is off-label (Geller et al., 2012). Only one case study exists in pediatric OCD, reporting considerable improvement after a combination treatment of fluoxetine and clonazepam (Leonard et al., 1994). Two double-blind placebo control studies in adult OCD showed no effect of clonazepam when added to an SSRI in SSRI nonresponders (Crockett, Churchill, & Davidson, 2004; Hollander, Kaplan, & Stahl, 2003). Thus in view of the current state of knowledge, this strategy is not recommended.

Other Possible Medications

There are several other potential strategies for treatment-refractory patients available but very few have showed some evidence (Geller et al., 2012). For instance, it has been suggested that switching to serotonin-norepinephrine reuptake inhibitors such as venlafaxine and duloxetine might be beneficial. However, RCTs among adult OCD do not suggest that venlafaxine is more effective than the SSRI paroxetine in adults with OCD (Denys, van der Wee, van Megen, & Westenberg, 2003). In a subsequent study of adult OCD nonresponders of these drugs, switching from venlafaxine to paroxetine was found to be significantly more effective than vice versa (Denys, van Megen, van der Wee, & Westenberg, 2004). However, serotonin-related genes may predict which patients respond to SSRIs and which patients respond to serotonin-norepinephrine reuptake inhibitors (Denys, Van Nieuwerburgh, Deforce, & Westenberg, 2007). Furthermore, increasing SSRI doses beyond the approved have been suggested to be an effective strategy in adults with OCD. One RCT in adult OCD SSRI nonresponders showed the benefits of 400 mg. of sertraline compared to 200 mg. daily (Ninan et al., 2006). Indeed, as stated in the most recent expert guidelines, these strategies are off-label and with the exception of riluzole they are at most based on a limited number of case reports (Geller et al., 2012). The other strategy is augmenting an SSRI with a serotonin 5-HT_3 receptor antagonist (Serata et al., 2015). One double-blind RCT has shown the benefits of augmenting an SSRI with granisetron in adult OCD (Askari et al., 2012) and two double-blind RCTs have shown the benefits of ondansetron in adult OCD (Heidari et al., 2014; Soltani et al., 2010). These treatments are clearly to be used by experts in true treatment-refractory OCD.

CHALLENGING/COMPLEX ISSUES

Challenges of Drug Treatment: Compliance

The child's and the parents' compliance with medication treatment is crucial and should be seen as a collaboration project with the family. There are different reasons for a child to avoid medication, all from dislike of the taste to a power struggle between child and parents. Some reasons are openly communicated, others are not. Therefore it is important to negotiate a medication contract directly with the child, of course with the consent of the parents. Some children are mainly concerned about what their peers might think about them taking medication. To help them to find out whether and what to tell friends usually solves the problem. Information about side effects needs to be given in a balanced and realistic way, as described previously. A special complex issue in adolescents is the importance to mention and review sexual side effects, usually best done without parents' presence. If they experience changes in their sexual reactions unprepared, this may lead them to stop medication without communicating the real reason to the therapist. Some children develop obsessions concerning harm of medication, for example, that the drugs may be toxic, contagious, or harmful in another way. It is then vital to identify this content as a part of OCD and to address it with exposure exercises, for example, taking the first prescription dose during a session.

Psychopharmacological Treatment of OCD Comorbidities: Indications, Pharmacodynamic and Kinetic Interaction With OCD Drugs

Comorbid disorders in children and adolescents with OCD are frequent (Ivarsson, Melin, & Wallin, 2008) and have profound influence on treatment outcome (Storch et al., 2008). In general, comorbid disorders should be assessed and, if they would likely impede treatment of OCD, they may need to be treated before addressing OCD to improve the final outcome (Storch et al., 2008). This is of particular importance when effective treatments are available that demand more than passive compliance, just as ERP-based treatment do, and the active combat against the symptoms that SSRI treatment, according to our current understanding, presupposes (Marks et al., 1988). In the following paragraphs, we discuss comorbid conditions which are frequently presenting together with OCD and that usually require psychopharmacological treatment.

ADHD

ADHD is a common comorbidity in OCD with prevalence from 10% (Geller et al., 2004; Ivarsson et al., 2008) up to 30% (Geller, Biederman, Griffin, Jones, & Lefkowitz, 1996). Patients with comorbid ADHD have problems in paying attention and in executive functioning (EF) causing a variety of problems for treatment compliance. Thus in CBT, but as well in SSRI treatment, it is a challenge for the patient to make plans, to follow them, and to pursue the treatment goal over time. As argued previously, the child's attitude to his/her illness during SSRI treatment need to include a sustained resistance to the OCD urges. In CBT, it is regularly difficult for the child to maintain attention and even more to comply with homework exercises, i.e., CBT puts the child's executive functioning resources to a severe test. Thus in contrary to the US practice parameter (Geller et al., 2012), recommending to treat OCD first in patients with OCD+ADHD, we argue that ADHD should be treated first or concurrently to provide an optimal base for successful CBT and SSRI treatments. In addition, treatment of comorbid ADHD before CBT/SSRI for OCD enables the evaluation of the effect of ADHD drug treatment, which is of relevance, not only with regard to the ADHD symptoms, but also for OCD symptoms, which may decrease as well in many children according to clinical experience. Also, a recent metaanalysis suggested that treatment with stimulants reduced the risk of anxiety when compared with placebo, possibly as a secondary effect of improved control of ADHD symptoms (Coughlin et al., 2015). However, worsening of anxiety symptoms as a possible side effect of stimulant medication may, according to industrial drug labeling, as well occur and need to be differentiated from the OCD. These symptoms occur probably coincidentally rather than being caused by stimulants, according to a recent metaanalysis (Coughlin et al., 2015). Nevertheless, if present, this problem could probably be addressed and solved with CBT and ERP exercises as it otherwise may lead to discontinuation of a potentially helpful stimulant treatment. In the presence of milder ADHD symptoms, CBT can be successfully conducted, if the treatment is adapted to the patient's shorter attention span, impulsivity, and limited patience, e.g., by reduced session length, firm and predictable structure of treatment sessions, breaks with play activities or games during sessions, and increased supervision of homework exercises by parents. With regard to the efficacy of drug treatments for ADHD, most patients respond well to stimulants, noradrenaline reuptake inhibitors, or alpha-adrenergic agonists. In all cases treatments need to be coordinated so that, for example, CBT for OCD starts when adequate compliance and better executive functioning is established. A different problem is that using a SSRI in patients with OCD plus ADHD may be associated with an attenuated SSRI response in the OCD treatment (Geller, Biederman, Stewart, Mullin, Farrell, et al., 2003). This may be due to patients not tolerating high enough doses, because of the side effects on EF, but other pharmacodynamical or treatment interaction effects are possible, but as yet not investigated. Some side effects of SSRI treatment are more often seen in children with, than without comorbid ADHD and/or Tourette's syndrome, for example "activation" (Murphy et al., 2008). Such nonspecific increase of all behaviors is often a reason for not increasing drug doses to appropriate levels for OCD. However, during SSRI treatment an increase of impulsive behaviors, for example, the use of inappropriate speech or aggressive acts for insufficient reasons compared with before SSRI treatment, can occur in the presence of, or without comorbid ADHD. This links SSRI treatment to a potentially increased vulnerability of executive functioning.

Atomoxetine alone had good effect on ADHD symptoms, but in addition to the ADHD effect, it improves anxiety symptoms in patients suffering from both ADHD and anxiety disorders (Geller et al., 2007). However, if atomoxetine is combined with a SSRI it has to be taken into consideration that SSRIs are potent inhibitors of the enzyme system CYP 2D6, which is important for the elimination of atomoxetine. Therefore elevated plasma concentration of atomoxetine is frequent and dose reduction has to be considered. It is also recommended that atomoxetine concentration is analyzed in blood samples during treatment with both atomoxetine and SSRI.

Tic Disorders/Tourette's Syndrome

Tic disorders are the most prevalent comorbid disorders in OCD occurring in about a third of patients (Ivarsson et al., 2008). Individuals with tic-related OCD report more aggressive, religious, and sexual obsessions as well as checking, counting, ordering, touching, and symmetry compulsions than those with nontic-related OCD do both in adult (Leckman et al., 1994; Worbe et al., 2010) and in pediatric samples (Masi et al., 2005). In addition, the comorbidity of TS with OCD is associated with elevated levels of ADHD and ODD (Lewin, Chang, McCracken, McQueen, & Piacentini, 2010). The differentiation between tic-related and nontic-related OCD is clinically important, as both choice of, and response to treatment, might diverge. This is demonstrated in medication trials and to a lesser extent in CBT trials (with ambiguous results). Thus in drug trials comorbid tics have been associated with poorer response (Ginsburg, Kingery, Drake, & Grados, 2008; March et al., 2007) but for CBT, comorbid TS seems to have little impact (Himle, Fischer, Van Etten, Janeck, & Hanna, 2003; Piacentini, Bergman, Jacobs, McCracken, & Kretchman, 2002; Torp et al., 2015). However, among CBT nonresponders, sertraline was superior to continued CBT in patients with comorbid TS (Skarphedinsson, Compton, et al., 2015), a finding that needs to be replicated. If treatment for tics is considered as necessary, i.e., that tics are causing functional impairment or significant discomfort, behavioral interventions are recommended as first-line treatment, and should be pursued vigorously as given medium to large effects (McGuire et al., 2014; Piacentini et al., 2002). Thus in cases that need pharmacological treatment for tics, lower doses may be enough, if at all needed. This is of value in itself due to the pharmacokinetic interactions with SSRI (see previously) and the high frequency of side effects of, e.g., atypical or second-generation antipsychotics and clonidine (Roessner et al., 2011). Furthermore, as atypical antipsychotics can be used as augmentation strategy for SSRI refractory OCD (see paragraph atypical antipsychotics previously) there might be a synergistic benefit of using both a SSRI and a SGA, in that we target both the tics and OCD in the treatment.

Autism Spectrum Disorders

Autism and autistic symptoms are common in children and adolescents treated for OCD, e.g., 8% fulfilled the diagnostic criteria for an Autism spectrum disorder (ASD) (Ivarsson et al., 2008) and subclinical ASD symptoms were more common in children with OCD than in controls (Weidle, Melin, Drotz, Jozefiak, & Ivarsson, 2012). On the other hand, among children and adolescents with ASD the prevalence of comorbid OCD is described to range from 8% to 37% (Leyfer et al., 2006; Simonoff et al., 2008). Thus because of the high comorbidity rate and symptom overlap with ASD, OCD symptoms must be distinguished from repetitive behaviors and special interests and diagnosed wherever or whenever the patient comes for treatment, as patients with ASD and OCD may benefit from standard treatments.

However, treatment of OCD in children with ASD needs to be adjusted to the deficits in executive functioning, social development, and to their perception of the environment. In addition to the lacking understanding of social clues and the inability to comply with social demands from the environment, comorbid ADHD is present in about 50% of children with ASD, aggravating their problems to a great extent (Mattila et al., 2010). Thus arguments for ADHD treatment in these complex cases are in place as well. Moreover, due to impaired ability for introspection, literal perception of language (e.g., exaggerated alerts of danger in the media) and impaired social judgment, children with OCD and ASD frequently lack insight into the irrational and unreasonable nature of their obsessions (DSM-5 specification poor or absent insight). This may have a negative impact on drug treatment as well as on CBT (Garcia et al., 2010). Another problem is that incentives to cooperate in treatment in order to get rid of OCD are mostly social, i.e., being able to join friends, might not be a rewarding goal for children with ASD. This facet needs to be taken into account when negotiating the drug treatment contract with the child. Also, the tendency to repetitive behavior and rigidity, i.e., the reduced ability for cognitive flexibility may overlap with OCD symptoms and can be a serious obstacle for complying with exposure treatment and the need to actively combat the OC urges in SSRI treatment.

Pharmacological treatment of ASD symptoms may be of value in these complex situations. Risperidone and aripiprazole are the two best-studied medications for ASD and found to be beneficial to reduce challenging and repetitive behavior, although the evidence base for medication on the whole is weak (McPheeters et al., 2011). SSRIs have shown some benefit in a few studies, but in general there is no evidence to support the use of SSRIs to treat autism in children (Williams, Brignell, Randall, Silove, & Hazell, 2013). Furthermore, a well-designed trial did not support the use of citalopram for the treatment of repetitive behavior in children and adolescents with ASD (King et al., 2009). The SGA drugs which are found to be most beneficial in ASD are the same which are used as augmentation strategy for SSRI refractory OCD (see paragraph atypical antipsychotics previously), so in children with OCD and ASD who are not able to comply with the demands of exposure therapy or have only insufficient effect from CBT and a SSRI trial, there might be an additional benefit of these compounds both to augment weak SSRI response and to reduce rigidity and repetitive behavior.

Disruptive Behavior Disorders

Diagnoses of comorbid disruptive disorders, mainly oppositional defiant disorder (ODD), are found with prevalence below 10% in most studies (Ivarsson et al., 2008; Piacentini et al., 2011), with few exceptions (Geller et al., 1996). However, aggressive outbursts are quite frequent in children with OCD even without comorbid disruptive behavior, often involving limit-setting situations (Storch et al., 2012). Clinical and subclinical disruptive behavior is associated with increased severity of OCD symptoms and poorer treatment outcome (Storch, Lewin, Geffken, Morgan, & Murphy, 2010). Treatment for ODD, for example, Parent Management Training (PMT), might establish a base for subsequent CBT (Sukhodolsky, Gorman, Scahill, Findley, & McGuire, 2013), but for those who do not respond drug treatment can be considered, e.g., in patients with high levels of aggression and high parental accommodation. The pharmacological intervention against disruptive behaviors is SGA, usually risperidone and aripiprazole, which may be beneficial, albeit the documentation is weak (Pringsheim, Hirsch, Gardner, & Gorman, 2015).

CONCLUSIONS

The treatment literature on pediatric OCD has gone a long way since Rapoport's first clomipramine study (Rapoport et al., 1980), and recent metaanalyses and systematic reviews now show, not only that we have evidence-based treatments in CBT and SSRI as first-line treatments, they show their relative value, the limitations of the evidence base, and the extent to which pediatric data are in consonance with adult evidence (Ivarsson et al., 2015; McGuire et al., 2015; Romanelli et al., 2014; Skarphedinsson, Hanssen-Bauer, et al., 2015). We conclude that drug treatment should be used as a second-line treatment, albeit the evidence base in that situation is limited, and that in nonresponders to both evidence-based treatments, the combination of different drugs may bring some additional benefit. However, due to the absence of controlled trials and the presence of problematic side effects, the benefits and the risks of using them must be carefully weighed against the risks involved in the illness itself.

REFERENCES

Alexander, G. E., & Crutcher, M. D. (1990). Functional architecture of basal ganglia circuits: Neural substrates of parallel processing. *Trends in Neurosciences*, *13*(7), 266–271.

Arumugham, S. S., & Reddy, J. Y. (2013). Augmentation strategies in obsessive-compulsive disorder. *Expert Review of Neurotherapeutics*, *13*(2), 187–202. quiz 203.

Asbahr, F. R., Castillo, A. R., Ito, L. M., Latorre, M. R., Moreira, M. N., & Lotufo-Neto, F. (2005). Group cognitive-behavioral therapy versus sertraline for the treatment of children and adolescents with obsessive-compulsive disorder. *Journal of the American Academy of Child and Adolescent Psychiatry*, *44*(11), 1128–1136.

Asberg, M., Ringberger, V. A., Sjoqvist, F., Thoren, P., Traskman, L., & Tuck, J. R. (1977). Monoamine metabolites in cerebrospinal fluid and serotonin uptake inhibition during treatment with chlorimipramine. *Clinical Pharmacology and Therapeutics*, *21*(2), 201–207.

Askari, N., Moin, M., Sanati, M., Tajdini, M., Hosseini, S. -M. -R., Modabbernia, A., et al. (2012). Granisetron adjunct to fluvoxamine for moderate to severe obsessive-compulsive disorder: A randomized, double-blind, placebo-controlled trial. *CNS Drugs*, *26*(10), 883–892.

Basham, R. B. (1986). Scientific and practical advantages of comparative design in psychotherapy outcome research. *Journal of Consulting and Clinical Psychology*, *54*(1), 88–94.

Black, K., Shea, C., Dursun, S., & Kutcher, S. (2000). Selective serotonin reuptake inhibitor discontinuation syndrome: Proposed diagnostic criteria. *Journal of Psychiatry and Neuroscience*, *25*(3), 255–261.

Bloch, M. H., Landeros-Weisenberger, A., Kelmendi, B., Coric, V., Bracken, M. B., & Leckman, J. F. (2006). A systematic review: Antipsychotic augmentation with treatment refractory obsessive-compulsive disorder. *Molecular Psychiatry*, *11*(7), 622–632.

Bussing, R., Murphy, T. K., Storch, E. A., McNamara, J. P., Reid, A. M., Garvan, C. W., et al. (2013). Psychometric properties of the treatment-emergent activation and suicidality assessment profile (TEASAP) in youth with OCD. *Psychiatry Research*, *205*(3), 253–261.

Bylund, D. B., & Reed, A. L. (2007). Childhood and adolescent depression: Why do children and adults respond differently to antidepressant drugs? *Neurochemistry International*, *51*(5), 246–253.

Carli, M., & Invernizzi, R. W. (2014). Serotoninergic and dopaminergic modulation of cortico-striatal circuit in executive and attention deficits induced by NMDA receptor hypofunction in the 5-choice serial reaction time task. *Frontiers in Neural Circuits*, *8*, 58.

Carlsson, A., Corrodi, H., Fuxe, K., & Hokfelt, T. (1969). Effect of antidepressant drugs on the depletion of intraneuronal brain 5-hydroxytryptamine stores caused by 4-methyl-alpha-ethyl-meta-tyramine. *European Journal of Pharmacology*, *5*(4), 357–366.

Cook, E. H., Wagner, K. D., March, J. S., Biederman, J., Landau, P., Wolkow, R., et al. (2001). Long-term sertraline treatment of children and adolescents with obsessive-compulsive disorder. *Journal of the American Academy of Child and Adolescent Psychiatry*, *40*(10), 1175–1181.

Coughlin, C. G., Cohen, S. C., Mulqueen, J. M., Ferracioli-Oda, E., Stuckelman, Z. D., & Bloch, M. H. (2015). Meta-analysis: Reduced risk of anxiety with psychostimulant treatment in children with attention-deficit/hyperactivity disorder. *Journal of Child and Adolescent Psychopharmacology*, *25*(8), 611–617.

Crockett, B. A., Churchill, E., & Davidson, J. R. (2004). A double-blind combination study of clonazepam with sertraline in obsessive-compulsive disorder. *Annals of Clinical Psychiatry*, *16*(3), 127–132.

Denys, D., van der Wee, N., van Megen, H. J., & Westenberg, H. G. (2003). A double blind comparison of venlafaxine and paroxetine in obsessive-compulsive disorder. *Journal of Clinical Psychopharmacology*, *23*(6), 568–575.

Denys, D., van Megen, H. J., van der Wee, N., & Westenberg, H. G. (2004). A double-blind switch study of paroxetine and venlafaxine in obsessive-compulsive disorder. *Journal of Clinical Psychiatry*, *65*(1), 37–43.

Denys, D., Van Nieuwerburgh, F., Deforce, D., & Westenberg, H. G. M. (2007). Prediction of response to paroxetine and venlafaxine by serotonin-related genes in obsessive-compulsive disorder in a randomized, double-blind trial. *Journal of Clinical Psychiatry*, *68*(5), 747–753.

Diniz, J. B., Shavitt, R. G., Fossaluza, V., Koran, L., Pereira, C. A. D. B., & Miguel, E. C. (2011). A double-blind, randomized, controlled trial of fluoxetine plus quetiapine or clomipramine versus fluoxetine plus placebo for obsessive-compulsive disorder. *Journal of Clinical Psychopharmacology*, *31*(6), 763–768.

Dold, M., Aigner, M., Lanzenberger, R., & Kasper, S. (2013). Antipsychotic augmentation of serotonin reuptake inhibitors in treatment-resistant obsessive-compulsive disorder: A meta-analysis of double-blind, randomized, placebo-controlled trials. *International Journal of Neuropsychopharmacology*, *16*(3), 557–574.

Farrell, L. J., Waters, A. M., Boschen, M. J., Hattingh, L., McConnell, H., Milliner, E. L., et al. (2013). Difficult-to-treat pediatric obsessive-compulsive disorder: Feasibility and preliminary results of a randomized pilot trial of D-cycloserine-augmented behavior therapy. *Depression and Anxiety*, *30*(8), 723–731.

Fernandez, C. E., & Lopez-Ibor, J. J. (1967). Monochlorimipramine in the treatment of psychiatric patients resistant to other therapies. *Actas Luso-Españolas de Neurología, Psiquiatría y Ciencias Afines*, *26*, 119–147.

Figueroa, Y., Rosenberg, D. R., Birmaher, B., & Keshavan, M. S. (1998). Combination treatment with clomipramine and selective serotonin reuptake inhibitors for obsessive-compulsive disorder in children and adolescents. *Journal of Child and Adolescent Psychopharmacology*, *8*(1), 61–67.

Fitzgerald, K. D., Stewart, C. M., Tawile, V., & Rosenberg, D. R. (1999). Risperidone augmentation of serotonin reuptake inhibitor treatment of pediatric obsessive compulsive disorder. *Journal of Child and Adolescent Psychopharmacology*, *9*(2), 115–123.

Franklin, M. E., Sapyta, J., Freeman, J. B., Khanna, M., Compton, S., Almirall, D., et al. (2011). Cognitive behavior therapy augmentation of pharmacotherapy in pediatric obsessive-compulsive disorder: The Pediatric OCD Treatment Study II (POTS II) randomized controlled trial. *JAMA*, *306*(11), 1224–1232.

Garcia, A. M., Sapyta, J. J., Moore, P. S., Freeman, J. B., Franklin, M. E., March, J. S., et al. (2010). Predictors and moderators of treatment outcome in the pediatric obsessive compulsive treatment study (POTS I). *Journal of the American Academy of Child and Adolescent Psychiatry*, *49*(10), 1024–1033.

Garland, E. J., & Baerg, E. A. (2001). Amotivational syndrome associated with selective serotonin reuptake inhibitors in children and adolescents. *Journal of Child and Adolescent Psychopharmacology*, *11*(2), 181–186.

Geller, D. A., Biederman, J., Griffin, S., Jones, J., & Lefkowitz, T. R. (1996). Comorbidity of juvenile obsessive-compulsive disorder with disruptive behavior disorders. *Journal of the American Academy of Child and Adolescent Psychiatry*, *35*(12), 1637–1646.

Geller, D. A., Biederman, J., Stewart, S. E., Mullin, B., Farrell, C., Wagner, K. D., et al. (2003a). Impact of comorbidity on treatment response to paroxetine in pediatric obsessive-compulsive disorder: Is the use of exclusion criteria empirically supported in randomized clinical trials? *Journal of Child and Adolescent Psychopharmacology*, *13*(Suppl. 1), S19–S29.

Geller, D. A., Biederman, J., Stewart, S. E., Mullin, B., Martin, A., Spencer, T., et al. (2003b). Which SSRI? A meta-analysis of pharmacotherapy trials in pediatric obsessive-compulsive disorder. *American Journal of Psychiatry*, *160*(11), 1919–1928.

Geller, D., Donnelly, C., Lopez, F., Rubin, R., Newcorn, J., Sutton, V., et al. (2007). Atomoxetine treatment for pediatric patients with attention-deficit/hyperactivity disorder with comorbid anxiety disorder. *Journal of the American Academy of Child and Adolescent Psychiatry*, *46*(9), 1119–1127.

Geller, D., March, J. S., & CQI, The AACAP Committee on Quality Issues. (2012). Practice parameter for the assessment and treatment of children and adolescents with obsessive compulsive disorder. *Journal of the American Academy of Child and Adolescent Psychiatry*, *51*(1), 98–113.

Geller, D. A., Wagner, K. D., Emslie, G., Murphy, T., Carpenter, D. J., Wetherhold, E., et al. (2004). Paroxetine treatment in children and adolescents with obsessive-compulsive disorder:

A randomized, multicenter, double-blind, placebo-controlled trial. *Journal of the American Academy of Child and Adolescent Psychiatry*, *43*(11), 1387–1396.

Ginsburg, G. S., Kingery, J. N., Drake, K. L., & Grados, M. A. (2008). Predictors of treatment response in pediatric obsessive-compulsive disorder. *Journal of the American Academy of Child and Adolescent Psychiatry*, *47*(8), 868–878.

Haynes, R. B., Sackett, D. L., Guyatt, H. H., & Tugwell, P. (2006). *Clinical epidemiology: How to do clinical practise research: Vol. 3*. Philadelphia: Lippincott Williams & Wilkins.

Heidari, M., Zarei, M., Hosseini, S. M., Taghvaei, R., Maleki, H., Tabrizi, M., et al. (2014). Ondansetron or placebo in the augmentation of fluvoxamine response over 8 weeks in obsessive-compulsive disorder. *International Clinical Psychopharmacology*, *29*(6), 344–350.

Himle, J. A., Fischer, D. J., Van Etten, M. L., Janeck, A. S., & Hanna, G. L. (2003). Group behavioral therapy for adolescents with tic-related and non-tic-related obsessive-compulsive disorder. *Depression and Anxiety*, *17*(2), 73–77.

Hollander, E., Kaplan, A., & Stahl, S. M. (2003). A double-blind, placebo-controlled trial of clonazepam in obsessive-compulsive disorder. *World Journal of Biological Psychiatry*, *4*(1), 30–34.

Ivarsson, T., Melin, K., & Wallin, L. (2008). Categorical and dimensional aspects of co-morbidity in obsessive-compulsive disorder (OCD). *European Child and Adolescent Psychiatry*, *17*(1), 20–31.

Ivarsson, T., Skarphedinsson, G., Kornør, H., Axelsdottir, B., Biedilæ, S., Heyman, I., et al. (2015). The place of and evidence for serotonin reuptake inhibitors (SRIs) in obsessive compulsive disorder (OCD) in children and adolescents: Views based on a systematic review and meta-analysis (e-pub). *Psychiatry Research*, *227*(1), 93–103.

King, B. H., Hollander, E., Sikich, L., McCracken, J. T., Scahill, L., Bregman, J. D., et al. (2009). Lack of efficacy of citalopram in children with autism spectrum disorders and high levels of repetitive behavior: Citalopram ineffective in children with autism. *Archives of General Psychiatry*, *66*(6), 583–590.

Leckman, J. F., Grice, D. E., Barr, L. C., de Vries, A. L., Martin, C., Cohen, D. J., et al. (1994). Tic-related vs. non-tic-related obsessive compulsive disorder. *Anxiety*, *1*(5), 208–215.

Leonard, H. L., Swedo, S. E., Lenane, M. C., Rettew, D. C., Cheslow, D. L., Hamburger, S. D., et al. (1991). A double-blind desipramine substitution during long-term clomipramine treatment in children and adolescents with obsessive-compulsive disorder. *Archives of General Psychiatry*, *48*(10), 922–927.

Leonard, H. L., Swedo, S., Rapoport, J. L., Coffey, M., & Cheslow, D. (1988). Treatment of childhood obsessive compulsive disorder with clomipramine and desmethylimipramine: A double-blind crossover comparison. *Psychopharmacology Bulletin*, *24*(1), 93–95.

Leonard, H. L., Topol, D., Bukstein, O., Hindmarsh, D., Allen, A. J., & Swedo, S. E. (1994). Clonazepam as an augmenting agent in the treatment of childhood-onset obsessive-compulsive disorder. *Journal of the American Academy of Child and Adolescent Psychiatry*, *33*(6), 792–794.

Lewin, A. B., Chang, S., McCracken, J., McQueen, M., & Piacentini, J. (2010). Comparison of clinical features among youth with tic disorders, obsessive-compulsive disorder (OCD), and both conditions. *Psychiatry Research*, *178*(2), 317–322.

Leyfer, O. T., Folstein, S. E., Bacalman, S., Davis, N. O., Dinh, E., Morgan, J., et al. (2006). Comorbid psychiatric disorders in children with autism: Interview development and rates of disorders. *Journal of Autism and Developmental Disorders*, *36*(7), 849–861.

Lombroso, P. J., Scahill, L., King, R. A., Lynch, K. A., Chappell, P. B., Peterson, B. S., et al. (1995). Risperidone treatment of children and adolescents with chronic tic disorders: A preliminary report. *Journal of the American Academy of Child and Adolescent Psychiatry*, *34*(9), 1147–1152.

Maayan, L., & Correll, C. U. (2010). Management of antipsychotic-related weight gain. *Expert Review of Neurotherapeutics*, *10*(7), 1175–1200.

March, J. S., Biederman, J., Wolkow, R., Safferman, A., Mardekian, J., Cook, E. H., et al. (1998). Sertraline in children and adolescents with obsessive-compulsive disorder: A multicenter randomized controlled trial. *JAMA: The Journal of the American Medical Association*, *280*(20), 1752–1756. http://www.mrw.interscience.wiley.com/cochrane/clcentral/articles/606/CN-00157606/frame.html.

March, J. S., Franklin, M. E., Leonard, H., Garcia, A., Moore, P., Freeman, J., et al. (2007). Tics moderate treatment outcome with sertraline but not cognitive-behavior therapy in pediatric obsessive-compulsive disorder. *Biological Psychiatry*, *61*(3), 344–347.

Marks, I. M., Lelliott, P., Basoglu, M., Noshirvani, H., Monteiro, W., Cohen, D., et al. (1988). Clomipramine, self-exposure and therapist-aided exposure for obsessive-compulsive rituals. *British Journal of Psychiatry*, *152*, 522–534.

Masi, G., Millepiedi, S., Mucci, M., Bertini, N., Milantoni, L., & Arcangeli, F. (2005). A naturalistic study of referred children and adolescents with obsessive-compulsive disorder. *Journal of the American Academy of Child and Adolescent Psychiatry*, *44*(7), 673–681.

Masi, G., Millepiedi, S., Perugi, G., Pfanner, C., Berloffa, S., Pari, C., et al. (2009). Pharmacotherapy in pediatric obsessive-compulsive disorder: A naturalistic, retrospective study. *CNS Drugs*, *23*(3), 241–252.

Masi, G., Pfanner, C., & Brovedani, P. (2013). Antipsychotic augmentation of selective serotonin reuptake inhibitors in resistant tic-related obsessive-compulsive disorder in children and adolescents: A naturalistic comparative study. *Journal of Psychiatric Research*, *47*(8), 1007–1012.

Mataix-Cols, D., Turner, C., Monzani, B., Isomura, K., Murphy, C., Krebs, G., et al. (2014). Cognitive-behavioural therapy with post-session D-cycloserine augmentation for pediatric obsessive-compulsive disorder: Pilot randomised controlled trial. *British Journal of Psychiatry*, *204*, 77–78.

Mattila, M. L., Hurtig, T., Haapsamo, H., Jussila, K., Kuusikko-Gauffin, S., Kielinen, M., et al. (2010). Comorbid psychiatric disorders associated with Asperger syndrome/high-functioning autism: A community- and clinic-based study. *Journal of Autism and Developmental Disorders*, *40*(9), 1080–1093.

McGuire, J. F., Piacentini, J., Brennan, E. A., Lewin, A. B., Murphy, T. K., Small, B. J., et al. (2014). A meta-analysis of behavior therapy for Tourette syndrome. *Journal of Psychiatric Research*, *50*, 106–112.

McGuire, J. F., Piacentini, J., Lewin, A. B., Brennan, E. A., Murphy, T. K., & Storch, E. A. (2015). A meta-analysis of cognitive behavior therapy and medication for child obsessive-compulsive disorder: Moderators of treatment efficacy, response, and remission. *Depression and Anxiety*, *32*, 580–593.

McPheeters, M. L., Warren, Z., Sathe, N., Bruzek, J. L., Krishnaswami, S., Jerome, R. N., et al. (2011). A systematic review of medical treatments for children with autism spectrum disorders. *Pediatrics*, *127*(5), e1312–e1321.

Murphy, T. K., Segarra, A., Storch, E. A., & Goodman, W. K. (2008). SSRI adverse events: How to monitor and manage. *International Review of Psychiatry*, *20*(2), 203–208.

Neziroglu, F., Yaryura-Tobias, J. A., Walz, J., & McKay, D. (2000). The effect of fluvoxamine and behavior therapy on children and adolescents with obsessive-compulsive disorder. *Journal of Child and Adolescent Psychopharmacology*, *10*(4), 295–306.

National Institute for Health and Clinical Excellence (NICE). (2005). *Obsessive compulsive disorder (OCD) and body dysmorphic disorder (BDD)*. London: National Institute for Health and Clinical Excellence.

Nieuwenhuys, R. (2012). The insular cortex: A review. *Progress in Brain Research, 195*, 123–163.

Ninan, P. T., Koran, L. M., Kiev, A., Davidson, J. R., Rasmussen, S. A., Zajecka, J. M., et al. (2006). High-dose sertraline strategy for nonresponders to acute treatment for obsessive-compulsive disorder: A multicenter double-blind trial. *Journal of Clinical Psychiatry, 67*(1), 15–22.

Norberg, M. M., Krystal, J. H., & Tolin, D. F. (2008). A meta-analysis of D-cycloserine and the facilitation of fear extinction and exposure therapy. *Biological Psychiatry, 63*(12), 1118.

Oliver, G., Dean, O., Camfield, D., Blair-West, S., Ng, C., Berk, M., et al. (2015). N-acetyl cysteine in the treatment of obsessive compulsive and related disorders: A systematic review. *Clinical Psychopharmacology and Neuroscience, 13*(1), 12–24.

Pauls, D. L., Abramovitch, A., Rauch, S. L., & Geller, D. A. (2014). Obsessive-compulsive disorder: An integrative genetic and neurobiological perspective. *Nature Reviews. Neuroscience, 15*(6), 410–424.

Piacentini, J., Bergman, R. L., Chang, S., Langley, A., Peris, T., Wood, J. J., et al. (2011). Controlled comparison of family cognitive behavioral therapy and psychoeducation/relaxation training for child obsessive-compulsive disorder. *Journal of the American Academy of Child and Adolescent Psychiatry, 50*(11), 1149–1161.

Piacentini, J., Bergman, R. L., Jacobs, C., McCracken, J. T., & Kretchman, J. (2002). Open trial of cognitive behavior therapy for childhood obsessive-compulsive disorder. *Journal of Anxiety Disorders, 16*(2), 207–219.

Piacentini, J., Peris, T. S., Bergman, R. L., Chang, S., & Jaffer, M. (2007). Functional impairment in childhood OCD: Development and psychometrics properties of the child obsessive-compulsive impact scale-revised (COIS-R). *Journal of Clinical Child and Adolescent Psychology, 36*(4), 645–653.

Piras, F., Piras, F., Chiapponi, C., Girardi, P., Caltagirone, C., & Spalletta, G. (2015). Widespread structural brain changes in OCD: A systematic review of voxel-based morphometry studies. *Cortex, 62*, 89–108.

Pittenger, C. (2015). Glutamatergic agents for OCD and related disorders. *Current Treatment Options in Psychiatry, 2*(3), 271–283.

POTS Treatment Study Team. (2004). Cognitive-behavior therapy, sertraline, and their combination for children and adolescents with obsessive-compulsive disorder: The Pediatric OCD Treatment Study (POTS) randomized controlled trial. *Journal of American Medical Association, 292*(16), 1969–1976.

Pringsheim, T., Hirsch, L., Gardner, D., & Gorman, D. A. (2015). The pharmacological management of oppositional behavior, conduct problems, and aggression in children and adolescents with attention-deficit hyperactivity disorder, oppositional defiant disorder, and conduct disorder: A systematic review and meta-analysis. Part 2: Antipsychotics and traditional mood stabilizers. *Canadian Journal of Psychiatry, 60*(2), 52–61.

Rapoport, J., Elkins, R., & Mikkelsen, E. (1980). Clinical controlled trial of chlorimipramine in adolescents with obsessive-compulsive disorder. *Psychopharmacology Bulletin, 16*(3), 61–63.

Reid, J. M., Storch, E. A., Murphy, T. K., Bodzin, D., Mutch, P. J., Lehmkuhl, H., et al. (2010). Development and psychometric evaluation of the treatment-emergent activation and suicidality assessment profile. *Child & Youth Care Forum, 39*(2), 113–124.

Roessner, V., Plessen, K. J., Rothenberger, A., Ludolph, A. G., Rizzo, R., Skov, L., et al. (2011). European clinical guidelines for Tourette syndrome and other tic disorders. Part II: Pharmacological treatment. *European Child and Adolescent Psychiatry, 20*(4), 173–196.

Romanelli, R. J., Wu, F. M., Gamba, R., Mojtabai, R., & Segal, J. B. (2014). Behavioral therapy and serotonin reuptake inhibitor pharmacotherapy in the treatment of obsessive-compulsive disorder: A systematic review and meta-analysis of head-to-head randomized controlled trials. *Depression and Anxiety*, *31*(8), 641–652.

Rynn, M. A., Walkup, J. T., Compton, S. N., Sakolsky, D. J., Sherrill, J. T., Shen, S., et al. (2015). Child/Adolescent anxiety multimodal study: Evaluating safety. *Journal of the American Academy of Child and Adolescent Psychiatry*, *54*(3), 180–190.

Serata, D., Kotzalidis, G. D., Rapinesi, C., Janiri, D., Di Pietro, S., Callovini, G., et al. (2015). Are 5-HT3 antagonists effective in obsessive-compulsive disorder? A systematic review of literature. *Human Psychopharmacology*, *30*(2), 70–84.

Shipp, S. (2016). The functional logic of corticostriatal connections. *Brain Structure and Function*, *222*, 669–706.

Simeon, J. G., Thatte, S., & Wiggins, D. (1990). Treatment of adolescent obsessive-compulsive disorder with a clomipramine-fluoxetine combination. *Psychopharmacology Bulletin*, *26*(3), 285–290.

Simonoff, E., Pickles, A., Charman, T., Chandler, S., Loucas, T., & Baird, G. (2008). Psychiatric disorders in children with autism spectrum disorders: Prevalence, comorbidity, and associated factors in a population-derived sample. *Journal of the American Academy of Child and Adolescent Psychiatry*, *47*(8), 921–929.

Simpson, H. B., Foa, E. B., Liebowitz, M. R., Huppert, J. D., Cahill, S., Maher, M. J., et al. (2013). Cognitive-behavioral therapy vs risperidone for augmenting serotonin reuptake inhibitors in obsessive-compulsive disorder: A randomized clinical trial. *JAMA Psychiatry*, *70*(11), 1190–1199.

Skarphedinsson, G., Compton, S., Thomsen, P. H., Weidle, B., Dahl, K., Nissen, J. B., et al. (2015). Tics moderate sertraline, but not cognitive-behavior therapy response in pediatric obsessive-compulsive disorder patients who do not respond to cognitive-behavior therapy. *Journal of Child and Adolescent Psychopharmacology*, *25*(5), 432–439.

Skarphedinsson, G., De Nadai, A. S., Storch, E. A., Lewin, A. B., & Ivarsson, T. (2017). Defining cognitive-behavior therapy response and remission in pediatric OCD: A signal detection analysis of the Children's Yale Brown Obsessive Compulsive Scale. *European Child and Adolescent Psychiatry*, *26*, 47–55.

Skarphedinsson, G., Hanssen-Bauer, K., Kornor, H., Heiervang, E. R., Landro, N. I., Axelsdottir, B., et al. (2015). Standard individual cognitive behavior therapy for pediatric obsessive-compulsive disorder: A systematic review of effect estimates across comparisons. *Nordic Journal of Psychiatry*, *69*(2), 81–92.

Skarphedinsson, G., & Ivarsson, T. (2015). Evidence-based treatments in treatment-naïve and treatment-resistant pediatric obsessive-compulsive disorder. *Current Behavioral Neuroscience Reports*, *2*(3), 127–136.

Skarphedinsson, G., Weidle, B., & Ivarsson, T. (2015). Sertraline treatment of nonresponders to extended cognitive-behavior therapy in pediatric obsessive-compulsive disorder. *Journal of Child and Adolescent Psychopharmacology*, *25*(7), 574–579.

Skarphedinsson, G., Weidle, B., Thomsen, P. H., Dahl, K., Torp, N. C., Nissen, J. B., et al. (2015). Continued cognitive behavior therapy versus sertraline for children and adolescents with obsessive-compulsive disorder that were non-responders to cognitive behavior therapy—A randomized controlled trial. *European Child and Adolescent Psychiatry*, *24*(5), 591–602.

Soltani, F., Sayyah, M., Feizy, F., Malayeri, A., Siahpoosh, A., & Motlagh, I. (2010). A double-blind, placebo-controlled pilot study of ondansetron for patients with obsessive-compulsive disorder. *Human Psychopharmacology*, *25*(6), 509–513.

Stahl, S. M. (2013). *Stahl's essential psychopharnacology: Neuroscientific basis and practical applications* (4th ed.). Cambridge: Cambridge University Press.

Storch, E. A., Bussing, R., Small, B. J., Geffken, G. R., McNamara, J. P., Rahman, O., et al. (2013). Randomized, placebo-controlled trial of cognitive-behavioral therapy alone or combined with sertraline in the treatment of pediatric obsessive-compulsive disorder. *Behaviour Research and Therapy*, *51*(12), 823–829.

Storch, E. A., Jones, A. M., Lack, C. W., Ale, C. M., Sulkowski, M. L., Lewin, A. B., et al. (2012). Rage attacks in pediatric obsessive-compulsive disorder: Phenomenology and clinical correlates. *Journal of the American Academy of Child and Adolescent Psychiatry*, *51*(6), 582–592.

Storch, E. A., Lewin, A. B., De Nadai, A. S., & Murphy, T. K. (2010a). Defining treatment response and remission in obsessive-compulsive disorder: A signal detection analysis of the Children's Yale-Brown Obsessive Compulsive Scale. *Journal of the American Academy of Child and Adolescent Psychiatry*, *49*(7), 708–717.

Storch, E. A., Lewin, A. B., Geffken, G. R., Morgan, J. R., & Murphy, T. K. (2010b). The role of comorbid disruptive behavior in the clinical expression of pediatric obsessive-compulsive disorder. *Behaviour Research and Therapy*, *48*(12), 1204–1210.

Storch, E. A., Merlo, L. J., Larson, M. J., Geffken, G. R., Lehmkuhl, H. D., Jacob, M. L., et al. (2008). Impact of comorbidity on cognitive-behavioral therapy response in pediatric obsessive-compulsive disorder. *Journal of the American Academy of Child and Adolescent Psychiatry*, *47*(5), 583–592.

Storch, E. A., Murphy, T. K., Goodman, W. K., Geffken, G. R., Lewin, A. B., Henin, A., et al. (2010). A preliminary study of D-cycloserine augmentation of cognitive-behavioral therapy in pediatric obsessive-compulsive disorder. *Biological Psychiatry*, *11*, 1073–1076. http://www.mrw.interscience.wiley.com/cochrane/clcentral/articles/829/CN-00768829/frame.html.

Storch, E. A., Wilhelm, S., Sprich, S., Henin, A., Micco, J., Small, B. J., et al. (2016). Efficacy of augmentation of cognitive behavior therapy with weight-adjusted d-cycloserine vs placebo in pediatric obsessive-compulsive disorder: A randomized clinical trial. *JAMA Psychiatry*, *73*(8), 779–788.

Sukhodolsky, D. G., Gorman, B. S., Scahill, L., Findley, D., & McGuire, J. (2013). Exposure and response prevention with or without parent management training for children with obsessive-compulsive disorder complicated by disruptive behavior: A multiple-baseline across-responses design study. *Journal of Anxiety Disorders*, *27*(3), 298–305.

Thomsen, P. H. (2004). Risperidone augmentation in the treatment of severe adolescent OCD in SSRI-refractory cases: A case-series. *Annals of Clinical Psychiatry*, *16*(4), 201–207.

Thoren, P., Asberg, M., Cronholm, B., Jornestedt, L., & Traskman, L. (1980). Clomipramine treatment of obsessive-compulsive disorder. I. A controlled clinical trial. *Archives of General Psychiatry*, *37*(11), 1281–1285.

Torp, N. C., Dahl, K., Skarphedinsson, G., Compton, S., Thomsen, P. H., Weidle, B., et al. (2015). Predictors associated with improved cognitive-behavioral therapy outcome in pediatric obsessive-compulsive disorder. *Journal of the American Academy of Child and Adolescent Psychiatry*, *54*(3), 200–207. e201.

Twohig, M. P., Hayes, S. C., Plumb, J. C., Pruitt, L. D., Collins, A. B., Hazlett-Stevens, H., et al. (2010). A randomized clinical trial of acceptance and commitment therapy versus progressive relaxation training for obsessive-compulsive disorder. *Journal of Consulting and Clinical Psychology*, *78*(5), 705–716.

Wagner, K. D., Cook, E. H., Chung, H., & Messig, M. (2003). Remission status after long-term sertraline treatment of pediatric obsessive-compulsive disorder. *Journal of Child and Adolescent Psychopharmacology*, *13*(Suppl. 1), S53–S60.

Walkup, J., Labellarte, M., Riddle, M. A., Pine, D. S., Greenhill, L., Fairbanks, J., et al. (2002). Treatment of pediatric anxiety disorders: An open-label extension of the research units on pediatric psychopharmacology anxiety study. *Journal of Child and Adolescent Psychopharmacology*, *12*(3), 175–188.

Watson, H. J., & Rees, C. S. (2008). Meta-analysis of randomized, controlled treatment trials for pediatric obsessive-compulsive disorder. *Journal of Child Psychology and Psychiatry*, *49*(5), 489–498.

Weidle, B., Melin, K., Drotz, E., Jozefiak, T., & Ivarsson, T. (2012). Preschool and current autistic symptoms in children and adolescents with obsessive-compulsive disorder (OCD). *Journal of Obsessive-Compulsive and Related Disorders*, *1*, 168–174.

Williams, K., Brignell, A., Randall, M., Silove, N., & Hazell, P. (2013). Selective serotonin reuptake inhibitors (SSRIs) for autism spectrum disorders (ASD). *Cochrane Database of Systematic Reviews*, *8*, Cd004677.

Worbe, Y., Mallet, L., Golmard, J. L., Behar, C., Durif, F., Jalenques, I., et al. (2010). Repetitive behaviours in patients with Gilles de la Tourette syndrome: Tics, compulsions, or both? *PLoS ONE*, *5*(9), e12959.

Chapter 10

Relapse Prevention Strategies for Young People With OCD (After CBT)

Georgina Krebs[*,†] and Angela Lewis[†]

[*]*King's College London, London, United Kingdom,* [†]*South London and Maudsley NHS Foundation Trust, London, United Kingdom*

INTRODUCTION

Relapse prevention is a core component of evidence-based protocols of cognitive behavior therapy (CBT) for obsessive-compulsive disorder (OCD) in young people. It encompasses a range of techniques which usually form the focus of the final one or two sessions in a course of CBT (e.g., March & Mulle, 1998; Turner et al., 2014). Research in the field of relapse prevention is limited and therefore the techniques that are used are largely based on clinical understanding and prior utilization in evidence-based treatment protocols, rather than having a formal evidence-base themselves. However, there is evidence that the inclusion of relapse prevention strategies in CBT improves long-term outcomes in OCD patients, which highlights their importance (Hiss, Foa, & Kozak, 1994).

In this chapter we will first provide a brief overview of rates of relapse and predictors of long-term outcomes in OCD. We will then focus on outlining the process of relapse prevention, starting with how this concept can be introduced to a young person and their parents. We will describe the key components of a relapse prevention plan, namely, anticipating triggers, identifying signs of relapse early on, and writing an action plan of what to do if symptoms reemerge. We will also discuss the importance of tackling residual symptoms at the end of a course of CBT and optimizing functioning. Finally, we will consider the role of the therapist and family in supporting the prevention of relapse, as well as some complex issues that the therapist may need to consider. Of note, an assumption throughout this chapter is that relapse prevention strategies are implemented following successful treatment of OCD with CBT that is focused

The Clinician's Guide to Cognitive-Behavioral Therapy for Childhood Obsessive-Compulsive Disorder
http://dx.doi.org/10.1016/B978-0-12-811427-8.00010-1

on *exposure with response prevention* (E/RP). This is in line with the current evidence base of CBT for pediatric OCD (e.g., McGuire et al., 2015) and clinical guidelines (e.g., NICE, 2005).

RELAPSE IN OCD

Before discussing the concept of relapse prevention, it is first important to clarify what is meant by the term "relapse." A relapse can be defined as a return of OCD symptoms following a period of improvement. This period of improvement does not necessarily have to be a full remission, during which the patient no longer meets diagnostic criteria for OCD; a relapse can occur in any patient who has shown a response to treatment, often defined as at least a 35% reduction in OCD symptoms (Mataix-Cols et al., 2016). Many clinicians have suggested that to truly qualify as a relapse, a return of symptoms should be present for at least a month in order to distinguish relapse from a transient flair up or lapse in symptoms (Mataix-Cols et al., 2016). In this chapter, the principles and techniques that are discussed apply to relapse in the broadest sense. In other words, they are applicable to preventing and managing any setback or return of symptoms.

Relatively few prospective studies have been conducted to establish relapse rates in OCD and the majority of these studies have been conducted in small samples and over relatively short follow-up periods. The Brown Longitudinal Obsessive-Compulsive Study (BLOCS) is the largest prospective study to date that has sought to establish long-term outcomes in OCD across the life span. This study found relatively high relapse rates of 59% within a 5-year period among a group of 83 adults who had achieved a full or partial remission from their OCD (Eisen et al., 2013). Encouragingly, BLOCS found lower relapse rates in young people with OCD; a third of young people (12 out of 38) aged 6–18 years who achieved a full or partial remission subsequently relapsed within a 2-year follow-up period (Mancebo et al., 2014). Of note, treatment was uncontrolled in this study, although most patients reported having received both CBT and SSRI medication.

Lower relapse rates have been found among young people who have received CBT for OCD in the highly controlled context of clinical trials (e.g., Asbahr et al., 2005; Barrett, Farrell, Dadds, & Boulter, 2005). For example, Barrett and colleagues found that 16.7% (8 out of 48) young people who received a course of family-based CBT relapsed within 18 months after treatment (Barrett et al., 2005). This may be somewhat of an underestimate of true rates given that individuals who were functioning well may have been more likely to remain in the study therefore biasing the sample. Nevertheless, the results are positive and suggest that relapse rates may be relatively low after protocol-driven CBT that incorporates relapse prevention strategies. Interestingly, in Barrett et al. (2005), all young people who relapsed by the 18-month follow-up did so within the first 12 months following the end of CBT, raising the possibility that if gains can be maintained for a year a more positive prognosis can be expected. Studies comparing relapse rates associated with different modalities of treatment have found better outcomes following CBT as compared to SSRI medication in youth. For example, Asbahr et al. (2005) found relapse rates of 5.3% (1 out of 19) following group CBT compared to 55.6% (10 out of 18) following SSRI treatment by 9-month follow-up.

Understanding the factors associated with relapse in OCD is important as it could help to identify individuals at risk of deterioration and elucidate new effective strategies for its prevention. Most studies that have examined long-term outcomes following CBT have analyzed outcomes at a single time point (e.g., at 12-month follow-up) rather than examining the course of symptoms over time (e.g., from posttreatment to 12-month follow-up). As such they do not differentiate patients who initially respond to treatment and then relapse from those who do not respond to treatment in the first place. A number of factors have been shown to be associated with poorer long-terms outcomes among young people with OCD including earlier age of onset, longer duration of illness, psychiatric comorbidity, higher family dysfunction, and more severe OCD symptoms at pretreatment (Barrett et al., 2005; Micali et al., 2010; Stewart et al., 2004). However, it is not clear whether these variables predict relapse per se as opposed to chronic, persistent symptoms. Importantly, among the few studies that have looked specifically at relapse, it has emerged that individuals who improve during CBT but have residual symptoms remaining at the end of treatment are more likely to relapse than those who achieve a full remission (i.e., have no symptoms or minimal symptoms) (Braga, Cordioli, Niederauer, & Manfro, 2005; Eisen et al., 2013). This finding makes sense from a clinical perspective. If the patient has made progress in overcoming their OCD, but is still harboring some obsessional worries and/or compulsive behaviors, it means that they are still "buying into" the OCD way of thinking to some extent and this is a slippery slope to be on; one extra hand wash can easily become two, then three, and so on. An important part of relapse prevention therefore is to ensure that the young person continues to tackle any residual OCD symptoms, as discussed later in this chapter.

INTRODUCING THE CONCEPT OF RELAPSE PREVENTION IN CBT

Introducing the concept of relapse prevention after successful treatment must be managed with sensitivity. The clinician needs to strike the right balance between being optimistic about the young person's prognosis and reinforcing their achievements, while simultaneously ensuring that the family understands that there is inevitably some risk of relapse. Following successful CBT, some young people and their families will be all too aware of the possibility that OCD may reemerge and will be feeling terrified at the prospect of being left right back where they started. Others will feel so delighted at the incredible progress made in treatment that the possibility of relapse seems remote. The first job of the therapist is therefore to manage these expectations. This can be done by ensuring that a comprehensive understanding of the realities of relapse is shared. In particular, it is important that the young person and their family understand the following:

- Relapse is a real, but manageable, possibility following recovery from OCD.
- Slips can be time limited and easily resolved if relapse prevention strategies are implemented.
- Relapse is less likely to occur if all residual symptoms have been tackled.
- Writing a relapse prevention plan is an effective way to help protect against relapse in the future.

THE RELAPSE PREVENTION PLAN

Toward the end of a successful course of CBT, the young person should feel that they have all the tools that they need to fight OCD. Writing a relapse prevention plan is an opportunity to consolidate these skills and consider how they could be used in the future if needed. The relapse prevention plan is a written document that the young person keeps and serves as a permanent, personalized guide for fighting OCD. The relapse prevention plan will be most effective if it also serves as an engaging reminder of the child's journey toward their eventual triumph over OCD. If they can remember all those really scary things that they were able to do in order to fight OCD, they will feel more confident about doing it again in the future if they need to. Photographs can be a particularly powerful way of achieving this. Any pictures that have been taken of the young person completing their most challenging exposure tasks can be used to decorate their plan. If these are not available, perhaps they can take some pictures of the hobbies or activities that they most enjoy doing now that OCD is not getting in their way.

On a practical note, in order to be useful the relapse prevention plan needs to be easily accessible. The therapist can ensure this by agreeing with the child where they will keep it and who they will share it with. They might want copies to give to family members or others in their support network. Lots of young people like to have a special folder in which they keep their relapse prevention plan or to laminate it in order to make sure that it is kept safe and well looked after.

There are three key components to the relapse prevention plan: anticipating potential triggers, identifying the warning signs, and generating an action plan. Each of these will be explained in detail as follows.

Anticipating Potential Triggers

It is widely accepted among clinicians working with OCD that relapses often occur within the context of stressful life events. For most young people who have successfully completed CBT, the goal in relapse prevention is not to minimize potential future stressors. After all, by this point in treatment the young person will have learnt that anxiety is not something to be feared and avoided but rather it should be confronted and tolerated. Therefore the focus in relapse prevention is on anticipating likely upcoming stressors so that the young person knows to be "on red alert" for OCD at these times, in case symptoms begin to reemerge. This way the young person is much less likely to be caught off guard and they can be prepared to fight back straight away using the CBT tools that they have learnt.

There are two broad categories of life stressors for young people to consider: generalized stressors and idiosyncratic stressors. Generalized stressors are the sorts of transitions, challenges, and events which most young people go through at some point and typically find anxiety provoking. This might include exams, school transitions, moving house, arguments with friends, breakdown of romantic relationships, death of a grandparent, or going to college/university. Many young people will also be able to identify idiosyncratic stressors. In contrast to generalized triggers, these are particular to the young person as they relate to their specific OCD symptoms. In other words, they are situations that are not generally considered to be stressful by all young people but are stressful for the individual due to the nature of their previous or residual OCD symptoms. For example, 14-year-old Jack had been successfully treated for OCD focused on contamination fears. During his relapse prevention sessions, he talked about an upcoming holiday in America where the family would be staying in a recreational vehicle and he anticipated this could be stressful for various reasons. Jack knew that due to practical restrictions the toilet would not be kept as clean as the bathrooms at home and that he would be expected to help out with emptying and contamination dimension out the septic tank with his father, which could possibly trigger some of his contamination fears. In another example, Sian was a 17-year old with a history of obsessions based on fear of harm coming to others and a range of compulsions including tapping, repeating, and mental rituals. During relapse prevention, she said she was planning on starting driving lessons soon and she thought this might be a potential stressor. She suspected that while driving she would be likely to feel an exaggerated sense of responsibility for the safety of pedestrians and other drivers and she wondered whether her OCD might latch onto this with a strong urge to carry out compulsions.

Identifying the Warning Signs

Once any upcoming generalized and idiosyncratic stressors in the young person's life have been discussed and written down, attention can turn toward establishing what the signs of relapse are likely to be. The aim here is to anticipate which symptoms would reemerge first if a setback were to occur, and how the young person would recognize them. Young people might ask why they need to do this: surely if it comes to it, recognizing the return of OCD will be easy? In reality, however, symptoms are not always immediately obvious. While young people are usually capable of identifying their warning signs at a time when they are in recovery and able to take an objective stance, it is much trickier to do this once OCD has started to take a hold and is impacting on their insight.

When identifying warning signs, the primary focus is usually on obsessions and compulsions. Ideally, these warning signs will be as concrete as possible so that the young person and their family know exactly what they need to keep an eye out for. The young person and their family can work together to list the obsessions and compulsions that they suspect could be early indicators of OCD. This exercise is of course about making a best guess; there will be no way of knowing for sure what OCD will look like in the case of a relapse. Thinking through the following questions can help guide this process:

- Which were the initial symptoms to develop the first time around?
- What was the hardest symptom to tackle in CBT?
- Are there any residual symptoms?
- What would other people such as parents and siblings notice first?

Thirteen-year-old Cassie had been treated for OCD, which presented mainly as obsessions and compulsions regarding contamination. She felt that her early warning signs would be cutting her nails very short and starting to wash her hands a second time. These were two of Cassie's first ever compulsions and she still had trouble challenging them from time to time. By the end of treatment Cassie was able to resist cutting her nails excessively short, but she had not managed to grow them long as part of an anti-OCD task. She suspected a second hand wash would be an early warning sign because it would be such a simple, quick behavior that she could quite easily fail to spot it as a compulsion if it crept in.

Sometimes young people say they are not sure what to look out for because their OCD has shifted and changed in the past, so if it comes back it may well look different again. In this case the therapist can explain that although compulsions sometimes do change with time, evidence suggests that any new compulsions would most likely still fall within the same symptom dimensions (e.g., the cleaning/contamination dimension; de la Cruz et al., 2013).

Other significant people in the young person's life, in particular parents and siblings, should always be included in the discussion about warning signs as they too will need to be vigilant for relapse indicators. Anecdotally, parents sometimes report that they notice compulsions before their child does, particularly where insight is poor (e.g., younger children, children with comorbid ASD, young people with chronic OCD). Sixteen-year-old Katie's mother was convinced that if OCD reemerged, the earliest signs of this would be that Katie would start asking her mother to put things away for her (e.g., packing up school books, folding away her laundry). She also predicted that she and Katie's dad would start receiving more text messages throughout the day asking whether they were ok.

If a child struggles to predict which obsessions and compulsions are most likely to reemerge first in a relapse, it can be helpful to focus on the additional warning signs such as broader changes in behavior, mood, and functioning. For example, 15-year-old Paulo's OCD presented predominantly as repeating rituals, but the compulsions themselves had changed significantly over the course of his illness (tapping, walking compulsions, repeating phrases in his head, and excessive blinking). He had also at times engaged in repetitive hand washing and some checking rituals. Paulo felt that his OCD could sneak back with completely new compulsions and he did not feel confident that he would be able to notice these straight away. He did feel sure, however, that one of the most obvious changes that he would notice would be that he would start to have less time to do the things that he enjoys, in particular playing on his computer and going out with his friends. He predicted that his school work would also suffer and that he would probably notice himself feeling more agitated than usual.

Generating an Action Plan

Once the young person and their family feel confident in identifying the warning signs of a relapse, it is time to think through the specifics of what they would actually do in this scenario. This is called the *action plan* (Derisley, Heyman, Robinson, & Turner, 2008) and it is a central component of relapse prevention as it outlines the set of strategies that the young person will actually use should they encounter a setback (see Box 1, for an example). Every action plan will be unique to the child, but there are a number of points that should always be incorporated. These include the following:

- Key learning points from psychoeducation about anxiety (e.g., anxiety is a protective mechanism and not harmful; anxiety always subsides over time naturally, without doing a ritual; if you repeatedly confront a feared situation, anxiety eventually extinguishes altogether)
- What they know about intrusive thoughts (e.g., intrusive thoughts are normal and experienced by everyone)
- Fundamental principles of how to set up an E/RP task (e.g., carrying out exposure in a graded way, staying in the feared situation long enough for anxiety to habituate, keeping an eye out for covert compulsions)
- The need to act early when fighting back
- The importance of letting significant people know about the OCD (e.g., parents, siblings, friends, therapist, teachers)
- How other people can help (e.g., what should they say back to OCD)

This information should be elicited from the child as much as possible through Socratic questioning and written down in the child's own words. An engaging way to generate and consolidate this information can be to do an OCD quiz. Children can even compete against their parents to see who scores the most points by remembering what they have learnt about anxiety, OCD, and fighting

BOX 1 Ten-Year-Old Charlotte's Action Plan

If OCD tries to sneak back - my fighting back plan!

- Tell Mum and Dad straight away
- Use my golden rules
  1. Always do the opposite of what OCD says
  2. If it is hard then break it down into small steps
  3. Keep practising everyday
- My anxiety will go in the end and it won't hurt me
- OCD talks rubbish so don't listen!
- I beat OCD before so I can again!

back. Pretend interviews and role-plays can also be effective ways to bolster what young people and their families already know. Children might like to interview their parents, siblings, or therapist to find out what they think they could do to support the young person's recovery. This should include the specifics of what other people need to say back to OCD if they notice any subtle requests for reassurance or accommodation. Role-plays can be used in various ways. One popular format involves the therapist pretending to be OCD, verbalizing all the scary intrusive thoughts that the young person could experience in the future if they experienced a setback (Waite & Williams, 2009). In this role-play, the young person's task is to practice ignoring OCD and/or using positive self-talk to cope with the intrusive thoughts (e.g., "This is just OCD trying to trick me").

TACKLING RESIDUAL SYMPTOMS AND OVERCOMING CORE FEARS

After generating an action plan that the young person can utilize *in the future* if needed, it is helpful to focus on what can be done in the *here and now* to reduce the likelihood of relapse. In most cases, young people will have some residual symptoms at the end of treatment. As described earlier, residual symptoms are likely to increase the risk of relapse and therefore the goal should be to overcome any remaining obsessions and compulsions. There may be clinical, social, or practical reasons for ending the course of CBT despite residual symptoms, rather than continuing sessions until they have been eliminated. In these instances, the therapist can emphasize to the young person that the end of the course of CBT does not mean the end of treatment, and that they now have the skills to be their own therapist. They can therefore continue to tackle any remaining symptoms independently, with support from their parents if needed. In order to optimize this process, the therapist and young person should make a concrete and specific plan of how the residual symptoms will be tackled over the weeks and months following the end of therapy. This will primarily involve planning suitable E/RP tasks and problem-solving any potential obstacles to completing these tasks. At this stage in treatment, it is important that the therapist allows the young person to take the lead with designing their own exposure tasks, in order to build their confidence in fighting OCD independently.

In addition, during relapse prevention sessions, the therapist should encourage the young person to consider more extreme E/RP tasks in order to confront and overcome their core fear/s. To this end, the therapist can introduce the concept of *overlearning* as described later.

Overlearning

Overlearning is the process whereby new skills are practiced passed the point of initial mastery. In the context of exposure-based CBT, overlearning refers to carrying out relatively extreme exposure tasks that push the patient beyond the limits of normal, day-to-day life. For example, a patient with a fear of contamination might be encouraged to put their hand down a toilet. The rationale for overlearning is that it enables the patient to fully confront and overcome their core fear. In contrast to other E/RP tasks, overlearning tasks are not something that the young person would be expected to do regularly. In fact, an overlearning task may be a one-off E/RP task that is performed as the "ultimate proof" that the young person has beaten their OCD. For example, Katie was a 12-year-old girl who had an obsessional fear of sticky substances, particularly chewing gum. Katie made fantastic progress in CBT and for her "ultimate fighting back task" she chose to put on a swimsuit and cover her entire body in chewing and bubble gum. Jonny was a 14-year-old boy who had obsessional thoughts about symmetry accompanied by extreme "evening out" rituals, as well as contamination fears and avoidance of any possible source of germs. For his overlearning task, he decided to eat a sandwich off a toilet seat, while standing asymmetrically on one leg and with one arm behind his back. Daneesh was a 16-year old with an obsessional fear of leaving behind a trace of himself wherever he went. At the end of therapy, Daneesh wrote his name down on pieces of paper and left these in all sorts of places: tucked under car windscreen wipers, buried in rubbish bins, nestled in a flower bed. He even posted some of the slips of paper through mail boxes.

Given that overlearning tasks usually involve doing something out of the ordinary, it is particularly important that identifying an overlearning task is a collaborative process involving the young person, therapist, and parents/carers. It is usually important to have parental approval for overlearning tasks given the relatively extreme nature of the exposure. Moreover, it is essential that the rationale for overlearning is clear to both the young person and parent, otherwise they are likely to wonder why on earth you are talking about putting your hand down a toilet, for example, given that no "normal" person does that anyway. The following height phobia analogy can be helpful when introducing the notion of overlearning:

> *Therapist:* "I want to tell you about Fred. Fred was a man who had a terrible fear of heights. He was so scared of heights that he always stayed on the ground floor in buildings. This meant that he couldn't go to visit his friend who lived on the fourth floor in a block of flats. He really wanted to overcome his fear so that he could visit his friend, so bit by bit he started facing his fear of heights. He practiced going up to the first floor, then the second floor, then the third floor, until eventually he could go all the way up to the fourth floor of a building. He was so pleased that he went straight around to see his friend. He got into the lift to go up to the fourth floor but accidentally pressed the button for the sixth floor. The lift took him all the way up and before he knew it he was on the sixth floor. What do you think happened when he realized?"
>
> *Young person:* "He probably panicked."
>
> *Therapist:* "Yes! Why?"
>
> *Young person:* "Because he had only practiced going up to the fourth floor, not any higher."
>
> *Therapist:* "Yes, that's right. So what do you think he needed to do to truly overcome him fear of heights once and for all?"
>
> *Young person:* "Go skydiving?"
>
> *Therapist:* "Exactly! So how do you think this relates to fighting OCD?"
>
> *Young person:* "In order to really beat OCD I need to do an extreme challenge."

Planning overlearning tasks can often raise ethical dilemmas for therapists. The therapist might wonder "Is this exposure task *too* extreme?" and question where they should draw the line. For example, for a young person with contamination fears, the therapist might feel that eating off a toilet seat is an appropriate overlearning task whereas putting their hand down the toilet is too extreme. Of course there is no absolute right or wrong when it comes to deciding how far to go with overlearning tasks, and the rationale and appropriateness needs to be carefully considered with the young person and family.

Although overlearning tasks are of course anxiety provoking for the young person, they can often be approached with humor particularly given that they usually involve doing something bizarre or over the top. Overlearning tasks should also be framed as a celebration and the final stage in the young person's journey of fighting OCD, a message which is often motivating for the patient. Many young people like to photograph their overlearning task as a permanent record of their victory over OCD. Such an image can serve as a powerful reminder of CBT and recovery if a relapse of symptoms occurs in the future.

Motivation to Tackle Residual Symptoms

Anecdotally, it is relatively common that young people with OCD lose motivation to fight OCD toward the end of treatment once their symptoms have significantly improved. By this point, the young person might be functioning very well and experiencing minimal impairment in day-to-day life as a result of OCD. It is understandable therefore that the "pros" of continuing to fight OCD (i.e., marginal improvement in daily life) start to feel outweighed by the "cons" (i.e., the effort required and distress experienced by ongoing E/RP). For example, Ruby was a 16-year old with obsessions and compulsions related to a fear of harm coming to her family. Her compulsions were wide ranging and included mental rituals, checking behaviors, and tapping and rubbing compulsions. She worked hard in CBT and managed to challenge most of her compulsions with fantastic results. By the end of treatment however, Ruby still engaged in a few low-level compulsions such as wiggling her toes and rubbing her fingers together. She described these as "habits" which did not really bother her, and so she felt it was more effort than it was worth to try to stop them. When this situation arises, it is important to communicate the notion that continuing to tackle residual symptoms is essential to optimize *long-term outcome*, not just improve *current functioning*. This discussion can be facilitated by use of the following analogy:

> *Therapist:* "OCD is a bit like a weed. You really want to get rid of it, and so you start cutting it down. You cut away and it is gets smaller and smaller and less and less noticeable. Once you have cut the weed right down so that you can barely see it, it might be tempting to stop and leave it as it is. After all, if you can hardly see it, that's good enough isn't it? But what do you think would happen if you did leave it?"
> *Young person:* "I suppose the weed would eventually grow back"
> *Therapist:* "Exactly. If you leave a bit of the weed there, it will start to grow back. So to get rid of a weed for good, what do you think you need to do?"
> *Young person:* "You need to get rid of *all* of it."
> *Therapist:* "Yes, you're right. You need to pull the weed out at the roots. And that is the same with OCD. If we leave a few worries and habits, even

> little ones, they might grow and get bigger and bigger. To make sure that OCD stays out of your life, we need to pull it out at the roots. In other words, we need to completely get rid of even the small worries and habits."

A similar analogy is treating an infection, whereby the therapist asks the young person what would be the problem with stopping taking antibiotics before an infection is 100% better (i.e., there is a risk that the infection would return and spread; Challacombe, Oldfield, & Salkovskis, 2011). Both analogies are helpful because they highlight the need to continue using treatment strategies in order to protect the future, even when the problem feels largely under control in the here and now. It can be helpful to explicitly discuss overcoming residual symptoms in terms of being an "investment for the future," maximizing the young person's chance of achieving their long-term goals.

LOOKING TO THE FUTURE: FILLING THE OCD GAP

Time-consuming rituals, distressing obsessions, and anxious avoidance mean that OCD can have a devastating impact on young people's lives. In the most severe cases, young people completely withdraw from education and social functioning, and may need substantial assistance to carry out even basic daily living tasks such as toileting and getting dressed. Even in less severe cases, it is common for young people with OCD to become restricted in their functioning and engage in a limited range of activities (Piacentini, Bergman, Keller, & McCracken, 2003). A key part of recovery, in addition to tackling OCD symptoms themselves, is rebuilding activities and "reclaiming life" (Challacombe et al., 2011; Derisley et al., 2008). For some young people, this happens relatively effortlessly and spontaneously as they experience their OCD symptoms improve. However, other young people require significant support to reintegrate into educational, social, and leisure activities. Reinstating general functioning is important from a relapse prevention perspective because it provides motivation to carry on resisting OCD and without it, there is a risk that obsessional thinking and rituals will gradually creep back in to fill the void that was left by OCD. For example, Tony was a 17-year old with OCD involving unwanted intrusive sexual thoughts about children. At its worst, his OCD had led to him becoming housebound. He had previously responded well to a course of CBT for OCD, but remained out of education and with no social activities. His days were spent largely at home watching films and playing video games. At the point of rereferral, he reported an increasing level of OCD symptoms. He remembered the CBT strategies he had learnt, but was struggling to implement them and felt "what is the point?" It was agreed that he would receive another course of treatment, with the main focus being on functional goals. With the support of his therapist, he joined two film clubs, applied for a part-time job, and gained a place on a higher education course. Through these activities he made a network of friends and developed a good social life. He began using CBT strategies to fight his OCD symptoms again and by the end of treatment his OCD symptoms were in the subclinical range. These gains were maintained over a 12-month follow-up period.

In order to encourage improved global functioning, it is helpful to revisit and update the young person's long-term goals that were set at the beginning of therapy. For some patients, it may be necessary to provide practical support and guidance to help them to take the necessary steps toward achieving their goals, particularly if their OCD has been relatively severe and chronic. For example, if they are interested in pursuing further education after a period of absenteeism, they may require assistance in navigating the educational system.

In thinking about rebuilding their life, some young people report feeling sad about the time they wasted with OCD and key events in their childhood or adolescence that they missed. In such cases, it is helpful to normalize this perspective and encourage the young person to see this as all the more reason for them to achieve their future goals and to not let OCD rob them of their life any longer. In most cases, looking forward to the future is a bright note to end on. The young person can reflect on what they are now looking forward to doing without OCD standing in their way. Young children can be presented with a certificate of achievement to punctuate the end of treatment and to celebrate their triumph over OCD (March & Mulle, 1998).

THE CONTINUING ROLE OF THE THERAPIST AND FAMILY

Given that relapse following CBT for OCD is a very real possibility, continued support might be necessary. As discussed earlier, there is some indication that the 12 months following treatment may be a critical period and that if young people maintain gains during this time they are less likely to subsequently experience a relapse in OCD (Barrett et al., 2005). Wherever possible, therefore, the young person should be offered periodic reviews over the first year posttreatment to assess their progress and refresh their knowledge of CBT strategies (NICE, 2005). It may be optimal to offer these follow-up appointments at progressively longer intervals (e.g., 1 month, 3 months, 6 months, and 12 months following treatment completion) in order to offer a graded approach to withdrawal from therapeutic support.

Parents can support their child as they transition away from regular therapeutic input by carrying out periodic reviews at home. By the end of treatment parents will have probably practiced taking the role of cotherapist and they will be well versed in the treatment of OCD. They can use this valuable experience to help their child tackle any residual symptoms. Weekly family meetings can be set up at home, ideally at the same time each week to ensure adherence. The aim here is for parents to have an opportunity to "check in" on OCD, congratulate their child on his or her efforts to fight OCD that week, and to help their child set up E/RP tasks for the coming week.

What Happens If a Relapse Does Occur?

A comprehensive relapse prevention plan does not, of course, guarantee that relapse will not occur. Sometimes it does despite everyone's best efforts. In this case the therapist will be crucial in supporting a rapid return to recovery. When tackling a relapse, the young person and family are likely to feel understandably dejected. The therapist can help by using language such as "setback" or "slip" which implies that this is a temporary episode. It can be powerful for the therapist to positively reframe the relapse as a useful opportunity to consolidate what has been learnt, which can ultimately contribute to a more robust recovery. By independently practicing the skills they have learnt when OCD does reappear, the young person can truly become fully accomplished at fighting OCD. Therefore while these episodes can be frightening, they are also really valuable learning experiences. Without going through a setback, how else would they know that they can cope with it?

The first step for the therapist is to assess the extent of the setback and to consider the level of intervention which may be required. To do this they might consider:

- Symptom severity and current functional impairment
- Duration of the lapse or relapse
- Risk (e.g., harm caused by compulsions, suicidality)
- Any strategies that have already been tried (e.g., from the relapse prevention plan)

In the first instance, directing the young person back through their relapse prevention plan—the action plan in particular—is often all that is needed in order to help them get back on track. At times, however, more substantial intervention may be required. For example, booster sessions might be offered if symptoms continue to persist for a number of weeks despite the implementation of relapse prevention strategies, or where relapse is so severe that risk is high (e.g., food restriction) or there is marked functional impairment (e.g., complete school refusal).

In order to ensure that booster sessions are as effective as possible, the therapist should establish whether there are particular aspects of the CBT protocol which need to be focused on. There may have been a cluster of symptoms which were not adequately challenged in treatment. Perhaps certain obsessions or compulsions were not disclosed due to feelings of shame and embarrassment. Alternatively, the young person may not have fully engaged in the more challenging E/RP tasks or overlearning tasks, leaving their core fear intact. For example Jack, described earlier, relapsed approximately 6 months following the end of his course of CBT. His relapse was sudden and his symptoms quickly escalated to a severe level. He had felt so overwhelmed that he had not been able to utilize his relapse prevention plan. Upon reviewing his previous treatment with his therapist, they realized that although Jack had reached the top of his compulsions hierarchy, he had struggled to complete any overlearning tasks because he found the prospect too scary. His therapist explained that this probably meant that his core fear about contamination from feces had not been fully challenged. Jack was offered a course of six booster sessions with the agreement that the focus would be on extreme exposure tasks which would involve Jack pushing himself beyond what might be considered normal limits. Jack engaged well and achieved a full remission from his OCD, which was maintained over a subsequent 12-month follow-up period.

Following recovery from a relapse, it is important that the young person reflects on their experience. There are often immensely valuable lessons to be learnt; what did they do well and what could they do even better if there is a "next time"? They might want to make changes to their relapse prevention plan now that they have direct experience of relapse. Fundamentally, though, the young person has learnt that they *can* recover from a relapse. Acknowledging this alone can be remarkably powerful. Following a brief lapse 3 months after she had recovered from OCD, 16-year-old Yolanda reflected on her experience of fighting back without her therapist's help: "*After treatment you're in a sort of bubble of recovery where everything's great and you don't really want to think about relapse. Then you have your first dip and the bubble bursts. But I'm glad that it happened because now I've tested the waters and I know that I can cope and resist OCD all by myself. I can use this experience next time to remind myself of what I'm able to do—a bit like when I ate chocolate off a toilet seat!.*"

COMPLEX ISSUES IN RELAPSE PREVENTION

In more complex cases, additional factors may require consideration at the relapse prevention stage of CBT in order to optimize long-term outcomes. Although not an exhaustive list, three common issues are outlined here.

First, comorbid psychiatric disorders may need to be considered at the relapse prevention stage of CBT. Comorbidity is highly common in pediatric OCD, affecting up to 80% of patients (POTS, 2004). In some cases, comorbidity occurs secondary to OCD and improves as OCD symptoms reduce. For example, depressive symptoms commonly improve following CBT for OCD (Brown, Lester, Jassi, & Krebs, 2015). In other cases, the comorbid disorder/s will persist despite remission of OCD and clinical experience suggests that this may render the young person vulnerable to relapse. It is important that clinicians reassess comorbid psychopathology toward the end of CBT, consider whether further intervention is indicated and if so, facilitate access to appropriate treatment.

Second, certain developmental profiles may make some individuals more vulnerable to an OCD relapse. For example, young people with autism spectrum disorders or learning disabilities are likely to find it harder to learn the abstract principles that are central to CBT for OCD (e.g., anxiety habituation) and will therefore struggle to generalize their application to any new symptoms that emerge following successful treatment. These individuals may require more intensive and longer term support from parents and therapists to maintain treatment gains. Furthermore, individuals with neurodevelopmental disorders may require a more systemic approach to relapse prevention. In particular, it is important to ensure that their full range of emotional, social, and education needs are being met. This is not only to optimize functioning in these domains, but also to minimize excessive and unnecessary levels of stress that might otherwise be experienced and could trigger an OCD relapse. For example, if a young person has learning difficulties and is not receiving adequate educational support, this is likely to be an understandable source of anxiety for them which could increase their risk of relapse.

Third, some young people who complete a course of CBT for OCD will be taking concurrent SSRI medication. Indeed, SSRI medication is another evidence-based treatment for OCD (Watson & Rees, 2008). For young people who are taking medication, relapse prevention sessions at the end of a successful course of CBT should include agreeing a medication management plan. This should be made in collaboration with the prescribing doctor, the young person, and their parents. Clinical guidelines recommend that young people should remain on a stable dose of medication for 6–12 months following recovery from OCD to consolidate treatment gains and then withdrawn gradually over several months (Geller & March, 2012; NICE, 2005). Where possible, CBT booster sessions should be offered at the point of medication withdrawal as this may reduce the risk of relapse (Geller & March, 2012; NICE, 2005).

CONCLUSIONS

In summary, even after a successful course of CBT young people are vulnerable to experiencing a relapse in their OCD. For this reason, relapse prevention is a crucial component of CBT for children and adolescents with OCD. It involves minimizing the risk of relapse in the future by tackling residual symptoms and optimizing current functioning, in conjunction with anticipating and planning for potential setbacks (see Box 2). The therapist and parents play a central role in relapse prevention. In more complex cases, other professionals may be involved in a relapse prevention plan, including other mental health professionals and school personnel. Following relapse prevention work, the young person and their parents should feel optimistic about their future and confident that they can tackle any OCD challenges that may emerge. Further research is needed to identify factors associated with relapse in pediatric OCD, which may inform the development of more effective relapse prevention strategies and ultimately improve long-term outcomes in this population.

BOX 2 Key Components of Relapse Prevention

- Anticipating *potential triggers* to relapse, including generalized and idiosyncratic stressors
- Identifying the *warning signs* of relapse, including spotting the recurrence of obsessions and compulsions, changes in mood and functioning
- Generating an *action plan* of what to do if a setback occurs, including knowledge of anxiety and E/RP
- *Tackling residual symptoms,* including introducing extreme exposure and overlearning tasks to overcome core fears
- *Optimizing current functioning*—reinstating activities and interests to fill the OCD gap
- *Regular follow-up appointments* with therapist for 12 months after CBT

REFERENCES

Asbahr, F. R., Castillo, A. R., Ito, L. M., Latorre, M. R., Moreira, M. N., & Lotufo-Neto, F. (2005). Group cognitive-behavioral therapy versus sertraline for the treatment of children and adolescents with obsessive-compulsive disorder. *Journal of the American Academy of Child and Adolescent Psychiatry*, *44*(11), 1128–1136. http://dx.doi.org/10.1097/01.chi.0000177324.40005.6f.

Barrett, P., Farrell, L., Dadds, M., & Boulter, N. (2005). Cognitive-behavioral family treatment of childhood obsessive-compulsive disorder: Long-term follow-up and predictors of outcome. *Journal of the American Academy of Child and Adolescent Psychiatry*, *44*(10), 1005–1014.

Braga, D. T., Cordioli, A. V., Niederauer, K., & Manfro, G. G. (2005). Cognitive-behavioral group therapy for obsessive–compulsive disorder: A 1-year follow-up. *Acta Psychiatrica Scandinavica*, *112*(3), 180–186. http://dx.doi.org/10.1111/j.1600-0447.2005.00559.x.

Brown, H. M., Lester, K. J., Jassi, A., Heyman, I., & Krebs, G. (2015). Paediatric obsessive-compulsive disorder and depressive symptoms: Clinical correlates and CBT treatment outcomes. *Journal of Abnormal Child Psychology*, *43*(5), 933.

Challacombe, F., Oldfield, V. B., & Salkovskis, P. M. (2011). *Break free from OCD: Overcoming obsessive compulsive disorder with CBT*. London: Vermillion.

de la Cruz, L. F., Micali, N., Roberts, S., Turner, C., Nakatani, E., Heyman, I., & Mataix-Cols, D. (2013). Are the symptoms of obsessive-compulsive disorder temporally stable in children/adolescents? A prospective naturalistic study. *Psychiatry Research*, *209*(2), 196–201.

Derisley, J., Heyman, I., Robinson, S., & Turner, C. (2008). *Breaking free from OCD: A CBT guide for young people and their families*. London: Jessica Kingsley Publishers.

Eisen, J. L., Sibrava, N. J., Boisseau, C. L., Mancebo, M. C., Stout, R. L., Pinto, A., et al. (2013). Five-year course of obsessive-compulsive disorder: Predictors of remission and relapse. *The Journal of Clinical Psychiatry*, *74*(3), 233–239. http://dx.doi.org/10.4088/JCP.12 m07657.

Geller, D. A., & March, J. (2012). Practice parameter for the assessment and treatment of children and adolescents with obsessive-compulsive disorder. *Journal of the American Academy of Child and Adolescent Psychiatry*, *51*(1), 98–113. http://dx.doi.org/10.1016/j.jaac.2011.09.019.

Hiss, H., Foa, E. B., & Kozak, M. J. (1994). Relapse prevention program for treatment of obsessive-compulsive disorder. *Journal of Consulting and Clinical Psychology*, *62*(4), 801–808.

Mancebo, M. C., Boisseau, C. L., Garnaat, S., Eisen, J. L., Greenberg, B., Sibrava, N. J., et al. (2014). Long-term course of pediatric obsessive-compulsive disorder: Three years of prospective follow-up. *Comprehensive Psychiatry*, *55*, 1498–1504.

March, J. S., & Mulle, K. (1998). *OCD in children and adolescents: A cognitive-behavioral treatment manual*. New York: Guilford Press.

Mataix-Cols, D., de la Cruz, L. F., Nordsletten, A. E., Lenhard, F., Isomura, K., & Simpson, H. B. (2016). Towards an international expert consensus for defining treatment response, remission, recovery and relapse in obsessive-compulsive disorder. *World Psychiatry*, *15*(1), 80–81. http://dx.doi.org/10.1002/wps.20299.

McGuire, J. F., Piacentini, J., Lewin, A. B., Brennan, E. A., Murphy, T. K., & Storch, E. A. (2015). A meta-analysis of cognitive behavior therapy and medication for child obsessive-compulsive disorder: Moderators of treatment efficacy, response and remission. *Depression and Anxiety*, *32*(8), 580–593. http://dx.doi.org/10.1002/da.22389.

Micali, N., Heyman, I., Perez, M., Hilton, K., Nakatani, E., Turner, C., et al. (2010). Long-term outcomes of obsessive–compulsive disorder: Follow-up of 142 children and adolescents. *The British Journal of Psychiatry*, *197*(2), 128–134.

NICE. (2005). *Obsessive-compulsive disorder: Core interventions in the treatment of obsessive-compulsive disorder and body dysmorphic disorder*. London: NICE.

Piacentini, J., Bergman, R. L., Keller, M., & McCracken, J. (2003). Functional impairment in children and adolescents with obsessive-compulsive disorder. *Journal of Child and Adolescent Psychopharmacology*, *13*(2, Suppl. 1), 61–69.

POTS. (2004). Cognitive-behavior therapy, sertraline, and their combination for children and adolescents with obsessive-compulsive disorder: The Pediatric OCD Treatment Study (POTS) randomized controlled trial. *The Journal of the American Medical Association*, *292*(16), 1969–1976. http://dx.doi.org/10.1001/jama.292.16.1969.

Stewart, S., Geller, D., Jenike, M., Pauls, D., Shaw, D., Mullin, B., et al. (2004). Long-term outcome of pediatric obsessive–compulsive disorder: A meta-analysis and qualitative review of the literature. *Acta Psychiatrica Scandinavica*, *110*(1), 4–13.

Turner, C. M., Mataix-Cols, D., Lovell, K., Krebs, G., Lang, K., Byford, S., et al. (2014). Telephone cognitive-behavioral therapy for adolescents with obsessive-compulsive disorder: A randomized controlled non-inferiority trial. *Journal of the American Academy of Child and Adolescent Psychiatry*, *53*(12), 1298–1307, . http://dx.doi.org/10.1016/j.jaac.2014.09.012.e1292.

Waite, P., & Williams, T. (2009). *Obsessive compulsive disorder: Cognitive behaviour therapy with children and young people (CBT with children, adolescents and families)*. London: Routledge.

Watson, H. J., & Rees, C. S. (2008). Meta-analysis of randomized, controlled treatment trials for pediatric obsessive-compulsive disorder. *Journal of Child Psychology and Psychiatry*, *49*(5), 489–498.

Chapter 11

Addressing Common Myths and Mistaken Beliefs in the Treatment of Youth With OCD

Shannon M. Blakey*, Benjamin E. Thomas†, and Nicholas R. Farrell†
**University of North Carolina, Chapel Hill, NC, United States, †Rogers Memorial Hospital, Oconomowoc, WI, United States*

Marked by significant impairment in academic, social, and familial functioning (Piacentini, Bergman, Keller, & McCracken, 2003), obsessive-compulsive disorder (OCD) affects about 1%–2% of youth (Piacentini, Peris, Bergman, Chang, & Jaffer, 2007). Without treatment, the disorder tends to follow a chronic, unremitting course that often persists into adulthood and is responsible for further morbidity. Accordingly, there is increasing emphasis on early intervention to effectively address OCD in youth.

Cognitive-behavioral therapy (CBT) with exposure and response prevention (ERP) has been identified as an effective intervention to treat OCD in youth. However, in spite of its effectiveness, the successful dissemination of CBT has been hindered by a number of commonly held yet mistaken beliefs about the treatment's safety, tolerability, and overall applicability to youth with OCD. Importantly, these beliefs negatively influence prospective youth clients' and their parents' willingness to engage in ERP. It is therefore very important that clinicians amply prepare themselves to identify these beliefs and address them efficiently.

The aim of this chapter is to provide guidance to clinicians for effectively addressing notable myths about the use of ERP to treat OCD in youth. Herein, we present six relatively common albeit mistaken beliefs about the treatment. For each belief, we review extant literature on the nature of the concern as well as empirical research that counters the concern. We then offer readers a summary of suggestions for effectively addressing each mistaken belief in the context of clinical practice. Finally, such suggestions are illustrated via hypothetical dialogs between a concerned youth client and a clinician.

The Clinician's Guide to Cognitive-Behavioral Therapy for Childhood Obsessive-Compulsive Disorder
http://dx.doi.org/10.1016/B978-0-12-811427-8.00011-3

BELIEF 1: ERP POSES UNACCEPTABLY HIGH RISK OF HARM

Nature and Validity of This Belief

Clinicians treating OCD in youth are likely to be confronted with concerns about the potential for ERP to result in harmful consequences. This belief is well documented among clinicians (e.g., Deacon, Farrell, et al., 2013; Deacon, Lickel, Farrell, Kemp, & Hipol, 2013) and is likely to be held by some youth and their family members. Regarding the nature of the anticipated consequences, it appears one of the foremost concerns is that ERP could directly result in a medical emergency, such as a seizure or loss of consciousness (Deacon & Farrell, 2013). Relatedly, some individuals may endorse the belief that approaching feared stimuli during exposure can lead to harm (e.g., acquiring a serious illness from a public toilet). The general idea of harm resulting from exposure to feared stimuli underlies many OCD symptoms and is thus likely to be held by many youth with OCD. Additionally, it is plausible that some parents as well as clinicians harbor similar concerns, which presents a critical barrier to effective implementation of ERP (Deacon & Farrell, 2013). Physical and medical concerns aside, there is also the belief that ERP poses a high risk for *psychological* harm. To illustrate, previous research has identified several notable concerns about exposure causing acute exacerbation of symptoms or other forms of mental "decompensation" (e.g., severe dissociation or psychosis; Feeny, Hembree, & Zoellner, 2003).

From a broad perspective, the likelihood of ERP causing harm to youth with OCD appears to be very minimal. There is ample literature highlighting that physical and/or psychological harm are very unlikely to occur as a result of experiencing heightened anxiety. For example, a survey study of clinicians found that among over 6500 clients receiving intensive ERP, the occurrence of highly severe physical or psychological consequences was nonexistent (e.g., heart attack, permanent psychosis), and the occurrence of less serious mishaps (e.g., vomiting, passing out) was extremely low (i.e., less than 0.1% chance; Deacon, Lickel, et al., 2013). Moreover, much has been written about the theoretical incompatibility of heightened anxiety and physical harm (e.g., Barlow & Craske, 2007). Anxiety serves an important evolutionary function (i.e., preparing to escape threat) aiding humans in adapting to their environment, and it is therefore improbable that anxiety could cause direct physical or psychological harm.

With regard to the belief that encountering feared stimuli in ERP can harm youth with OCD, there are some important considerations. It is inherent within ERP that confronting exposure stimuli does involve some—albeit minimal—risk for harm. However, it is important that the clinician, parent, and youth have a mutual understanding that the primary objective of ERP is to help the youngster learn to accept minor risks that most individuals regularly encounter without ever being certain that feared outcomes cannot occur (Abramowitz, Deacon, & Whiteside, 2011). When conducted properly, exposure to feared stimuli entails acceptably low risk for harm, which is accomplished through clinicians considering youths' safety in creating and implementing ERP tasks. It is outside the scope of this chapter to provide a comprehensive guide to ensuring maximal safety in effectively delivering ERP; however, we refer readers to the helpful suggestions put forth by Olatunji, Deacon, and Abramowitz (2009).

Addressing This Belief in Clinical Practice

Clinicians who encounter concerns among youth with OCD and/or their parents about ERP being harmful are encouraged to first normalize this concern; past research has shown that many clients are initially apprehensive about the potential for ERP to cause harm (Rowa et al., 2014). Depending on the specific nature of the belief, the clinician may then select a strategy aimed at refuting this concern.

For youth and parents fearful of being harmed either physically or psychologically by the mere experience of elevated anxiety, the clinician may describe the extremely low likelihood of these occurrences (Deacon, Lickel, et al., 2013). Given that many youths are likely to have difficulty understanding even the most well-described summaries of empirical studies, it would be prudent for the clinician to instead use an anecdotal example of a previous youth who encountered heightened levels of anxiety but did not experience any significant harm. The clinician may also elect to implement an abbreviated course of interoceptive exposure to disconfirm the belief that intense anxiety can be physically or psychologically harmful (Barlow & Craske, 2007).

It can be somewhat of a delicate "dance" to address youths' concerns about being harmed by their exposure stimuli. As mentioned previously, these concerns often underlie core OCD symptomatology (e.g., believing that one will be responsible for a house fire when using an electrical appliance). Thus the clinician must use caution in attempting to refute these concerns without reassuring the youth of absolute safety. In our experience, it works well to discuss the *seemingly low likelihood* of negative consequences with the youth (and parent if needed) while still remaining open to all outcomes—safe and unsafe—that could possibly occur. In this manner, the clinician can impart confidence in the youth's ability to confront feared stimuli while still allowing for the belief to be disconfirmed via direct experience.

The suggestions outlined previously are depicted in the following dialog between a clinician and a 15-year-old client (Marco), who recently obtained his driver's learning permit but was fearful that he would cause serious accident.

Clinician: It sounds like you have some concerns about ERP, Marco.

Marco: Yes. I understand it, but it freaks me out to even think about driving. I know I'll be really scared. What if it gets so bad that something terrible happens?

Clinician: What are you concerned could happen during your driving exposures?
Marco: Well, I'm worried I will jerk the wheel and steer into another car. I know we've discussed how that's probably not going to happen, but part of me still believes it will.
Clinician: Yes, we've discussed your intrusive thoughts about jerking the wheel and your fear that you'll actually do it if the thoughts come while you're driving. That is a prediction that ERP will help you "test." Are there other concerns you have about ERP, Marco?
Marco: This might sound silly, but I'm nervous about just my anxiety in general because I don't deal with it well. When I get anxious in school, I get really lightheaded and have to leave class because I'm afraid I'll pass out. What if that happened while driving? Then I'd definitely crash!
Clinician: Your concern doesn't sound silly to me. A lot of adolescents struggle with the idea that anxiety could be dangerous in some way—like making you pass out while driving. How likely does it seem to you that you'll get so anxious that you'll lose consciousness while driving?
Marco: Pretty likely. Sometimes it feels I'm on the verge of passing out when I'm really anxious.
Clinician: I understand why you're afraid this will happen. However, are you aware that the likelihood of passing out due to anxiety—even really intense anxiety—is extremely low?
Marco: Really? I thought it was the opposite. Like higher anxiety means higher chance of passing out. At least that's how it seems to go in movies and TV! (laughs)
Clinician: (laughs) I can see why you'd get that idea, but it's pretty inaccurate. Anxiety and passing out just don't go together. I've helped a lot of kids like you beat their OCD by using ERP, and I can't remember a time where a kid passed out even during really hard exposures.
Marco: That's good to know. I feel better about it now. So, what do you think I should do?
Clinician: I think we should stick to our plan of having you start exposure by driving around an empty parking lot. You'll probably feel some anxiety and lightheadedness, but that will give you an opportunity to see that you probably won't pass out behind the wheel. How does that sound?

BELIEF 2: ERP CREATES DISTRESS THAT IS INTOLERABLE

Nature and Validity of This Belief

Related to the concern that ERP will cause harm, another mistaken belief about ERP is that it creates distress to such an extent that youth cannot tolerate the treatment. This belief appears to be of significant concern among clinicians who treat OCD in youth (Reid et al., 2016) and is associated with selection of treatment strategies that are less efficacious than ERP in the treatment of OCD (Whiteside, Deacon, Benito, & Stewart, 2016). As one clinician put it while being interviewed for a *New York Times* article on exposure-based therapies: "I think very few patients can tolerate that adrenaline-based approach" (Slater, 2003). Such concerns appear to reflect a more general belief that clients are too psychologically "fragile" to endure even mild levels of distress, an idea that the influential psychologist Paul Meehl (1973) derided and labeled as the "spun-glass theory of the mind."

Clinicians aside, there is some evidence that clients with OCD believe ERP will create debilitating distress (Rowa et al., 2014), and it is plausible that parents will share these concerns (Taboas, McKay, Whiteside, & Storch, 2015). In light of the widespread concerns about the tolerability of the treatment, it comes as little surprise that many individuals assume ERP to be associated with exceedingly high dropout rates (Deacon, Farrell, et al., 2013) although this is not nearly the case. It is therefore important for clinicians to be prepared for youth and/or their parents to raise questions about the tolerability of ERP.

Despite the apparent pervasiveness of concerns about ERP creating intolerable distress for clients, research indicates that clients' psyches are considerably stronger than "spun glass." That is, clients receiving ERP generally report being able to successfully tolerate the distress evoked within the treatment. One recent study comparing clients' and clinicians' perceptions of ERP found that although youth with OCD endorsed very low concerns about the tolerability of the treatment, clinicians significantly underestimated their youth clients' ability to tolerate ERP (Riemann, Deacon, Farrell, & Kinnear, 2014). When compared to other treatment approaches, ERP is generally perceived as equally tolerable as other traditional psychotherapies (e.g., cognitive therapy; Norton, Allen, & Hilton, 1983). Furthermore, both clients and the parents of youth with OCD report ERP to be a more tolerable treatment approach than pharmacotherapy (Brown, Deacon, Abramowitz, Dammann, & Whiteside, 2007). It is therefore unsurprising that parents of youth seeking treatment for OCD preferred CBT with ERP overwhelmingly to pharmacotherapy (Lewin, McGuire, Murphy, & Storch, 2014). Finally, there appear to be no reliable differences in dropout rates when exposure-based therapies are compared to alternative psychotherapy (Hembree & Cahill, 2007).

Addressing This Belief in Clinical Practice

Clinicians need not be alarmed when youth express concern about engaging in ERP due to anticipating the treatment to be intolerable. In fact, clinical experience suggests this is a relatively common occurrence and presents a convenient opportunity for the clinician to begin instilling confidence in the youth about his/her ability to endure the distress evoked in ERP. We have found it helpful to draw upon youths' previous experiences of tolerating distressing scenarios that they initially feared were intolerable. To illustrate, many youth will be able to recall an unpleasant visit to the dentist or an anxiety-ridden night trying to sleep away from their parents that was nonetheless more bearable than anticipated. These and other similar experiences can be used to begin gently challenging the youth's perspective that he/she is incapable of facing the distress that comes with exposure to feared stimuli.

Clinicians are also encouraged to present several pieces of information that may prove helpful in assuaging youths' concerns about ERP being intolerable. First, upon normalizing the youth's perceptions of ERP being intolerable *prior to beginning the treatment* (Rowa et al., 2014), the clinician can quickly pivot to pointing out that a substantial majority of youth with OCD (as well as their parents) report that ERP is quite tolerable after they have begun treatment (i.e., started confronting feared stimuli; Riemann, Deacon, Farrell, & Kinnear, 2014). Thus it can be explained to youth that initial apprehension about tolerating ERP is normal but seems to quickly fade upon beginning the treatment. This may be in part because youth learn they have a fair amount of influence regarding the nature and pacing of ERP and will not be "forced" to confront their most feared scenarios (i.e., flooding) early in the course of ERP.

Consider the following dialog between a clinician and an 11-year-old client, Hannah, who was concerned that she would not be able to tolerate any type of exposure in which she could have potentially be responsible for a house fire (e.g., preheating the oven).

Clinician: Hannah, I'm hearing that you're unsure if you're willing to do any house fire exposures. What's making you feel that way?

Hannah: I just don't think I can do it. (Begins crying) I mean look, I even get upset just talking about it. I think doing the exposures would be too much.

Clinician: Can you help me understand what you mean when you say "too much?"

Hannah: Like I won't be handle being that upset or scared. I'll be overwhelmed.

Clinician: I see. It sounds like you're not confident that you can tolerate being anxious during the house fire exposures. Is that it?

Hannah: (Nods)

Clinician: That's understandable, Hannah. Many kids are worried about the same thing—that they won't be able to handle facing their fears. I'm wondering if you can think of a time when you did face your fears in a different situation. Does anything come to mind?

Hannah: Umm (pauses), I guess I did at my friend Katie's pool party. Her family has a diving board, and all my friends were jumping off it, but I was really scared and I almost chickened out.

Clinician: So, what did you do?

Hannah: I just kind of made myself do it. Like, I just kept my feet moving even though in my head I was saying "stop!"

Clinician: It sounds like you were really scared even though you made up your mind to do it.
Hannah: Oh yeah. I'm pretty sure I screamed, but at least I didn't chicken out. It was kind of fun.
Clinician: That sounds to me like you actually tolerated your anxiety pretty well. Do you agree?
Hannah: I think so. I wasn't afraid after that. I actually jumped off it a lot more times.
Clinician: You see? Even though you weren't sure you could handle it, you did it and showed yourself that you *could* handle it!
Hannah: (Smiles)
Clinician: Do you remember how I said that a lot of kids worry they won't be able to handle facing their fears in ERP? What's really cool is that most kids who decide to try it learn that they actually *can* tolerate being scared during exposure—just like how you learned you could handle being scared to go off the diving board. Do you think trying ERP might be similar for you?
Hannah: I guess it could. I just know it'll be super hard.
Clinician: It might be hard at times, but let's remember a couple of important things. We created that exposure hierarchy so that we can begin doing exposures that aren't super scary right away. We'll keep working on them until they get easier and you feel ready to try something a little harder. This way, you can help me make sure that the exposures aren't overwhelming for you.
Hannah: Okay. So I don't have to start with the one where I light a match inside my house?
Clinician: Not if you tell me you're not ready for it yet. We can be patient and work our way up to that exposure gradually. I might challenge you at times to go beyond your "comfort zone," but I'll never force you to do any exposures you're unwilling to try.

BELIEF 3: THE USE OF ERP PRECLUDES AN EFFECTIVE THERAPEUTIC ALLIANCE

Nature and Validity of This Belief

In pediatric OCD, the therapeutic alliance refers to the personal bond that contextualizes the working relationship between a clinician, youth, and occasionally the youth's parents. A strong therapeutic relationship is generally characterized by a clinician attending to a client's experience as well as being flexible, honest, warm, and respectful (Ackerman & Hilsenroth, 2003) and is important in the treatment of any psychological condition, including pediatric OCD (e.g., Keeley, Geffken, McNamara, & Storch, 2011). Moreover, a strong therapeutic alliance might be *especially* important when working with youth with OCD, who are often brought into treatment by their caregivers and may be less engaged in the early stages of treatment.

Given that ERP involves the deliberate induction of obsessional anxiety, some critics of ERP argue that using ERP precludes an effective therapeutic alliance. Specifically, some worry that exposures will be intolerable and/or that a youth's distress will become "too high" during session, which might damage the therapeutic relationship and hamper progress. Concerns that ERP is "cruel" because it involves confronting feared stimuli are not uncommon among clinicians (Deacon, Farrell, et al., 2013); furthermore, such perceptions extend beyond clinicians into the general public (e.g., Slater, 2003). This concern about ERP is often sustained by a lack of experience with the treatment. Fortunately, psychoeducation and experience using ERP for youth with OCD may correct this mistaken belief (akin to exposure *for the clinician*; Abramowitz et al., 2011).

To investigate the effects of ERP on therapeutic alliance, researchers have examined differences in alliance change between CBT with ERP and psychoeducational/supportive therapy among youth with anxiety disorders. One such study utilized youth-, therapist-, and parent-rated alliance ratings to examine the overall mean difference in therapeutic alliance as a function of treatment approach, as well as potential differences between treatment approaches over the full course of therapy (Kendall et al., 2009). Results showed that alliance ratings increased over the course of treatment regardless of treatment approach, even after in-session exposures were introduced mid-treatment for the ERP group. Furthermore, youth receiving ERP showed greater symptom improvement than did youth who received psychoeducational/supportive therapy (Kendall, Hudson, Gosche, Flannery-Schroeder, & Suveg, 2008). Although this study included youth with diagnoses other than OCD, these findings nevertheless contradict the mistaken belief that ERP precludes an effective therapeutic alliance in youth with OCD (and other anxiety-related conditions).

It is possible that ERP may *enhance,* rather than weaken, the therapeutic alliance between clinician and youth (e.g., Kendall et al., 2009). That is, clinicians and youth collaborate during multiple stages of ERP, including (a) the development of a hierarchy, (b) negotiating between-session exposure homework, and (c) deciding how much to involve the parents in the treatment process.[1] Additionally, the positive social reinforcement value of verbal praise or a "high five" following a successful exposure trial may also foster an effective therapeutic alliance. Clinicians may also incorporate enjoyable activities into sessions to make exposure tasks less laborious and more "game-like." Examples include doing tasks that activate the need for perfectionism (e.g., coloring inside/outside the lines), eating treats that trigger contamination obsessions (e.g., "dirt cup" pudding snacks), and creating an "exposure BINGO card" to encourage repeated and varied exposure practices at home between sessions.

1. Although clinicians should take care to honor the limits of confidentiality (Gola, Beidas, Antinoro-Burke, Kratz, & Fingerhut, 2016).

Addressing This Belief in Clinical Practice

In our own clinical experience, it is challenging for "pro-ERP" clinicians to effectively persuade a skeptical colleague that ERP does not preclude an effective therapeutic alliance. Research in social psychology suggests that clinicians aiming to modify others' beliefs about ERP should provide critics with information about the treatment that balances empirical and emotional appeals. Empirical findings and case examples may both be used to provide persuasive evidence for exposure's nondeleterious effects on the therapeutic alliance (Farrell, Deacon, Dixon, & Lickel, 2013).

Consider Eleanor, a pediatric psychologist who was asked by her colleague, Darius, to explain why she utilized ERP when treating youth with OCD, despite the fact that "it inherently harms the therapeutic alliance."

Eleanor: What about helping clients face their fears sounds harmful to the therapeutic alliance?
Darius: You're making a client feel awful. If I were a kid and my therapist triggered my OCD anxiety, I'd hate them and wouldn't want to come or participate in the session at all.
Eleanor: So you're saying that encouraging a child to bring on OCD-related anxiety when they are trying to overcome their OCD harms the therapeutic alliance?
Darius: Right—you're having them do things in session that they try to avoid in everyday life.
Eleanor: I see. After your knee surgery last year, you saw a physical therapist, right?
Darius: That's right.
Eleanor: Okay. So once you had a few physical therapy sessions under your belt, did your physical therapist only have you do exercises that felt comfortable or enjoyable?
Darius: No. After a while, he had me build up to more and more repetitions of each exercise so that I could get my full strength and range of motion back.
Eleanor: I see. That must have hurt a little.
Darius: It was uncomfortable, yes, but I knew it wasn't causing me physical harm. I could always say "no" or pause if he was asking too much. But a little bit of discomfort was good; it meant I was rebuilding muscle that had atrophied since my surgery.
Eleanor: Couldn't he have just told you what exercises to do, and let you do them by yourself so that he wasn't the one pushing you to increase your repetitions?
Darius: Yes, but without him there, I probably would have quit once I started feeling tired or sore, which wouldn't have helped me recover. Or worse, I could have aggravated my injury by doing the exercises using improper form.

Eleanor: That makes sense—*he* had to be the one guiding you through the tasks. And how would you describe your relationship with your physical therapist?

Darius: Honestly, I really liked him. He challenged me to put more effort into my recovery than I would have if left unsupervised, which helped me improve faster.

Eleanor: My role as an exposure therapist is similar to what you described. I also push my clients to "go further" than they would on their own, but I also root for them every step of the way. My end goal mirrors that of your physical therapist: to help my client function as best as possible so that they can pursue the life that they want to, free of the symptoms that bring them into treatment in the first place.

Darius: Okay, that analogy makes sense. But how do you know that you couldn't take a softer treatment approach and still get the same results?

Eleanor: Actually, several research groups have examined this question. Not only do studies show that the therapeutic alliance in exposure-based treatments is comparable to that seen in alternative treatments, but youth receiving ERP for their OCD actually fare better after therapy compared to approaches most would consider "softer."

Darius: I had no idea.

BELIEF 4: PARENTS SHOULD DO EVERYTHING POSSIBLE TO EASE THEIR CHILD'S OCD-RELATED ANXIETY

Nature and Validity of This Belief

Many parents of youth with OCD try to do anything they can to calm their child's OCD-related anxiety. Parents may also be prone to feel guilty if they do not (or cannot) alleviate their child's distress (e.g., "I should be able to soothe him") and may blame themselves if their efforts are unsuccessful (e.g., "I'm a bad parent"). *Parental accommodation* refers to the ways in which parents change their behavior in response to a youth's OCD symptoms (Lebowitz, Panza, Su, & Bloch, 2012) and is often intended to help youth avoid or neutralize OCD-related distress.

As any parent knows, a child's behavior occurs within a larger familial context. The relationship between a youth's OCD and family functioning is bidirectional; not only might a youth's OCD symptoms affect daily living (e.g., refusing to eat at *that* restaurant), but family members are often drawn into the youth's numerous avoidant and compulsive behaviors. A scan of online parent support group forums shows that families of youth with OCD frequently feel compelled to "save" youth from encountering OCD triggers and/or avoid the socially awkward predicament of explaining their child's compulsive rituals. Parental accommodation can range from active/obvious behaviors (e.g., excessively sanitizing a child's toy before and after every use) to passive/subtle actions (e.g., avoiding discussing certain topics), such that some parents do not even realize they are accommodating their child's OCD symptoms.

From a behavioral perspective, parental accommodation is negatively reinforced: distress (the youth's OCD-related anxiety and/or the parent's distress at seeing his or her child become anxious) prompts parents to "give in" to the youth's demands to accommodate avoidance/rituals, which neutralizes both the youth's and parent's distress. Although parental accommodation is often motivated by a desire to mitigate the child's fear, such behaviors serve to reinforce OCD symptoms by preventing the youth from learning that (a) feared outcomes are less likely/severe than anticipated and (b) obsessional anxiety declines naturally over time.

Substantial research evidence shows that accommodation is ubiquitous among parents of youth with OCD (up to 99% of parents; Flessner et al., 2011) and is associated with OCD symptom severity as well as other behavior problems (Storch et al., 2007). Importantly, parental accommodation is also associated with poorer OCD treatment outcome (e.g., Merlo, Lehmkuhl, Geffken, & Storch, 2009). In fact, family accommodation was one of only five factors that significantly predicted treatment outcomes in the largest OCD treatment study for youth (Garcia et al., 2010). Therefore fading parental accommodation in the context of OCD is critical.

Addressing This Belief in Clinical Practice

Few parents recognize the deleterious long-term effects of their symptom accommodation prior to seeking therapy for their child; therefore clinicians should be careful not to blame parents for causing or worsening their child's OCD symptoms. Clinicians should instead help parents develop alternative ways to respond to their child's OCD-related distress that are consistent with rationale of ERP. Eliminating accommodation requires psychoeducation (i.e., explaining that accommodation relieves OCD-related anxiety in the short term but serves to maintain the "vicious cycle" of OCD in the long term), self-monitoring of accommodation, and replacing accommodation behaviors with alternative responses that may help the youth overcome his/her OCD in the long run. Although some clinicians and parents find that devoting an entire session to parental accommodation prevention is helpful, other clinicians will instead spend 10–15 min at the start of several treatment sessions meeting with the parent(s) alone to cover this material before meeting with the youth individually for the remainder of the session.

Given that parental accommodation may become automatic—and such behaviors also effectively neutralize a *parent's* distress in response to their child's OCD-related anxiety—eliminating accommodation behaviors is akin to exposure and response prevention *for the parent*. Consider Priya, who accommodated her son Dev's rituals related to obsessions that someone would break into their home and hurt their pets and family:

Clinician: Last week, I asked you to self-monitor the accommodation behaviors you did to help Dev perform his compulsive rituals. Were you able to do that?
Priya: Yes, I was.
Clinician: That's great. What did you notice?
Priya: Well, I learned that I accommodate all the time—way more than I thought. I also realized that I'm most likely to give in when we're in a rush to get somewhere and I don't want to be late.
Clinician: I see. Did any other patterns emerge during your week of self-monitoring?
Priya: Yes—in keeping track of the behaviors I was doing, I realized that I also accommodate Dev's OCD concerns even if he doesn't ask me to.
Clinician: Interesting. Tell me more about that.
Priya: Well, yesterday, we were late leaving for school and Dev was putting his backpack in the car as I was exiting the house. I locked the front door like I always do, but then I shook the door knob several times *loudly* so that Dev knew I had checked that the door was locked behind me.
Clinician: What was that like for you?
Priya: I was shocked! I had no idea that Dev's rituals had become my own habits. It was like I was preemptively avoiding his pleading or doubling-back to check the door himself so that we could avoid being later than we already were.
Clinician: I can see how checking the door locks might become incorporated into your own behavior. Thinking back to our discussion last week of how accommodation backfires long-term, what do you think you might have tried instead?
Priya: Not rattle the locked doorknob, because that is equivalent to my doing Dev's rituals for him, and he's trying to fade his rituals out in therapy now.
Clinician: I agree. How would resisting accommodation behaviors make you feel?
Priya: Well, it would be difficult. Dev would probably start crying or yelling, which would be pretty tough to sit with. And I'd feel guilty for knowingly causing him to feel so upset.
Clinician: So by locking the door but not checking it, you're "knowingly" causing Dev harm?
Priya: Well, no. But I'd just feel bad, especially at first.
Clinician: What do you think would happen after a few minutes into the drive?
Priya: Honestly, he'd probably get so exhausted from crying or he'd become distracted by what was happening out the window that he would eventually calm down and forget about it. And then that would help me to eventually calm down too.
Clinician: That sounds reasonable to me. What do you think Dev would learn from your *resisting* accommodating his rituals and letting the situation play out instead?

Priya: Well, it would kind of be like an exposure. He would learn that it's okay to feel upset because his anxiety would fade naturally after a little while. Plus, when we got back home, he'd get to see that no one broke into our house. Not to mention, it might help us to make appointments on time if we don't have to delay leaving the house due to Dev's checking rituals.
Clinician: Exactly! Do you think you could try not giving into Dev's checking rituals this week?
Priya: I could definitely try—I could start with not checking when the house is empty and build up to not checking for him when the rest of the family is still inside.
Clinician: That's a great idea! Why don't you keep track of your accommodation behaviors again this week, this time noting whether you resisted versus gave in to accommodating. We can review your progress and troubleshoot any difficulties you're still having next week.

BELIEF 5: ERP ONLY ADDRESSES THE SYMPTOMS OF OCD WITHOUT TREATING THE "ROOT CAUSE"

Nature and Validity of This Belief

Some clinicians claim that ERP addresses OCD's superficial symptoms without treating its root cause. Specifically, psychoanalytically oriented clinicians argue that ignoring the putative subconscious source of a youth's OCD symptoms (e.g., disruption in psychosexual development) causes him or her to repress their original symptoms and develop alternative symptoms instead. The belief that ERP promotes such "symptom substitution" depicts OCD as Hydra—the mythological multiheaded water monster that regenerates more heads for every head that is severed—such that for every ritual prevented, another compulsion is assumed to take its place.

In contrast to this myth, symptom substitution is not common in clinical practice (e.g., Foa & Steketee, 1987; Peterson et al., 2016). Although some youth may report new OCD symptoms during a course of ERP, it is more likely that these supplementary symptoms reflect pretreatment obsessions not reported during the initial assessment. Alternatively, OCD symptoms that are arise during the course of ERP may reveal that the youth has not corrected his or her general tendency to misinterpret a broad range of mental intrusions as particularly significant or meaningful. In either instance, "new" OCD symptoms may be targeted via continued ERP. Functional assessment of the triggers, fearful predictions, and compulsive rituals performed in response to these "new" obsessions might suggest additional exposure tasks that can be integrated into the youth's treatment plan (e.g., Abramowitz et al., 2011). To summarize, eliminating OCD symptoms in one dimension (e.g., need for symmetry) does not necessarily result in the development of OCD symptoms in another domain (e.g., contamination fears). Rather, ERP helps youth to adaptively respond to a variety of unwanted intrusive thoughts, images, doubts, and impulses, regardless of specific OCD symptom domain.

Addressing This Belief in Clinical Practice

Some youth who experience a change in their primary obsessions mistakenly conclude that they cannot benefit from ERP. Not only is ERP the most empirically supported intervention for OCD in youth (Freeman et al., 2014), but other research has found that more positive treatment expectations are linked to better treatment response, retention, and compliance (Lewin, Peris, Bergman, McCracken, & Piacentini, 2011). Therefore clinicians working with youth who endorse the pessimistic belief that ERP causes symptom substitution should correct this misconception and reestablish confidence in the treatment plan. Consider Amelia, a 16-year-old who believed her OCD was "untreatable" because she noticed a shift in her obsessional content.

Amelia: I don't think I should keep coming to therapy. I'm doing better with thinking that something bad will happen to my mom if I'm not around to protect her, but now I'm worried that *I* will accidentally do something to harm my mom.

Clinician: I see—you're afraid that because you're having a new type of obsession than you didn't have before coming to treatment, this means you'll never get better.

Amelia: That's right. It's like I scratched one itch, but that only caused another.

Clinician: Let's see if we can look at your new fears using the cognitive-behavioral diagram that we learned about in our first session. What do you remember about how we think about OCD?

Amelia: Well, there are negative beliefs that cause me to misinterpret my thoughts or triggers as dangerous. And that makes me feel anxious or afraid.

Clinician: Exactly. And how did that apply to you when you first came to see me?

Amelia: I was afraid that something bad would happen to my mom, and I thought I was responsible for protecting her. So when she didn't text me back or wasn't on time to pick me up, I'd get really upset thinking something bad happened to her that I'm responsible for.

Clinician: Great job, you understand how we think about OCD. So help me understand the new obsessions that are causing you problems now.

Amelia: Well, I'm afraid that instead of being my mom's protector, I'm actually the bad guy. Like yesterday, she was vacuuming the carpet at the top of the stairs, and I had the thought that I could push her down the stairs. I was so afraid. What if deep down, *I'm* a dangerous person?

Clinician: And what did you do once you had that thought?

Amelia: I locked myself in my room. It felt like the only thing I could do to avoid acting on the thought was to get away from her. I was trying to protect her from something awful.
Clinician: Okay, I see how that would seem really scary. You felt like you would have been responsible for hurting her if you didn't stop from acting on your unwanted impulse to hurt her.
Amelia: That's right.
Clinician: Thank you for sharing. May I try to summarize your new obsessions using that same cognitive-behavioral diagram you described to me a moment ago?
Amelia: Yes.
Clinician: It sounds like you are afraid that something bad will happen to your mom, and that you are the one responsible for protecting her. And when you have these unwanted thoughts of hurting her, you become really upset. Is that right?
Amelia: That's right.
Clinician: Do you notice anything familiar about the summary I just shared with you?
Amelia: It's almost the same as how my OCD was before I started seeing you. Only now instead of thinking someone else will hurt my mom, I'm afraid that *I'll* hurt her.
Clinician: Exactly. How does that make you feel, hearing that your new obsessions seem to be just like your old obsessions, only with a little plot twist?
Amelia: I guess it doesn't mean that my OCD is changing that much. It sounds like I'm just making the same thinking mistakes as before, but in different situations now.
Clinician: I agree. So what do you think we should do?
Amelia: I guess we could keep trying exposures that trigger my fears of something bad happening to my mom. That way I can test whether my obsessions are true.
Clinician: I think that's an excellent idea. It's not necessarily a bad sign that you're noticing new obsessions that didn't bother you before. It just means we have more work to do to help you see that thoughts are just thoughts, which don't necessarily mean anything.

BELIEF 6: OCD IS A BIOLOGICAL DISEASE THAT CANNOT BE TREATED EFFECTIVELY WITH PSYCHOTHERAPY

Nature and Validity of This Belief

Many clinicians who treat youth with OCD will undoubtedly encounter clients and/or parents who endorse doubts about the treatability of OCD using any psychotherapy, such as ERP, due to perceptions of the disorder as a biological "brain disease." Recent research attests to the increasing popularity of biologically oriented conceptions of mental disorders among both the general public (e.g., Pescosolido et al., 2010) as well as individuals afflicted with a mental disorder (e.g., Lebowitz, 2014). These conceptions are actively promoted by influential health organizations, leading figures in mental health, and many popular media outlets (Deacon, 2013).

Although biological contributions to the development of OCD are well documented (e.g., Rosenberg, Russell, & Fougere, 2005), it is widely acknowledged that the etiology of OCD likely involves a complex interaction of biological, psychosocial, and environmental factors (e.g., Taylor & Jang, 2011). In other words, whereas biological variables cannot be discounted in conceptual models of OCD, many other nonbiological variables are also part of the equation. This begs the question: what is the harm if youth and/or their parents subscribe to a "brain disease" model of OCD?

There are several potential drawbacks to youth and their parents conceptualizing OCD as *only* a biological disease. First and foremost, this belief is likely to dampen enthusiasm for and perceived effectiveness of ERP relative to pharmacotherapy (Taylor, McKay, & Abramowitz, 2010). Indeed, previous research indicates that clients who endorse biologically based models of mental disorders tend to perceive psychotherapy as a less credible option than medication (e.g., Kemp, Lickel, & Deacon, 2014). This is problematic given that ERP is recommended as a first-line treatment for OCD in youth, and medication has not been shown to reliably augment ERP (Storch et al., 2013). Clients and/or parents who believe OCD to be biologically determined are also likely to be more pessimistic about the likelihood of overcoming OCD regardless of the selected modality (Lebowitz, 2014). Finally, given that greater beliefs in biological etiologies of mental disorders are associated with diminished perceptions of controlling one's own mood and behavior (Kemp et al., 2014), it is plausible that youth who believe their OCD to be a brain disease will be less willing to put forth the considerable effort that is required for ERP to be maximally beneficial.

Addressing This Belief in Clinical Practice

Effectively confronting youths' views of their OCD as a biological illness can be a rather difficult task. In our experience, rather than addressing the notion that biology is involved in the development of OCD, we have found it more advantageous to directly address the secondary belief that ERP will ultimately prove unhelpful. Previous work has shown that among youth with OCD, greater expectancies for ERP to be helpful are significantly associated with superior treatment gains (Lewin et al., 2011). Consequently, it is important for clinicians to instill positive expectancies for the effectiveness of ERP regardless of whether clients maintain the idea that their OCD is biologically based.

Clinical experience suggests that a highly effective "sales pitch" clinicians can make is to describe how ERP reliably produces changes in the structure and function of brain areas believed to be involved in OCD (e.g., Porto et al., 2009); these changes are highly resemblant of the changes produced by medications commonly used in the treatment of OCD (Baxter et al., 1992). Such a description will not discredit youths' and parents' view of OCD as a biological illness, but instead alter their perspective on the treatability of OCD using ERP. It appears that the critical piece of this description is conveying to youth and parents that whatever the involvement of biological factors in the development of OCD, these factors are more *malleable* than may be anticipated (Lebowitz, Ahn, & Nolen-Hoeksema, 2013). Thus although we do not disagree with other authors' recommendations to highlight the biological underpinnings of OCD as a means to "externalize" the disorder (Franklin, Rynn, Foa, & March, 2003), we strongly advocate that clinicians who take this approach make certain to emphasize the malleability of these biological factors. Doing so will ensure that youth and their parents' perceptions of ERP as an effective approach will remain high.

Our suggestions outlined previously for addressing youths' beliefs about ERP being unable to counteract a biologically based illness are illustrated in the following dialog between a clinician, a 13-year-old client with OCD (Brady), and his mother. In this conversation, both Brady and his mother expressed their view of his OCD as a biologically determined illness unlikely to respond to ERP.

Clinician: During our last session, we discussed ERP and how it works. Before we move on today, are there any questions you have about last week's session?

Brady: I guess I've been thinking a lot about whether ERP will work for me, and I don't think it will. It just seems like it's too simple for such a severe illness.

Mother: You see, we have a lot of OCD in our family tree, so it makes sense that Brady has it. It's just in our genes, I guess. But maybe that's the problem. If this is really a genetic thing, we're worried if ERP can help.

Clinician: It sounds like you attribute Brady's OCD to genetics, which leads you to question if ERP is right for you. Do I have that right?

Brady: Yeah. I mean, if OCD is an illness in my brain, I just don't think ERP is enough. I probably need to take pills or maybe shock treatment—something like that.

Mother: Shock treatment sounds a little extreme, but we are concerned that ERP won't be enough. I know you said last week it's effective for OCD, but is it really enough to fix a serious brain malfunction? We've seen a lot of pictures of brain scans comparing OCD brains to healthy ones, and the differences were pretty clear. Brady's aunt also read something about certain brain chemicals being imbalanced in kids with OCD.

Clinician: I can tell you're both very concerned about OCD involving a lot of biological problems. And you're not wrong—there is some research backing it up. However, it's important to know that OCD isn't all genes and chemical imbalances. There are many other factors involved too, like the way a person responds when they're afraid of something.

Brady: I guess it makes sense. If OCD was only genetic, then all my family would have it!

Clinician: Here's something else that's important to consider: Not only does ERP help many kids get past their OCD, but research shows it actually makes changes in the brain. Remember those photos you've seen of OCD brains compared to non-OCD brains? In a lot of cases, ERP results in the person's brain looking healthier at the end of treatment.

Brady: That's pretty neat.

Mother: I wasn't aware of that. You're saying that the brain can change that much from just therapy and no medications?

Clinician: Exactly. You see, a lot of people assume that biological factors like brain functioning are permanent and can't change. But the environment can strongly influence our biology. Our genes are no exception. They can be sort of turned on and off—just like a light switch.

Mother: That's fascinating.

Brady: I want to do a brain scan before and after I do ERP so I can see if mine changes, too!

SUMMARY

Despite the efficacy of ERP in treating youth OCD, the treatment's successful implementation is impeded by a collection of mistaken beliefs about its use. In particular, ERP is often viewed as posing unacceptable risk for harm to youth or exceedingly difficult for them to tolerate. Additionally, there are concerns that ERP can cultivate relational disharmony, whether it be between client and clinician or parent and child. Finally, ERP is assumed by some to be an inadequate intervention for OCD out of concern that it merely leads to "substitution" of symptoms or is incapable of influencing the neurobiological underpinnings of OCD. Given that clinicians who treat youth with OCD are likely to encounter one or more of these myths in their clinical practice, it is important to be prepared to address these myths in a nonconfrontational yet assured manner. This chapter presents many suggestions—some generated from empirical research and others from clinical experience—that are helpful in instilling views of ERP as a safe, tolerable, and effective intervention.

In summarizing our suggestions across each of the six mistaken beliefs reviewed in this chapter, we advocate clinicians to first take the step of choosing to address rather than ignore the concern and to normalize and validate the youth and/or parent's concern. We also encourage clinicians to become familiar with this chapter's summaries of empirical literature refuting mistaken beliefs about ERP and to communicate these summaries to youth and parents in easy-to-understand language. Additionally, it is helpful to reinforce empirical findings with anecdotal evidence (e.g., case examples). Finally, clinicians may employ behavioral strategies to address concerns that can be immediately disconfirmed, such as using interoceptive exposure to demonstrate that anxiety does not cause harm. It is our hope that the suggestions in this chapter aid clinicians in imparting positive expectancies for ERP in overcoming OCD among youth and their families.

REFERENCES

Abramowitz, J. S., Deacon, B. J., & Whiteside, S. P. (2011). *Exposure therapy for anxiety: Principles and practice*. New York, NY: Guilford Press.

Ackerman, S. J., & Hilsenroth, M. J. (2003). A review of therapist characteristics and techniques positively impacting the therapeutic alliance. *Clinical Psychology Review*, *23*, 1–33.

Barlow, D. H., & Craske, M. G. (2007). *Mastery of your anxiety and panic: Workbook* (4th ed.). New York: Oxford University Press.

Baxter, L. R., Schwartz, J. M., Bergamon, K. S., Szuba, M. P., Guze, B. H., Mazziotta, J. C., et al. (1992). Caudate glucose metabolic rate changes with both drug and behavior therapy for obsessive–compulsive disorder. *Archives of General Psychiatry*, *49*, 681–689.

Brown, A., Deacon, B. J., Abramowitz, J. S., Dammann, J., & Whiteside, S. P. (2007). Parents' perceptions of pharmacological and cognitive-behavioral treatments for childhood anxiety disorders. *Behaviour Research and Therapy*, *45*, 819–828.

Deacon, B. J. (2013). The biomedical model of mental disorder: A critical analysis of its validity, utility, and effects on psychotherapy research. *Clinical Psychology Review*, *33*, 846–861.

Deacon, B. J., & Farrell, N. R. (2013). Therapist barriers to the dissemination of exposure therapy. In D. McKay & E. Storch (Eds.), *Handbook of treating variants and complications in anxiety disorders*. New York, NY: Springer Press.

Deacon, B. J., Farrell, N. R., Kemp, J. J., Dixon, L. D., Sy, J. T., Zhang, A. R., et al. (2013). Assessing therapist reservations about exposure therapy for anxiety: Development and validation of the therapist beliefs about exposure scale. *Journal of Anxiety Disorders*, *27*, 772–780.

Deacon, B. J., Lickel, J. J., Farrell, N. R., Kemp, J. J., & Hipol, L. J. (2013). Therapist perceptions and delivery of interoceptive exposure for panic disorder. *Journal of Anxiety Disorders*, *27*, 259–264.

Farrell, N. R., Deacon, B. J., Dixon, L. J., & Lickel, J. J. (2013). Theory-based training strategies for modifying practitioner concerns about exposure therapy for anxiety. *Journal of Anxiety Disorders*, *27*, 781–787.

Feeny, N., Hembree, E., & Zoellner, L. (2003). Myths regarding exposure therapy for PTSD. *Cognitive and Behavioral Practice*, *10*, 85–90.

Flessner, C. A., Freeman, J. B., Sapyta, J., Garcia, A., Franklin, M. E., March, J. S., et al. (2011). Predictors of parental accommodation in pediatric obsessive-compulsive disorder: Findings from the POTS trial. *Journal of the American Academy of Child and Adolescent Psychiatry*, *50*, 716–725.

Foa, E. B., & Steketee, G. S. (1987). Emergent fears during treatment of three obsessive-compulsives: Symptom substitution or de-conditioning? *Journal of Behavior Therapy and Experimental Psychiatry*, *8*, 353–358.

Franklin, M. E., Rynn, M., Foa, E. B., & March, J. S. (2003). Treatment of obsessive-compulsive disorder. In M. A. Reinecke, F. M. Dattilio, & A. Freeman (Eds.), *Cognitive therapy with children and adolescents: A casebook for clinical practice* (2nd ed., pp. 162–188). New York, NY: Guilford Press.

Freeman, J., Garcia, A., Frank, H., Benito, K., Conelea, C., Walther, M., et al. (2014). Evidence base update for psychosocial treatments for pediatric obsessive-compulsive disorder. *Journal of Clinical Child & Adolescent Psychology*, *43*, 7–26.

Garcia, A. M., Sapyta, J. J., Moore, P. S., Freeman, J. B., Franklin, M. E., March, J. S., et al. (2010). Predictors and moderators of treatment outcome in the pediatric obsessive compulsive treatment study (POTS I). *Journal of the American Academy of Child & Adolescent Psychiatry*, *49*, 1024–1033.

Gola, J. A., Beidas, R. S., Antinoro-Burke, D., Kratz, H. E., & Fingerhut, R. (2016). Ethical considerations in exposure therapy with children. *Cognitive and Behavioral Practice*, *23*, 184–193.

Hembree, E. A., & Cahill, S. P. (2007). Obstacles to successful implementation of exposure therapy. In D. C. S. Richard & D. Lauterbach (Eds.), *Comprehensive handbook of the exposure therapies* (pp. 389–408). New York, NY: Academic Press.

Keeley, M. L., Geffken, E. R., McNamara, J. P. H., & Storch, E. A. (2011). The therapeutic alliance in the cognitive behavioral treatment of pediatric obsessive-compulsive disorder. *Journal of Anxiety Disorders*, *25*, 855–863.

Kemp, J. J., Lickel, J. J., & Deacon, B. J. (2014). Effects of a chemical imbalance causal explanation on individuals' perceptions of their depressive symptoms. *Behaviour Research and Therapy*, *56*, 47–52.

Kendall, P. C., Comer, J. S., Marker, C. D., Creed, T. A., Puliafico, A. C., Hughes, A. A., et al. (2009). In-session exposure tasks and therapeutic alliance across the treatment of childhood anxiety disorders. *Journal of Consulting and Clinical Psychology*, *77*, 517–525.

Kendall, P. C., Hudson, J. L., Gosche, E., Flannery-Schroeder, E., & Suveg, C. (2008). Cognitive-behavioral therapy for anxiety disordered youth: A randomized clinical trial evaluating child and family modalities. *Journal of Consulting and Clinical Psychology*, *76*, 282–297.

Lebowitz, M. S. (2014). Biological conceptualizations of mental disorders among affected individuals: A review of correlates and consequences. *Clinical Psychology: Science and Practice*, *21*, 67–83.

Lebowitz, M. S., Ahn, W., & Nolen-Hoeksema, S. (2013). Fixable or fate? Perceptions of the biology of depression. *Journal of Consulting and Clinical Psychology*, *81*, 518–527.

Lebowitz, E., Panza, K., Su, J., & Bloch, M. H. (2012). Family accommodation on obsessive-compulsive disorder. *Expert Review of Neurotherapeutics*, *12*, 229–238.

Lewin, A. B., McGuire, J. F., Murphy, T. K., & Storch, E. A. (2014). The importance of considering parents' preferences when planning treatment for their children—The case of childhood obsessive-compulsive disorder. *Journal of Child Psychology and Psychiatry*, *55*, 1314–1316.

Lewin, A. B., Peris, T. S., Bergman, R. L., McCracken, J. T., & Piacentini, J. (2011). The role of treatment expectancy in youth receiving exposure-based CBT for obsessive-compulsive disorder. *Behaviour Research and Therapy*, *49*, 536–543.

Meehl, P. E. (1973). Why I do not attend case conferences. In P. E. Meehl (Ed.), *Psychodiagnosis: Selected papers* (pp. 225–302). Minneapolis, MN: University of Minnesota Press.

Merlo, L., Lehmkuhl, H., Geffken, G., & Storch, E. (2009). Decreased family accommodation associated with improved therapy outcome in pediatric obsessive-compulsive disorder. *Journal of Consulting and Clinical Psychology*, *72*, 355–360.

Norton, G. R., Allen, G. E., & Hilton, J. (1983). The social validity of treatments for agoraphobia. *Behaviour Research and Therapy*, *21*, 393–399.

Olatunji, B. O., Deacon, B. J., & Abramowitz, J. S. (2009). The cruelest cure? Ethical issues in the implementation of exposure-based treatments. *Cognitive and Behavioral Practice*, *16*, 172–180.

Pescosolido, B. A., Martin, J. K., Long, J. S., Medina, T. R., Phelan, J. C., & Link, B. G. (2010). A disease like any other? A decade of change in public reactions to schizophrenia, depression, and alcohol dependence. *The American Journal of Psychiatry*, *167*, 1321–1330.

Peterson, A. L., McGuire, J. F., Wilhelm, S., Piacentini, J., Woods, D. W., Walkup, J. T., et al. (2016). An empirical examination of symptom substitution associated with behavior therapy for Tourette's disorder. *Behavior Therapy*, *47*, 29–41.

Piacentini, J., Bergman, R. L., Keller, M., & McCracken, J. (2003). Functional impairment in children and adolescents with obsessive-compulsive disorder. *Journal of Child and Adolescent Psychopharmacology*, *13*, S61–S69.

Piacentini, J., Peris, T. S., Bergman, R. L., Chang, S., & Jaffer, M. (2007). Functional impairment in childhood OCD: Development and psychometric properties of the child obsessive-compulsive impact scale-revised (COIS-R). *Journal of Clinical Child and Adolescent Psychology*, *36*, 645–653.

Porto, P. R., Oliveria, L., Mari, J., Volchan, E., Figueria, I., & Ventura, P. (2009). Does cognitive behavioral therapy change the brain? A systematic review of neuroimaging in anxiety disorders. *Journal of Neuropsychiatry & Clinical Neurosciences*, *21*, 114–125.

Reid, A. M., Guzick, A., Fernandez, A. G., Deacon, B., McNamara, J. P. H., Geffken, G. R., et al. (2016). *Exposure therapy for youth with anxiety: Utilization rates and predictors of dissemination in a sample of practicing clinicians in the United States.* [submitted for publication].

Riemann, B., Deacon, B. J., Farrell, N. R., & Kinnear, K. (2014, November). Myth #4: Patients participating in exposure perceive treatment as unethical, intolerable, and harmful. In Farrell, N. R., & Kemp, J. J. (Chairs), *Myth-busting exposure therapy for anxiety. Symposium presented at the annual meeting of the Association for Behavioral and Cognitive Therapies*, Nashville, TN.

Rosenberg, D. R., Russell, A., & Fougere, A. (2005). Neuropsychiatric models of OCD. In J. S. Abramowitz & A. C. Houts (Eds.), *Concepts and controversies in obsessive-compulsive disorder* (pp. 209–228). New York, NY: Springer Press.

Rowa, K., Gifford, S., McCabe, R., Milosevic, I., Antony, M. M., & Purdon, C. (2014). Treatment fears in anxiety disorders: Development and validation of the treatment ambivalence questionnaire. *Journal of Clinical Psychology*, *70*, 979–993.

Slater, L. (2003). *The cruelest cure.* The New York Times. p. 34.

Storch, E. A., Bussing, R., Small, B. J., Geffken, G. R., McNamara, J. P., Rahman, O., et al. (2013). Randomized, placebo-controlled trial of cognitive-behavioral therapy alone or combined with sertraline in the treatment of pediatric obsessive–compulsive disorder. *Behaviour Research and Therapy*, *51*, 823–829.

Storch, E. A., Geffkin, G. R., Merlo, L. J., Jacob, M. L., Murphy, T. K., Goodman, W. K., et al. (2007). Family accommodation in pediatric obsessive-compulsive disorder. *Journal of Clinical Child Psychology*, *36*, 207–216.

Taboas, W. R., McKay, D., Whiteside, S. P. H., & Storch, E. A. (2015). Parental involvement in youth anxiety treatment: Conceptual bases, controversies, and recommendations for intervention. *Journal of Anxiety Disorders*, *30*, 16–18.

Taylor, S., & Jang, K. L. (2011). Biopsychosocial etiology of obsessions and compulsions: An integrated behavioral–genetic and cognitive–behavioral analysis. *Journal of Abnormal Psychology*, *120*, 174–186.

Taylor, S., McKay, D., & Abramowitz, J. (2010). More on the brain disease model of mental disorders. *The Behavior Therapist*, *33*, 16–17.

Whiteside, S. P. H., Deacon, B. J., Benito, K., & Stewart, E. (2016). Factors associated with practitioners' use of exposure therapy for childhood anxiety disorders. *Journal of Anxiety Disorders*, *40*, 29–36.

Chapter 12

OCD in School Settings

Michael L. Sulkowski*, Cary Jordan†, Stacey Rice Dobrinsky‡, and Rachel E. Mathews§
*University of Arizona, Tucson, AZ, United States, †St. Elizabeth Boardman Hospital, Youngstown, OH, United States, ‡McLean Hospital, Belmont, MA, United States, §Kent State University, Kent, OH, United States

Obsessive-compulsive disorder (OCD) is the fourth most common psychiatric disorder in the United States (Kessler et al., 2012), affecting about 6–9 million or about 3% of US children (Rapoport et al., 2000; Reinherz et al., 1993). While OCD can be a debilitating disorder, evidence-based treatment such as Cognitive-Behavior Therapy (CBT) using Exposure Response Prevention (ERP) has been found to be effective at reducing symptom severity and distress caused by anxiety. ERP has been established as a particularly efficacious treatment, with metaanalyses demonstrating that 60%–80% of individuals experience significant reduction in symptoms (defined by 35% or more reduction in symptom severity; Björgvinsson, Hart, & Heffelfinger, 2007). Research also suggests that treatment gains derived from ERP often are maintained at a 2-year follow-up (Himle & Franklin, 2009). ERP is considered a short-term therapeutic intervention, and symptom improvement is usually seen within 12–15 sessions (Himle & Franklin, 2009).

Despite the effectiveness of CBT, the majority of youth with OCD do not receive these first-line treatments and as a result they experience impairments in functioning (CBT; Jordan, Reid, Mariaskin, Augusto, & Sulkowski, 2012; Marazziti & Consoli, 2010). Several barriers to treatment contribute to the discrepancy between the large number of youth with OCD and the small number who actually receive efficacious treatment. Most saliently, these include a lack of knowledge of treatment options; logistical complications associated with treatment access; the limited number of trained OCD providers; and fear, distrust, or unfamiliarity with accessing psychiatric, medical, or behavioral health services (Jordan, De Nadai, Sulkowski, & Storch, 2013; Jordan et al., 2012). Without receiving effective treatment, children often struggle at school and experience impairments in their academic functioning.

With the goal of helping support children with OCD at school, this chapter first covers ways to overcome treatment barriers. Second, school-based service

The Clinician's Guide to Cognitive-Behavioral Therapy for Childhood Obsessive-Compulsive Disorder
http://dx.doi.org/10.1016/B978-0-12-811427-8.00012-5

delivery is discussed to help inform clinicians how they can work effectively with school-based professionals. Additionally, content on relevant laws that influence school-based delivery is covered as well as how these laws can be utilized. Lastly, seven specific recommendations on how clinicians can help with children with OCD at school are provided.

HOW TO OVERCOME TREATMENT BARRIERS

Extant Barriers

Many barriers to psychiatric and behavioral health treatment are related to structural, social, and environmental factors. Structural barriers include lack of qualified clinicians, long wait lists, and lack of insurance coverage. Additional barriers include stigma related to mental health and barriers related to perceptions of mental health services (e.g., child's resistance to receiving services, lack of trust of providers; Owens et al., 2002).

While knowledge of evidence-based treatments for OCD might be growing in the psychiatric, psychological, and medical community, this knowledge does not often translate back to the general public and many mental health providers struggle to identify effective treatments for a range of different mental health problems (Sulkowski, Wingfield, Jones, & Coulter, 2011). Moreover, in areas with few specialized providers such as in rural communities, children and families may see several nonspecialized providers for psychiatric care, medication management, and supportive psychotherapy (Sulkowski, in press).

Specialized OCD treatment is often provided at medical centers, many of which tend to be located in large metropolitan areas. OCD is also treated in specialty clinics scattered across the United States and at university clinics located in college towns. Thus to receive evidence-based treatment for OCD, patients and caregivers might have to travel hours to and from a clinic to meet with a provider, which can be cost and time prohibitive for many individuals and families (Nakatani, Mataix-Cols, Micali, Turner, & Heyman, 2009). However, according to research by Eberhardt et al. (2001), about 90% of the United States is classified as "rural" and approximately 19.3% of the US population resides in a rural community, a community that is traditionally underserved by health and mental health providers. Despite this phenomenon, the President's New Freedom Commission Report (2003) concluded that: "...rural issues are often misunderstood, minimized, and not considered in forming national mental health policy ... Too often, policies and practices developed for metropolitan areas are erroneously assumed to apply to rural areas" (p. 50).

Specialized and supervised training is needed to treat OCD effectively. Often, generalist psychology, psychiatry, social work, and counseling programs do not have flexibility in coursework, practicum, or clinical training opportunities; as a result, there are limited opportunities for such specialization or supervised clinical experience, didactics, and other structured training experiences for providers to develop competence in specializing in treating OCD. Additionally, treatment studies often prescribe an intensive ERP regimen based on 15 sessions across 3 weeks (Abramowitz, Foa, & Franklin, 2003). However, less intensive treatment (e.g., 2 sessions weekly) has been found to produce similar levels of symptom reduction (Abramowitz et al., 2003). The intensive nature of ERP often makes it difficult for clinicians to include this type of specialized treatment into their practice. Because of these barriers, many communities are relatively devoid of OCD specialists—and in communities with these providers, long wait-lists often exist that forestall treatment access. Simply stated, there are far many more children, adolescents, and adults with OCD than can currently receive treatment by existing specialized providers in clinical, medical, behavioral health, or community centers (Sulkowski, Jordan, & Nguyen, 2009; Sulkowski, Mancil, et al., 2011; Sulkowski, Wingfield, et al., 2011).

Lastly, many individuals and families fear, distrust, or are unfamiliar with medical, psychiatric, and behavioral health service delivery. Such service models are often criticized for failing to be sensitive to cultural, linguistic, spiritual, socioeconomic, and other factors that influence comfort associated with service access, treatment engagement, and clinical outcomes (Hernandez, Nesman, Mowery, Acevedo-Polakovich, & Callejas, 2009). Additionally, because of a history of illegal; unethical; and unscrupulous research, clinical practice, and service delivery (or the lack thereof), some racial and ethnic groups such as African Americans and Indigenous Americans are reluctant to access health and mental health treatment in clinical settings (Corbie-Smith, Thomas, & George, 2002; Gone & Kirmayer, 2010; Kroll & Erickson, 2002).

Overcoming Barriers Through School-Based Service Delivery

In contrast to medical centers and specialty clinics, schools are located in virtually all communities across the United States and, regardless of their size or location, are frequently viewed as trusted institutions. Additionally, schools are often centrally located in communities and provide transportation services to students within districted zoned areas. Therefore as part of a federal mandate to provide all students with a "free and appropriate education" (FAPE), schools must provide students with psychoeducational services and proactively work toward increasing access to these services. Current estimates suggest that approximately 20% of school-aged children experience emotional or behavioral symptoms that would qualify them for a psychiatric diagnosis each year (Dowdy, Ritchey, & Kamphaus, 2010). However, the vast majority of these children do not receive any mental health services. Barriers to receiving appropriate outpatient care include parental psychopathology and decreased quality of life (Owens et al., 2002). As such, schools remain an appropriate context to provide wraparound and collaborative mental health services. Expanding on this notion, research suggests that youth who traditionally do not seek mental health services in community settings may be amenable to receiving them in school or educational settings (Sulkowski & Michael, 2014).

Schools also employ individuals who can be utilized to provide mental health services to students and families. To be compliant with federal law, Local Education Agencies (LEAs) or districts and schools that receive federal monies must employ specific personnel to assist with identifying students with disabilities and provide them with behavioral, academic, and mental health supports (IDEIA, 2004). Additionally, students must be periodically reevaluated to ensure that they are making adequate progress toward goals that are determined by a multidisciplinary team of educational and related professionals. Individuals who often fit the aforementioned role and serve on multidisciplinary teams include school psychologists, counselors, and social workers. Although these individuals are usually generalists and must shoulder a range of responsibilities, they can be utilized to help with mental health service delivery or consulted to ensure effective treatment generalization.

Lastly, although more research is needed, preliminary findings suggest that the provision of mental health services in schools can reduce disparities in service use among minority and culturally diverse students (Cummings, Ponce, & Mays, 2010). Furthermore, results from a study by Chandra and Minkovitz (2007) suggest that the stigma associated with seeking metal health services can be reduced through psychoeducation with school-based practitioners. Therefore engaging school-based mental health professionals in facilitating treatment and psychoeducation can help some youth become more amenable to receiving treatment for their OCD symptoms. Overall, as illustrated previously, utilizing school-based service delivery options can help with supporting youth with OCD who might otherwise not receive any support.

HOW DOES SCHOOL-BASED SERVICE DELIVERY WORK?

It is important for clinicians, regardless of the setting in which they practice, to understand the components of school-based service delivery. Although some variability exists across states, schools can provide academic, behavioral, and mental health services in three predominant ways that are driven by extant laws. These service delivery options are driven by different laws, policies, and best practices including the Individuals with Disabilities Education Improvement Act (IDEIA; Individuals with Disabilities Education Improvement Act, P.L. 101–476) and Section 504 of the Rehabilitation Act (Section 504; P.L. 93–112, amended P.L. 93–516) (Fig. 1). In addition, a multitiered intervention service delivery framework known as multitiered systems of support (MTSS) can also influence the provision of services to students displaying an array of needs, vulnerabilities, or problems (Sulkowski & Michael, 2014).

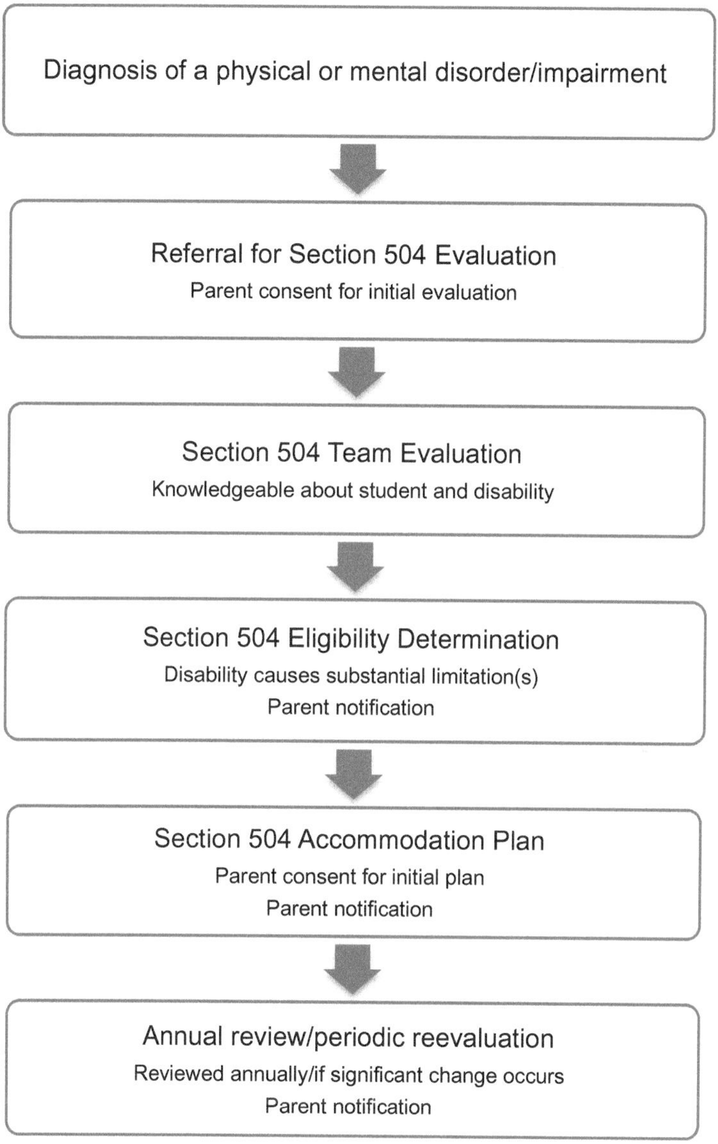

FIG. 1 Section 504 Plan/Intervention Accommodation Plan evaluation procedures flowchart.

The Individuals With Disabilities Education Improvement Act

The IDEIA is a federal special education law that mandates how federally funded public agencies, such as public districts and schools, provide early intervention, special education, and related services to children with disabilities (or suspected disabilities). Listing the 13 disability categories included in IDEIA, the Office of Special Education and Rehabilitative Services (OSERS, 2006) of the Federal Department of Education delineates criteria that must be met for a student to be classified as having a disability. However, because state departments of education are tasked with interpreting and implementing IDEIA's federal mandate, some variability exists across states in how students are evaluated for disabilities and provided with supportive interventions (U.S. Department of Education, § 300.8 (4) (i), p. 46756).

For example, states differ in how they describe students who could classify as having a disability because of severe emotional and behavioral problems, which may be relevant for some students with OCD. In addition, states can also vary in terms of eligibility criteria that must be met in order for a student to receive services. For example, some states require a note from a physician for a student to be eligible to receive services under an Other Health Impairment [OHI] classification (Sulkowski & Joyce-Beaulieu, 2014). Therefore in addition to being aware of IDEIA, clinicians also must know specific aspects of IDEIA that are dictated by the departments of education in the states in which they practice.

Out of the extant IDEIA disability categories, youth with OCD are most likely to be classified as having an Emotional Disturbance (ED) or OHI to receive special education services. It is important to note that youth should not be identified as having more than one classification and that the aforementioned disability categories are not diagnostically specific. In other words, many youth with a range of presenting psychiatric disorders, problems, or symptoms can be classified as meeting criteria for an IDEIA-recognized disability. According to federal criteria, students with ED should display one or more of the following characteristics over a long period of time and to a marked degree that adversely affects education performance:

> *(A) An inability to learn that cannot be explained by intellectual, sensory, or health factors; (B) an inability to build or maintain satisfactory interpersonal relationship with peers and teachers; (C) inappropriate types of behavior or feelings under normal circumstances; (D) a general pervasive mood of unhappiness or depression; and (E) a tendency to develop physical symptoms or fears associated with personal or school problems.*
>
> (OSERS, 2006, p. 46756).

In contrast, the OHI disability category is intended for youth with "acute or chronic health conditions" (OSERS, 2006, p. 46540). Although not an exhaustive list, federal OHI criteria further specify that the condition must result in the following: (p. 46550).

> *Having limited strength, vitality, or alertness, including a heightened alertness to environmental stimuli, that results in limited alertness with respect to the educational environment, that—(i) Is due to chronic or acute health problems such as asthma, attention deficit disorder or attention deficit hyperactivity disorder,*

> *diabetes, epilepsy, a heart condition, hemophilia, lead poisoning, leukemia, nephritis, rheumatic fever, sickle cell anemia, and Tourette syndrome; and (ii) Adversely affects a child's educational performance.*
>
> (OSERS, 2006, p. 46757).

Thus although core OCD symptoms are not explicitly included in IDEIA classification criteria, school personnel can argue that a student meets eligibility criteria for ED or OHI based on the student's symptom presentation and related impairment on educational performance (e.g., grades, psychosocial functioning); subsequently, the student is identified as having a disability and should be provided with special education services. Additionally, information provided from outside clinicians (e.g., psychological reports, treatment summaries, etc.) can be used by members of school-based multidisciplinary teams to help make eligibility determinations.

If a student is classified as having a disability under IDEIA, he or she is mandated to receive special education services on an Individualized Educational Program (IEP). These plans delineate the specific interventions, accommodations, and supports that the school will directly provide and/or financially cover to help a student meet specific educational and behavioral goals. Further, these plans must be maintained and updated annually until the student graduates high school or reaches his or her 21st birthday. In addition to listing specific services, IEPs also state where services will be provided (e.g., in a general education class, in a special education classroom, etc.) and who will provide the services (e.g., an Intervention Specialist, Speech-Language Pathologist, Occupational Therapist, etc.).

How to Help With the IEP Process

Mental health clinicians such as psychologists, social workers, and psychiatrists are accustomed to diagnosing psychopathology. However, as noted previously, educational professionals and school-based mental health professionals generally identify students as having a disability under one of the aforementioned IDEIA categories. Although these respective assessment or evaluation practices differ in terms of considered criteria (e.g., disorder symptoms, disability criteria, etc.), they are not entirely independent and can actually be complementary. For example, a diagnosis of OCD from an outside practitioner can be considered and used by school personnel for making classification decisions about whether a student should be identified as ED or OHI.

The decision to qualify a student with a disability must be made by a multidisciplinary team of individuals and the student must be assessed in all domains of the suspected disability. This team of professionals must include a legal guardian of the student and can involve outside practitioners. Therefore clinicians can be integral to the IDEIA-related classification process, as well as the process of determining possible accommodations or supports to be included on an IEP. In this role, clinicians can discuss recommendations for helping a student with OCD meet important and measurable academic and behavioral goals (provided the clinician has obtained consent from the legal guardian). Moreover, the inclusion of a therapist with experience treating OCD may be fundamental to ensure that appropriate accommodations and supports are provided, while potentially contraindicated ones are avoided.

Consistent with the last point, it is important to exclude any IEP accommodations that could exacerbate compulsions, increase behavioral avoidance, or interfere with treatment gains. For example, providing a student with a special seat cover may seem like an intuitive way to reduce contamination-related worry. However, carrying around such a cover may be unwieldy and, even worse, it might interfere with the habituation process associated with treatment. Therefore it is important for clinicians and school-based personnel to discuss and carefully consider the potential impacts that those specific accommodations will likely have on multiple outcomes. Ultimately, this discussion will involve weighing the relative advantages associated with supporting a student's academic functioning with progress in treatment or ability to cope with OCD symptoms.

To help with the IDEIA classification or IEP process, clinicians should communicate with legal guardians to ensure that appropriate consent procedures are being followed. In addition to the Health Insurance Portability and Accountability Act (HIPAA; Pub.L. 104–191, 110 Stat. 1936) of 1999, care is also needed to respect the confidentiality of a child's educational records. Therefore written consent must be obtained by different individuals and agencies for different reasons. For example, the clinician must obtain consent to share protected health information (PHI) with members of the school. Conversely, the school will need consent to share educational records with the clinician that are protected under IDEIA and the Family Educational Rights and Privacy Act (FERPA; 20 U.S.C. § 1232g; 34 CFR Part 99), as well as any PHI for which the school might be responsible (e.g., medications the student receives from the nurse, previous diagnoses). Additionally, schools are required to obtain consent from a legal guardian prior to evaluating a student for a potential disability, and again before providing the student with accommodations or interventions.

School psychologists often know the most about psychology in schools and education in the psychological community. Therefore it behooves clinicians to reach out to school psychologists (as they are consistently involved with classification decisions for students with emotional, behavioral, and mental health problems). School psychologists have training in educational law; assessment, diagnosis, and classification; functional behavior assessment and behavior modification; school-based consultation; and an increasing number now have (or are seeking) experience with mental health service delivery, including counseling and therapy (Joyce-Beaulieu & Sulkowski, 2015). Thus school psychologists can serve as a natural conduit for bridging the clinic-school gap.

Section 504 of the Rehabilitation Act

Section 504 of the Rehabilitation Act of 1973 guarantees various rights to individuals with disabilities; it also prohibits discrimination against those who are enrolled in federally funded programs (Rehabilitation Act of 1973, 1973). "Individuals with Disabilities" are defined by Section 504 as: "Persons with a physical or mental impairment which substantially limits one or more major life activities." Major life activities involve "caring for oneself, walking, seeing, hearing, speaking, breathing, working, performing manual tasks, and learning" (Section 504 of the Rehabilitation Act of 1973, as amended 29 U.S.C. § 794, 34 C.F.R. 104.3(j)(2)(i)).

Within the context of school-based service delivery, Section 504 aims to promote equal educational opportunities and decrease discrimination by requiring schools to provide reasonable accommodations to students with disabilities (e.g., preferential seating, extra time on assignments, use of assistive technology). However, in contrast to receiving services under IDEIA, no specific disability classification criteria need to be met for a student to receive accommodations under Section 504. Therefore such accommodations can be provided for temporary problems such as reintegrating a student with OCD and school avoidance, or chronic problems such as extensive school refusal associated with contamination concerns. Furthermore, accommodations under Section 504, which are listed on an Individualized Accommodation Plan (IAP), can be easily modified, augmented, or removed to meet the needs of a student as they vary over time. However, in contrast to IDEIA, schools must cover all expenses associated with Section 504 accommodations; no direct federal or state funding is available to cover these services. Because of this, schools with limited funding may struggle to provide Section 504-related accommodations, even if they may be beneficial (Sulkowski, Joyce, & Storch, 2012). This issue may be particularly problematic in rural communities where schools often lack full-time and within-building health service providers and mental health professionals.

To assist with the Section 504 and IAP process, similar concerns exist with regard to ensuring confidentiality under HIPAA and FERPA. However, less rigid procedures are needed when making modifications to or updating IAPs. Therefore clinicians can monitor a child's progress in treatment and make periodic suggestions about which accommodations or school-based interventions should be in place. For example, through collaboration a clinician and members of the school-based multidisciplinary team might decide that a student could benefit from carrying a safety object to and from classes during transition times and add this accommodation to an IAP. However, because of the importance of limiting the use of such safety objects in treatment, the safety object could eventually be removed from the IAP after the child experiences success in treatment.

MULTITIERED MENTAL HEALTH SERVICE DELIVERY

Multitiered Systems of Support (MTSS), also commonly called Response-to-Intervention (RtI), is a contemporary multitiered school-based service delivery framework. This framework is applied in order to address students displaying various academic, behavioral, and mental health needs that may or may not be related to any particular disability (Sulkowski & Michael, 2014; Wheeler & Mayton, 2010). Currently, no federal law mandates the implementation of MTSS; however, many state departments of education recently have incorporated MTSS-related language into their bulletins for intervention service delivery. For example, the following criterion must now be considered for classifying a student with ED in Louisiana: "Behavioral patterns, consistent with the definition, exist after behavior intervention and/or counseling and educational assistance implemented through the RTI process which includes documented research-based interventions targeting specific behaviors of concern" (Part C.L. Bulletin 1508–Pupil Appraisal Handbook, 2009). Thus in some states, in addition to meeting ED classification criteria, students also must fail to respond to an intervention that is designed to remediate their academic, behavior, or mental health problem(s).

The MTSS process generally involves the use of universal screening for academic and behavioral problems, the provision of evidence-based early intervention, team-based collaborative problem solving, progress monitoring of intervention effectiveness, and intervention scaffolding as needed (National Association of State Directors of Special Education, 2008; Sulkowski, Joyce, & Storch, 2012). Additionally, most MTSS frameworks include three tiers of intervention delivery that vary by intensity: Tier I (universal), Tier II (targeted), and Tier III (intensive).

Tier I service delivery generally involves the provision of research-based primary prevention or early intervention services to all students. Tier II intervention services are provided to students who do not respond adequately to Tier I services. These services are targeted in that they are delivered to at-risk students who display unaddressed needs and often are provided in small groups. Lastly, Tier III services intensively target problems displayed by students who do not effectively respond to Tier I and II interventions. These are often delivered individually to students who display symptoms or problems that significantly impair their educational performance and can be provided in collaboration with special education services if a student is classified with a disability (Sulkowski & Michael, 2014).

As the latest school-based service delivery model, MTSS is less familiar to noneducational professionals and only has been discussed within the context of mental health service delivery within the past decade or so (Sulkowski et al., 2013; Sulkowski & Michael, 2014). However, as the most flexible model, great potential exists for supporting the needs of students with OCD using MTSS. To help with such efforts, clinicians can communicate with members of MTSS or RTI teams[1] to determine what types of Tier I and II supports can be provided to help stabilize a student with OCD. Additionally, for students with more

1. Some other commonly used terms for such teams across different states include the multidisciplinary team (MDT), the multidisciplinary evaluation team (MET), school-building level committee (SBLC), and student study team (SST).

intensive problems or symptoms, clinicians can discuss providing targeted Tier III services, either directly or in collaboration with a school-based mental health provider. With the aforementioned model in mind, a child might meet with a clinician at his or her outpatient office for weekly CBT and then do additional behavioral exposures with a school psychologist at school in between appointments. Of course, the success of such an approach would depend on clear information sharing between parties, as well as involving caregivers in treatment to help with generalization and ensure that the child is not receiving contradictory information from different providers.

HOW CAN CLINICIANS ASSIST WITH SCHOOL-BASED SERVICE DELIVERY?

As discussed previously, a lot of leeway exists in how schools can support students with disabilities or problems that have a deleterious impact of their educational performance. Because of this, outside mental health providers often find school-based service delivery confusing, inconsistently implemented, and even counterintuitive at times (Joyce-Beaulieu & Sulkowski, 2015). However, it is critically important for these individuals to be involved with school-based service delivery efforts. School is one of the most important environments in children's lives—it is where they learn, grow, and forge important relationships. Additionally, it is where OCD symptoms often present and can be most functionally impairing. Thus consistent with the goal of bridging the clinic-school gap, the remaining sections of this chapter focus on ways that clinicians can provide a larger role in addressing OCD in school settings. In particular, 10 specific strategies on how clinicians can assist with school-based service delivery are delineated.

How to Identify OCD Symptoms in School Settings

OCD symptoms are highly heterogeneous and some are very context specific. For example, a child with contamination-related obsessions associated with exposure to people with physical disabilities might function relatively normally at home, yet struggle at school where many students have physical impairments and limitations. Similarly, school can be particularly stressful for a child with sexual obsessions related to younger children, the opposite sex, the same sex, one's teacher, or others more generally.

However, despite being highly variable, some common signs exist that OCD symptoms might be impacting a student at school. Although no single sign is suggestive of having OCD, when a cluster of functionally related signs are present, it is important for clinicians and supportive adults at school to take notice and assess whether a child is experiencing educational or other functional impairments. Some common signs that a child might be struggling with OCD at school include frequent cleaning/hand washing (red, chapped hands);

long frequent trips to the bathroom; avoidance of the playground, art supplies, sticky substances; frequently having untied shoelaces (may be contaminated); engaging in safety behaviors (e.g., carrying paper towels); refusing to sit in public places or use playground equipment; turning in assignments with excessive erasing, words/numbers retraced, or needless corrections; inability to turn in "imperfect" assignments as well as purposely not turning in assignments; not participating in swimming or refusing to change in the locker room; having to carry a seat cushion or pad (not for a legitimate medical reason); avoiding scissors, sharpened pencils, compasses, and pens; taking excessive time to take tests; and appearing distracted, preoccupied, or engaged in other mental activities during instruction.

How to Collaborate With School Personnel?

Clinicians can reach out to school personnel to inform them of certain signs of symptoms of impairment to look for in students with OCD. Often, OCD symptoms are baffling and difficult for educators and even school-based mental health professionals to identify, understand, and address (Sloman, Gallant, & Storch, 2007). The presence of intrusive thoughts and high levels of anxiety can appear as inattention or distractibility and be misperceived by educators. Additionally, some youth with OCD engage in anxiety-driven acting out and avoidant behavior, which can be misunderstood as being deliberately oppositional or disruptive to instruction.

Through interdisciplinary collaboration, clinicians can provide psychoeducation on OCD symptoms and how these symptoms might manifest in school settings. Furthermore, they can inform school personnel about effective and available treatment options in the community. Individuals with OCD, especially children, often do not receive evidence-based treatments such as cognitive-behavioral therapy (CBT) with exposure and response prevention (ERP) as a core component (Jordan et al., 2013). Instead, they often receive supportive psychotherapy or psychopharmacological treatment, which are nonoptional stand-alone treatments. Thus through engaging members of school communities, practitioners can establish their skill set for treating OCD and be a primary referral source for children and families impacted by OCD.

OCD treatment and collaboration in school settings is a salient issue and crucial for comprehensive care to achieve optimal symptom reduction. In this vein we offer the following recommendations:

THERAPIST RECOMMENDATIONS

1. Identify the school psychologist who provides services in your patient/client's school. Currently, there is a critical need for school psychologists nationwide, which has led to very high school psychologist to student ratios. Schools psychologists often work in several different schools within a

particular district (e.g., elementary, middle, and high) and may only be in any one school 1–2 times a week. Therefore it is recommended to also identify the school counselor who will typically be at the same school every day as a potential collaborative resource. Additionally, obtaining releases of information from the school and providing your practice's release to talk to the school initially helps to address the barrier of confidential communication between all parties. Finally, exchange of direct contact numbers helps to prevent communication delays or barriers.

2. Working collaboratively with schools and providing lectures or trainings on OCD can help facilitate communication and partnerships in the community. Offering to provide a lecture at a Parent-Teacher Association (PTA) meeting or staff/faculty in-service/continuing education can be a valuable service to the school that continues to break down barriers to multidisciplinary collaboration and treatment. These lectures can also serve as a way to help school personnel identify children who display OCD symptoms/behaviors and facilitate referrals for treatment to qualified therapists.
3. Once a collaborative relationship has been established with the school, participation in IEP or 504 meetings can play a crucial role in providing comprehensive treatment and remove barriers to school-based exposure engagement. IEP meetings provide a forum in which parents, teachers, school psychologists, counselors, and school personnel can work collaboratively to create a comprehensive plan to help a patient/client maximize academic achievement through appropriate accommodations and school-based interventions. OCD therapists can advocate for reasonable and appropriate accommodations (e.g., taking a break in a quiet office, more frequent bathroom passes, early release between classes, preferred seating, etc.). It is important to clarify that these accommodations will change and be reduced as the patient/client progresses through exposure therapy. IEP meetings also provide an excellent opportunity to answer questions from all parties that have contact with a patient/client and clarify ways to help with treatment and respond to ritual engagement.
4. In the context of multidisciplinary collaboration, discussion of the exposure hierarchy can help with understanding patient/client's treatment goals and the importance of working specific items. Several questions can arise related to how a school teacher, counselor, or psychologist can or should react to ritualistic behaviors. A formal discussion of the hierarchy helps demonstrate the proposed progress through treatment and how accommodating some symptoms initially may be important in order to not engage in more difficult exposures before the patient/client is ready. Often, it may be important to say, "Yes, I agree that is challenging in the classroom and is a part of our treatment, but we will address that when Billy is ready and has conquered his easier items on the exposure hierarchy list." We have found that is it important to confirm that school impairment and disruptions are a crucial part of treatment and will be addressed, but gradual progression

from easier items to harder exposure items is vital to successful treatment and significant symptom reduction.

5. Providing psychoeducation on accommodation and reassurance can help teachers and school psychologists identify appropriate strategies for managing OCD symptoms. For example, a student who demonstrates symptoms related to perfectionism may repeatedly ask a teacher if they completed an assignment correctly. Providing teachers with information related to why a student might engage in these behaviors, as well as how to respond to them, create consistency in treatment and help minimize frustration that teachers may experience when working with a child with OCD. Children who are able to receive consistent messages about accommodation, both at home and at school, may be able to better generalize learning across different environments.
6. Utilization of school psychologists or counselors as therapists in the school can truly help with adherence to exposure homework and provide another setting for generalization and habituation to anxiety-provoking stimuli. School psychologists or counselors can help with advising teachers and staff therapist's recommendations for addressing accommodations of symptoms and encouraging ritual resistance/exposure engagement. From our clinical experience, we have been able to work collaboratively with schools to help facilitate exposures or achieve solutions to accommodations that are appropriate for the school environment and require minimal effort/school resources.
7. Finally, open communication and collaborative relationship with schools can ultimately lead to more informed school personnel on proper OCD treatment and referrals. OCD therapists can serve as an expert information source for treatment recommendations and advocacy beyond therapy services.

REFERENCES

Abramowitz, J. S., Foa, E. B., & Franklin, M. E. (2003). Exposure and ritual prevention for obsessive-compulsive disorder: Effects of intensive versus twice weekly sessions. *Journal of Consulting and Clinical Psychology*, *71*, 394–398. http://dx.doi.org/10.1037/0022-06X.71.2.394.

Björgvinsson, T., Hart, J., & Heffelfinger, S. (2007). Obsessive compulsive disorder: An update on assessment and treatment. *Journal of Psychiatric Practice*, *13*, 362–372. http://dx.doi.org/10.1097/01.pra.0000300122.76322.ad.

Chandra, A., & Minkovitz, C. S. (2007). Factors that influence mental health stigma among 8th grade adolescents. *Journal of Youth and Adolescence*, *36*, 763–774. http://dx.doi.org/10.1007/s10964-006-9091-0.

Corbie-Smith, G., Thomas, S. B., & George, D. M. M. S. (2002). Distrust, race, and research. *Archives of Internal Medicine*, *162*, 2458–2463. http://dx.doi.org/10.1001/archinte.162.21.2458.

Cummings, J. R., Ponce, N. A., & Mays, V. M. (2010). Comparing racial/ethnic differences in mental health service use among high-need subpopulations across clinical and school-based settings. *Journal of Adolescent Health*, *46*, 603–606. http://dx.doi.org/10.1016/j.jadohealth.2009.11.221.

Dowdy, E., Ritchey, K., & Kamphaus, R. W. (2010). School based screening: A population-based approach to inform and monitor children's mental health needs. *School Mental Health*, *2*, 166–176. http://dx.doi.org/10.1007/s12310-010-9036-3.

Eberhardt, M., Freid, V. M., Harper, S., Ingram, D. D., Makuc, D. M., Pamuk, E., et al. (2001). *Urban and rural health chartbook*. Health Hyattsville, MD: National Center for Health Statistics.

Family education rights: Privacy ACT (FERPA) of 1974. (2012). 20 6.S.C. § 34 CFR Part 99.

Gone, J. P., & Kirmayer, L. J. (2010). On the wisdom of considering culture and context in psychopathology. In T. Millon, R. F. Krueger, & E. Simonsen (Eds.), *Contemporary directions in psychopathology: Scientific foundations of the DSM-V and ICD-11* (pp. 72–96). New York, NY: Guilford.

Hernandez, M., Nesman, T., Mowery, D., Acevedo-Polakovich, I. D., & Callejas, L. M. (2009). Cultural competence: A literature review and conceptual model for mental health services. *Psychiatric Services*, *60*, 1046–1050. http://dx.doi.org/10.1176/ps.2009.60.8.1046.

Himle, M. B., & Franklin, M. E. (2009). The more you do it, the easier it gets: Exposure and response prevention for OCD. *Cognitive and Behavioral Practice*, *16*, 29–39. http://dx.doi.org/10.1016/j.cbpra.2008.03.002.

Individuals with Disabilities Education Improvement Act of 2004. 20 U.S.C. § 1400 et seq.

Jordan, C., De Nadai, A., Sulkowski, M. L., & Storch, E. A. (2013). Predictors of treatment history in youth with obsessive-compulsive disorder. *Minerva Psichiatrica*, *54*, 31–40.

Jordan, C., Reid, A. M., Mariaskin, A., Augusto, B., & Sulkowski, M. L. (2012). First-line treatment for pediatric obsessive–compulsive disorder. *Journal of Contemporary Psychotherapy*, *42*, 243–248. http://dx.doi.org/10.1007/s10879-012-9210-z.

Joyce-Beaulieu, D., & Sulkowski, M. L. (2015). *Cognitive behavioral therapy in K-12 school settings: A practitioner's toolkit*. New York, NY: Springer Publishing Company.

Kessler, R. C., Avenevoli, S., Costello, E. J., Georgiades, K., Green, J. G., Gruber, M. J., et al. (2012). Prevalence, persistence, and sociodemographic correlates of DSM-IV disorders in the National Comorbidity Survey Replication Adolescent Supplement. *Archives of General Psychiatry*, *69*, 372–380. http://dx.doi.org/10.1001/archgenpsychiatry.2011.160.

Kroll, J., & Erickson, P. (2002). Religion and psychiatry. *Current Opinion in Psychiatry*, *15*, 549–554.

Louisiana Department of Education. (2009). *Bulletin 1508: Louisiana pupil appraisal handbook. Retrieved from http://www.doe.state.la.us/divisions/specialp/bulletin_1508_training.html.*

Marazziti, D., & Consoli, G. (2010). Treatment strategies for obsessive-compulsive disorder. *Expert Opinion on Pharmacotherapy*, *11*, 331–343.

Nakatani, E., Mataix-Cols, D., Micali, N., Turner, C., & Heyman, I. (2009). Outcomes of cognitive behaviour therapy for obsessive compulsive disorder in a clinical setting: A 10-year experience from a specialist OCD service for children and adolescents. *Child and Adolescent Mental Health*, *14*, 133–139. http://dx.doi.org/10.1111/j.1475-3588.2008.00509.x.

National Association of State Directors of Special Education. (2008). *Response to intervention: Blueprints for implementation. Retrieved from https://www.nasdse.org/Portals/0/DISTRICT.pdf.*

Office of Special Education and Rehabilitative Services, & Department of Education. (2006). *Federal register: Part II Department of Education, 34 CFR Parts 300 and 301, Assistance to states for the education of children with disabilities and preschool grants for children with disabilities; Final rule*. Author.

Owens, P. L., Hoagwood, K., Horwitz, S. M., Leaf, P. J., Poduska, J. M., Kellam, S. G., et al. (2002). Barriers to children's mental health services. *Journal of American Academy of Child and Adolescent Psychiatry*, *41*, 731–738. http://dx.doi.org/10.1097/00004583-200206000-00013.

President's New Freedom Commission on Mental Health (2003). *Achieving the promise: Transforming mental health in America Final report*. Rockville, MD: DHHS Publication.

Rapoport, J. L., Inoff-Germain, G., Weissman, M. M., Greenwald, S., Narrow, W. E., Jensen, P. S., et al. (2000). Childhood obsessive–compulsive disorder in the NIMH MECA Study: Parent versus child identification of cases. *Journal of Anxiety Disorders, 14*, 535–548. http://dx.doi.org/10.1016/S0887-6185(00)00048-7.

Rehabilitation Act of 1973. Pub. L. 93–112. 26 Sept. 1973. H.R. 8070.

Reinherz, H. Z., Giaconia, R. M., Pakiz, B., Silverman, A. B., Frost, A. K., & Lefkowitz, E. S. (1993). Psychosocial risks for major depression in late adolescence: A longitudinal community study. *Journal of the American Academy of Child & Adolescent Psychiatry, 32*, 1155–1163. http://dx.doi.org/10.1097/00004583-199311000-00007.

Sloman, G. M., Gallant, J., & Storch, E. A. (2007). A school-based treatment model for pediatric obsessive-compulsive disorder. *Child Psychiatry and Human Development, 38*, 303–319. http://dx.doi.org/10.1007/s10578-007-0064-7.

Sulkowski, M. L. (in press). Legal and ethical issues related to rural school mental health. In K. Michael & J. P. Jameson (Eds.), *Handbook of rural school mental health*. New York, NY: Springer.

Sulkowski, M. L., Jordan, C., & Nguyen, M. L. (2009). Current practices and future directions in psychopharmacological training and collaboration in school psychology. *Canadian Journal of School Psychology, 24*, 237–244. http://dx.doi.org/10.1177/0829573509338616.

Sulkowski, M. L., Joyce, D. J., & Storch, E. A. (2012). Treating childhood anxiety in schools: Service delivery in a response to intervention paradigm. *Journal of Child and Family Studies, 21*, 938–947. http://dx.doi.org/10.1007/s10826-011-9553-1.

Sulkowski, M. L., & Joyce-Beaulieu, D. K. (2014). School-based service delivery for homeless students: Relevant laws and overcoming access barriers. *American Journal of Orthopsychiatry, 84*, 711–719. http://dx.doi.org/10.1037/ort0000033.

Sulkowski, M. L., Mancil, T. L., Jordan, C., Reid, A., Chakoff, E., & Storch, E. A. (2011). Validation of a classification system of obsessive-compulsive spectrum disorder symptoms in a non-clinical sample. *Psychiatry Research, 188*, 65–70. http://dx.doi.org/10.1016/j.psychres.2011.01.015.

Sulkowski, M. L., & Michael, K. (2014). Meeting the mental health needs of homeless students in schools: A multi-tiered system of support framework. *Children and Youth Services Review, 44*, 145–151. http://dx.doi.org/10.1016/j.childyouth.2014.06.014.

Sulkowski, M. L., Wingfield, R. J., Jones, D., & Coulter, W. A. (2011). Response to intervention and interdisciplinary collaboration: Joining hands to support children's healthy development. *Journal of Applied School Psychology, 27*, 118–133. http://dx.doi.org/10.1080/15377903.2011.565264.

Wheeler, J. J., & Mayton, M. R. (2010). *Other innovative techniques: Positive behavior supports and response to intervention. Current issues and trends in special education: Identification, assessment and instruction: Vol. 19* (pp. 175–195). http://dx.doi.org/10.1108/S0270-4013(2010)0000019015.

FURTHER READING

Abramowitz, J. S., Taylor, S., & McKay, D. (2009). Obsessive compulsive disorder. *Lancet, 374*, 491–499. http://dx.doi.org/10.1016/S0140-6736(09)60240-3.

Grant, J. E. (2014). Obsessive compulsive disorder. *New England Journal of Medicine, 201*, 646–653.

Tolin, D. F., Diefenbach, G. J., & Gilliam, C. M. (2011). Stepped care versus standard cognitive behavioral therapy for obsessive-compulsive disorder: A preliminary study of efficacy and costs. *Depression and Anxiety, 28*, 314–323. http://dx.doi.org/10.1002/da.20804.

U.S. Department of Health and Human Services. (1996). *Health Insurance Portability and Accountability Act of 1996 (HIPAA). Retrieved from: http://www.hhs.gov/hipaa/.*

Chapter 13

Addressing Family Accommodation in Childhood Obsessive-Compulsive Disorder

Eli R. Lebowitz
Yale Child Study Center, New Haven, CT, United States

WHAT IS FAMILY ACCOMMODATION?

Childhood Obsessive-Compulsive Disorder: A Systemic Perspective

The impact of Obsessive-Compulsive Disorder (OCD) is not limited to the individual patient and extends in most cases to those closest to them, in particular family members. This is true for OCD across the life span and is particularly the case when it is a young person, a child or an adolescent, who is coping with OCD. Indeed, OCD in childhood may be best conceptualized as a systemic rather than individual phenomenon. Like most other mammals, young humans cope with threat and distress through a complex set of interpersonal signaling and behavior involving both the child and their caregivers. Caregivers (chiefly parents) are predisposed to respond to their child's threat and distress cues by providing essential functions relating to protection and regulation. As such, any disorder that causes chronic activation of the threat system, or that causes repeated experiences of internal distress and negative arousal in a child, will inevitably also trigger aspects of this complex interpersonal system of reciprocal signaling and social behavior.

When a child experiences an obsessive thought, and its associated anxiety, they signal that anxiety to parents, who in turn are motivated to aid their child in alleviating the distress. Over time, parents will often act preemptively to avoid situations that would cause distress to the child. Likewise, a child's need to perform a compulsive ritual will often engage parents in attempts to provide the child with assistance in completing the ritual and achieving relief. The term *family accommodation* encompasses the myriad changes that parents make to

The Clinician's Guide to Cognitive-Behavioral Therapy for Childhood Obsessive-Compulsive Disorder
http://dx.doi.org/10.1016/B978-0-12-811427-8.00013-7

their own behavior in their attempts to help their child avoid or alleviate distress related to the symptoms of their disorder.

Family Accommodation—A Brief History

Family accommodation was first introduced as a formal description of caregiver involvement in the symptoms of OCD by Calvocoressi et al. (1995). That study, and another that followed (Calvocoressi et al., 1999), focused on parents and relatives of adults with OCD. Subsequent studies soon established that family accommodation is also highly prevalent among parents of children with OCD. Tools for the identification and assessment of family accommodation in childhood OCD were developed (and are described in this chapter), and several studies underscored the importance of family accommodation for both the clinical course and the treatment outcomes of childhood OCD (Caporino et al., 2012; Farrell & Barrett, 2007; Flessner et al., 2011; Futh, Simonds, & Micali, 2012; Stewart et al., 2008; Strauss, Hale, & Stobie, 2015).

Family accommodation is consistently linked to more severe OCD symptoms and to greater degrees of impairment related to those symptoms. The presence of high levels of family accommodation prior to treatment has also been identified as a prognostic marker of high importance. In an analysis of outcomes from the largest randomized controlled trial of childhood OCD treatment (Pediatric OCD Treatment Study Team, 2004), family accommodation was the only family-level variable to be identified as a significant predictor of treatment results (Garcia et al., 2010). High levels of family accommodation predicted poor response to treatment, and the pattern held regardless of whether the child received individual cognitive-behavior therapy (CBT), medication, or a combination of both treatments. In contrast, parental psychopathology, family history of OCD, and family functioning were not significant predictors of child outcomes across treatment conditions, although family history of OCD moderated results, with poorer outcomes for children who received only behavioral treatment and no medication. Other studies have also implicated family accommodation in poor response to treatment and demonstrated that successful treatment is associated with reductions in family accommodation (Rudy, Lewin, Geffken, Murphy, & Storch, 2014; Storch et al., 2007). A study in adults found that OCD patients who did not respond to treatment had higher levels of family accommodation compared to treatment responders (Ferrao et al., 2006).

In recent years, family accommodation has also been established as a key construct across anxiety disorders in addition to OCD (Jones, Lebowitz, Marin, & Stark, 2015; Lebowitz, Panza, & Bloch, 2016; Lebowitz, Scharfstein, & Jones, 2015; Lebowitz et al., 2013; Norman, Silverman, & Lebowitz, 2015; Storch et al., 2015). A comparison of family accommodation in childhood OCD and childhood anxiety disorders revealed overall similar levels and patterns of accommodation and confirmed the association between family accommodation and symptom severity (Lebowitz, Scharfstein, &

While superficially comparable situations, there are several theoretical reasons and substantial empirical evidence indicating that family accommodation of childhood OCD can actually contribute to the symptoms and impede treatment.

Frontline treatments for childhood OCD, in particular Cognitive-Behavioral Therapy (CBT), emphasize confronting OCD triggers rather than avoiding them, and gaining the skills to better regulate the distress they cause. Family accommodation can act in the opposite direction. By accommodating a child with OCD, parents may be promoting avoidant behavior and reinforcing a pattern of the child's reliance on them for regulation, rather than developing the skills for self-regulation. Family accommodation may also provide the child with confirmation that their obsessive thoughts or beliefs are true and valid, thereby impeding the development of better insight into the pathological nature of those thoughts (Adelman & Lebowitz, 2012). For example, a child who fears they will become ill if the whole family does not engage in a hand washing ritual may perceive their parent's acquiescence as confirmation of the worrying belief. Family accommodation may also provide the child with an alternative to the hard work of therapy and lead to reduced motivation for treatment or to lower treatment compliance. For example, a child whose parents agree not to drive a certain route because it triggers the child's distress may be less motivated for therapy than a child who is experiencing distress because their parents drive the route anyway.

The remainder of this chapter focuses on tools and strategies for addressing family accommodation in cases of childhood OCD. Reducing family accommodation is a goal in several interventions for childhood OCD with varying degrees of emphasis and specificity of tools or strategies (Comer et al., 2014; Freeman et al., 2014; Thompson-Hollands, Abramovitch, Tompson, & Barlow, 2015). The steps described in this chapter draw most heavily from a program developed with the primary purpose of reducing family accommodation. The SPACE Program (Supportive Parenting for Anxious Childhood Emotions) is a parent-based approach to childhood OCD and anxiety that aims to reduce family accommodation as a means of treating the child's disorder (Lebowitz & Omer, 2013). Case studies and two open trials of The SPACE Program have been published, one in OCD, and have demonstrated the potential of accommodation reduction as an effective therapeutic approach (Lebowitz, 2013, 2015; Lebowitz, Omer, Hermes, & Scahill, 2014). These tools, however, need not be implemented as an alternative to working directly with the child and, as described in more detail in this chapter, can be used in concert with other therapeutic interventions to address this key aspect of childhood OCD.

ADDRESSING FAMILY ACCOMMODATION IN TREATMENT

Assessment of Family Accommodation

Assessment of family accommodation should be part of any assessment for childhood OCD. Nonstructured assessment of family accommodation can include a frank conversation with parents about the ways in which their lives have changed as a result of their child's difficulty. Informing parents that some level of family accommodation is almost inevitable, and that they are not being blamed for providing it, may help to facilitate the conversation. Since many parents will not immediately identify or recall all the accommodations they provide, it is useful to describe some common accommodations, and also to ask about accommodations related to the various OCD symptoms that have been described in other parts of the assessment.

> *You told me about Jason's symptoms and now I'd like to ask you a little bit about how those symptoms have been affecting you and the rest of your family. Children typically rely on their parents for help with these kinds of problems and as a parent you probably want to help Jason feel as good as he can. Have you ever felt like you need to help Jason with his OCD, or like his OCD is causing you to do things differently? Can you tell me more about that?*
>
> *One of the things you described to me is that Jason gets very upset if he hears the word Zika, or any reference to the Zika virus on the news or in other places. What would you do if the television was on and a report about Zika came on, for example? Has Jason ever asked you not to say that word? Or to make any other changes because it freaks him out so much?*

Another useful line of questioning is to ask parents if they feel like the OCD is "taking over" other parts of the family life. Many parents of children with OCD recognize themselves in this description and will relate to the sense that OCD is gradually taking over their time, their personal space, or their ability to act as they wish.

Family accommodation can also be assessed using more formal and structured assessment tools. The interviewer rated Family Accommodation Scale (FAS-IR) consists of two parts (Calvocoressi et al., 1999). First, a checklist of symptoms adapted from the Yale-Brown Obsessive Compulsive Scale is administered and provides a list of current OCD symptoms. Then, a series of questions pertaining to different forms of family accommodation is administered. Specific reference is made to accommodations relating to each of the symptoms endorsed during the first part of the interview. The scores from these items provide an overall index for the extent of family accommodation. A self-rated version of the instrument has also been developed (FAS-SR) and requires approximately 20 min to complete (Pinto, Van Noppen, & Calvocoressi, 2013). Finally, a patient-rated version of the same instrument has also been developed (FAS-PV) and tested in adults (Wu et al., 2015). Asking children with OCD about their parents' accommodation can provide useful information beyond what is provided by the parents themselves, as has also been demonstrated in the assessment of family accommodation in anxiety disorders (Lebowitz et al., 2015).

In addition to the tools and instruments described previously, it is often useful to use a daily schedule to map out (and later to monitor) parents' accommodating behaviors. A daily schedule, listing the various times of day during which parents interact with the child and the various accommodations that occur can significantly enhance the overall clinical picture. Particular attention should be paid to "accommodation hotspots"—moments and situations that are likely to elicit family accommodation either because of the nature of the situation or in light of the child's particular symptoms. For example, meal times often elicit a lot of accommodation, as do transitions and separation, washing and showering, and bedtime. The schedule should be completed separately for each parent, and it is often useful to have separate ones for weekdays and for weekends or holidays. In addition to asking about the parents' family accommodation, clinicians can ask about the ways in which siblings and others in the home (e.g., grandparents) accommodate the child. It is common for a sibling to either explicitly or inadvertently accommodate their sibling's OCD. Though the opposite, namely, deliberate and provocative triggering of OCD symptoms by a sibling, is also not unheard of.

Identifying a Target Accommodation

Most parents of children with OCD will describe multiple forms of family accommodation. Recommending that parents cease all accommodation at once is unlikely to prove effective. Such an approach is akin to trying to modify many aspects of a child's defiant behavior at once or to attempting to learn multiple new and complex skills at the same time. In short, it is likely to backfire. Parents who are advised to refrain from all forms of accommodation will most likely adopt a haphazard approach, accommodating some of the time and attempting not to at others. Not only will such behavior not provide the child with a consistent and predictable pattern from which to learn, but the inconsistency will be guided by nontherapeutic factors. For example, the parents may choose not to accommodate at certain times because they are tired, busy, or angry with the child for reasons unrelated to the accommodation. This will most likely send the child the message that they are not accommodating as a form of punishment, rather than because they believe the child is able to cope independently or because they believe that the accommodation is unhelpful in the longer term. For all these reasons, choosing a specific target in which to reduce the family accommodation, and choosing wisely, is of great importance.

Several considerations can facilitate the selection of a target as the first focus of a plan to reduce family accommodation. Firstly, it is useful to choose to concentrate on an accommodation that the parents feel interferes with their lives, or impedes their functioning, in a meaningful way. Choosing a target of only minor importance may seem easier, but is also likely to elicit a lower sense of commitment and determination on the part of the parents. Parents will need this determination if they are to persist at withholding the accommodating behavior. Asking parents to reflect on the accommodations that most get in the way of other activities, or that cause them the most exasperation can help in this regard.

Secondly, the target should be an accommodation that happens frequently. Preferably on a daily, or even multiple times per day, basis. This will ensure that there are sufficient opportunities to practice the new behavioral pattern and to correct their implementation of the plan, or to make changes to the plan itself if their early attempts do not go well. For example, some parents may highlight the child's need of accommodations in getting to school. This may be a useful target to choose if school is in session but is unlikely to provide ample opportunity for work over the summer vacation. Finally, it is important that the target be a parental behavior, and that it be a parental behavior that the parents can choose to change. For example, parents may describe a child's endless need for reassurance as a target of choice. The therapist would have to clarify that while a child asking for reassurance is not an example of family accommodation, the parents providing that reassurance is.

Maintaining Transparency and Setting the Stage

Central to the goal of reducing family accommodation is that the child be aware of the reasons for the change in the parents' behavior, and that this change be framed as part of an attempt to help the child overcome OCD. Merely modifying the parental behavior in the absence of such a frame may be effective in combatting OCD symptoms but is also likely to cause frustration, confusion, and resistance on the part of the child. Informing the child of the plan to reduce the accommodation can also help to solidify the parents' commitment to the plan and to reduce the risk of backpedaling should the process prove more difficult than expected.

Alongside the commitment to transparency and openness about the accommodation reduction plan, it is also important not to make the implementation of such a plan contingent on the child's approval or consent. A key benefit of focusing on modifications to parental behavior, rather than attempting to directly shape the child's behavior, is the potential for effective intervention even in the absence of child collaboration. As noted previously, high levels of family accommodation can be conducive to lower treatment motivation and to lower compliance in the child. When this is the case it may be most beneficial to focus first on modifying the parental behavior before persisting with attempts to directly engage the child.

When possible, engaging the child in a collaborative effort is preferable. A frank discussion, led by the therapist, about family accommodation and the reasons to reduce it is a good starting point. The child should not be held responsible for the family accommodation and there is no need to assign blame for existing behavioral patterns. Rather, the family accommodation should be described as a choice the parents have made in their attempts to help and care for the child. A choice which they now understand to be misguided, and which they aim to change. The specific target problem should be described, followed by a discussion of the changes the parents will make to their behavior.

A collaborative child can have useful input into designing the specifics of the plan to reduce family accommodation. For example, a child who relies on parents to perform regular checks can provide input into the degree of initial change they believe they can cope with. The child may also suggest alternative parental responses which they believe will be useful and encouraging for them.

Forming a collaborative plan in this manner should not be confused by parents (or therapists) with a need for the child to provide consent to implementing the plan at every step of the way. A child who rationally understands the importance of reducing the accommodation may cooperate on designing a plan in the therapeutic session. The same child however may feel too anxious when experiencing the acute OCD symptoms to agree that their parents should abide by that plan. Parents should be advised not to seek the child's approval in the moment but to act on the agreed-upon plan regardless of the child's consent or disapproval.

When a child is too anxious, or otherwise disinclined, to collaboratively work on reducing the family accommodation the therapist can work with the parents to do so nonetheless. Informing the child in advance, and correctly framing the parents' intent as an attempt to help the child, is important. This communication, and all communication about the child's symptoms, should be *supportive*.

Supportive Communication

Supportive communication about a child's anxiety combines an acknowledgment and acceptance of the child's difficulty, with a confidence in the child's ability to cope with and to tolerate OCD-related distress. When parental messages convey only acceptance of the child's difficulty, they are empathic and may be comforting. They are not however supportive (as defined here) because they do not promote better coping or guide the child toward overcoming the problem. When a message denies or trivializes the child's difficulty, it is likewise not supportive as the child senses that their parents don't "get it" and is likely to feel misunderstood or rejected. Even among very empathic and sensitive parents, it is not uncommon to hear statements and messages that deny the child's actual experience. Statements such as "it's not scary" or "don't think about it" are well intentioned, but for a child who is, in fact, experiencing the acute distress of OCD symptoms, these statements can seem detached and unhelpful. Furthermore, implying that a child "should" be able to better control their thoughts or feelings can elicit unhelpful frustration and a sense of failure. By combining the validation of the child's experience, with confidence in the child's ability to withstand and overcome that experience, parents can express their support and provide the framework for the reduced accommodation.

Therapists can help parents to ensure that they communicate their plan to reduce family accommodation in a supportive manner by planning with the parents precisely what they are going to say. Role-play can be incorporated into the session and delivery of the message to the child can be practiced. Role playing of this kind may feel artificial at first, but it also provides significant benefits. First, it ensures that the first time parents actually talk about reducing family accommodation will not be to the child, when both parents and child may be under stress. Second, it provides opportunities to plan for possible child reactions to their message and devise positive responses to these reactions. For example, while role playing parents may realize that their child is likely to react with emotional distress. Others may predict that their child will become aggressive and some parents will expect their child to react by simply by ignoring them. If not planned for in advance, these responses may lead to negative outcomes such as parents shifting the topic of the conversation (e.g., talking about the need to be respectful rather than about family accommodation), or to escalation and argument.

Another tool for ensuring supportive communication, and avoiding conflict and escalation is the use of written messages. Therapists can draft a brief and supportive note to the child, discussing the need to reduce the accommodation. Parents can then either give the note to the child or read it to them. Written communication also feels unnatural and forced to many parents, but helps to ensure that they will "stay on message." What follows is one example of a supportive statement parents can make to a child, explaining their intent to reduce family accommodation at home:

> *Laine, we love you and we know how awful your OCD can make you feel. We understand that you get so uncomfortable when you have OCD thoughts, like the thought that somebody sneezed on you and you could get sick. We know that you want us to promise you that you won't get sick and we have been doing that a lot recently. But we also know that by making all those promises we are not actually helping you to get better. We have realized that we are actually helping your OCD to get worse! We love you and we have decided we are going to stop helping OCD and start helping you! Instead of promising you that you won't get sick we will remind you that this is just an OCD thought. We are 100% confident in how strong you are and we know you will be able to cope. Love, Mom and Dad.*

Formulating a Plan to Reduce Family Accommodation—Practical Considerations

"A goal without a plan is just a wish." This quote, attributed to the French writer Antoine de Saint-Exupery, captures the importance of formulating a concrete plan and operationalizing the goal of reducing parental accommodation. Identifying a target accommodation, and advising parents to refrain from accommodating, without translating that goal into a clearly defined set of steps is akin to advising a person to eat healthier food without equipping them with a specific series of changes to implement. Worse, it places parents in the unhelpful position of having to determine the precise action under the stress of a child requesting, or demanding, accommodation. The absence of a clearly defined plan also places stress on the ability of two parents to cooperate with each other, as each of them may have a different interpretation and understanding of how to achieve the goal.

A well-formulated plan will include concrete descriptions of when and how parents will behave differently compared to their past behavior. Will parents completely remove the accommodation or will they reduce it gradually? If they are to reduce it gradually, what is the precise sequence of graded steps they will take? Which behaviors, exactly, are included under the accommodation being targeted? In an illustrative example, two parents were accustomed to accommodating their child with OCD by not opening windows in the home because the child feared exposure to possible radiation from electric lines outside. They soon realized that "we will not agree to not open windows" was too vague a statement for them to implement effectively. They needed to define when exactly they would open windows, which windows would be opened and which would not, how frequently would they open them, and would the child be allowed to keep their own window shut.

The plan should also specify how parents *will* respond in those situations where they would previously have provided accommodation. Deciding on an agreed upon and supportive phrase that both parents will use consistently can help the child to adapt to the new behavioral pattern with less difficulty. For example, parents may say "We know OCD is really making you upset right now and you feel like you need us to [accommodate] but we know that doesn't really help you and we're sure you'll be ok." The section on *Troubleshooting and Coping with Challenging Circumstances*, later in this chapter, includes suggestions for parents whose child responds with aggression or extreme distress to the behavioral changes.

Here is one example of an accommodation reduction plan formulated with the parents of an 8-year-old child. The parents had been providing family accommodation by checking the child's backpack multiple times each school night and morning to confirm the right things were packed. They also had been repeatedly re-covering the child's books and notebooks to ensure they were "perfectly" covered.

Accommodation Plan

1. *Mom or Dad (not both) will check your backpack one time in the evening.*
2. *Mom and Dad will not check the backpack in the morning.*
3. *Mom and Dad will not answer more than one question each, every day, relating to school equipment.*
4. *Mom and Dad will not cover any more books or notebooks unless they are new (even if you remove the covers completely).*
5. *Mom and Dad will not buy more covers for school things.*

Implementation

Once parents have formulated a detailed plan and informed the child about it, the process of reducing family accommodation begins in earnest. Monitoring the actual implementation of the plan through a written log, and recording difficulties and expected or unexpected challenges, will help the therapist to make modifications to the plan and to maximize compliance. For example, if parents report that they were able to refrain from accommodating the child while at home, but were unable to do so in other settings, the therapist can problem-solve the specific situational difficulties that impeded their success outside the home. In one example a child would become distraught and call attention to themselves in public when not accommodated, leading the parents to feel pressured to accommodate to avoid embarrassment. The therapist was able to problem-solve the issue and the parents agreed that they would either ignore the behavior, apologize to those around them, or leave the situation, rather than resuming the accommodating behavior. In another example, parents were able to implement the plan some of the time but not other times, and did not initially report a specific pattern determining this. A detailed discussion of the circumstances under which they accommodated revealed that they were able to cope with the child nagging or even becoming aggressive, but were not able to persist when the child became sad and appeared emotionally distressed and self-critical. They described feeling guilty about not accommodating when the child made statements such as "I'm the worst kid in the world," "I suck," or "I'll never get better." The therapist worked with the parents to formulate some supportive statements they could make during such moments. Parents were then able to use those statements to convey to the child their appreciation of the difficulty and their pride in the efforts the child was making, while still adhering to the plan of not accommodating.

When parents do consistently refrain from engaging in the family accommodation, the child is likely to become accustomed to the new pattern and to discover that they are able to cope better than they previously believed. Over time, parents will see their child coping without the accommodation and will observe the corresponding increase in self-regulation, leading to increased confidence for them as well. When the new pattern has been established, additional target accommodations can become the focus of ongoing work, following a similar program to that used for the initial target.

TROUBLESHOOTING AND COPING WITH CHALLENGING CIRCUMSTANCES

Reducing family accommodation is rarely easy, but some circumstances can add to and compound the difficulty. Identifying these circumstances and equipping parents for practical tools for dealing with them can enable effective accommodation reduction in situations where it would otherwise be unlikely to succeed. A (partial) list of common challenges and suggestions for coping with them follows and is the focus of the next part of this chapter.

Disruptive and Aggressive Child Behavior

Disruptive or aggressive behaviors on the part of a child whose parents are reducing family accommodation are not uncommon. These behaviors are better coped with if parents are prepared for them in advance. Disruptive or aggressive behaviors can take various forms from extreme and intense nagging, to verbal aggression, and to physical violence against property or persons. Many of these behaviors may be conceptualized in behavioral terms as an extinction burst due to the absence of expected reinforcement.

Parents will likely cope better with disruptive and aggressive behaviors if they are reminded of three key points. First, the behaviors are a reflection of the child's anxiety and distress rather than of disrespect, bad character, or additional psychopathology. When conceptualized in this way, as expressions of anxiety and distress, the behaviors can evoke empathy and understanding for a child coping with a new difficulty, rather than anger, blame, or punishment. Second, the behaviors are likely to be short-lived, conditional on them not being reinforced through a return to accommodation on the part of the parents. Bearing this in mind, parents may be better able to withstand the behaviors. Conversely, parents who believe the behaviors will not cease unless the accommodation is restored will be motivated in the opposite direction—to resume the family accommodation. Third, it is the parents who have chosen, correctly, to change their behavior. The parents have essentially unilaterally changed the "rules of engagement." The parents also have a rationale for this change and an understanding of its importance, which has developed over time with an opportunity to prepare for the change. The child, on the other hand, despite parental efforts to provide information and to frame the plan supportively, is experiencing a novel behavior which they have not chosen and which they likely do not agree with. Moreover, from the child's perspective it may appear as though their parents have suddenly decided to withhold the one thing that can help them to feel better. Faced with this situation it is unremarkable that they would be incensed and would express that anger verbally and behaviorally.

In many cases, parents are best advised not to respond to the disruptive or aggressive behaviors at all. Rather, it may be best to view these behaviors as the child adapting to the new rules and to simply express that the behavior is not acceptable. Distancing themselves physically from the child in that moment will often speed the ending of the outburst. In other cases, a child may exhibit behaviors that the parent cannot reasonably ignore. For example, the child may be physically aggressive or may have caused significant destruction of property. In those cases, parents are still advised to delay their reaction until they have had a chance to plan (preferably with the therapist) a determined, but cool-headed, response. This response should be resolute rather than punitive and it should still reflect the attitude of support for the child. In other words, it should still convey to the child that the parents understand the valid difficulty driving the behavior, but that they are confident in the child's ability to cope, and to do so without engaging in inappropriate behaviors.

One such response involves the use of parties outside the immediate family circle. Uncles, grandparents, family friends, and others can be enlisted in an effort to convey the supportive message to the child. Receiving several visits or phone calls from such individuals, all of whom convey to the child the same message of "I know how hard this is for you, but I also heard that you acted in this way and I want you to know that it is not acceptable," can have a powerful impact. It is not a punishment and it adheres to the supportive message, but it can be an effective inhibitor of additional displays of disruptive or aggressive behavior on the part of the child.

Threats of Self Harm

Claire's parents, Jay and Betta, informed Claire that they would no longer consent to serving as her "confessor". Her daily ritual of confessions, including many details of everything she had done and said that day had escalated to the point that it dominated the family's evenings and took up several hours each time. Jay and Betta would have to listen to her entire recitation, and reassure her many times that what she was describing was not a sin, that God was not angry with her, and that she would not be punished. Oftentimes, Claire would quiz them about details of her confession to ensure they were paying sufficient attention. Claire was distraught when her parents informed her of their decision to stop the accommodation. She initially went to her room and sobbed, staying there for over an hour. Soon after she attempted to start the confession ritual as usual, as though nothing had been said. When her parents reminded her of their decision she again began to cry. Claire accused Jay and Betta of not caring about her, and about whether she lived or died, went to heaven or hell. She told them she would not be able to live without their help and that if they did not hear her confession she would not be able to get to sleep, to go to school the next day, or to function at all. When the parents did not respond, Claire told them that since she could not live like this, and since they clearly did not care, she was going to end her life. She told them she knew where they kept her medication (an SSRI), and that she was going to take the whole bottle and be done with it all.

Some children, like Claire in this example, will respond to the parental decision not to provide family accommodation with threats to themselves, either explicit or implied. For example, a child may state that they "cannot live" without the accommodation. Or, they may say directly that they will kill themselves if their parents do not accommodate. Statements such as these naturally exert a powerful, and oftentimes paralyzing, effect on parents. Parents may feel that while important in principle, they cannot risk a child's physical well-being to reduce family accommodation. Therapists too can feel helpless in the face of this kind of threat.

It is never advisable to take threats of self-harm lightly. A reasoned approach to coping with these situations requires a delicate balance. On the one hand, a child's safety is of paramount importance. On the other hand, abandoning the goal of reducing the accommodation is detrimental to the child's prospects of overcoming the OCD and can reinforce a maladaptive coping pattern. A child whose parents react to suicidal statements by resuming accommodation may be motivated to use similar threats in other situations involving parental behaviors that cause them distress or anxiety.

A key to striking this delicate balance involves reframing the decision faced by parents. Therapists can help parents to shift their frame away from one that equates reducing accommodation with child risk. Rather, parents can fully commit to protecting their child's safety to their utmost ability, but doing so through means other than aborting their attempts to help the child by reducing family accommodation. This message can be made explicitly clear to the child. For example, a parent can respond to such a threat by stating unequivocally that "We will do everything in our power to keep you safe, but we will not stop trying to help you—and we will not go back to doing things that we know make your OCD worse."

Once the issue is framed in this way, various new possibilities become available. One such possibility is to respond to suicidal statements or threats of self-harm by increasing observation and protection of the child, all while adhering to the nonaccommodation plan. Parents can decide to arrange for complete observation of the child for a predetermined time period (e.g., 24 h) following any suicidal threat, and explain to the child with OCD that they are concerned for their safety and therefore watching them to ensure they do not come to harm. Relatives and friends of the family can be called upon to assist in the observation, even taking "shifts" over the decided upon time period. This kind of response can send a strong message to the child that their parents take suicidal statements very seriously, and that they are resolved to keep them safe, but does not enter into a negotiation about the accommodation. As such, it is less likely to act as reinforcement for the threat. Consequentially, it does not contribute to the recurrence of the suicidality.

An alternative to this kind of home-based protective observation is to have the child evaluated at an emergency room or psychiatric acute care center. A child who is taken to the hospital because of suicidal statements, but whose parents then resume their family accommodation reduction plan, can learn that threats to the self have serious consequences and that they do not achieve the goal of halting the parental actions.

Coping With Parental Conflict and Fostering Collaboration

Disagreement between parents poses a challenge for any parent-focused intervention. It is common for two parents to have very different views and opinions about a child's OCD, and the family accommodation. The difficulty inherent in these disagreements is often compounded by additional factors. One parent may blame the other for the child's difficulties, or for the way they respond to them; parents may have unrelated marital conflict; parents may have different views regarding parenting overall; and parents may have very different experiences with the child due to spending different amounts and kinds of time with them, or because the child behaves differently with each parent.

Underlying many of the disagreements between parents attempting to reduce their family accommodation is a key question: whether an anxious child with OCD should be "pushed" to cope better, or whether allowances should be made for the child's disorder. It is common for one parent to express the view that because the child is truly ill this should be accepted and parental behavior should be modulated accordingly and for the other parent to express the view that the child needs to overcome their difficulty and not "give in" to it.

The concept of support described earlier in this chapter provides a path for navigating this kind of conflict. Support exists when parents successfully integrate *both* messages: acceptance and validation of the child's symptoms and difficulty, and confidence in the child's ability (and need) to tolerate the difficulty. Essentially, these are the two perspectives being represented in the parental disagreement. Each parent may actually be representing one half of the supportive message. Since both halves are needed, the therapist can validate both parents and help them to see that they are each providing a crucial ingredient that is necessary for helping the child to overcome OCD. Replacing the belief that one parent is "right" while the other is "harmful" with an understanding that both parents are contributing to the solution, can pave the way for more collaborative work and for greater mutual appreciation between the parents.

CONCLUSION

Family accommodation is highly prevalent among the parents of children with OCD and represents a natural response to the child's symptoms and distress. However, family accommodation can contribute to maintaining the OCD symptoms, to increased severity and greater impairment, and can impede the likelihood of successful treatment.

Integrating an assessment of family accommodation into the evaluation procedures for childhood OCD can highlight those cases where family accommodation is most prominent and can reveal important aspects of the child's disorder that would otherwise go unidentified. Assessment of family accommodation can include unstructured conversation with guided questions, the use of structured interviews, rating scales and questionnaires, and daily schedules for mapping the specific forms of accommodation being provided.

Reducing family accommodation is an important therapeutic goal and can be done alongside other interventions such as CBT or psychopharmacological therapy. Family accommodation can also be addressed in the absence of direct child treatment. This is particularly useful in cases where a child is unwilling or otherwise unable to actively participate in direct therapy. The tools and strategies described in this chapter form part of the SPACE Program, a parent-based intervention for addressing family accommodation in childhood OCD and anxiety disorders.

REFERENCES

Adelman, C. B., & Lebowitz, E. R. (2012). Poor insight in pediatric obsessive compulsive disorder: Developmental considerations, treatment implications, and potential strategies for improving insight. *Journal of Obsessive-Compulsive and Related Disorders*, *1*(2), 119.

Albert, U., Bogetto, F., Maina, G., Saracco, P., Brunatto, C., & Mataix-Cols, D. (2010). Family accommodation in obsessive-compulsive disorder: Relation to symptom dimensions, clinical and family characteristics. *Psychiatry Research*, *179*(2), 204–211.

Calvocoressi, L., Lewis, B., Harris, M., Trufan, S. J., Goodman, W. K., McDougle, C. J., et al. (1995). Family accommodation in obsessive-compulsive disorder. *American Journal of Psychiatry*, *152*(3), 441–443.

Calvocoressi, L., Mazure, C. M., Kasl, S. V., Skolnick, J., Fisk, D., Vegso, S. J., et al. (1999). Family accommodation of obsessive-compulsive symptoms: Instrument development and assessment of family behavior. *Journal of Nervous and Mental Disease*, *187*(10), 636–642. http://dx.doi.org/10.1097/00005053-199910000-00008.

Caporino, N., Morgan, J., Beckstead, J., Phares, V., Murphy, T., & Storch, E. (2012). A structural equation analysis of family accommodation in pediatric obsessive-compulsive disorder. *Journal of Abnormal Child Psychology*, *40*(1), 133–143.

Comer, J. S., Furr, J. M., Cooper-Vince, C. E., Kerns, C. E., Chan, P. T., Edson, A. L., et al. (2014). Internet-delivered, family-based treatment for early-onset OCD: A preliminary case series. *Journal of Clinical Child and Adolescent Psychology*, *43*(1), 74–87. http://dx.doi.org/10.1080/15374416.2013.855127.

Farrell, L. J., & Barrett, P. M. (2007). The function of the family in childhood obsessive-compulsive disorder: Family interactions and accommodation. In *Handbook of child and adolescent obsessive-compulsive disorder* (pp. 313–332). Mahwah, NJ: Lawrence Erlbaum Associates Publishers.

Ferrao, Y. A., Shavitt, R. G., Bedin, N. R., de Mathis, M. E., Carlos Lopes, A., Fontenelle, L. F., et al. (2006). Clinical features associated to refractory obsessive-compulsive disorder. *Journal of Affective Disorders*, *94*(1–3), 199–209. http://dx.doi.org/10.1016/j.jad.2006.04.019.

Flessner, C. A., Freeman, J. B., Sapyta, J., Garcia, A., Franklin, M. E., March, J. S., et al. (2011). Predictors of parental accommodation in pediatric obsessive-compulsive disorder: Findings from the pediatric obsessive-compulsive disorder treatment study (POTS) trial. *Journal of the American Academy of Child and Adolescent Psychiatry*, *50*(7), 716–725.

Freeman, J., Sapyta, J., Garcia, A., Compton, S., Khanna, M., Flessner, C., et al. (2014). Family-based treatment of early childhood OCD: The pediatric OCD treatment study junior (POTS Jr.) randomized controlled trial. *JAMA Psychiatry*, *71*(6), 689.

Futh, A., Simonds, L. M., & Micali, N. (2012). Obsessive-compulsive disorder in children and adolescents: Parental understanding, accommodation, coping and distress. *Journal of Anxiety Disorders*, *26*(5), 624–632. http://dx.doi.org/10.1016/j.janxdis.2012.02.012.

Garcia, A. M., Sapyta, J. J., Moore, P. S., Freeman, J. B., Franklin, M. E., March, J. S., et al. (2010). Predictors and moderators of treatment outcome in the pediatric obsessive compulsive treatment study (POTS I). *Journal of the American Academy of Child and Adolescent Psychiatry*, *49*(10), 1024–1033.

Jones, J. D., Lebowitz, E. R., Marin, C. E., & Stark, K. D. (2015). Family accommodation mediates the association between anxiety symptoms in mothers and children. *Journal of Child & Adolescent Mental Health*, *27*(1), 41–51. http://dx.doi.org/10.2989/17280583.2015.1007866.

Lebowitz, E. R. (2013). Parent-based treatment for childhood and adolescent OCD. *Journal of Obsessive-Compulsive and Related Disorders*, *2*(4), 425–431. http://dx.doi.org/10.1016/j.jocrd.2013.08.004.

Lebowitz, E. R. (2015). Treatment of extreme family accommodation in a youth with obsessive-compulsive disorder. In E. A. Storch & A. B. Lewin (Eds.), *Clinical handbook of obsessive-compulsive and related disorders. A case-based approach to treating pediatric and adult populations* (pp. 321–335). New York, NY: Springer.

Lebowitz, E. R., Leckman, J. F., Feldman, R., Zagoory-Sharon, O., McDonald, N., & Silverman, W. K. (2016). Salivary oxytocin in clinically anxious youth: Associations with separation anxiety and family accommodation. *Psychoneuroendocrinology*, *65*, 35–43. http://dx.doi.org/10.1016/j.psyneuen.2015.12.007.

Lebowitz, E. R., & Omer, H. (2013). *Treating childhood and adolescent anxiety: A guide for caregivers*. Hoboken, NJ: Wiley.

Lebowitz, E. R., Omer, H., Hermes, H., & Scahill, L. (2014). Parent training for childhood anxiety disorders: The SPACE program. *Cognitive and Behavioral Practice*, *21*(4), 456–469. http://dx.doi.org/10.1016/j.cbpra.2013.10.004.

Lebowitz, E. R., Omer, H., & Leckman, J. F. (2011). Coercive and disruptive behaviors in pediatric obsessive—Compulsive disorder. *Depression and Anxiety*, *28*(10), 899–905. http://dx.doi.org/10.1002/da.20858.

Lebowitz, E. R., Panza, K. E., & Bloch, M. H. (2016). Family accommodation in obsessive-compulsive and anxiety disorders: A five-year update. *Expert Review of Neurotherapeutics*, *16*(1), 45–53. http://dx.doi.org/10.1586/14737175.2016.1126181.

Lebowitz, E. R., Panza, K. E., Su, J., & Bloch, M. H. (2012). Family accommodation in obsessive—Compulsive disorder. *Expert Review of Neurotherapeutics*, *12*(2), 229–238. http://dx.doi.org/10.1586/ern.11.200.

Lebowitz, E. R., Scharfstein, L. A., & Jones, J. (2014). Comparing family accommodation in pediatric obsessive-compulsive disorder, anxiety disorders, and nonanxious children. *Depression and Anxiety*, *31*(12), 1018–1025. http://dx.doi.org/10.1002/da.22251.

Lebowitz, E. R., Scharfstein, L., & Jones, J. (2015). Child-report of family accommodation in pediatric anxiety disorders: Comparison and integration with mother-report. *Child Psychiatry and Human Development*, *46*(4), 501–511. http://dx.doi.org/10.1007/s10578-014-0491-1.

Lebowitz, E. R., Storch, E. A., MacLeod, J., & Leckman, J. F. (2014). Clinical and family correlates of coercive—Disruptive behavior in children and adolescents with obsessive—Compulsive disorder. *Journal of Child and Family Studies*, *24*(9), 2589–2597. http://dx.doi.org/10.1007/s10826-014-0061-y.

Lebowitz, E. R., Vitulano, L. A., Mataix-Cols, D., & Leckman, J. (2011a). Editorial Perspective: When OCD takes over…the family! Coercive and disruptive behaviours in paediatric obsessive compulsive disorder. *Journal of Child Psychology and Psychiatry and Allied Disciplines*, *52*(12), 1249–1250.

Lebowitz, E. R., Vitulano, L. A., & Omer, H. (2011b). Coercive and disruptive behaviors in pediatric obsessive compulsive disorder: A qualitative analysis. *Psychiatry*, *74*(4), 362–371. http://dx.doi.org/10.1521/psyc.2011.74.4.362.

Lebowitz, E. R., Woolston, J., Bar-Haim, Y., Calvocoressi, L., Dauser, C., Warnick, E., et al. (2013). Family accommodation in pediatric anxiety disorders. *Depression and Anxiety*, *30*(1), 47–54. http://dx.doi.org/10.1002/da.21998.

McGuire, J. F., Small, B. J., Lewin, A. B., Murphy, T. K., De Nadai, A. S., Phares, V., et al. (2013). Dysregulation in pediatric obsessive compulsive disorder. *Psychiatry Research*, *209*(3), 589–595. http://dx.doi.org/10.1016/j.psychres.2013.04.003.

Norman, K. R., Silverman, W. K., & Lebowitz, E. R. (2015). Family accommodation of child and adolescent anxiety: Mechanisms, assessment, and treatment. *Journal of Child and Adolescent Psychiatric Nursing*, *28*(3), 131–140. http://dx.doi.org/10.1111/jcap.12116.

Pediatric OCD Treatment Study Team. (2004). Cognitive-behavior therapy, sertraline, and their combination for children and adolescents with obsessive-compulsive disorder. *JAMA*, *292* (16), 1969–1976. http://dx.doi.org/10.1001/jama.292.16.1969.

Pinto, A., Van Noppen, B., & Calvocoressi, L. (2013). Development and preliminary psychometric evaluation of a self-rated version of the family accommodation scale for obsessive-compulsive disorder. *Journal of Obsessive-Compulsive and Related Disorders*, *2*(4), 457–465.

Rudy, B. M., Lewin, A. B., Geffken, G. R., Murphy, T. K., & Storch, E. A. (2014). Predictors of treatment response to intensive cognitive-behavioral therapy for pediatric obsessive-compulsive disorder. *Psychiatry Research*, *220*(1–2), 433–440. http://dx.doi.org/10.1016/j.psychres.2014.08.002.

Stewart, S. E., Beresin, C., Haddad, S., Stack, D. E., Fama, J., & Jenike, M. (2008). Predictors of family accommodation in obsessive-compulsive disorder. *Annals of Clinical Psychiatry*, *20*(2), 65–70.

Stewart, S. E., Hu, Y. P., Hezel, D. M., Proujansky, R., Lamstein, A., Walsh, C., et al. (2011). Development and psychometric properties of the OCD family functioning (OFF) scale. *Journal of Family Psychology*, *25*(3), 434–443. http://dx.doi.org/10.1037/a0023735.

Storch, E. A., Geffken, G. R., Merlo, L. J., Jacob, M. L., Murphy, T. K., Goodman, W. K., et al. (2007). Family accommodation in pediatric obsessive-compulsive disorder. *Journal of Clinical Child and Adolescent Psychology*, *36*(2), 207–216.

Storch, E. A., Salloum, A., Johnco, C., Dane, B. F., Crawford, E. A., King, M. A., et al. (2015). Phenomenology and clinical correlates of family accommodation in pediatric anxiety disorders. *Journal of Anxiety Disorders*, *35*, 75–81. http://dx.doi.org/10.1016/j.janxdis.2015.09.001.

Strauss, C., Hale, L., & Stobie, B. (2015). A meta-analytic review of the relationship between family accommodation and OCD symptom severity. *Journal of Anxiety Disorders*, *33*(33), 95–102. http://dx.doi.org/10.1016/j.janxdis.2015.05.006.

Thompson-Hollands, J., Abramovitch, A., Tompson, M. C., & Barlow, D. H. (2015). A randomized clinical trial of a brief family intervention to reduce accommodation in obsessive-compulsive disorder: A preliminary study. *Behavior Therapy*, *46*(2), 218–229. http://dx.doi.org/10.1016/j.beth.2014.11.001.

Wu, M. S., Pinto, A., Horng, B., Phares, V., McGuire, J. F., Dedrick, R. F., et al. (2015). Psychometric properties of the family accommodation scale for obsessive-compulsive disorder-patient version. *Psychological Assessment*. http://dx.doi.org/10.1037/pas0000165.

Chapter 14

Working With Challenging Young People and Families

Amita Jassi* **and Georgina Krebs***[,†]
South London and Maudsley NHS Foundation Trust, London, United Kingdom, †King's College London, London, United Kingdom

Cognitive-behavior therapy (CBT) with exposure with response prevention (E/RP) is an effective and recommended treatment for obsessive-compulsive disorder (OCD) in young people. However, therapists can encounter a range of challenges when delivering CBT that may compromise outcomes if not addressed. In this chapter, we will consider common challenges relating to characteristics of the young person, their family, and broader environment (see Fig. 1). We will draw on the available evidence base as well as clinical experience to highlight each issue and propose strategies for managing these challenges in order to optimize treatment outcomes. Throughout this chapter we assume an E/RP-based model of CBT, in line with the existing evidence base.

DIFFICULT OCD SYMPTOMS

OCD is a highly heterogeneous disorder associated with a wide range of symptoms. Studies examining symptom dimensions (e.g., symmetry/ordering, contamination/cleaning, sexual/religious), each of which encompasses a range of obsessions and compulsions, as predictors of CBT outcomes have yielded mixed results. Some studies have found differential effects of symptom dimension on CBT outcomes (e.g., Abramowitz, Franklin, Schwartz, & Furr, 2003) and others have found no differences (e.g., Storch, Merlo, et al., 2008). However, clinical experience suggests that some obsessions and compulsions can be particularly challenging when delivering CBT for a number of reasons discussed below.

Difficulty Disclosing Symptoms

Young people may struggle to disclose symptoms for several reasons; they may fear that if they disclose their obsession it will come true

The Clinician's Guide to Cognitive-Behavioral Therapy for Childhood Obsessive-Compulsive Disorder
http://dx.doi.org/10.1016/B978-0-12-811427-8.00014-9

(thought-action-fusion)[1] or they may be reluctant to communicate it for fear of being judged (e.g., they may be scared that the therapist will think they are crazy, dangerous, perverted, or immoral). In relation to the latter, this can be particularly relevant when the content of obsessions is highly embarrassing and/or bizarre in nature. Among the most embarrassing OCD symptoms for young people are sexual obsessions, which can include unwanted thoughts of sexual acts with children, family members, and animals or sexual acts that go against one's own sexual preference. It has been reported that 24% of young people with OCD experience sexual obsessions (Fernández de la Cruz et al., 2013). Additionally, unusual or bizarre obsessions are also common among youth. One such example are transformation obsessions, which are defined as a fear of turning into someone or something else or taking on unwanted characteristics (Volz & Heyman, 2007). Monzani et al. (2015) reported that 10% of young people with OCD attending a specialist clinic presented with transformation obsessions.

In cases where there are issues in disclosing symptoms, it is important that the therapist *asks directly* about embarrassing and unusual symptoms, providing lots of examples and checking if there are thought-action-fusion fears. It may be helpful to ask the young person without a parent present, if developmentally appropriate, as they may be hesitant to disclose symptoms in front of their parents. In addition to this, externalizing OCD is a powerful technique to help young people disclose symptoms, i.e., highlighting that OCD is separate from them. Furthermore, it is crucial that in psychoeducation sessions, intrusive thoughts are normalized, and the therapist emphasizes how common they are in the context of OCD and in general. The therapist can share published surveys (e.g., Purdon & Clark, 1993; Rachman & de Silva, 1978), which provide examples of intrusive thoughts in OCD and non-OCD populations, and highlight that both bizarre and "taboo" intrusive thoughts are common. For example, Nadine was a 12-year-old girl who experienced obsessions that she may hurt her younger brother. She struggled to disclose this obsession as she was worried that she would get into trouble with her parents and that they would think she was a bad person. The therapist met with Nadine alone explaining to the family that it was routine clinical practice to discuss any symptoms they may find difficult/embarrassing to talk about. The therapist first shared surveys that illustrated *everyone* experiences intrusive thoughts that they do not like and to show the range of thoughts people without OCD experience. The therapist then explained that OCD plays tricks on people's minds and makes them experience these thoughts over and over and that this was OCD's fault and not the person themselves. As well as sharing examples from the survey, the therapist gave examples of types of obsessions other

1. Refers to cognitive process where one believes thinking about action is the equivalent to actually carrying out the action or that having the thought is as bad as carrying out the action, e.g., intrusive thought about murdering someone is the same as actually murdering them.

young people with OCD had shared with her, giving the most extreme examples so Nadine understood this was common. The therapist asked directly, while sharing examples, whether Nadine had experienced anything similar and this enabled Nadine to disclose her obsession.

In some cases clinicians only become aware that a symptom has not been disclosed at a later stage in treatment. One indicator is when E/RP tasks do not appear to be effective in reducing symptoms. This may indicate that the core fear has not been addressed or understood. For example, Kathy was a 17-year-old girl engaged in touching contaminated objects identified on her hierarchy. However, at the end of treatment, her OCD remained in the severe range. When a new therapist reviewed her OCD and asked directly about transformation obsessions, she discovered that the core fear was not dirt or germs but transforming into someone less intelligent. Therefore the previous E/RP tasks had not targeted the underlying fear hence it persisted. Once identified, E/RP tasks were targeted at this (e.g., coming into contact with less intelligent people), which ultimately led her to achieving a full remission.

Ethical Challenges in E/RP Tasks

Some OCD symptoms can be difficult to tackle because exposing the young person to their core fear raises ethical issues. For example, when working with a young person with aggressive obsessions, the therapist may wonder whether it is appropriate to encourage the patient to take a knife into a public place as part of an exposure task. Similarly, in treating a child with contamination fears, the therapist may struggle to decide what is appropriate and inappropriate—is it acceptable to encourage the child to lick the bottom of their shoe or is that a step too far? Setting up exposure tasks with young people with sexual obsessions can be particularly anxiety provoking for therapists in terms of considering ethical boundaries. There is no absolute right or wrong when making decisions about the appropriateness of E/RP tasks; however young people should be pushed as far as they can manage to face their fears in order to fully overcome OCD. At times therapists can be concerned when setting up tasks that the young person may act on their obsession; however this is not a true risk in that people with OCD are the least likely to act on their obsessions, in fact they find the obsessions abhorrent. Decisions on tasks should be made in collaboration with the young person and parents, ideally with the young person taking the lead, however at times therapists may need to come up with tasks which will involve doing something out of the ordinary, and pushing them beyond "normal limits" for the sake of fighting OCD. For example, Lorena was a 14-year-old girl with fears that she would stab someone or push someone on a train track, which led her to avoid both train stations and knives. Her therapist suggested a task where she had a knife in her pocket while walking up and down a train station platform. Lorena was understandably very anxious about this, as were her parents, by the thought of her carrying a knife around which was not a behavior they condoned. The rationale for the task was explained by the therapist and it is was highlighted that the task was directly linked to her core fear and that this was a task to help her overcome OCD, not something that Lorena would be encouraged to do in everyday life. Lorena was encouraged to do the task and she practiced it until it no longer caused anxiety; this was a catalyst for Lorena's full recovery from OCD.

Difficulty in Setting up E/RP Tasks

Some symptoms pose difficulties when setting up E/RP tasks. For example, some obsessional fears are very abstract in nature (e.g., a fear of "something" bad happening) or relate to a distant event (e.g., going to hell after dying) and it can therefore be tricky to develop tasks that fully expose the young person to their core fear. In such cases, a useful tool is to do exposure to thoughts (e.g., by young person writing down obsessions or recording them on loop tape) or imaginal exposure (e.g., writing a script of what it would be like to be in hell; see Box 1). It is important when working with abstract obsessions not to get drawn into conversations about the likelihood of the feared outcome occurring

BOX 1 Imaginal Exposure Script for Fear of Going to Hell (Written by 13-Year-Old Brad)

I am dead now. I see the devil in front of me; he is twice as tall and wide as me, he is red with horns on his head, he has an angry face and is gritting his teeth. It is really hot in here as there are flames surrounding me from all around. The devil is shouting at me telling me I am a bad person and I have done bad things and that is why I am here. I hear screaming from other people as they are being pushed by the devil and his scary helpers into a red hot lava. I try to run away, but the devil pushes me towards the lava and tells his helper to burn me in there as I am bad person. I scream asking him to stop but I cannot push back and I get hotter and hotter as I get closer to the lava. I am pushed in and then flames surround me; I cannot take the heat, it's too much.

because it will be impossible to disprove (e.g., you cannot prove that nothing bad will happen or that the young person will not burn in hell).

Mental rituals can pose challenges in setting up tasks. They include a range of things such as repeating words or phrases, praying, counting, mental checking, thinking "good" or "safe" thoughts, giving self-reassurance, and neutralizing distressing mental images. Mental rituals are common; in an adult study they were the primary presenting compulsion in 12.9% of OCD sufferers, with the reported age of onset between 9 and 13 years old (Sibrava, Boisseau, Mancebo, Eisen, & Rasmussen, 2011). This therefore suggests that mental rituals are likely to be common in young people. Abramowitz et al. (2003) found mental compulsions were most prevalent among patients with intrusive religious, violent, or sexual thoughts.

Mental rituals can interfere with E/RP as young people may struggle to identify mental rituals as compulsions and confuse them with obsessions or other thought processes. For example, Anna attended seven sessions of CBT and engaged in E/RP tasks where she touched contaminated objects. Each time her anxiety came down very quickly, however each time she did the task, her anxiety started at the same point despite lots of practicing. It was noticed that Anna would be distracted at times and would ask for the therapist to repeat herself. Given this, the therapist suspected Anna was engaging in mental rituals. Halfway through treatment Anna disclosed that she was giving herself reassurance that she would not get ill if she touched contaminated items.

Lots of examples will be needed to support a young person to recognize and identify mental rituals. Once identified, mental rituals can still be tricky to tackle. They are often harder to resist compared to overt rituals and more difficult to monitor as they are not observable. To start challenging them, it is vital that the young person and their family understand that mental rituals work in exactly the same way as overt rituals. As it is often hard initially to resist mental rituals altogether, the first step may be to ask the young person to try to "mess up" or change the ritual somehow or to replace it with another mental activity in order to inhibit the response. It must be made clear that this is a temporary measure and ultimately the goal is to eliminate the ritual altogether. For example, Anna, described previously, started by singing a song in her head, then, when she felt that she had more control, she listened to the obsessions on a loop tape while resisting other compulsions.

Symptoms Causing High Levels of Family Distress and Conflict

It is common for OCD to impact on the family, but some symptoms can have a particularly profound effect on parents and siblings. For example, constant reassurance seeking is difficult as families can get drawn into rituals of having to respond in a certain way and being contacted when not with the young person so that reassurance can be obtained. Many young people engage in compulsive confessing, which can involve family members hearing about difficult topics that can be distressing for them. This may include the young person confessing they may have touched a young child inappropriately or that they may have stabbed someone. In addition, families may get drawn into other rituals such as washing the young person or checking for them. It can be exhausting and difficult for families to engage in these rituals. Another example of symptoms that can cause distress and conflict for the family is when obsessional worries relate specifically to family members, including siblings (Barrow, Heyman, Scott, & Krebs, 2014) and parents. The nature of the obsession can include sexual obsessions, transformation obsessions, and contamination fears relating to a specific family member.

Symptoms that cause distress and conflict in the family can be challenging to work with as they frequently result in major disruption to family relationships and functioning (Barrow et al., 2014). In extreme cases, obsessions related to family members, or compulsions involving them, can escalate to the point of complete family breakdown. These symptoms can cause issues for CBT in that the focus of sessions may become about the impact on family life and relationships therefore reducing the focus on E/RP, or the obsession may be focused on the parent who is needed as a co-therapist, making it difficult for them to attend sessions or help with homework tasks. The treatment should follow the same structure as for other compulsions and obsessions. However, if the impact on family starts to take center stage, then therapists may wish to consider focusing on the most distressing and impairing symptoms for the family as a whole, even if it is higher on the hierarchy for the young person or considering including a co-therapist to address issues. For example, Anil was a 16 year old with fears that he would pick up negative characteristics from his brother if he came into contact with him, heard his voice, or saw him. This had a major impact on the family functioning; the family could not eat together, Anil had to be driven to school separately, he slept in his parents' room as he could not share a room with his brother and there were arguments between the parents on how to manage the situation as his father did not see the behavior as part of his OCD. Discussions on the impact on family life began to take up most of the sessions meaning in vivo E/RP tasks were not completed and the impact of symptoms worsened at home. The therapist decided it was important for the parents to have a shared understanding of the problem in order to effectively manage it, as well as Anil engaging in E/RP tasks to do with his brother. Given these were formulated as equally important but it felt both could not be done in the same session, a co-therapist was enlisted to work directly with the parents to give them space to discuss the impact it was having on the family as well as them developing a shared understanding of the problem and discuss ways to manage home life. In the meantime, Anil was able to concentrate on E/RP tasks with his brother joining sessions. At the end of their parallel sessions, the family would meet together with the therapists to set homework based on session task and clearly highlighting how parents would support tasks as home.

LACK OF "MOTIVATION"

Children and adolescents with OCD commonly express ambivalence about CBT. In some cases, clinicians encounter substantial resistance and struggle to engage the young person in treatment. A recent metaanalysis estimated that 18.7% of adults with OCD either refuse or dropout of CBT (Ong, Clyde, Bluett, Levin, & Twohig, 2016) and it has been suggested that rates may be similar in young people (Lebowitz, 2013). In addition to those who refuse or dropout of CBT, some patients continue to attend appointments but do not fully participate in key aspects of therapy. Young people may be more likely than adults to attend sessions "half-heartedly" given that they are typically brought along by parents, sometimes under duress.

Young people who are reluctant to engage in CBT are often described as "*unmotivated*." Although this can be a convenient shorthand, the term "unmotivated" is often unhelpful because (a) it has negative connotations and implicitly attributes blame to the patient; and (b) it does not help others to understand *why* the young person is not engaging in treatment and what can be done to help. It is therefore often more clinically useful to identify the specific factors that are interfering with engagement, as these may be amenable to therapeutic change. Outlined below are some of the common factors that can undermine willingness to engage in CBT and strategies that can be used to address them.

Anxiety About Treatment

Anxious avoidance is a common reason why young people with OCD do not engage in CBT. The young person might be fearful of CBT if they simply do not understand what the treatment involves. Perhaps even more commonly, the young person has some understanding of what CBT for OCD entails and they are anxious about the prospect of confronting their fears (Maltby & Tolin, 2005). If anxiety is a barrier to engaging in CBT, it is important that the therapist identifies and addresses underlying beliefs that are driving the anxiety. As well as using discussion techniques to challenge unhelpful beliefs, it has been suggested that constructing a sample hierarchy can be a helpful way of providing concrete evidence that exposure is a graded process (Maltby & Tolin, 2005). Showing patients a video of an E/RP session can also be a powerful way of demonstrating that it is a collaborative, graded process (Maltby & Tolin, 2005). If the young person is unwilling to attend an initial appointment, it will be necessary to attempt to have these discussions via telephone or email. For example, Alisha was a 17-year-old girl with OCD symptoms that were centered on a fear of contamination. She refused to attend an initial CBT session but eventually agreed to speak to a therapist on the telephone. She disclosed that she was fearful of treatment because a doctor who she had seen previously had told her that CBT involved "facing your fear head on by doing things like putting your hand down the toilet." The therapist explained that although confronting fears was a key part of CBT, it would be done in a graded way with Alisha setting her own goals and determining the pace. The therapist described an example of a contamination exposure hierarchy, and Alisha was surprised and pleased that the tasks at the bottom of the hierarchy seemed achievable. She subsequently agreed to start CBT.

Limited Insight Into OCD Symptoms

Poor insight can be another barrier to engaging youth with OCD in CBT. Individuals with OCD have varying levels of insight into the irrationality and excessiveness of their obsessions and compulsions (American Psychiatric Association, 2013). Young people with OCD routinely exhibit poor insight into their symptoms (Storch, Milsom, et al., 2008) and this has been shown to be associated with a poorer response to CBT (Garcia et al., 2010).

Broadly, there are three approaches that can be taken when insight is limited. First, the therapist can attempt to increase insight prior to starting E/RP though psychoeducation about OCD (Adelman & Lebowitz, 2012). Sometimes providing information about common obsessions and compulsions can help a young person to recognize their difficulties as being OCD. For example, a young person with pedophilic obsessions may be convinced that they are an emerging pedophile but providing evidence (e.g., from published studies and/or surveys) that sexual obsessions are common in OCD may help them to better understand their difficulties (Fernández de la Cruz et al., 2013). In other instances, it may be helpful to provide information about normative behaviors, in order to help the young person with OCD to realize that their rituals are excessive. For example, Jade was a 16-year-old girl with severe OCD which had emerged when she was 7 years old. She had an obsessional fear of dirt and excessive washing routines, including a time-consuming hand washing ritual. Jade viewed her hand washing as being reasonable and in line with normal, hygienic behavior, and did not want to change it. Jade agreed to let her therapist carry out a survey asking people for information about their hand washing habits. She was shocked to discover the brevity with which most people wash their hands, following which she agreed that her behavior was in fact excessive and was willing to try reducing it.

A second approach to dealing with low levels of insight is to attempt to engage the young person in E/RP by using concrete rewards. Contingency management is commonly used to promote compliance with E/RP in young people with OCD but may be particularly beneficial in those with little insight. Carrying out E/RP tasks may improve insight as it enables the individual to learn that when they resist a ritual, their feared event does not occur, thereby demonstrating that their obsessions and compulsions are irrational and unnecessary (Adelman & Lebowitz, 2012). For example, 12-year-old Nathan had a fear of being poisoned by chemicals and engaged in excessive washing rituals, but generally felt that his concerns and behaviors were reasonable and he was reluctant to tackle them. His therapist set up a reward system whereby Nathan would earn 20 min of iPad time for every attempt he made to carry out an E/RP task. Nathan was highly motivated by this incentive and began to complete E/RP tasks, initially largely for the sake of earning iPad time. However, after several weeks he was able to reflect on the fact that the E/RP tasks were becoming easier and that nothing bad had happened to him as a result, which helped him to recognize that his worries had been unrealistic. Of note, when introducing the concept of a reward system to families in the context of CBT for OCD, it is often helpful to frame it as a way of acknowledging the hard work that the young person is putting into fighting OCD, especially in the early stages of treatment. It is important that parents see rewards as an extra incentive for the young person to fight OCD rather than a bribe, the latter of which implies that the young person has no desire to change. To this end, it can be helpful for the therapist to normalize the value that tangible, immediate rewards when we are faced with a difficult challenge, whether it is revising for an exam, preparing a presentation for work, or training for a marathon.

A third approach for poor insight is to work with parents. Poorer insight is known to be associated with higher levels of family accommodation (Storch, Milsom, et al., 2008) and although the nature of this relationship is uncertain, it is possible that when parents accommodate their child's OCD they are inadvertently conveying the message that their symptoms are reasonable, thereby reducing insight (Lebowitz, 2013; Storch, Milsom, et al., 2008). For example, if a parent carries out excessive washing and cleaning routines to placate their child, the child may come to think that their obsessional worries about germs are valid. Furthermore, when parents facilitate rituals, they are effectively making life with OCD easier for their child and so they may be less likely to recognize that they have a problem that requires treatment. Lebowitz (2013) developed the Supporting Parenting for Anxious Childhood Emotions (SPACE) program. The main target for parents of young people with OCD is to reduce parental accommodation in order to improve child functioning. Furthermore, as accommodation is withdrawn, youth will be forced to confront fears and/or experience the full magnitude of OCD-related impairment, which may improve their insight and motivation for subsequent treatment. The first step in the SPACE program is addressing any misconceptions or concerns that the parents might have including reassuring them that the program is a treatment for their child's OCD, and explaining that while the treatment involves working with parents this is in no way implying parental blame. The therapist helps parents to understand that their child is finding it too hard to fight OCD and therefore they need to start the fight for them, and that this process will involve making decisions which their child may be resistant to but ultimately will be in their child's best interest. Parents then receive guidance on graded withdrawal from rituals and strategies for managing their child's reactions. Accommodating behaviors are targeted one by one and detail plans are written on how the parent will change their behavior. Parents are encouraged to share all plans with their child prior to implementation, either via a discussion or written communication if needed. A case series including six young people aged 10–13 years demonstrated the

SPACE program to be effective in reducing OCD symptoms and increasing the likelihood of subsequent successful individual child treatment (Lebowitz, 2013). Anecdotally, when clinicians are considering working solely with parents, it is important to consider the possibility that in the short term the child may become more impaired and distressed as they struggle to manage their OCD symptoms without their parents' assistance. It is essential that parental expectations are managed accordingly and that they make an informed, realistic decision about whether they feel able to manage.

Hopelessness About Treatment

Another factor that can undermine motivation to engage in CBT is hopelessness about recovery (Maltby & Tolin, 2005). Hopelessness about treatment may be particularly common in young people with treatment-resistant OCD who have failed to respond to previous attempts at treatment; chronic OCD who may have come to view OCD as being part of who they are; very severe symptoms who may think they are "beyond help"; and those with comorbid depressive symptoms who have a generalized sense of hopelessness about their future. In such cases, an initial aim for the therapist is to instill a sense of therapeutic optimism by providing information about the efficacy of CBT for OCD. For young people who view OCD as being part of their character, it is important to externalize OCD. Furthermore, speaking to a recovered patient can be a powerful way of bolstering therapeutic optimism (Maltby & Tolin, 2005), particularly if they had similar symptoms. For example, 10-year-old Billy had had OCD since early childhood and he felt it was part of his personality. This was further compounded by the fact that his father also had chronic OCD, and Billy thought he was destined to have OCD in the long term. Billy's therapist explained to him that OCD was not part of his personality and that OCD was like a bully who was controlling him and making him carry out rituals even when he did not want to. They drew a picture of the OCD bully and Billy named it "Big Mouth." The therapist informed him that he could learn to stand up to Big Mouth with a treatment called "CBT," and the therapist explained that about 8 out of 10 people who have CBT beat their "OCD bullies." In addition, the therapist asked a previous client to write a letter (anonymously) to Billy, explaining how hopeless she had felt at the start of treatment but how she had managed to overcome her OCD. Billy subsequently agreed to engage in a course of CBT. For young people who have previously received CBT and failed to respond, this is most likely to be because CBT was not delivered in an optimal form and there was an insufficient focus on E/RP (Krebs et al., 2015; Stobie, Taylor, Quigley, Ewing, & Salkovskis, 2007). In such cases, it is important that the therapist first empathizes with the young person's reluctance to attempt another course of CBT. The therapist should then explain that CBT is an umbrella term for a range of different techniques and that when it comes to fighting OCD very specific techniques, which the young person has not yet had an opportunity to fully utilize, are known to be effective.

Motivational Interviewing

In addition to the strategies described previously, a formal motivational interviewing (MI) approach can serve as a helpful adjunct to CBT for OCD (Merlo et al., 2010). In this context, a key MI strategy is the use of staging rulers to assess the young person's confidence in completing planned E/RP tasks and their perceived importance. For example, a young person may rate their confidence in completing an E/RP task as being 4/10 and its importance as being 5/10. The therapist can then ask why they rated their confidence as 4/10 as opposed to 3/10, and why they rated the importance as 5/10 instead of 4/10. In this way, the young person is encouraged to focus on reasons that they can successfully complete E/RP tasks and why E/RP is important. Decision balance worksheet can be used to map out the costs and benefits associated with changing versus not changing, and goal statements can be utilized to encourage self-motivation. In a preliminary randomized controlled trial (RCT), Merlo et al. (2010) evaluated MI versus additional psychoeducation sessions as an adjunct to CBT for OCD in young people. The MI group displayed more rapid improvements during treatment, although by posttreatment the two groups were equivalent with respect to OCD symptom reduction. However, it is of note that participants were not selected because they had expressed ambivalence about treatment and it is possible that the added benefits of MI would be greater among difficult-to-engage cases.

COMORBIDITY

Psychiatric comorbidity is very common in pediatric OCD, with a recent study reporting 67% having one, 20.5% having two, and 2.6% having three comorbid Axis I disorders (Ortiz et al., 2016). Storch, Merlo, et al. (2008) found that having one or more comorbidities is associated with poorer CBT response. Some comorbidities are more likely to impede treatment than others. For example, disruptive behavior disorders and attention deficit hyperactivity disorder (ADHD) have been found to be associated with poorer treatment response (Storch, Merlo, et al., 2008), as have autism spectrum disorders (ASD) (Murray, Jassi, Mataix-Cols, Barrow, & Krebs, 2015). However, a number of studies have indicated that generalized anxiety disorder, depressive symptoms, and tics do not impact on CBT response (Krebs & Heyman, 2010).

A challenge for clinicians is deciding whether the comorbidity presents a genuine barrier in CBT for OCD and therefore needs addressing in its own right. This needs to be balanced against the risk of becoming unnecessarily side-tracked by comorbidities or related issues, which can lead to diluting the important ingredients needed to effectively treat OCD (particularly E/RP). If the comorbidity is viewed as significantly interfering with the young person's ability to engage in CBT for OCD, clinicians may need to use a modified CBT approach (e.g., for young people with ASD and OCD; Russell et al., 2013), or they may need to treat the comorbidity first or in parallel with OCD (e.g., parent management training for comorbid oppositional defiant disorder). Chapter 16 provides in-depth description for dealing with common comorbid problems.

ATYPICAL DEVELOPMENTAL PROFILES

Atypical developmental profiles, such as ASD, ADHD, and learning difficulties are common in those with OCD. A metaanalysis of data from 31 studies found the prevalence of OCD among youth with ASD to be over 17% (van Steensel, Bögels, & Perrin, 2011). ADHD has been found to be common among young people with OCD, with one study reporting 26% of those with OCD also had ADHD (Storch, Merlo, et al., 2008). In terms of low IQ, Gothelf and colleagues reported that 11% of adolescents with mild to moderate intellectual disabilities had OCD (Gothelf et al., 2008).

There are several challenges that exist when undertaking CBT for OCD with young people who have neuro-developmental difficulties. For those with ASD, barriers in CBT include difficulties recognizing and reporting thoughts, feelings, and behaviors (Attwood, 2004); cognitive rigidity (Hill, 2004); difficulties with generalizing principles from one situation to another (National Research Council, 2001); and impaired executive functioning leading to poor organization and planning (Attwood, 2004). Challenges in the ADHD group may include executive functioning difficulties which may lead to difficulties in planning and organizing both within and outside of sessions, and also decreased ability to concentrate in sessions which may result in poor comprehension of key concepts discussed within therapy (Rapee, 2003). Those with low IQ may struggle with the same issues stated previously in addition to a more global impairment in understanding the principles of CBT. Consistent with these clinical impressions, a number of studies have found neuro-developmental disorders to be associated with poorer outcomes following CBT for OCD. For example, a recent study found that young people with ASD and co-occurring OCD responded less well to standard CBT compared to their typically developing counterparts (Murray et al., 2015). Storch and colleagues found young people with comorbid ADHD had significantly lower response rates to standard CBT for OCD compared to those without comorbidities and indeed those with other comorbidities, e.g., generalized anxiety disorder, depression, social phobia, Tourette syndrome, or panic disorder (Storch, Merlo, et al., 2008).

In recent years increasing empirical attention has been given to developing *modified CBT protocols* for young people who have OCD in the context of atypical developmental profiles, in an attempt to improve outcomes. A number of single case studies (e.g., Farrell, James, Maddox, Griffiths, & White, 2016) and one RCT (Russell et al., 2013) have evaluated modified CBT protocols in individuals with OCD and ASD and found promising results. The literature on modifying CBT for those with low IQ has been largely drawn from ASD studies. One case series describing three adults with borderline IQ found modified CBT to be beneficial (Pence, Aldea, Sulkowski, & Storch, 2011). There is less reported on modifications for those with ADHD and OCD, although modified CBT can be effectively delivered in this group when treating ADHD directly (Antshel, Farone, & Gordon, 2012). An individual formulation of a young person's strengths and difficulties will be needed to decide which modifications need to be utilized and which would not be needed, rather than basing it solely on the diagnosis of ASD, ADHD, or IQ level. Drawing on existing literature, Table 1 summarizes the main modifications to CBT that may be included.

TABLE 1 Modifications to CBT to Accommodate Atypical Developmental Profiles

Modification to Standard CBT	Reason for Modification
Format of CBT	
Greater use of visual materials and worksheets	Language and/or communication difficulties
Simplify language and concepts	Difficulties in understanding information
Greater repetition of key psychological concepts	Processing speed and/or working memory impairments
Short breaks throughout sessions, particularly psychoeducation sessions	Impairments in attention, processing speed, and/or working memory
Sessions highly structured with agenda and timings explicitly shared	Need for routine and predictability Executive functioning difficulties
Directive, explicit, and factual style of therapy	Literal communication style
Rules for conversations, e.g., turn taking, interrupting, etc.	Difficulties in reading social situations
"Download time" at end of every session to discuss special interests	To reduce tangential conversations during session and reward at end of session
Content of CBT	
Extended psychoeducation about anxiety, e.g., education on different emotions, where anxiety presents in the body	Poor emotional recognition and understanding Attention difficulties Difficulty understanding information
Use of special interests anxiety rating scale	Poor emotional understanding and communication. Difficulties seeing emotions on continuous scale

Continued

TABLE 1 Modifications to CBT to Accommodate Atypical Developmental Profiles—cont'd

Modification to Standard CBT	Reason for Modification
Hierarchies developed around specific goals	Concrete thinking style Limited motivation
Mini-hierarchies for each OCD domain	Distress intolerance
Increased involvement of parents, i.e., leading E/RP tasks in sessions	Difficulty generalizing
Regular home-based E/RP sessions	Difficulty generalizing
Working with school and other systems	Difficulty generalizing Need to optimize functioning in all domains by ensuring appropriate support in place for neurodevelopmental needs
Developing social activities in parallel with CBT	Poor social functioning leading to limited opportunities to confront certain obsessional fears
Contingency management, i.e., reward charts	Limited motivation
Parents/therapist modeling tasks	Difficulties in carrying out task with instructions only

CHALLENGING BEHAVIOR ASSOCIATED WITH OCD

OCD is often associated with challenging and coercive behaviors which include verbal attacks, physical aggression, destructive behavior, temper outbursts, imposing rules on others, forcing others to participate in rituals, and demanding that they perform certain behaviors (e.g., Krebs et al., 2013; Lebowitz, Omer, & Leckman, 2011; Storch et al., 2012). Outbursts are often triggered by the disruption of rituals or refusal to comply with compulsive routines, and parents frequently report having to "tread on eggshells" around their child. In a worldwide survey, OCD experts reported that coercive and disruptive behaviors were present in at least a quarter of their pediatric OCD cases (Lebowitz et al., 2011). Importantly, these experts viewed these difficult behaviors as being *secondary to OCD* rather than being indicative or a comorbid disruptive behavior disorder. Consistent with this view, temper outbursts have been found to occur in over a third of pediatric OCD cases and are related to depressed mood but not externalizing symptoms (Krebs et al., 2013). Similarly, rage attacks have been show to occur in half of pediatric OCD cases and are related to OCD severity but not comorbid externalizing disorders (Storch et al., 2012).

Young people with OCD who display frequent temper outbursts can be challenging to engage in CBT. For example, behavioral outbursts may occur when attempting E/RP tasks. Furthermore, parents are often preoccupied with the temper tantrums and this can easily dominate sessions. Despite the challenges, there is evidence to indicate that temper outbursts do not impede response to family-based CBT and the outbursts themselves improve as OCD symptoms reduce (Krebs et al., 2013). This suggests that in these cases CBT should not deviate significantly from evidence-based protocols, but involving parents in sessions is likely to be particularly important in order to:

- Externalize OCD and encourage parents to blame OCD, not the child.
- Normalize temper outbursts, by framing them as the "fight" part of the anxiety "fight or flight" response
- Reassure parents that temper outbursts will subside as OCD gets better and therefore joint efforts should be focused on fighting back at OCD
- Ensure that parents understand that OCD might be the *reason* for outbursts but it is not an *excuse* for unacceptable behavior and OCD should not get in the way of sensible parenting (e.g., putting boundaries in place for unacceptable behavior such as hitting)
- Encourage parents to praise the young person when they manage their anxiety without an outburst during E/RP tasks

A proportion of young people with OCD present with a broader range of externalizing symptoms (e.g., stealing, lying, vindictiveness) and meet diagnostic criteria for a comorbid disruptive behavior disorder. Estimated rates of disruptive behavior disorders in pediatric OCD vary greatly between studies, ranging from 9% (Ivarsson, Melin, & Wallin, 2008) to 57% (Geller, Biederman, Griffin, Jones, & Lefkowitz, 1996). It is important to differentiate temper outbursts from a true comorbid disruptive behavior disorder, because the latter predicts a poorer response to CBT for OCD (Garcia et al., 2010; Storch, Merlo, et al., 2008). In these cases, it has been suggested that outcomes can be improved by including parent management training (PMT) as an adjunct to CBT for OCD. Sukhodolsky and colleagues randomly allocated six patients with OCD and comorbid oppositional defiant disorder, aged 9–14 years, to receive either 6 weekly sessions of PMT followed by 12 sessions of E/RP, or to remain on a waitlist for 6 weeks and then receive 12 sessions of E/RP (Sukhodolsky, Gorman, Scahill, Findley, & McGuire, 2013). The PMT+E/RP group displayed significantly greater improvement in OCD symptoms compared with the E/RP only group, suggesting that PMT may successfully augment CBT in this patient group. When combining PMT with CBT for OCD, it is usually most helpful to initiate a brief course of PMT to increase compliance prior to starting CBT. However, in some cases the two treatments may be best offered concurrently, for example, when the disruptive behaviors and OCD are difficult to disentangle. When clinicians consider PMT to be the most appropriate initial intervention, this needs to be discussed carefully with families in order to promote engagement. Families may be hesitant about commencing PMT if they had sought treatment specifically for OCD. The therapist can explain that the young person's recovery from OCD is a two-step process. First, the young person and parents need to learn to work well together as a team, and this is easiest to practice initially in a non-OCD context. Second, the child and parent team will work together to fight the OCD bully—the stronger they are as a team, the easier it will be to fight OCD.

UNHELPFUL FAMILY DYNAMICS

Pediatric OCD is associated with critical and overinvolved parenting style (Barrett, Shortt, & Healy, 2002), parental hostility and blame (Peris, Sugar, et al., 2012; Peris, Yadegar, Asarnow, & Piacentini, 2012), and high levels of expressed emotion (Hibbs et al., 1991). A growing body of research suggests that these types of unhelpful family dynamics can impede CBT response. High levels of expressed emotion (characterized by hostility, criticism, and/or emotional overinvolvement) have been found to predict a greater OCD-related functional impairment following CBT (Peris, Yadegar, et al., 2012; Przeworski et al., 2012). Similarly, family conflict, blame, and cohesion have been shown to be predictors of poorer response to family-based CBT (Peris, Sugar, et al., 2012; Peris, Yadegar, Asarnow, & Piacentini, 2012). In a study of long-term outcomes following CBT, higher levels of family dysfunction at pretreatment were found to predict inferior outcomes 18 months after treatment (Barrett, Farrell, Dadds, & Boulter, 2005).

The optimal approach for managing unhelpful family dynamics is likely to depend on the extent of associated impairment. Clinical experience suggests that lower level parental criticism and overinvolvement can often be successfully addressed in the context of family-based CBT without deviating from standard, evidence-based protocols. For example, parents are often blaming of their child and critical of compulsive behaviors because they do not have a good understanding of OCD. Highlighting that compulsions are anxiety driven and not something that the child is doing to be awkward or taking pleasure in is therefore important. Similarly, externalizing OCD and framing it as a bully that the child is struggling to stand up to can help the parent to develop empathy and reduce criticism. For overinvolved parents, learning about the importance of confronting fears and anxiety habituation can be helpful.

In cases with higher levels of family dysfunction, additional family interventions may be required in combination with CBT in order to optimize outcomes. Peris and Piacentini developed "Positive Family Interaction Therapy" (PFIT), designed as an adjunct to CBT for OCD in highly distressed and impaired families with difficult dynamics (Peris & Piacentini, 2016). As well as providing parent-focused psychoeducation about OCD and the reduction of family accommodation, PFIT also includes techniques specifically aimed at reducing conflict and blame, and promoting family cohesion. For example, functional analysis is used to understand patterns of behavior that trigger and maintain conflict. Families are taught more helpful techniques for managing difficult situations including problem-solving, effective negotiation, and emotion regulation strategies (e.g., emotion labeling, relaxation, and disengagement from arousing situations). Implementation of these techniques is practiced through experiential exercises, supported by the therapist. In an initial pilot study, families characterized by high conflict, high blame, and poor cohesion were randomly allocated to receive standard CBT, or standard CBT plus six 1-h PFIT sessions. The PFIT condition was associated with a 70% response rate, in contrast to a 40% response rate in the CBT condition, and gains were maintained up to 3-month follow-up (Peris & Piacentini, 2013).

PARENTAL MENTAL HEALTH PROBLEMS

Mental health problems are common in parents of young people with OCD. For example, one study found that 45% of fathers and 65% of mothers meet diagnostic criteria for at least one psychiatric disorder (Lenane et al., 1990). Little empirical attention has been given to the extent to which parental mental health problems impact on CBT response in pediatric OCD (Ginsburg, Kingery, Drake, & Grados, 2008). However, clinical experience suggests that parental psychopathology can impact on the child's recovery in a number of ways. First, parents with mental health problems may struggle to act as co-therapists. They may be less able to attend appointments consistently and when they do attend they may struggle to fully engage in the session (e.g., if their concentration is impaired). Parents with mental health problems may also be less consistent at implementing CBT strategies with their child at home. Anxious parents, in particular, may find it difficult to implement E/RP as they may find it hard to tolerate their child becoming distressed. Second, parental psychiatric illness can be a significant source of anxiety for the child, which can fuel their OCD. This is particularly the case when parents have severe and enduring mental health problems as these may involve periods of marked functional impairment, unemployment, financial hardship, and/or repeated inpatient admissions.

Given that OCD is a highly familial disorder (Nestadt et al., 2000), a significant proportion of parents of young people with OCD will also meet diagnostic criteria for OCD themselves (Lenane et al., 1990; Nestadt et al., 2000). This can be particularly challenging in treatment, especially when the parent's OCD symptoms are similar in content to their child's. For example, 8-year-old Ahmed had a fear of germs, as did his father who had more severe OCD. Ahmed was highly motivated to fight his OCD and engaged well with E/RP tasks in sessions, which generally involved exposure to perceived contamination. Ahmed's father always attended the sessions and was supportive of Ahmed carrying out E/RP tasks in this context. However, half-way through treatment, when Ahmed was making slower progress than expected, it transpired that his father would always make him take his clothes off and shower when they got home after any exposure task. Ahmed's father understood that this was undermining the effect of E/RP but felt unable to resist.

Assessment of young people with OCD should always include screening for parental psychopathology, given the high prevalence and clinical significance of parental mental health problems in this population. Screening for parental mental health problems can form part of an unstructured clinical interview, and ideally this will be supplemented by use of a validated screening instrument (e.g., the Psychiatric Diagnostic Screening Questionnaire; Zimmerman & Mattia, 2001) and/or a symptom measure (e.g., the Depression Anxiety Stress Scale; Brown, Chorpita, Korotitsch, & Barlow, 1997). For all parental mental health problems, clinicians should assess whether the difficulty is impairing or distressing enough to warrant a referral for their own mental health support and treatment. If a referral is clinically indicated, this should be approached sensitively with the parent. Some parents will already be linked in with mental health services but not receiving optimal treatment, in which case the therapist may need to act as advocate for the parent in accessing the appropriate intervention. In cases of parental OCD or anxiety disorders specifically, involving parents in the child's CBT sessions may confer some therapeutic effect as the parent may acquire CBT strategies that they can use themselves. However, the therapist must ensure that treatment remains focused on the child and the parent's expectations for treatment should be managed accordingly. In cases where parental mental health problems are viewed as impeding CBT, consideration should be given to putting treatment on hold until the parent's mental health has improved. This decision needs to be based on realistic expectations of if, when, and how the parent is likely to improve. An alternative model is to treat the parental psychopathology and child OCD concurrently, with two therapists. In such instances it is important that therapist liaise closely in order to ensure that the two treatments are compatible and optimize outcomes.

SOCIAL DEPRIVATION

Family financial income has not found to be associated with CBT response for OCD in one of the largest RCTs to date (Garcia et al., 2010). However, clinical experience suggests that in certain circumstances, including issues relating to social deprivation, can present a challenge in CBT for OCD. For example, families (particularly parents) may be preoccupied with significant, ongoing life difficulties (e.g., relating to finances or housing), which may limit their capacity to focus on and engage in CBT sessions or do homework tasks. In addition, families may face barriers in accessing treatment in the first place or may live in deprived environments that are anxiety provoking for the young person and therefore fuel their OCD.

Financial Problems/Practical Barriers to Accessing Therapy

It may be difficult for some families to access CBT for OCD due to financial constraints. For example, parents may not be able to take time off from work to bring their child to sessions or pay for transport to get to the clinic. Therapists may be able to assist in accessing funds for transportation. This may be available through government benefits, charitable resources, or private insurance. Alternatively, CBT could be offered via the telephone, internet, Skype, or FaceTime. Studies have indicated these modalities to be effective in reducing OCD (e.g., Pozza, Andersson, & Dèttore, 2016; Storch et al., 2011; Turner et al., 2014) and there is evidence that remote delivery is as effective as face-to-face CBT for OCD in youth (Turner et al., 2014). Clinicians should consult their local and national regulatory bodies before using these alternative methods of treatment delivery to ensure they are not breaching guidelines in place to maintain patient confidentiality and protecting sensitive information.

Tackling OCD Symptoms in the Context of Real-Life Risk

OCD is typically characterized by unrealistic and irrational fears. However, for some young people their obsessional fear, although excessive, may have some basis in reality. For example, 13-year-old Charlie lived in housing owned by the local authority where he had been physically attacked by others living there. Charlie developed a range of compulsions and avoidance behaviors, which he believed would reduce the likelihood of this happening again (e.g., avoiding reading the housing estate name, tapping, and mental rituals). While this was a very challenging situation where the likelihood of the feared outcome is higher than usual, CBT for OCD was carried out in the same way while acknowledging how scary this can feel given past events and the context. The focus of treatment was around challenging the usefulness of compulsions as a way of reducing threat. Charlie was able to recognize that while the threat was still present, the compulsions did not serve to reduce the likelihood of the attack happening again and actually gave him a false sense of security. In general when the young person is living in the context of a real risk, it is crucial to consider the magnitude of the threat versus the worry. If there is a substantial, real risk, then the young person's worries may well be valid and they may not meet diagnostic criteria for OCD. In such cases, the focus has to be on dealing with the threat and supporting family to reduce risk. More commonly, there may be some degree of real risk but the young person's fear is still excessive, as was the case with Charlie. In such cases, ways of reducing the threat could be explored but, as with Charlie, the focus in CBT would be on reducing compulsions as a way of managing distress and reducing likelihood of feared outcome coming true.

RISK AND OCD

In some cases of OCD, patients present with risky compulsive and/or avoidant behaviors that are challenging to manage in CBT. For example, excessive washing can lead to skin infections and restrictive eating can lead to malnutrition (Veale, Freeston, Krebs, Heyman, & Salkovskis, 2009). In CBT, therapists need to be mindful that risk could increase when E/RP begins (e.g., a young person may go home and wash with bleach after exposing themselves to "contamination" in a session). If increased risk is a possibility, explicit plans need to be made with the family to manage this risk. One option could be to do more graded tasks so there is not an OCD "backlash" after sessions or perhaps come up with an alternative less risky compulsion to be carried out in the short term.

In some cases, risk may need to be stabilized before even starting E/RP. One example is when young people are underweight due to restrictive eating. For example, Amar had an extreme fear of sugar due to believing even small amounts would rot his teeth. This led him to eat very little; his Body Mass Index dropped to 16 (underweight) and he was losing weight each week. As a result, he struggled to engage in CBT due to the effects of malnutrition. Restrictive eating to this extreme can cause various health issues and can potentially be life threatening. CBT for OCD in such cases is not as effective compared to healthy weight counterparts (Jassi, Patel, Lang, Heyman, & Krebs, 2016). This information was shared with Amar and his family to set up the rationale for the priority to be given to stabilizing risk before exposure work i.e., to improve his dietary intake and restore his weight. The therapist, in collaboration with Amar and his family, came up with a plan to work around his OCD, i.e., eating more "safe foods" but also to allow some compulsions, i.e., he was able to seek reassurance from his parents that there was no sugar in his food. It was made clear to them that this was a temporary measure to reduce risk. Once his weight was back in a healthy range, graded exposure begun to tackle the compulsions, in parallel with risk assessment and management (e.g., weekly weight check in).

COMPLEX ISSUES

This chapter has focused on challenges therapists face in delivering CBT for OCD and ideas to address them within the context of CBT. However, some young people, particularly those with severe or complex OCD, are likely to require pharmacotherapy in conjunction with CBT. If medication is considered, Selective Serotonin Reuptake Inhibitors (SSRIs) are recommended for pediatric OCD (e.g., NICE, 2005). When considering combined treatment, it may be advisable to commence medication first and optimize the dose before starting CBT, particularly for those young people who struggle to engage in CBT. This is partly to promote engagement with exposure-based CBT and partly so that the young person and clinicians are able to monitor which treatment has had which effect. It is important that young people receiving combined treatment recognize the progress that they make with CBT in order to increase their sense of self-efficacy and ensure that they do not inaccurately attribute their progress solely to medication.

This chapter has focused on ways of managing challenges in the context of outpatient treatment. In some cases inpatient or residential treatment may be warranted. This is often the case when there are risk issues that cannot be managed in the community, which could arise as a direct result of OCD (e.g., self-neglect) or as a consequence of a comorbid condition (e.g., depression with suicidality). There are advantages to inpatient/residential treatment, in addition to risk management. It allows other interventions to be offered to the young person including nursing, occupational therapy, and medical support. It can also enable a more intensive format of CBT to be delivered, which in itself could improve outcomes.

CONCLUSION

This chapter has highlighted challenges therapists may face when delivering CBT for OCD to young people and their families. These are summarized in Fig. 1. There are several strategies that have been outlined that can be employed within the context of CBT to overcome these issues. However, in some cases, additional treatment interventions may need to be added, e.g., behavior management techniques, medication or inpatient/residential treatment may be warranted. A thorough, exploratory assessment of an OCD case can help therapists to preempt and prepare for any potential challenges that the young person may face in CBT. Regular reviews with the young person and their family during treatment, as well as effective use of clinical supervision, may reduce the likelihood of therapy becoming "stuck" thus allowing for better clinical outcomes. We encourage therapists to reflect on and discuss challenging cases with their colleagues in order to provide the best treatment possible for young people and their families.

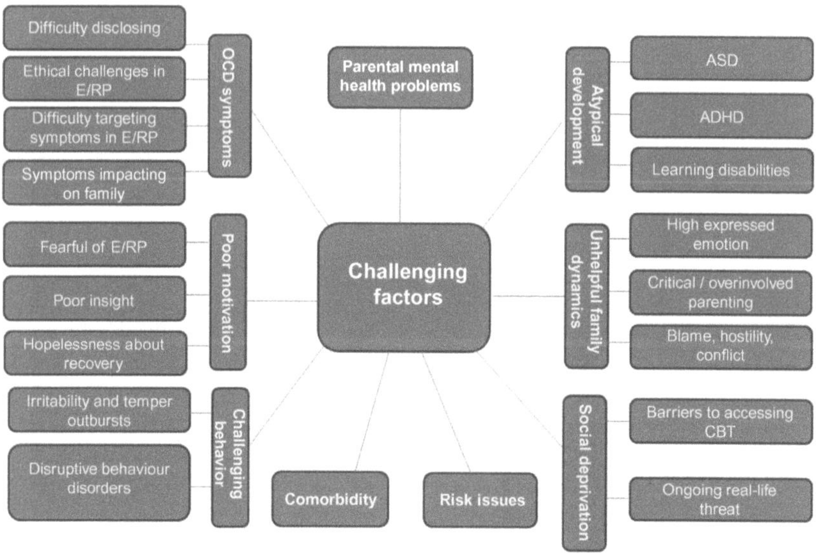

FIG. 1 Common challenges encountered when delivering CBT to young people with OCD.

CONFLICTS OF INTEREST

None.

REFERENCES

Abramowitz, J. S., Franklin, M. E., Schwartz, S. A., & Furr, J. M. (2003). Symptom presentation and outcome of cognitive-behavioral therapy for obsessive-compulsive disorder. *Journal of Consulting and Clinical Psychology*, *71*(6), 1049.

Adelman, C. B., & Lebowitz, E. R. (2012). Poor insight in pediatric obsessive compulsive disorder: Developmental considerations, treatment implications, and potential strategies for improving insight. *Journal of Obsessive-Compulsive and Related Disorders*, *1*(2), 119–124. http://dx.doi.org/10.1016/j.jocrd.2012.02.003.

American Psychiatric Association. (2013). *The diagnostic and statistical manual of mental disorders: DSM 5*. Arlington, VA: American Psychiatric Publishing.

Antshel, K. M., Farone, S. V., & Gordon, M. (2012). Cognitive behavior treatment outcomes in adolescent ADHD. *Focus*, *10*(3), 334–345.

Attwood, T. (2004). Cognitive behaviour therapy for children and adults with Asperger's syndrome. *Behaviour Change*, *21*(03), 147–161.

Barrett, P., Farrell, L., Dadds, M., & Boulter, N. (2005). Cognitive-behavioral family treatment of childhood obsessive-compulsive disorder: Long-term follow-up and predictors of outcome. *Journal of the American Academy of Child & Adolescent Psychiatry*, *44*(10), 1005–1014. http://dx.doi.org/10.1097/01.chi.0000172555.26349.94.

Barrett, P., Shortt, A., & Healy, L. (2002). Do parent and child behaviours differentiate families whose children have obsessive-compulsive disorder from other clinic and non-clinic families? *Journal of Child Psychology and Psychiatry*, *43*(5), 597–607.

Barrow, F., Heyman, I., Scott, S., & Krebs, G. (2014). "Rituals or rivalry?" The phenomenology and treatment of sibling specific obsessions in paediatric obsessive-compulsive disorder. *Journal of Obsessive-Compulsive and Related Disorders*, *3*(3), 209–214.

Brown, T. A., Chorpita, B. F., Korotitsch, W., & Barlow, D. H. (1997). Psychometric properties of the Depression Anxiety Stress Scales (DASS) in clinical samples. *Behaviour Research and Therapy*, *35*(1), 79–89.

Farrell, J. L., James, C. S., Maddox, B. B., Griffiths, D., & White, S. (2016). Treatment of comorbid obsessive-compulsive disorder in youth with ASD: The case of MAX. In A. E. Storch & B. A. Lewin (Eds.), *Clinical handbook of obsessive-compulsive and related disorders: A case-based approach to treating pediatric and adult populations* (pp. 337–355). Cham: Springer International Publishing.

Fernández de la Cruz, L., Barrow, F., Bolhuis, K., Krebs, G., Volz, C., Nakatani, E., et al. (2013). Sexual obsessions in pediatric obsessive-compulsive disorder: Clinical characteristics and treatment outcomes. *Depression and Anxiety*, *30*(8), 732–740.

Garcia, A. M., Sapyta, J. J., Moore, P. S., Freeman, J. B., Franklin, M. E., March, J. S., et al. (2010). Predictors and moderators of treatment outcome in the Pediatric Obsessive Compulsive Treatment Study (POTS I). *Journal of the American Academy of Child & Adolescent Psychiatry*, *49*(10), 1024–1033.

Geller, D. A., Biederman, J., Griffin, S., Jones, J., & Lefkowitz, T. R. (1996). Comorbidity of Juvenile obsessive-compulsive disorder with disruptive behavior disorders. *Journal of the American Academy of Child & Adolescent Psychiatry*, *35*(12), 1637–1646. http://dx.doi.org/10.1097/00004583-199612000-00016.

Ginsburg, G. S., Kingery, J. N., Drake, K. L., & Grados, M. A. (2008). Predictors of treatment response in pediatric obsessive-compulsive disorder. *Journal of the American Academy of Child & Adolescent Psychiatry*, *47*(8), 868–878. http://dx.doi.org/10.1097/CHI.0b013e3181799ebd.

Gothelf, D., Goraly, O., Avni, S., Stawski, M., Hartmann, I., Basel-Vanagaite, L., et al. (2008). Psychiatric morbidity with focus on obsessive–compulsive disorder in an Israeli cohort of adolescents with mild to moderate mental retardation. *Journal of Neural Transmission*, *115*(6), 929–936.

Hibbs, E. D., Hamburger, S. D., Lenane, M., Rapoport, J. L., Kruesi, M. J., Keysor, C. S., et al. (1991). Determinants of expressed emotion in families of disturbed and normal children. *Journal of Child Psychology and Psychiatry*, *32*(5), 757–770.

Hill, E. L. (2004). Evaluating the theory of executive dysfunction in autism. *Developmental Review*, *24*(2), 189–233.

Ivarsson, T., Melin, K., & Wallin, L. (2008). Categorical and dimensional aspects of co-morbidity in obsessive-compulsive disorder (OCD). *European Child & Adolescent Psychiatry*, *17*(1), 20–31. http://dx.doi.org/10.1007/s00787-007-0626-z.

Jassi, A. D., Patel, N., Lang, K., Heyman, I., & Krebs, G. (2016). Ritualised eating in young people with obsessive compulsive disorder: Clinical characteristics and treatment outcomes. *Journal of Obsessive-Compulsive and Related Disorders*, *8*, 1–8.

Krebs, G., Bolhuis, K., Heyman, I., Mataix-Cols, D., Turner, C., & Stringaris, A. (2013). Temper outbursts in paediatric obsessive-compulsive disorder and their association with depressed mood and treatment outcome. *Journal of Child Psychology and Psychiatry*, *54*(3), 313–322.

Krebs, G., & Heyman, I. (2010). Treatment-resistant obsessive-compulsive disorder in young people: Assessment and treatment strategies. *Child and Adolescent Mental Health*, *15*(1), 2–11.

Krebs, G., Isomura, K., Lang, K., Jassi, A., Heyman, I., Diamond, H., et al. (2015). How resistant is 'treatment-resistant' obsessive-compulsive disorder in youth? *British Journal of Clinical Psychology*, *54*(1), 63–75.

Lebowitz, E. R. (2013). Parent-based treatment for childhood and adolescent OCD. *Journal of Obsessive-Compulsive and Related Disorders*, *2*(4), 425–431. http://dx.doi.org/10.1016/j.jocrd.2013.08.004.

Lebowitz, E. R., Omer, H., & Leckman, J. F. (2011). Coercive and disruptive behaviors in pediatric obsessive-compulsive disorder. *Depression and Anxiety*, *28*(10), 899–905. http://dx.doi.org/10.1002/da.20858.

Lenane, M. C., Swedo, S. E., Leonard, H., Pauls, D. L., Sceery, W., & Rapoport, J. L. (1990). Psychiatric disorders in first degree relatives of children and adolescents with obsessive compulsive disorder. *Journal of the American Academy of Child & Adolescent Psychiatry*, *29*(3), 407–412. http://dx.doi.org/10.1097/00004583-199005000-00012.

Maltby, N., & Tolin, D. F. (2005). A brief motivational intervention for treatment-refusing OCD patients. *Cognitive Behaviour Therapy*, *34*(3), 176–184. http://dx.doi.org/10.1080/16506070510043741.

Merlo, L. J., Storch, E. A., Lehmkuhl, H. D., Jacob, M. L., Murphy, T. K., Goodman, W. K., et al. (2010). Cognitive behavioral therapy plus motivational interviewing improves outcome for pediatric obsessive–compulsive disorder: A preliminary study. *Cognitive Behaviour Therapy*, *39*(1), 24–27.

Monzani, B., Jassi, A., Heyman, I., Turner, C., Volz, C., & Krebs, G. (2015). Transformation obsessions in paediatric obsessive-compulsive disorder: Clinical characteristics and treatment response to cognitive behaviour therapy. *Journal of Behavior Therapy and Experimental Psychiatry*, *48*, 75–81.

Murray, K., Jassi, A., Mataix-Cols, D., Barrow, F., & Krebs, G. (2015). Outcomes of cognitive behaviour therapy for obsessive–compulsive disorder in young people with and without autism spectrum disorders: A case controlled study. *Psychiatry Research*, *228*(1), 8–13. http://dx.doi.org/10.1016/j.psychres.2015.03.012.

National Institute for Health and Care Excellence (NICE). (2005). *Obsessive-compulsive disorder and body dysmorphic disorder: Treatment*. London: NICE.

National Research Council. (2001). Educating children with autism. In C. Lord & J. P. McGee (Eds.), (2001). Washington, DC: National Academy Press.

Nestadt, G., Samuels, J., Riddle, M., Bienvenu, O. J., 3rd, Liang, K. Y., LaBuda, M., et al. (2000). A family study of obsessive-compulsive disorder. *Archives of General Psychiatry*, *57*(4), 358–363.

Ong, C. W., Clyde, J. W., Bluett, E. J., Levin, M. E., & Twohig, M. P. (2016). Dropout rates in exposure with response prevention for obsessive-compulsive disorder: What do the data really say? *Journal of Anxiety Disorders*, *40*, 8–17. http://dx.doi.org/10.1016/j.janxdis.2016.03.006.

Ortiz, A. E., Morer, A., Moreno, E., Plana, M. T., Cordovilla, C., & Lázaro, L. (2016). Clinical significance of psychiatric comorbidity in children and adolescents with obsessive–compulsive disorder: Subtyping a complex disorder. *European Archives of Psychiatry and Clinical Neuroscience*, *266*(3), 199–208.

Pence, S. L., Jr., Aldea, M. A., Sulkowski, M. L., & Storch, E. A. (2011). Cognitive behavioral therapy in adults with obsessive–compulsive disorder and borderline intellectual functioning: A case series of three patients. *Journal of Developmental and Physical Disabilities*, *23*(2), 71–85.

Peris, T. S., & Piacentini, J. (2013). Optimizing treatment for complex cases of childhood obsessive compulsive disorder: A preliminary trial. *Journal of Clinical Child and Adolescent Psychology*, *42*(1), 1–8. http://dx.doi.org/10.1080/15374416.2012.673162.

Peris, T. S., & Piacentini, J. (2016). *Helping families manage childhood OCD: Decreasing conflict and increasing positive interaction therapist guide*. New York, NY: Oxford University Press.

Peris, T. S., Sugar, C. A., Bergman, R. L., Chang, S., Langley, A., & Piacentini, J. (2012). Family factors predict treatment outcome for pediatric obsessive-compulsive disorder. *Journal of Consulting and Clinical Psychology*, *80*(2), 255–263. http://dx.doi.org/10.1037/a0027084.

Peris, T. S., Yadegar, M., Asarnow, J. R., & Piacentini, J. (2012). Pediatric obsessive compulsive disorder: Family climate as a predictor of treatment outcome. *Journal of Obsessive-Compulsive and Related Disorders*, *1*(4), 267–273. http://dx.doi.org/10.1016/j.jocrd.2012.07.003.

Pozza, A., Andersson, G., & Dèttore, D. (2016). Therapist-guided internet-based cognitive-behavioural therapy for adult obsessive-compulsive disorder: A meta-analysis. *European Psychiatry*, *33*, S276–S277.

Przeworski, A., Zoellner, L., Franklin, M., Garcia, A., Freeman, J., March, J., et al. (2012). Maternal and child expressed emotion as predictors of treatment response in pediatric obsessive–compulsive disorder. *Child Psychiatry & Human Development*, *43*(3), 337–353. http://dx.doi.org/10.1007/s10578-011-0268-8.

Purdon, C., & Clark, D. A. (1993). Obsessive intrusive thoughts in nonclinical subjects. Part I. Content and relation with depressive, anxious and obsessional symptoms. *Behaviour Research and Therapy*, *31*(8), 713–720.

Rachman, S., & de Silva, P. (1978). Abnormal and normal obsessions. *Behaviour Research and Therapy*, *16*(4), 233–248.

Rapee, R. M. (2003). The influence of comorbidity on treatment outcome for children and adolescents with anxiety disorders. *Behaviour Research and Therapy*, *4*, 105–112.

Russell, A. J., Jassi, A., Fullana, M. A., Mack, H., Johnston, K., Heyman, I., et al. (2013). Cognitive behavior therapy for comorbid obsessive-compulsive disorder in high-functioning autism spectrum disorders: A randomized controlled trial. *Depression and Anxiety*, *30*(8), 697–708. http://dx.doi.org/10.1002/da.22053.

Sibrava, N. J., Boisseau, C. L., Mancebo, M. C., Eisen, J. L., & Rasmussen, S. A. (2011). Prevalence and clinical characteristics of mental rituals in a longitudinal clinical sample of obsessive–compulsive disorder. *Depression and Anxiety*, *28*(10), 892–898.

Stobie, B., Taylor, T., Quigley, A., Ewing, S., & Salkovskis, P. M. (2007). "Contents may vary": A pilot study of treatment histories of OCD patients. *Behavioural and Cognitive Psychotherapy*, *35*(03), 273–282.

Storch, E. A., Caporino, N. E., Morgan, J. R., Lewin, A. B., Rojas, A., Brauer, L., et al. (2011). Preliminary investigation of web-camera delivered cognitive-behavioral therapy for youth with obsessive-compulsive disorder. *Psychiatry Research*, *189*(3), 407–412.

Storch, E. A., Jones, A. M., Lack, C. W., Ale, C. M., Sulkowski, M. L., Lewin, A. B., et al. (2012). Rage attacks in pediatric obsessive-compulsive disorder: Phenomenology and clinical correlates. *Journal of the American Academy of Child & Adolescent Psychiatry*, *51*(6), 582–592. http://dx.doi.org/10.1016/j.jaac.2012.02.016.

Storch, E. A., Merlo, L. J., Larson, M. J., Geffken, G. R., Lehmkuhl, H. D., Jacob, M. L., et al. (2008). Impact of comorbidity on cognitive-behavioral therapy response in pediatric obsessive-compulsive disorder. *Journal of the American Academy of Child & Adolescent Psychiatry*, *47*(5), 583–592.

Storch, E. A., Milsom, V. A., Merlo, L. J., Larson, M., Geffken, G. R., Jacob, M. L., et al. (2008). Insight in pediatric obsessive-compulsive disorder: Associations with clinical presentation. *Psychiatry Research*, *160*(2), 212–220. http://dx.doi.org/10.1016/j.psychres.2007.07.005.

Sukhodolsky, D. G., Gorman, B. S., Scahill, L., Findley, D., & McGuire, J. (2013). Exposure and response prevention with or without parent management training for children with obsessive-compulsive disorder complicated by disruptive behavior: A multiple-baseline across-responses design study. *Journal of Anxiety Disorders*, *27*(3), 298–305. http://dx.doi.org/10.1016/j.janxdis.2013.01.005.

Turner, C. M., Mataix-Cols, D., Lovell, K., Krebs, G., Lang, K., Byford, S., et al. (2014). Telephone cognitive-behavioral therapy for adolescents with obsessive-compulsive disorder: A randomized controlled non-inferiority trial. *Journal of the American Academy of Child & Adolescent Psychiatry*, *53*(12), 1298–1307.

van Steensel, F. J., Bögels, S. M., & Perrin, S. (2011). Anxiety disorders in children and adolescents with autistic spectrum disorders: A meta-analysis. *Clinical Child and Family Psychology Review*, *14*(3), 302–317.

Veale, D., Freeston, M., Krebs, G., Heyman, I., & Salkovskis, P. (2009). Risk assessment and management in obsessive–compulsive disorder. *Advances in Psychiatric Treatment*, *15*(5), 332–343.

Volz, C., & Heyman, I. (2007). Case series: Transformation obsession in young people with obsessive-compulsive disorder (OCD). *Journal of the American Academy of Child & Adolescent Psychiatry*, *46*(6), 766–772.

Zimmerman, M., & Mattia, J. I. (2001). The psychiatric diagnostic screening questionnaire: Development, reliability and validity. *Comprehensive Psychiatry*, *42*(3), 175–189. Chicago.

Chapter 15

Working With Young Children With OCD

Jenny Herren[*,†] **and Joseph Berryhill**[†]
[*]*Alpert Medical School of Brown University, Providence, RI, United States,* [†]*Bradley Hospital, Riverside, RI, United States*

Obsessive-compulsive disorder (OCD) is a neurobehavioral disorder that can present as fully developed OCD, rather than a prodromal stage of the illness, in early childhood (Skriner et al., 2016). Compared to older youth with OCD, young children (8–9 years of age and under) with the disorder have similar symptoms, severity levels, and comorbidity rates (Garcia et al., 2009; Selles, Storch, & Lewin, 2014; Skriner et al., 2016). However, symptom expression can vary, with younger children often presenting with higher rates of disruptive behaviors, tics, and hoarding compulsions, as well as having poorer insight (Frank et al., 2014; Selles et al., 2014; Skriner et al., 2016). Compulsions without expressed obsessions are also common among very young children (Freeman et al., 2012). Given their lack of cognitive maturation, young children may not understand or identify the connection between obsessional thoughts and subsequent compulsions or verbally report this pattern. Appropriate assessment and treatment of OCD in young children is paramount given the severity of symptoms, frequent comorbidity, adverse developmental consequences, and significant impairments the disorder causes at home and school (Piacentini, Bergman, Keller, & McCracken, 2003; Piacentini, Peris, Bergman, Chang, & Jaffer, 2007). Therefore a thorough assessment of OCD symptoms is the first step in working with children with OCD.

ASSESSMENT OF OCD IN YOUNG CHILDREN

Children presenting with concerns of intrusive thoughts, recurrent worries, excessive reassurance seeking, avoidance of certain situations and/or objects, or repetitive behaviors should be screened for OCD (Keeley, Storch, Dhungana, & Geffken, 2007). If none of these concerns is raised, then general probes should be considered (e.g., "Do you ever have worries or pictures that get stuck in your head and won't go away? Are there things you do over and over

The Clinician's Guide to Cognitive-Behavioral Therapy for Childhood Obsessive-Compulsive Disorder
http://dx.doi.org/10.1016/B978-0-12-811427-8.00015-0

and can't stop?"). Obtaining caregiver reports is also crucial when assessing pediatric OCD, as children's ability to report symptoms varies widely. Assessors should be particularly aware of developmental norms to differentiate developmentally appropriate behaviors from atypical ones (Geller & March, 2012). Younger children will often have routines around bedtime, meals, and dressing that may look similar to compulsions. Because interruption of such "normal" routines does not usually create significant distress for the child, assessors should examine children's emotional and behavioral response as well as the negative impact on family functioning with routine disruption. Additionally, providing psychoeducation during assessment can ensure families understand the definitions of obsessions and compulsions and help differentiate OCD behaviors from those that are not (Freeman et al., 2012).

If symptoms of OCD are endorsed, additional measures can be used to assess severity and impairment. Practitioners should be aware that some measures may not have been tested with a younger population or should be interpreted with caution given the patient's age. The Children's Yale-Brown Obsessive Compulsive Scale (CY-BOCS; Scahill et al., 1997) is the "gold standard" for assessing OCD severity in pediatric populations and has been shown to have good psychometric properties (Scahill et al., 1997; Storch et al., 2004). However, the CY-BOCS was originally tested for ages 8 and above, and studies with younger children have demonstrated less favorable technical properties (Cook, Freeman, Garcia, Sapyta, & Franklin, 2015; Freeman, Flessner, & Garcia, 2011). While the CY-BOCS can be administered separately or jointly with the child and parent, joint administration is most common among young patients.

Therapist understanding of the family context, especially patterns of accommodation, is crucial when treating younger patients with OCD (Freeman et al., 2012). Family accommodation refers to ways in which other family members assist or change their own behaviors in response to the child's OCD (e.g., providing reassurance, allowing the child to avoid certain activities, participating in rituals, changing family routines). Accommodation within the family occurs often with OCD and is especially common in young children with OCD. Research shows family accommodation adversely impacts treatment outcome and is positively related to symptom severity, behavior problems, and functional impairment (Lebowitz, Panza, Su, & Bloch, 2014; Storch et al., 2007). From a theoretical perspective, family accommodation reinforces the patient's symptoms, providing relief in the short term but maintaining or strengthening symptoms over time. Therapists can assess family accommodation by discussing it with parents and child. Another option is to administer the Family Accommodation Scale (FAS; Calvocoressi et al., 1995) or use a parent report version of the FAS (FAS-PR; Flessner et al., 2011).

Overall, the treatment of young children with OCD begins with appropriate and thorough assessment (for additional recommendations, see Lewin & Piacentini, 2010). When working with young children, therapists should be mindful of typical developmental patterns to distinguish atypical behavior, include caregivers as part of the assessment, choose measures suited for younger children and have been tested in that age group, and assess the role and impact of the family in symptoms.

COGNITIVE BEHAVIORAL THERAPY FOR YOUNG CHILDREN WITH OCD

Cognitive behavioral therapy (CBT) using exposure with response prevention (E/RP) has been identified as the first-line treatment for children and adolescents with OCD (Geller & March, 2012; Freeman et al., 2014). Developmentally modified CBT with young patients with OCD, ages 5–8 years, who have traditionally been excluded from larger trials has been shown to be extremely effective (Freeman et al., 2014). Furthermore, emerging evidence demonstrates that family-based CBT is efficacious, well tolerated, and acceptable for children as young as 3 years of age with OCD (Lewin et al., 2014). Treatment of OCD in young children marries tenets of traditional CBT treatment for OCD with family intervention and behavioral parent management techniques. Developmental modifications and caregiver involvement are crucial given the developmental limitations of young children and the impact OCD can have on family functioning (Choate-Summers et al., 2008).

The remainder of the chapter will provide a general overview of E/RP used with young children, including treatment elements that precede and follow it. An emphasis will be placed on integrating family process and delivering exposure in a developmentally sensitive manner for young children using a habituation and distress tolerance framework.

Using a theoretical orientation is important to guide the delivery of exposure; however, there is ongoing debate around the mechanisms that facilitate learning and make exposure effective (Abramowitz, 2013). Two common frameworks for approaching exposure include inhibitory learning (Craske, Treanor, Conway, Zbozinek, & Vervliet, 2014) and habituation (Benito & Walther, 2015; Foa & Kozak, 1986). According to both theories, one should approach anxiety-provoking situations without engagement in behaviors that function to reduce anxiety (e.g., negative reinforcement via rituals or avoidance). Optimally, exposures should activate fear and therapist behaviors should maintain or increase focus on the anxious trigger and associated obsessions. Therapist behaviors that actively reduce anxiety, such as distraction, should be avoided (Benito & Walther, 2015). This type of exposure will promote distress tolerance and allow for reduction in fear over time. While a distress tolerance model can be challenging for young kids, use of active coping strategies to reduce anxiety, such as relaxation, is thought to interfere with habituation (Benito & Walther, 2015). As discussed in this chapter, incorporation of other strategies such as therapist praise, encouraging positive self-talk, providing rewards, modeling distress tolerance and behavioral approach, and making the exposure more engaging help make this model more acceptable and feasible for young children and their families. Principles presented in this chapter are guided by the treatment manual *Family Based Treatment for Young Children with OCD: Therapist Guide* (Freeman & Garcia, 2008).

PSYCHOEDUCATION

The first step of treatment is to provide psychoeducation about OCD to caregivers and the child. With young children, it is typically helpful first to complete a separate psychoeducation session with caregivers to establish rapport, assess the impact of OCD on the family, and ensure caregivers have a clear understanding of the treatment model. Due to OCD symptoms, many families come to treatment in distress and with strained relationships. Goals in this initial session include removal of blame from the child and presenting a neurobehavioral framework. Comparing OCD to a medical illness, such as diabetes, can be especially helpful. An overview of treatment, including the rationale of E/RP also should be provided.

Family accommodation and caregiver response to rituals should be explored and identified as a part of the treatment process. It is important that caregivers take on the role of "home coach" and therapists set the stage for their active involvement in treatment. Caregivers should learn that a crucial part of treatment is giving them "tools" to respond to OCD and their child's behavior. While emphasized initially, psychoeducation should be used flexibly and revisited throughout treatment as often as necessary. Treating younger children means that this may be the family's first experience with the mental health system or psychotherapy. Therefore it will be especially important to assess and process the caregivers' emotional experiences as well as orient them to psychotherapy in general.

Developmentally appropriate psychoeducation should be used with the child. The main goals with the child are to build rapport, externalize OCD, and introduce the idea of E/RP. It is important not to underscore the value of positive rapport with the child given this treatment model asks the child to be uncomfortable. Having a strong and collaborative therapeutic relationship with the child can help facilitate E/RP. Therapists should externalize the disorder, a technique from narrative therapy in which problems are separated from people (Freeman, Epston, & Lobovits, 1997). Externalization removes blame and allows parents and children to align and work creatively together against the disorder. To externalize OCD, encourage children to name their OCD (e.g., Ms. Worry, The Trickster, Germinator) and draw a picture of it. Some younger children benefit from having a physical representation of OCD, such as a stuffed animal or puppet. This helps make the idea of obsessions or urges more concrete. If a child does not want to name OCD, continue to externalize by using the term OCD or another label the child chooses. E/RP should be introduced as the way to "boss back" OCD and do the opposite of what OCD wants. It is important to explain that s/he will feel uncomfortable at first when bossing back OCD but it will get easier over time. Some kids respond well to the concept of "bravery practice."

Depending on the developmental level of the child, a few different examples or metaphors can be used to illustrate exposure. For example, learning a new skill, such as a sport, can be used to illustrate how practice can help things get easier over time. Some children may also relate to an example of getting over a specific fear (such as a fear of dogs) or doing something scary (riding a roller coaster for the first time vs fifth time). To illustrate habituation, consider a metaphor of going into the cold ocean or pool and your body adjusting to the temperature. Lastly, a team approach should be conveyed and the child should know that you will decide the pace of exposures together. Given that understanding of OCD varies widely in young children, one key in treatment success is parents' ability to grasp exposure concepts and encourage their children to expose themselves to anxiety-provoking triggers (Freeman et al., 2012).

FUNCTIONAL ASSESSMENT OF SYMPTOMS

To optimally deliver exposure, one needs to understand the relationship between a patient's obsessions and rituals (Conelea, Freeman, & Garcia, 2012). Rituals that look similar topographically may serve different functions depending on the obsessions. Topography refers to what a behavior looks like when observed. Function is the relation between a behavior and its antecedents and consequences—or the "purpose" of a behavior. For example, two children's tapping rituals may "look" the same when observed (topography) but may reflect different functions, such as one child responding to a "just right" urge and the other trying to neutralize a harm obsession. Without understanding functional connections, it is difficult to design and titrate exposures appropriately. As a result, exposures may be too easy or difficult or may not activate the fear at all. The process of hypothesis testing and understanding the relation between obsessions and compulsions should start before initiating E/RP and occur throughout treatment.

The first step of a functional assessment is to identify both obsessions and compulsions at a topographical level. This information was likely gathered as part of the assessment process, such as the administration of the CY-BOCS symptom checklist. One way to organize this information is to make a two-column list with one side listing compulsions and the other listing specific obsessions (e.g., fear of getting sick, fear of parent dying). The next step is to connect the identified compulsions to their corresponding obsessions though functional assessment questions. Such questions may include: "If you didn't [do compulsion], what do you worry could happen?" *If there is no identified feared consequence*, ask, "Do you feel like you will just keep feeling uncomfortable, like something is 'not just right' or 'incomplete'?" "When you have [obsession], what makes it better/go away/reduces your anxiety?" and "Is there anything you have to do in a set way?" (Conelea et al., 2012, p. 115). When a connection is

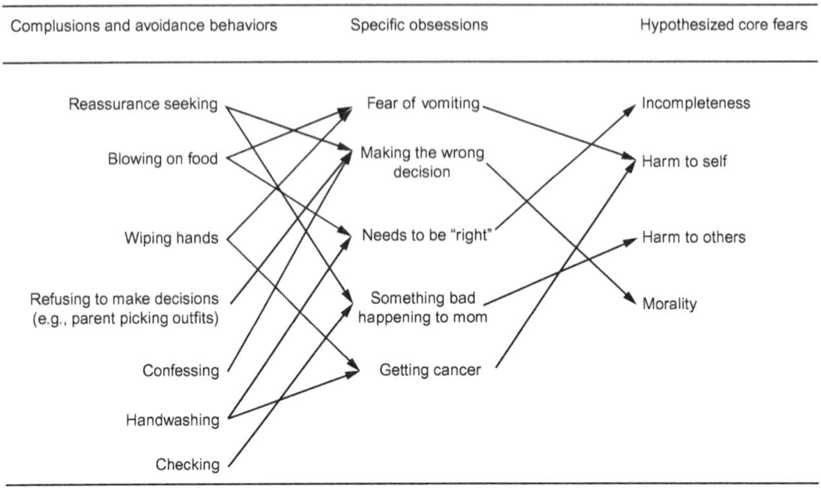

FIG. 1 Example functional assessment map.

identified, a line should be drawn connecting the two symptoms. Once there is an understanding of the relation between each compulsion and obsession, therapists should also consider the core fear or theme around a child's specific obsession. At the broadest level, there are two core dimensions of OCD obsessions: harm avoidance and incompleteness (Pietrefesa & Coles, 2009; Summerfeldt, 2004). Within harm avoidance, there are common subtypes of feared outcomes such as scrupulosity, aggression, and contamination. Children may present with both types of these core obsessions or just one. Once each step is completed, a therapist will have a "map" of the child's symptoms and their connections. Fig. 1 is an example of a functional assessment of symptoms for a child presenting with both contamination fears and incompleteness.

BUILDING A HIERARCHY

A thorough functional assessment will prepare a therapist to make a hierarchy with the family. A fear hierarchy is essentially an exposure treatment plan that lists out specific situations or feared stimuli the patient will gradually face (Abramowitz, Deacon, & Whiteside, 2012). To build a hierarchy, a scale measuring distress should be introduced to the child and family. For young children, the type of scale used will depend on their development. Some children will be able to use a traditional 10-point scale (0—no anxiety/distress, 10—extreme anxiety/distress); however, most young children will need a modified scale (e.g., smaller 3-point range, smiley faces with or without a point scale, types of animals from cuddly to aggressive, or visual scales such as use of hands or stacking cups). The scale serves as a communication tool around a child's distress both within and outside of exposure. It is important to practice using the scale with non-OCD situations to ensure the child understands how to use it. Young children often report an "all-or-nothing" experience of anxiety. If this is the case, look for subtle behavioral cues to help identify intermediate levels of distress and shape a child's accuracy using the scale (Choate-Summers et al., 2008).

The next step is to identify specific situations that trigger the child's anxiety/fear. You should choose items that the child will practice in the office or at home. Situations, places, or things that are avoided or result in ritualizing should be included on the hierarchy. When creating fear hierarchies for OCD, you should identify the obsession or fear the child should focus on during the exposure as well as any avoidance or ritual behavior the child should not engage in during or after the exposure. The child and/or caregiver rates the items based upon whatever rating scale you introduced to the family. The goal is to identify items that represent low, middle, and high ranges of distress for a particular fear. General task variations that may modify the difficulty of the exposure include changing the proximity of the stimulus, altering the amount of contact with the stimulus, combining more than one trigger/stimulus, having the caregiver present or not, and increasing or decreasing uncertainty around the task. An example item for a contamination exposure might be "touch outside of therapist's trashcan with hands without washing, wiping, or asking mom if I will be okay."

Caregiver perspective is especially important when creating hierarchies with younger children. Have the caregiver monitor and record OCD behaviors between sessions, including their response to the behavior, as a way to start building possible hierarchy items. Hierarchies for young children should include specific items around reducing family accommodation of symptoms. Increasing parental awareness around their response to behavior is a first step to building a hierarchy which reduces caregiver accommodation. Lastly, inquire about subtle avoidance behaviors or ways to make an exposure easier based upon a caregiver's experience with approaching difficult tasks at home.

When making the hierarchy, shy away from using specific time limits unless there is an OCD ritual involved with time. This is because many children will "white knuckle" through an exposure with the anticipation of escape at the end which then reinforces the anxious cycle. Items on a fear hierarchy should be ordered from least anxiety provoking to most with the intent to increase difficulty over the course of treatment; however, therapists should be flexible around the order of completing exposures as the hierarchy will change and evolve. Use discretion to determine how detailed a hierarchy should be before moving forward with exposure. Because hierarchies are not static and constantly evolve throughout treatment, a therapist should be mindful not to spend excessive amounts of time building hierarchies at the expense of moving forward with E/RP.

EXPOSURE WITH RESPONSE PREVENTION (E/RP)

As previously mentioned, E/RP is the critical ingredient for treating OCD. E/RP involves gradually exposing a child to situations that are distressing to them without engagement in rituals. E/RP should be guided by the functional assessment of symptoms and the hierarchy. Caregivers are most always present and involved with E/RP when treating young children with OCD because they will need to coach them in using E/RP at home. A possible exception is when a caregiver's presence serves as a safety behavior and needs to be removed to increase the difficulty of the exposure. Each section later will discuss how to prepare, implement, and process E/RP.

Preparing for E/RP

The first step in preparing for E/RP is choosing an exposure from the hierarchy. Choosing an item from the hierarchy should always be completed collaboratively with the family. Conducting "mini" hierarchy building prior to the start of the exposure can be helpful to ensure the exposure task is clear and appropriately challenging. For example, a child with hoarding symptoms may have "throwing away a paper from school" as an item on the hierarchy. The therapist should try to be as specific as possible around the expected exposure task. Further assessment might include what type of item the child has to throw away (e.g., particular subject, artwork), how many items, where s/he will throw the item away (e.g., trash can in room, locked recycle bin), and whether caregivers will be present. Additionally, the response prevention should be discussed and agreed upon prior to the exposure. For instance, this child may be asked to resist checking, removing the item from the trash, or seeking reassurance from the caregiver.

Therapists should be mindful of the pace of exposures when working with young children (Choate-Summers et al., 2008). The idea of "starting low and going slow" is helpful with younger children. For initial exposures, choose easier exposure items that activate mild distress to set the stage for a successful exposure, increase the child's confidence and self-efficacy, and gauge his or her ability to provide accurate ratings. Young children are often inaccurate reporters of how upsetting an exposure task might be; therefore starting with an easier item gives a therapist more flexibility. Increasing the difficulty of the exposure is easier than starting with something too hard.

Choosing an exposure with young children can prove challenging for a number of reasons including their motivation to engage in the task. As such, it is important to make the exposure task as fun and engaging as possible. This can be challenging when the ultimate goal is to evoke anxiety/distress. Humor and being silly can be effective tools to engage younger children. Table 1 offers examples of ways to make exposure tasks more engaging through play.

Implementing E/RP

For therapists new to exposure therapy, a looming question is often what they should be doing during the exposure. Using a theoretical model is helpful to

TABLE 1 Example Integrations of Exposure and Play for Young Children

Exposure Task/ Game	Brief Description	Potential Fear(s) Targeted
Uneven "Simon Says"	Have the child engage in triggering body movements or actions without "evening out"	Incompleteness
Scavenger Hunt	Go look for feared stimulus (e.g., bugs) and earn points for each bravery encounter	Contamination Phobias
"Messed up" artwork	Coloring outside the lines, choosing incorrect colors for objects (e.g., blue grass), leaving portion of drawing incomplete	Perfectionism Incompleteness
Contaminated Baking	Make a preferred treat to eat in presence of contaminant or with contaminated hands	Contamination
"Go Feel Uncomfortable" or Matching	Modified version of "Go Fish" with cards involving avoided words or phrases (e.g., swear words, body parts, cancers); use same cards to play matching game	Scrupulosity Sexual obsessions Harm to self or others Phobia Contaminate words/phrases
Modified board games	Change rules or contaminate game pieces and play game with new rules or contaminated pieces; stop game at random time	Contamination Perfectionism Incompleteness
Watching cartoon scenes	Watch cartoon involving avoided content (e.g., clip of Dora the Explorer vomiting)	Harm to self or others Phobias Scrupulosity

guide and anchor your own behavior. As previously stated, E/RP in this chapter is described using a distress tolerance and habituation framework. To review, the basic tenet of habituation is that anxiety/distress will naturally decrease over time in the absence of anxiety-reducing behaviors. Thus at a basic level therapists should engage in behaviors that promote the experience of habituation and minimize reducing anxiety through other mechanisms (e.g., coping behaviors, distraction). Common misconceptions about this model are that habituation must occur in session, must be evident to end the exposure, is an active process, and is "all or nothing" (Benito & Walther, 2015). A child's anxiety may not be fully reduced at the end of the exposure; however, that does not mean habituation did not occur. Therapists may feel like they need to "help the child habituate," suggesting it is an active process that can be controlled; however, natural anxiety reduction will occur in its own time without active strategies. A therapist is helping the child by creating optimal conditions that allow for habituation and the opportunity to learn distress tolerance.

Prior to starting the exposure, clear instructions should be given about the expected behaviors from the child, parent, and therapist. Again, reducing parent involvement in rituals is a key feature during exposures with young children. Parents should be coached prior to an exposure about how to respond to the child when requests around ritualizing during the exposure arise. An instruction about exposure with bleach may look like this after the exposure has been collaboratively decided with the family and rituals identified:

> *Today we are going to fight OCD by sitting in the room with an opened bleach bottle. OCD is likely going to tell you that you might have swallowed the bleach just like he does at home. He's really bossy and I bet he will want you to ask your mom if you are going to get sick or check your mouth in the mirror. Your job is to boss back OCD by not asking mom questions about being safe or the bleach and to not check your mouth. If you do ask me or your mom questions about the bleach, our job is to not answer OCD's questions. Remember, we are on your team and don't want OCD to get stronger. We aren't ignoring your question, we are ignoring OCD. I'm going to ask you to tell me how anxious or uncomfortable you are using our three faces. I know this is tough but you're so brave and can do it! Do you have any questions?*

Once the instructions are clear, have the child approach the exposure task. Once you start the exposure, engage in behaviors that maintain or increase a patient's contact with the exposure task (Benito & Walther, 2015). For example, use descriptive statements about the exposure itself (e.g., "Wow, I bet OCD doesn't like you being in a room with an opened bottle of bleach"), encourage the child to decrease avoidance (e.g., "Show OCD who is in charge and look at the bottle"), or increase the difficulty of the exposure task itself (e.g., "Come a bit closer to the bleach bottle," "Imagine there is bleach on your tongue right now"). To help engage the child and keep focus on the exposure task, it is often helpful for the therapist to play the role of OCD or use an object (e.g., puppet, stuffed animal) to represent OCD. You as OCD might make statements such as "Are you sure there isn't bleach in your mouth? Go ahead and check your mouth. Maybe you should ask mom to be sure you're safe. Bleach can make you sick." The child can "boss" back OCD by saying things like "No!" or "I don't have to listen to you" while resisting engaging in the rituals. Additionally, check in with patients about their anxiety during the exposure to help them focus on their anxious experience. Because young children typically aren't able to offer a wide range of ratings, use behavioral cues as an indicator of level of distress. If a child seems to be engaging in more approach behaviors and less avoidance, this is a good indicator that the exposure task is getting easier or they are tolerating their distress better.

Therapists should avoid using strategies to reduce anxiety during exposure as it will impede the process of habituation and distress tolerance. Anxiety-reducing behaviors may include using relaxation during exposure (e.g., encouraging progressive muscle relaxation, taking deep breaths), purposefully providing accommodation or allowing caregivers to accommodate (e.g., "It is impossible for bleach to be in your mouth, so you're safe"), engaging in distraction (e.g., playing a game of UNO while the bleach is out of sight), talking about unrelated topics (e.g., what the family is doing over the weekend), or encouraging cognitive strategies that are meant to reduce distress in the moment (e.g., evaluating and focusing on the likelihood of getting sick) (Benito & Walther, 2015). With young children, caregivers may be looking for these types of strategies to "help them manage the anxiety" in the moment. Therefore it is important for parents to understand the rationale for not engaging in these strategies during an exposure.

Being silly, humorous, or animated can make exposures more tolerable and fun, which may increase the likelihood a child will engage in them. Additionally, creating space for silliness and humor allows the child to have a different experience with a feared stimulus than they might have anticipated, which is a key tenet of the inhibitory learning approach (Craske et al., 2014). It is important, however, that the child is still exposed to the feared stimulus and that play or fun is not a complete distraction from anxiety. Playing UNO, for instance, may be less distracting if the exposure task is to contaminate each card drawn by having it touch the bleach bottle. Thus the child is frequently engaged with the stimulus and the therapist can keep redirecting the child back to the stimulus. This exposure is functionally different than introducing bleach and then shifting focus to a game. Additionally, children often engage in distraction by talking about topics other than the exposure. When this occurs, simply redirect the child back to the exposure task. Protecting time at the end of the session to talk about topics of importance or playing a game is helpful. If a child raises an important topic, say "I want to hear all about [topic] but we need to finish our bravery practice first. Let's remember to talk about that after this."

During exposure, therapists may engage in other behaviors that have a neutral effect on anxiety but are important to the therapeutic process (Benito & Walther, 2015). That is, these behaviors do not seem to increase or decrease anxiety. For young kids, encourage engagement through positive attention. Praise brave behavior and effort rather than reduction of fear. Externalize OCD to emphasize the separation between OCD and the child. Encourage positive self-talk (e.g., "I can do this") to promote confidence and self-efficacy. These behaviors may be especially helpful during exposures that are more difficult or when the child appears less motivated.

There is no set length or rule for ending an exposure. Optimally, exposure ends when the child's anxiety reduces, with the decrease not due to anxiety-reducing behaviors, such as ritualizing. Fear ratings alone should not determine when to end an exposure as some children will quickly learn the exposure will end if they say they aren't anxious anymore. While inhibitory learning theory suggests that subjective reports of distress do not need to be reduced for exposure to end (Abramowitz, 2013; Craske et al., 2014), you want to ensure that young children will continue to engage in response prevention after they leave your office. Young children with OCD may have more difficulty with resisting rituals if their anxiety is high at the end of session. It is important to leave time for processing and planning for ritual prevention after the session.

Processing E/RP

Processing the exposure experience can help build self-efficacy and pride around a child's accomplishment. Brave behavior and the ability to handle distress should be emphasized. As previously mentioned, discuss continued ritual prevention, especially if the child is still reporting some levels of anxiety or seems distressed. By creating a plan with the family, it will minimize the risk of the child ritualizing once they leave the office. "Reexposure" can be introduced in postsession planning as needed. For instance, if a child is resisting washing her hands and then uses the bathroom and washes them, encourage the child to reexpose herself to the original stimulus or an equivalent stimulus.

Assigning E/RP for homework is a crucial part of treatment. Some exposures are difficult to practice in the office and can only be completed at home. Additionally, repeating the same exposure at home will allow for "massed" practice and facilitate extinction. Given that E/RP may be conducted more slowly with young children and is often done through play, home practice is especially crucial to ensure treatment gains (Choate-Summers et al., 2008). Choate-Summers and colleagues recommend comparing OCD to juvenile diabetes for caregivers in that both are biologically based disorders that need consistency in management. Part of preparing for homework includes coaching parents on how to respond to their child around E/RP, especially with limiting family accommodation. Therapists should use the contingency management skills discussed in the next session to support caregivers in being the at home coach. Families should leave the session with clear E/RP homework outlining the exposure plan for the child and how the parent will support it.

CONTINGENCY MANAGEMENT OF BEHAVIOR

Exposure therapy is difficult for everyone and can be especially difficult for small children, particularly when they are not motivated to change their behavior. Therefore behavioral management strategies can be helpful in supporting treatment. The extent to which therapists integrate and use these strategies will depend on a child's presentation, motivation, and interactions within the family. Given that oppositional and disruptive behavior occurs more frequently in younger children than older ones with OCD (Selles et al., 2014; Skriner et al., 2016), therapists may find that addressing parent management and disruptive behavior is a necessary step to move forward with exposure. This approach may involve completing a full behavioral modification program (see *Defiant Children*, Barkley, 2013). However, many young children will respond well to the integration of contingency management within the exposure protocol.

Positive reinforcement strategies are encouraged first with verbal praise for brave behavior being the cornerstone. Teach praise to be specific, immediate, and labeled. Therapists can use praise to both promote in-session compliance and model for caregivers. Many young children will need additional positive reinforcement through a rewards system. Rewards can be tangible items (e.g., stickers, small toy from a prize box) or privileges (e.g., staying up 15–30 min past bedtime, choosing a movie or dinner, getting an extra play date, having special time with a caregiver). For younger children, an immediate reward will likely motivate them more powerfully than a delayed one. Some children, however, might want to earn a larger reward or privilege. In that case, setting up a point system or sticker chart would be beneficial. For example, create a "Bingo" chart that allows kids to put a sticker wherever they want. Once they get a line across, they can earn a privilege or toy. Some families even like to offer a special prize or treat for completing a whole chart of "Being Brave Bingo." Most importantly, be creative and identify rewards that are reinforcing for the child.

For some children, positive reinforcement alone is insufficient to get them to engage in exposures, especially if caregivers focus frequently on negative or anxious behavior. Caregiver attention is a powerful reinforcer whether that attention is positive or negative. Differential attention should be taught to caregivers to help them remove attention from unwanted behaviors (i.e., active ignoring) and shift attention to desired behaviors (e.g., praise). Caregivers need to understand you are not asking them to reduce the amount of attention they give the child but instead you would like them to choose the behaviors to which they give attention. Prepare the family for the possibility of an extinction burst and the importance of riding it out. To mitigate a major extinction burst, children should be told ahead of time that parents will no longer respond to X behavior and if they wish to get help, they should instead do Y behavior. Some behaviors, such as aggression, are not appropriate for active ignoring. If the child is engaging in unsafe behaviors, negative consequences should be employed. Time-out from positive reinforcement can be used for breaking of house rules. If the caregiver is already using time-out, spend some time assessing how it is administered. Small changes to time-out and using the protocol outlined in Defiant Children (Barkley, 2013) can help increase its effectiveness. Children who have a hard time engaging in exposure may need to have everyday privileges linked to exposure goals. For example, one 6 year old with OCD with "just right" rituals and avoidance of getting dressed needed to be ready by a certain time each day to earn T.V. privileges after school. The family also used time-out when she became aggressive in the morning. With clear expectations and consequences, this child was able to consistently be ready on time. Make sure that children are developmentally capable of the expectation and that you are choosing an appropriately titrated exposure or you may be unfairly setting them up for failure.

Two other helpful parenting strategies include modeling and scaffolding (Freeman & Garcia, 2008), especially when caregivers experiencing their own anxiety are telling children or inadvertently sending messages to feel afraid or avoid. Explain that one way children learn is by watching parent behavior. Caregivers have the opportunity to teach and model brave behavior by demonstrating approach to uncomfortable situations and by calmly encouraging children to do the same. Scaffolding is meant to help children take more responsibility and reduce family involvement with OCD. It follows specific steps that include: (1) identify the child's emotion and empathize with his/her feelings, (2) encourage approach to the situation by brainstorming options to limit avoidance, and (3) move forward with exposure and reward the child for brave behavior. Scaffolding can be particularly helpful when families encounter unexpected triggers that provoke a lot of anxiety.

RELAPSE PREVENTION

Toward the end of treatment, relapse prevention strategies should be taught. Relapse prevention commonly includes educating the family about the chronicity of OCD, emphasizing the importance of continued exposure practice, and preparing the family to manage reemergence of symptoms. OCD is biological in nature and is typically chronic but can be managed over time. During times of transition or stress, exacerbations in OCD symptoms may occur. Identify typical developmental stressors, such as starting a new school year, with families to develop awareness and plan for how to respond to OCD in case it worsens. Additionally, it is important for families to know that exposure does not end with treatment but should become part of a new lifestyle. Comparing anxiety to a weed in a garden exemplifies how anxiety returns if you do not keep engaging in exposure. Help the family identify signs of OCD and steps for addressing new or returning symptoms. Such steps should include encouraging approach and engaging in purposeful exposure. Encourage caregivers to use skills learned in therapy; however, if families are having difficulty applying the skills, they should consider returning to therapy for "booster" sessions.

TROUBLESHOOTING E/RP WITH YOUNG CHILDREN

This section offers suggestions to deal with common concerns and questions raised when treating young children with OCD. As always, use your clinical judgment when identifying the best solution for a particular child and family.

What If I Am Not Getting Enough Information for The Hierarchy?

As previously mentioned, young children may have a difficult time reporting their symptoms and have poorer insight than older youth (Selles et al., 2014). Potential solutions include:

- Collect information from multiple informants.
- Acknowledge it can feel embarrassing to share symptoms and say that you have heard these types of symptoms before.
- Make educated guesses about fears for the child to confirm or deny rather than using open-ended questions.
- Be curious about rituals or avoidance behavior observed in session (e.g., a child observed wiping his hands after touching markers may disclose that the therapist coughed and contaminated them).
- Listen for impromptu statements during session (e.g., if a child says, "I'm glad I didn't eat breakfast" during an exposure with vomit words then you may follow-up with questions about whether eating makes anxiety worse due to stomach uneasiness, fullness, etc. Exposures then can be made more difficult by combining eating with vomit triggers).

What If an Exposure Does Not Go as Planned?

While it can be challenging when exposures do not go as predicted, a child's response may give you valuable information about fears and symptoms. An exposure may be too easy if the child completes the task without any difficulty and you do not observe active avoidance or ritualizing. If an exposure appears too easy, consider the following options:

- Evaluate whether the exposure actually targets and elicits the child's fear (e.g., a child who avoids drinking from water bottles easily drinks from one she brought to session, leading to questions that reveal she only avoids bottles she left unattended).
- Revisit the hierarchy and brainstorm ways to make the exposure more difficult (e.g., increase the proximity or contact with the stimulus).
- Check to ensure the child is not ritualizing (e.g., doing a mental ritual, such as counting).

Signs that an exposure is too hard include children refusing to do it, ritualizing, rushing, having a tantrum, "white knuckling" with an intent to ritualize or escape later, or stopping; all of which block or interfere with habituation and distress tolerance. Suggested options include:

- If you already are in an exposure that is too hard, try to complete the original task by offering more praise and reducing focus on the fear.
- If the child is unable to continue the exposure task, use scaffolding steps (see the Contingency Management of Behavior section) to help identify a more

tolerable exposure, with the goal to have the child not totally escape and approach the feared stimulus to some degree.
- If the exposure is not yet under way, create more tolerable artificial or contrived conditions such as touching a "thing to a thing" (e.g., the child's holding a tissue against a contaminated object).

What If A Child Refuses to Engage in E/RP?

It is not uncommon for younger children to be more hesitant or less motivated than their caregivers to change their behavior. If a child is refusing to do an exposure:

- Create an incentive plan or consider additional incentives to engage in exposures.
- Ensure that offered rewards are desirable (menus selected by the child and approved by the parent are likely to work best).
- Integrate more play into the exposure to facilitate interest (see Table 1 for examples).
- Assess for additional oppositional behavior and, if present, consider a full parent training program before proceeding.

How Do I Deal With Parental Distress?

Perhaps the most difficult part of treatment for parents is seeing their child in distress. In fact, many families have made extensive accommodations to rescue their child from discomfort, and the E/RP model may feel counterintuitive to a caregiver's typical response. Unfortunately, parental distress can impede exposure. To prevent and assist with parental discomfort, you can:

- Take steps to ensure caregivers understand the rationale for exposure and agree with treatment.
- Assess how much child distress parents can tolerate and titrate exposures accordingly.
- Validate and normalize parental distress, including processing parental emotions and explaining that feeling bad in the short run leads to getting better in the long run.
- Incorporate more family process and parent training work (e.g., provide specific coaching and modeling on how to respond to a child's distress).
- Consider recommending individual treatment for parents who remain highly uncomfortable with the treatment model.

CONCLUSION

In summary, early treatment of OCD in young children is crucial given the chronicity and negative trajectory on function and impairment. CBT using E/RP is an efficacious and tolerable treatment for young children. Major developmental modifications include having the caregivers actively involved in treatment, addressing family process and accommodation, and modifying exposures to be engaging for a younger audience. Contingency management of behavior should be integrated within an E/RP protocol to help promote engagement in the model and address disruptive behavior. Lastly, therapists should use a theoretical framework to guide exposure, use strategies to maintain or increase anxiety during exposure rather than anxiety-decreasing behaviors, and have functional understanding of symptoms to better design and titrate exposures.

REFERENCES

Abramowitz, J. S. (2013). The practice of exposure therapy: Relevance of cognitive-behavioral theory and extinction theory. *Behavior Therapy*, *44*(4), 548–558.

Abramowitz, J. S., Deacon, B. J., & Whiteside, S. P. (2012). *Exposure therapy for anxiety: Principles and practice*. New York, NY: Guilford Press.

Barkley, R. A. (2013). *Defiant children: A clinician's manual for assessment and parent training*. New York, NY: Guilford Press.

Benito, K. G., & Walther, M. (2015). Therapeutic process during exposure: Habituation model. *Journal of Obsessive-Compulsive and Related Disorders*, *6*, 147–157.

Calvocoressi, L., Lewis, B., Harris, M., Trufan, S. J., Goodman, W. K., McDougle, C. J., et al. (1995). Family accommodation in obsessive-compulsive disorder. *American Journal of Psychiatry*, *152*(3), 441–443.

Choate-Summers, M. L., Freeman, J. B., Garcia, A. M., Coyne, L., Przeworski, A., & Leonard, H. L. (2008). Clinical considerations when tailoring cognitive behavioral treatment for young children with obsessive compulsive disorder. *Education and Treatment of Children*, *31*(3), 395–416.

Conelea, C. A., Freeman, J. B., & Garcia, A. M. (2012). Integrating behavioral theory with OCD assessment using the Y-BOCS/CY-BOCS symptom checklist. *Journal of Obsessive-Compulsive and Related Disorders*, *1*(2), 112–118.

Cook, N. E., Freeman, J. B., Garcia, A. M., Sapyta, J. J., & Franklin, M. E. (2015). Assessment of obsessive compulsive disorder in young children: Psychometric properties of the Children's Yale-Brown Obsessive Compulsive Scale. *Journal of Psychopathology and Behavioral Assessment*, *37*(3), 432–441.

Craske, M. G., Treanor, M., Conway, C. C., Zbozinek, T., & Vervliet, B. (2014). Maximizing exposure therapy: An inhibitory learning approach. *Behaviour Research and Therapy*, *58*, 10–23.

Flessner, C. A., Sapyta, J., Garcia, A., Freeman, J. B., Franklin, M. E., Foa, E., et al. (2011). Examining the psychometric properties of the family accommodation scale-parent-report (FAS-PR). *Journal of Psychopathology and Behavioral Assessment*, *33*(1), 38–46.

Foa, E. B., & Kozak, M. J. (1986). Emotional processing of fear: Exposure to corrective information. *Psychological Bulletin*, *99*(1), 20.

Frank, H., Stewart, E., Walther, M., Benito, K., Freeman, J., Conelea, C., et al. (2014). Hoarding behavior among young children with obsessive–compulsive disorder. *Journal of Obsessive-Compulsive and Related Disorders*, *3*(1), 6–11.

Freeman, J., Epston, D., & Lobovits, D. (1997). *Playful approaches to serious problems: Narrative therapy with children and their families*. New York, NY: W.W. Norton & Company.

Freeman, J., Flessner, C. A., & Garcia, A. (2011). The Children's Yale-Brown Obsessive Compulsive Scale: Reliability and validity for use among 5 to 8 year olds with obsessive-compulsive disorder. *Journal of Abnormal Child Psychology, 39*(6), 877–883.

Freeman, J. B., & Garcia, A. M. (2008). *Family based treatment for young children with OCD: Therapist guide.* Cary, NC: Oxford University Press.

Freeman, J., Garcia, A., Benito, K., Conelea, C., Sapyta, J., Khanna, M., et al. (2012). The pediatric obsessive compulsive disorder treatment study for young children (POTS Jr): Developmental considerations in the rationale, design, and methods. *Journal of Obsessive-Compulsive and Related Disorders, 1*(4), 294–300.

Freeman, J., Garcia, A., Frank, H., Benito, K., Conelea, C., Walther, M., et al. (2014). Evidence base update for psychosocial treatments for pediatric obsessive-compulsive disorder. *Journal of Clinical Child & Adolescent Psychology, 43*(1), 7–26.

Freeman, J., Sapyta, J., Garcia, A., Compton, S., Khanna, M., Flessner, C., et al. (2014). Family-based treatment of early childhood obsessive-compulsive disorder: The Pediatric Obsessive-Compulsive Disorder Treatment Study for Young Children (POTS Jr)—A randomized clinical trial. *JAMA Psychiatry, 71*(6), 689–698.

Garcia, A. M., Freeman, J. B., Himle, M. B., Berman, N. C., Ogata, A. K., Ng, J., et al. (2009). Phenomenology of early childhood onset obsessive compulsive disorder. *Journal of Psychopathology and Behavioral Assessment, 31*(2), 104–111.

Geller, D. A., & March, J. (2012). Practice parameter for the assessment and treatment of children and adolescents with obsessive-compulsive disorder. *Focus, 10*(3), 360–373.

Keeley, M. L., Storch, E. A., Dhungana, P., & Geffken, G. R. (2007). Pediatric obsessive-compulsive disorder: A guide to assessment and treatment. *Issues in Mental Health Nursing, 28*(6), 555–574.

Lebowitz, E. R., Panza, K. E., Su, J., & Bloch, M. H. (2014). Family accommodation in obsessive-compulsive disorder. *Expert Review of Neurotherapeutics 12*(2), 229–238.

Lewin, A. B., Park, J. M., Jones, A. M., Crawford, E. A., De Nadai, A. S., Menzel, J., et al. (2014). Family-based exposure and response prevention therapy for preschool-aged children with obsessive-compulsive disorder: A pilot randomized controlled trial. *Behaviour Research and Therapy, 56*, 30–38.

Lewin, A. B., & Piacentini, J. (2010). Evidence-based assessment of child obsessive compulsive disorder: Recommendations for clinical practice and treatment research. *Child & Youth Care Forum. 39*, 73–89.

Piacentini, J., Bergman, R. L., Keller, M., & McCracken, J. (2003). Functional impairment in children and adolescents with obsessive-compulsive disorder. *Journal of Child and Adolescent Psychopharmacology, 13*(2, Suppl. 1), 61–69.

Piacentini, J., Peris, T. S., Bergman, R. L., Chang, S., & Jaffer, M. (2007). BRIEF REPORT: Functional impairment in childhood OCD: Development and psychometrics properties of the child obsessive-compulsive impact scale-revised (COIS-R). *Journal of Clinical Child and Adolescent Psychology, 36*(4), 645–653.

Pietrefesa, A. S., & Coles, M. E. (2009). Moving beyond an exclusive focus on harm avoidance in obsessive-compulsive disorder: Behavioral validation for the separability of harm avoidance and incompleteness. *Behavior Therapy, 40*(3), 251–259.

Scahill, L., Riddle, M. A., McSwiggin-Hardin, M., Ort, S. I., King, R. A., Goodman, W. K., et al. (1997). Children's Yale-Brown obsessive compulsive scale: Reliability and validity. *Journal of the American Academy of Child & Adolescent Psychiatry, 36*(6), 844–852.

Selles, R. R., Storch, E. A., & Lewin, A. B. (2014). Variations in symptom prevalence and clinical correlates in younger versus older youth with obsessive-compulsive disorder. *Child Psychiatry & Human Development*, *45*(6), 666–674.

Skriner, L., Freeman, J., Garcia, A., Benito, K., Sapyta, J., & Franklin, M. (2016). Characteristics of young children with obsessive-compulsive disorder: Baseline features from the POTS Jr. sample. *Child Psychiatry & Human Development*, *47*(1), 83–93.

Storch, E. A., Geffken, G. R., Merlo, L. J., Jacob, M. L., Murphy, T. K., Goodman, W. K., et al. (2007). Family accommodation in pediatric obsessive-compulsive disorder. *Journal of Clinical Child and Adolescent Psychology*, *36*(2), 207–216.

Storch, E. A., Murphy, T. K., Geffken, G. R., Soto, O., Sajid, M., Allen, P., et al. (2004). Psychometric evaluation of the Children's Yale–Brown Obsessive-Compulsive Scale. *Psychiatry Research*, *129*(1), 91–98.

Summerfeldt, L. J. (2004). Understanding and treating incompleteness in obsessive-compulsive disorder. *Journal of Clinical Psychology*, *60*(11), 1155–1168.

Chapter 16

Strategies to Manage Common Co-occurring Psychiatric Conditions

Yolanda E. Murphy, Elle Brennan, Sarah Francazio, and Christopher A. Flessner
Kent State University, Kent, OH, United States

Pediatric obsessive-compulsive disorder (OCD) impacts a substantial proportion of the population (AACAP, 2012) and causes significant distress and psychosocial impairment (Piacentini, Bergman, Keller, & McCracken, 2003; Storch et al., 2010). Despite the fact that highly efficacious treatments exist for OCD (Öst, Riise, Wergeland, Hansen, & Kvale, 2016), many individuals who seek to reduce their symptoms do not receive the frontline treatments that are available (e.g., exposure with response prevention (ERP), pharmacotherapy; Torres et al., 2006). Further, large proportions of individuals (e.g., 50% of adults, 27%–79% of youth) do not fully benefit from treatment and continue to suffer with clinically significant symptoms even following OCD treatment (Abramowitz, 2006; Pallanti et al., 2002; Pediatric OCD Treatment Study (POTS) Team, 2004; Torp et al., 2015).

One challenge in treating pediatric OCD is the high levels of comorbidity common to the disorder, including anxiety, mood, and disruptive disorders (Langley, Lewin, Bergman, Lee, & Piacentini, 2010) among others. Understanding and managing these symptoms is of particular importance as comorbidity is largely considered to be the rule with pediatric OCD, rather than the exception (Ortiz et al., 2016; Pediatric OCD Treatment Study (POTS) Team, 2004). This is particularly worrisome as individuals who meet diagnostic criteria for multiple psychiatric disorders are generally less likely to respond to treatment and more likely to relapse following treatment. For example, Geller, Biederman, et al. (2004) found that youth with attention-deficit/hyperactivity disorder (ADHD), tic disorders, or oppositional defiant disorder (ODD) in addition to OCD showed a significantly worse response to treatment with paroxetine (56%, 53%, and 39%, respectively) than youth with OCD only (75%). The specific interface between OCD, its common comorbid diagnoses,

The Clinician's Guide to Cognitive-Behavioral Therapy for Childhood Obsessive-Compulsive Disorder
http://dx.doi.org/10.1016/B978-0-12-811427-8.00016-2

and treatment outcome is not fully understood. However, it is likely that these deficiencies in treatment efficacy are due, in part, to specific characteristics of the psychiatric disorders, as well as unique interactions between the demands of treating the respective comorbid conditions in addition to OCD.

ADHD, for instance, co-occurs in approximately 20%–30% of pediatric OCD cases (Geller, Biederman, Griffin, Jones, & Lefkowitz, 1996; Geller et al., 2007). As will be discussed further later in this chapter, the deficits associated with ADHD have been found to complicate treatment for pediatric OCD, such as by significantly reducing response rates (Storch et al., 2008)—though such findings are mixed (e.g., Masi et al., 2006). Other externalizing disorders, such as ODD and Conduct Disorder (CD), also commonly co-occur with pediatric OCD impacting 11%–43% or 7% of such youth, respectively (Geller et al., 1996). These disruptive behavioral patterns may be particularly detrimental to pediatric OCD treatment outcomes (Masi et al., 2006; Storch et al., 2007), as will be discussed further later.

Internalizing problems such as anxiety disorders are also extremely common in youth with OCD (Alvarenga et al., 2016), which is unsurprising as OCD has long been conceptualized alongside the anxiety disorders. Generalized anxiety disorder (GAD), in particular, is comorbid in 7%–59% of youth with OCD (Geller, Wagner, et al., 2004; Langley et al., 2010). Despite their distinctive natures, aspects of these two disorders are often conflated. As will be discussed, comorbid symptoms of GAD do not appear to negatively impact treatment outcome for OCD (Rapee, Lyneham, Hudson, Kangas, & Schniering, 2013). However, the unique contributions of each disorder must still be addressed in treatment.

Tic disorders (TD)—including chronic motor tics, chronic vocal tics, transient tics, and Tourette's Disorder—can be found in 10%–53% of youth with OCD (Conelea et al., 2014; Geller et al., 1996; Leckman et al., 2010). Similarly to GAD, the co-occurrence of TD with OCD has not been found to be disruptive of CBT for OCD (Conelea et al., 2014; March et al., 2007). However, the disruptive nature of tics (e.g., anger, embarrassment, etc.) could potentially complicate treatment when comorbid with OCD in youth.

The complexity described previously in the presentation of OCD and its common comorbid disorders, among others, is relevant to consider when determining how best to approach treatment. This is particularly important when determining where to focus treatment first and/or how to integrate aspects of treatment geared toward one disorder into the other. As such, it is critical that clinicians have a general working knowledge of OCD and its common comorbid disorders, as well as understand how best to approach such cases flexibly. What follows is a brief review of the extant literature on the treatment of OCD and each of its primary comorbid disorders, along with recommendations for how to approach the complexities of treating youth with these complex symptom presentations.

ATTENTION-DEFICIT/HYPERACTIVITY DISORDER

The DSM-5 defines ADHD as "a persistent pattern of inattention and/or hyperactivity-impulsivity that interferes with functioning or development, has symptoms presenting in two or more settings (e.g., at home, school, or work; with friends or relatives; in other activities), and negatively impacts directly on social, academic or occupational functioning" (American Psychiatric Association, 2013, p. 59). In the overwhelming majority of cases, onset of ADHD appears to be earlier than the age of onset for OCD (Geller et al., 2003). This comorbidity appears to be bidirectional, such that children and adolescents with ADHD report similar rates of co-occurring OCD (Moll et al., 2000). In addition, patients with comorbid OCD and ADHD are more likely to report additional diagnoses of tic disorder, bipolar disorder, and disruptive behavior disorders (Masi et al., 2006). Though such high rates of comorbidity in OCD and ADHD are well established, there is substantial debate as to whether the symptoms of ADHD—including inattention, impulsivity, and hyperactivity—are indicators of true comorbid ADHD or are simply consequences of OCD and its related anxiety (Masi et al., 2006).

The most commonly implemented treatment for ADHD is stimulant medication (Geller et al., 2002; Zuvekas & Vitiello, 2012), though behavioral interventions are also utilized (American Academy of Pediatrics, 2011; Daley et al., 2014; Evans, Schultz, DeMars, & Davis, 2011; Power et al., 2012). As mentioned previously, comorbid diagnosis of ADHD may have important implications for OCD treatment response. Studies have suggested that the core symptoms of ADHD—as well as the known deficits in executive functioning, emotion regulation, and social skills (Barkley, 1998; Hinshaw, 2003)—may interfere with E/RP (Garcia et al., 2010; Halldorsdottir & Ollendick, 2014; Storch et al., 2008). For example, habituation is considered to be the main process underlying improvement from CBT and requires sustained contact with the anxiety-eliciting stimulus until anxiety reduction is observed (Davis & Ollendick, 2005; Tryon, 2005). The inattentive and hyperactive symptoms observed in ADHD may disrupt or prevent this sustained anxious arousal, impeding habituation and decreasing the effectiveness of exposure treatments (Benito, Conelea, Garcia, & Freeman, 2012). ADHD symptoms may also interfere with the effectiveness of cognitive components of CBT. Children may have greater difficulty sustaining attention and staying involved during psychoeducation, therapist modeling, and more cognitively oriented components (Pelham & Fabiano, 2008). Given these unique challenges to treatment for children with comorbid ADHD, it is important to effectively treat ADHD symptoms so that children can fully benefit from CBT treatment to address their OCD symptoms.

In addition to having a negative impact on psychotherapy outcomes (Storch et al., 2008), comorbid ADHD may also have a deleterious impact on response to psychopharmacological treatment as well (Geller et al., 2003). For example, a study examining response to SRI treatment in a clinical sample of children and adolescents with co-occurring OCD and ADHD (Masi et al., 2006) found lower levels of improvement at 6-month follow-up. Studies have also found greater functional impairment (Bowen, Chavira, Bailey, Stein, & Stein, 2008), such as compromised educational functioning (Geller et al., 2003) in children with OCD and ADHD, even after SRI treatment (Masi et al., 2006). It is possible that the additive effects of a comorbid ADHD/OCD diagnosis may prevent children from receiving the full beneficial effects of psychopharmacological treatment on psychosocial functioning.

Considering research evidence herein, clinicians treating youths with comorbid ADHD and OCD should consider factors that might interfere with OCD treatment and/or impede symptom reduction. An initial treatment consideration should be the proper differentiation between inattentive/hyperactive symptoms due to the anxiety associated with OCD versus ADHD, given the substantial symptom overlap with these disorders (Jarrett & Ollendick, 2008). Self-report inventories such as the Swanson, Nolan, and Pelham (SNAP-IV) Teacher and Parent Rating Scale (Swanson, 1995) and the Children's Yale-Brown Obsessive Compulsive Scale (CY-BOCS; Scahill et al., 1997) should be utilized to identify symptoms attributable to ADHD and OCD, respectively. Obtaining a clear diagnostic picture is essential to planning treatment tailored to children's specific needs and difficulties (Weissman, Chu, Reddy, & Mohlman, 2012). Another early consideration should be concurrent pharmacological treatment for ADHD, given that psychostimulant medications have been found to be highly effective in reducing symptoms (MTA Cooperative Group, 1999). Management of ADHD symptoms early in OCD treatment may help to ensure experiences with success early on in treatment and consequently patient engagement, which is necessary during more challenging portions of OCD treatment (i.e., prolonged exposures). In addition to early pharmacological management of ADHD symptoms, Halldorsdottir and Ollendick (2014) recommend various behavioral strategies that should be implemented throughout the course of treatment. One such recommendation is that sessions be highly structured by providing children with an overview of the session and presenting children with explicit expectations for their involvement in each session. Highly engaging and interactive activities during sessions are also encouraged to prevent boredom. It is recommended that therapists be creative by introducing and practicing skills in a variety of different ways and to engage children as frequently as possible to gauge information retention. In addition, the cognitive load for youths demonstrating comorbid ADHD symptoms may need to be decreased, such that information is provided in multiple, small steps. Introduction of time management and organizational strategies into therapy may also facilitate the completion of homework assignments between sessions (Abikoff et al., 2013). It is important for treating clinicians to continuously evaluate the extent to which these strategies are effective in diminishing the effects of ADHD on treatment outcome or if further modification of the treatment approach is warranted.

Lastly, in addition to the creative and flexible modification of treatment for youths with ADHD and OCD, parental involvement is highly encouraged for success both in and outside the session. Parents should have an adequate understanding of the nature of both ADHD and OCD, and should receive psychoeducation on how ADHD symptoms could impede progress in OCD treatment, as well as how the parent might be able to reduce the potential disruptive effects of ADHD. For example, a clinician might instruct a parent in the following manner:

> *It is necessary for treatment that your child has the experience of their anxiety about [obsessive thought] going down without doing [compulsive behavior]. It is especially important that they sit with their anxiety and don't do anything to distract from it or make it go down prematurely. As they struggle with [inattention and/or hyperactivity], it might be hard for them to stay focused on the exposure task. Where you can help is to notice when they start to become distracted and help redirect them to what they are supposed to be doing.*

In sum, a comorbid ADHD diagnosis presents unique challenges to treating OCD in children and adolescents. It is important that clinicians have a comprehensive understanding of an individual's diagnoses before proceeding with treatment. Appropriate treatment planning is necessary to determine which symptoms have the greatest impact on a patient's psychosocial functioning and should be addressed initially. Strategies for managing ADHD symptoms should be implemented throughout treatment to ensure engagement and participation in session. In addition, parental psychoeducation and involvement in treatment will help to ensure success in managing symptoms of both disorders both in session and in the child's environment.

OPPOSITIONAL DEFIANT DISORDER

ODD is characterized by recurrent patterns of defiance, disobedience, angry/irritable mood, and hostile behavior that begins during childhood or adolescence (APA, 2013). Though some level of oppositional behavior typically occurs during normal development, ODD symptoms last for at least 6 months and cause significant problems in daily functioning. Similar to other disruptive behavior disorders, ODD may develop several years before the onset of comorbid OCD (Geller et al., 1996). This pattern seems to indicate that the disruptive and defiant behaviors symptomatic of ODD may be their own discrete diagnosis and may not entirely be an artifact of OCD. In other instances, oppositional and disruptive behavior may develop after the onset of OCD as an approach to coping with anxiety (e.g., disruptive behavior to avoid triggers). Nevertheless, differentiation between defiant behaviors attributable to ODD and similar behaviors often symptomatic of OCD (e.g., coerciveness, disruptive behavior) can be difficult (Lebowitz, Omer, & Leckman, 2011).

A comorbid ODD diagnosis appears to impact both the presentation of OCD symptoms and the resulting impairment. In a comparison study of children diagnosed with OCD with or without a comorbid disruptive behavior disorder (DBD)—including ODD—more severe OCD symptoms, higher levels of impairment, and greater family dysfunction were observed in the children with comorbid ODD (Langley et al., 2010; Storch et al., 2010). One such avenue through which family dysfunction occurs in this clinical population is family accommodation (Lebowitz et al., 2011). Family members often accommodate children with OCD by assisting in or providing materials needed for rituals, providing reassurance, or modifying daily routines to avoid or alleviate the child's distress (Lebowitz, Panza, Su, & Bloch, 2012; Storch et al., 2007). Family accommodation is highly prevalent among families of children with OCD and is an important predictor of severity, impairment, and treatment outcomes (Francazio et al., 2016; Garcia et al., 2010; Merlo, Lehmkuhl, Geffken, & Storch, 2009; Storch et al., 2010). Studies have found accommodation to be elevated in families of children with ODD and other DBDs (Flessner et al., 2011; Peris et al., 2008).

Consistent with other disruptive behavior disorders, comorbid ODD could complicate and increase the difficulty of implementing behavioral treatment for OCD and could have an impact on treatment gains. As with any psychotherapeutic treatment, comprehensive assessment of symptoms and proper differential diagnosis—in this case, of ODD and OCD—is a crucial first step in planning treatment and strategies for managing oppositional behavior in session. Knowledge of an ODD diagnosis has important implications for the therapeutic alliance. For instance, children and adolescents with ODD often experience anger outbursts and engage in vindictive behavior, often directed at an authority figure (Steiner & Remsing, 2007). Storch et al. (2012) indicated that children with OCD often report an increased sense of calmness after a "rage attack," suggesting that these outbursts are being negatively reinforced through successful avoidance of a trigger. Mental health professionals should keep this in mind when working with this population. Therapists should take extra steps to present the therapeutic relationship as a partnership in which therapist and client work together for the benefit of the client, thus minimizing the child's potentially negative perception of the therapist as an authority figure. For example, the therapist might explain to the child that:

> *You and I are going to be working together on your OCD, and I want you to know that it's okay to ask questions or tell me if you don't understand why I'm asking you to do something or if we're going too fast. There might be times where I'll ask you to do things that make you feel nervous or uncomfortable, and it's okay to feel that way. Just know that everything we do in therapy is very important, and we're going to do it together until you can do it all on your own.*

Throughout the process of treatment, it is also important to progress at a speed that feels appropriate for each individual child, so as not to increase anxiety unnecessarily. Children should be comfortable vocalizing their discomfort if at any time they become overwhelmed. This may be even more so true of children demonstrate more defiant or oppositional behavior. In addition, the treating clinician should focus additional effort on empathizing with what is likely to be a frustrated and angry child brought to therapy against their will by a parent, while not condoning any oppositional behaviors (Steiner &

Remsing, 2007). Though the capacity to do so is age dependent, most children with ODD have some insight into their behaviors (Steiner, 1997) and may be more amenable to modifying them through treatment in the context of a strong therapeutic alliance.

Fortunately, many of the treatment strategies utilized in treating ODD and other disruptive behavior disorders address the parent-child relationship and can easily be integrated into CBT for OCD. Parent management training and the use of contingency management strategies for handling disruptive behavior is a highly substantiated and frequently implemented treatment for ODD (Brestan & Eyberg, 1998; Kazdin, 2005). Contingency management strategies (e.g., rewarding children for completing in session exposure tasks and homework assignments) have also demonstrated success when used in combination with ERP for treating youth with OCD and disruptive behavior disorders (Piacentini, Gitow, Jaffer, Graae, & Whitaker, 1994). Contingency management techniques may have the benefit of decreasing not only ODD behaviors but parental accommodation as well, as parents receive psychoeducation on how to reinforce desirable behaviors (e.g., completion of at-home exposures) and decrease reinforcement of disruptive behaviors (e.g., removal of a reward if a child refuses to practice exposures at home). Parents can also increase child participation in homework outside of therapy through the use of reinforcement. Parent-child interaction therapy (PCIT; Eyberg, 1988) is another common intervention for ODD that can be integrated into and have benefits for CBT for OCD. This therapy focuses on improving the parent-child relationship and provides parents with skills to manage disruptive behavior (Nixon, Sweeney, Erickson, & Touyz, 2003). Parents learn effective parenting techniques (e.g., explicit description, praise, and imitation of children's positive actions) while engaging with their child while the therapist observes and instructs the parent. This technique could be combined with behavioral treatment for OCD, such that the parent could work with their child on OCD intervention strategies learned in session while also practicing parenting techniques under the guidance of a therapist observer/teacher.

A comorbid ODD diagnosis presents its own distinct challenges to OCD treatment both within and outside of the therapy environment. It is important that treatment plans and strategies for managing oppositional behaviors be established early in treatment. It may be necessary, depending on the severity of disruptive behaviors and in order to ensure success during OCD treatment, to first address the child's disruptive behavior problems prior to implementing treatment for OCD. While the therapeutic alliance is important in all treatment contexts, it may be particularly important in ensuring treatment success in children who are likely to be resistant and unmotivated to change. In addition, parental involvement in the session is critical and may have benefits that are twofold. Parents can learn effective parenting strategies to manage their child's ODD while gaining knowledge about and practice with OCD interventions that will ultimately require extension into the child's home life.

GENERALIZED ANXIETY DISORDER

OCD and GAD—though differing disorders—often manifest in similar symptoms (e.g., persistent worry, avoidance, etc.; Cohen, Mychailyszyn, Settipani, Crawley, & Kendall, 2011; Comer, Kendall, Franklin, Hudson, & Pimentel, 2004). Accompanying noted OCD criteria, youths with comorbid GAD are further characterized by increased general or "everyday" worries (lacking coinciding compulsions; e.g., worries in relation to school, finances, friends, etc.) and physiological symptoms (e.g., restlessness, fatigue, muscle tension, irritability, etc.; APA, 2013). Notably however, given several potential factors (e.g., client and/or therapist factors such as client age, lack of insight regarding OCD compulsions, lack of therapist experience with GAD and/or OCD, etc.), symptom disparities may remain elusive, potentially limiting comprehensive diagnoses (e.g., inability to detect when both disorders are present) and overall treatment efficacy. For example, previous literature suggests that both OCD and GAD demonstrate a positive response to CBT; however, efficacy levels for particular types of CBT vary among the disorders (Read, Puleo, Wei, Cummings, & Kendall, 2013). Specifically, while combined E/RP demonstrates efficacy for OCD-related symptoms, response prevention demonstrates no efficacy for GAD symptoms. Similar to preceding diagnoses, given such differences in symptom response, therapist acknowledgment of comorbidity (most often achieved through thorough diagnostic interview, self- and parent-reports, observations, etc.) is essential for developing efficacious interventions.

Subsequent to comorbid GAD and OCD diagnosis, an initial treatment concern will be determining an appropriate course of intervention. Differing from other comorbid diagnoses within this chapter, research suggests that comorbid OCD has no detrimental effect on GAD treatment, and comorbid GAD has no effect on OCD treatment (Rapee et al., 2013). Therefore clinicians may have a choice of several options moving forward. First, a clinician may wish to begin treatment initially targeting most distressing symptoms—whether this be GAD or OCD. In this context, symptom distress may be obtained through interviews with the child, as well as with the child's family. Within these interviews, it is important that clinicians discuss similarities and differences in OCD and GAD treatment, differentiate between OCD and GAD symptoms, and simultaneously acknowledge perspectives of each individual (e.g., individuals involved may have differences regarding which symptoms belong to which disorder, which symptoms are most distressing, etc.). Given similarity in disorder symptoms or preconceived understanding of disorder presentations, families may particularly struggle or disagree with symptom differentiation. As such, within the context of OCD and GAD, it is still important that clinicians spend sufficient time providing psychoeducation, validating such difficulties (e.g., acknowledge that there are many similarities between OCD and GAD and symptoms are often confused), and mapping out child's symptoms (this may be facilitated through lists, charts/diagrams, etc.). To initiate such a discussion, clinicians may wish to begin with the following dialog:

> *Today I would like to review some of [child's] symptoms and discuss potential treatment plans. To begin therapy, it's important that we are able to agree on steps moving forward and that includes deciding which symptoms we should work on first. While treatments are very similar there are some differences that are quite important. Let's start by looking at how each of these symptoms is affecting [child].*

Notably dialog should be modified appropriately depending upon child's presence, age, and/or cognitive level. Potential initial dialog for a young child is as follows:

> *Today I wanted to talk to you about some things you might think about or do that might bother you sometimes. Like [give 1-2 brief examples of relevant OCD and GAD symptoms the child or parent has already reported.]. It's my job to help you and I'd really like to know which of those things bugs you the most?*

In addition to discussion, parent and youth reports (i.e., self-report or clinician administered) may also facilitate understanding of symptom distress. Several GAD pediatric measures exist including the Spence Children's Anxiety Scale (SCAS; child and parent report; Spence, 1998), Penn State Worry Questionnaire for Children (PDSWQ-C; Chorpita, Tracey, Brown, Collica, & Barlow, 1997), and the Multidimensional Anxiety Scale for Children, 2nd Edition (MASC 2; child and parent report; March, 2013). Alternatively, clinicians may wish to begin treatment initially targeting symptoms most accessible (e.g., least severe symptoms, symptoms child is most willing to work on, etc.). For example, a child presenting with severe washing compulsions may demonstrate significant distress at the idea of challenging such symptoms; however, s/he may be more willing to work on techniques addressing anxiety (e.g., deep breathing, imagery, etc.). As demonstrated in this scenario, initially addressing less severe symptoms may increase child's comfort and confidence in therapy. Similar to steps taken with symptom distress, clinicians may utilize discussions and self-report to determine symptom accessibility. Within such discussions, given differences in functionality between GAD and OCD (i.e., while a child's GAD symptoms may lead to distress and avoidance, anxieties of OCD indicate obsessions which ultimately trigger related compulsions), it is important that clinicians provide further information regarding these differences. In addition to increasing parental knowledge regarding OCD and GAD symptoms, such a discussion may also facilitate symptom differentiation (as discussed previously within this section) and further highlight accessibility of the child's symptoms (e.g., compared to GAD, OCD symptoms with numerous triggers may be more severe given additional components of compulsions).

The examples provided previously presume that comorbid GAD and OCD diagnoses are identified at treatment onset; however, as alluded to previously there are numerous instances in which comorbidities of GAD and OCD remain unclear—thus comorbidity is identified within the course of treatment. For clinicians in this context (e.g., clinicians uncertain as to whether comorbid GAD and OCD are present, clinicians deciding between a GAD or OCD diagnosis, etc.), considering increased base rates of GAD compared to OCD as well as similarities between GAD and OCD treatments, research suggests that treatment begin with exposure-based interventions for anxiety (Comer et al., 2004). Such interventions for youth often consist of multiple components including psychoeducation (i.e., provide developmentally modified information for both child and parent), skills training (e.g., teach both child and parent deep breathing, muscle relaxation, imagery, etc.), exposure activities (e.g., expose child to graded imaginal and in vivo exposures), cognitive restructuring (e.g., teach and practice positive self-talk to build confidence), and relapse prevention (see evidenced-based treatment manuals such as Coping Cat and the C.A.T Project for explicit examples of all components; Connolly & Bernstein, 2007; Kendall, Choudhury, Hudson, & Webb, 2002; Kendall & Hedtke, 2006). Should OCD symptoms become more apparent, subsequent to anxiety treatment, clinicians may then use E/RP, in lieu of cognitive restructuring or efforts to a priori decrease the child's anxiety (e.g., relaxation training), to address OCD symptoms.

As a final consideration, regardless of initial treatment approach, clinicians should remain cognizant of several factors throughout treatment. These factors include normal developmental worries and fears, individual child characteristics (e.g., environmental context, developmental level, etc.), fluctuating presentations of anxiety and OCD in youths (anxiety presenting as increased temper tantrums in younger children vs adolescents), current treatment symptom response (e.g., low symptom response may require increased efforts in particular treatment components or may suggest treating other disorder first), and additional factors related to GAD and OCD (e.g., familial and cognitive factors). Awareness of these factors may inform both treatment development and further treatment modifications (e.g., clinicians may opt to add additional family or cognitive components to treatment, clinicians may develop tailored mechanisms for determining treatment progress, etc.).

TIC DISORDERS

As highlighted previously, TD, which are clusters of brief intermittent movements and/or sounds that serve no observable purpose, also commonly co-occur with pediatric OCD suggesting common etiological factors between the disorders. While understanding the pathophysiology of TD and OCD is important (e.g., may inform future conceptualizations and research), managing comorbid symptoms and distress is most relevant to providing appropriate psychotherapeutic intervention. As such, it is important that clinicians are familiar with both common and disparate aspects of presentations of both disorders in order to best understand what comorbid OCD and TD may look like in youths. TD often develop prior to the onset of OCD symptoms and frequently attenuate during the childhood years (80% symptom cessation by age 20 years; Bloch et al., 2006; Bloch & Leckman, 2009; Eisen et al., 2013). Additionally, although severe tics can cause considerable embarrassment and may be physically limiting, most tics are also fairly mild. Despite the characteristic differences between tics and OCD (e.g., tics are involuntary which contrasts with the effortful performance of compulsions in OCD), there are many links between the two, including needing to achieve a sense of "just right" (Roessner, Becker, Banaschewski, & Rothenberger, 2005). These phenotypic similarities between tics and some compulsions (e.g., symmetrical tapping) make it possible for TD symptoms to be mistaken for compulsive acts (Lewin & Piacentini, 2010).

This can be problematic as the frontline treatments for each disorder are quite different in practice. Habit reversal training (HRT) and the Comprehensive Behavioral Intervention for Tics (CBIT), which have been shown to be highly effective in treating TD, involve increased awareness of tic urges paired with a competing response (e.g., pressing one's arms to one's sides; Dutta & Cavanna, 2013; McGuire et al., 2014) and relaxation training (in the case of CBIT; Piacentini et al., 2010). Contrastingly, ERP focuses on exposure to feared stimuli paired with the prevention of completion of the associated compulsive action (Abramowitz, 2006). Research does suggest that "tic-related OCD" responds well to ERP (Conelea et al., 2014); however, co-occurring tics that are not associated with the OCD symptoms are likely to require HRT or CBIT. Thus in order to best manage associated symptoms, it is important that a clinician determine whether a behavior serves to reduce distress (i.e., a compulsion) or can be better explained as a response to an urge (i.e., a tic). Avoidance of such confusion through proper assessment of symptoms can aid clinicians in selecting the appropriate approach to best alleviate the distress associated with comorbid pediatric TD and OCD.

Individuals with both OCD and TD have also been found to experience greater overall dysfunction and distress than those without comorbid symptoms (Swain, Scahill, Lombroso, King, & Leckman, 2007; Wanderer et al., 2012). For instance, longitudinal research has found that the presence of TD in childhood predicts worse OCD symptomatology later in adolescence and young adulthood (Peterson, Pine, Cohen, & Brook, 2001). Identifying whether one disorder is responsible for greater impairment than the other (e.g., additional impairment associated with TD may fall secondary to impairment associated with OCD) is likely to facilitate treatment effectiveness.

There are several additional considerations clinicians may keep in mind when implementing CBT for these youth. For example, it is possible for stress—such as that experienced during ERP—to exacerbate a child's tics temporarily during treatment (Buse, Kirschbaum, Leckman, Münchau, & Roessner, 2014; Lin et al., 2007). Though this does not necessarily have a lasting impact on the child's prognosis or long-term benefits from treatment, it can be discouraging and frustrating for the child and his/her family. As such, it is recommended that clinicians remain cognizant of the frequency and magnitude of a child's tics throughout treatment to best determine what behaviors to focus on as treatment progresses. There is also the possibility that a child's tics might become distracting to him/her during ERP and take focus away from the exposure exercise. If this is the case, it is important for the clinician to ensure the child is not relying on his/her tics as a means to divert their focus or effort in treatment (particularly if they come to serve the purpose of reducing the child's experience of distress). Accordingly, it is critical that a clinician be mindful of a child engaging in tics during ERP so that the child does not take on similar tic-like behaviors in substitution for his/her familiar compulsions.

Considering the information presented here, it would seem most prudent to either focus on the cessation of OCD symptoms with HRT/CBIT to follow, or to treat OCD and TD concurrently if a child's tics are too severe or acutely interfere with treatment. Notably however, it is very important that a clinician explain to a child and his/her parents why such a decision has been made. This is especially the case if, for example, the parents are more aware of and concerned with the behavioral interference presented by TD than a more subtle set of obsessions and compulsions (e.g., mental counting). With the child, a clinician might wish to engage in dialog regarding the importance of focusing on one aspect of treatment at a time, facilitating the child's level of engagement in an age-appropriate manner. For example, a clinician could say

> *First we are going to work together on stopping the behaviors that keep your worries coming back and that you feel like you must do, and then we are going to work on stopping the behaviors that you just can't seem to control. I know it can be scary to think about doing this, but together we can get you feeling a lot better by working to stop these behaviors.*

Reducing a child's reliance on compulsions and improving control over obsessive worries may also reduce the child's emotional and cognitive load in order to better enable him/her to then subsequently focus on reducing tics through effortful opposite action, as prescribed through HRT. This approach is further supported as not all TD respond to HRT/CBIT (Piacentini et al., 2010). As such, postponing the treatment of impairing OCD while TD symptoms may not remit fully regardless of treatment may not be the most responsible option and supports the importance of monitoring a child's progress through treatment and adjusting the focus of sessions accordingly. Initially focusing on the treatment of OCD is also likely to reduce the shame and guilt that many individuals experience due to the nature of their obsessions and their dependence upon compulsions (Hennig-Fast et al., 2015).This may empower the child to better engage in treatment and increase efforts in reducing symptoms for both disorders.

Alternatively, clinicians may choose to treat both pediatric OCD and TD concurrently, particularly if a child's TD is highly impairing or causing significant interference during initial ERP sessions. In this context, it may best serve to work with the child briefly on TD psychoeducation and building an arsenal of competing responses through HRT in order to begin reducing tics. Once competing responses have been established, agreed upon, and practiced, clinicians may want to shift the focus of treatment toward ERP, reminding and encouraging the child to engage in HRT as tics become present throughout sessions. This approach to treatment may help reduce the distraction caused by a child's tics during ERP treatment; however, asking a child to effortfully engage in competing responses during exposures could in itself become quite distracting and must be managed cautiously. Engaging parents in treatment (e.g., utilizing CBIT) to help remind a child to use his/her competing response(s) when not in session may help expedite reductions in TD symptoms while also improving a child's ability to focus during exposures.

Finally, it is important to note that some evidence does suggest that TD in youth with OCD may impair their ability to benefit from pharmacological treatment for their OCD symptoms (March et al., 2007; McDougle et al., 1993), though this finding is not demonstrated across all studies (Husted et al., 2007; Riddle, Hardin, King, Scahill, & Woolston, 1990). As pharmacotherapy is commonly utilized in the treatment of pediatric OCD (Abramowitz, Whiteside, & Deacon, 2005) and combination treatment (CBT + medication) has shown strong efficacy for pediatric OCD (Pediatric OCD Treatment Study (POTS) Team, 2004), some parents may question the use of CBT alone. In such a case (i.e., decision to utilized CBT alone at the start of treatment), clinicians may benefit from explaining the treatment rationale to parents and engaging in a healthy conversation with the family in regards to the evidence base for the various treatment options available to them.

Ultimately, efficacious CBT-oriented treatments exist for both pediatric OCD and TD. These treatments can be applied consecutively or concurrently, at the clinician's discretion, and can lead to positive outcomes for youth who suffer from both OCD and TD. A qualified clinician is likely able to successfully make the decision of what symptoms to treat first and how to manage any symptom-related interference in treatment, while encouraging participation and commitment from the child to engage in treatment, and support from the parent(s) to work toward recovery from both OCD and TD.

SUMMARY

Several disorders (e.g., ADHD, ODD, GAD, and TD) demonstrate increased comorbidity with pediatric OCD. Understandably, such comorbidities are of critical concern to clinicians and necessitate appropriate approaches to treatment. Collectively, recommendations provided herein highlight a number of factors important to comorbid treatment development including severity and interference of symptoms and effects of comorbid symptoms on OCD treatment response. While not the only method of approaching pediatric comorbidity, the recommendations given provide a guiding framework for effectively targeting complex symptom presentations.

REFERENCES

Abikoff, H., Gallagher, R., Wells, K. C., Murray, D. W., Huang, L., Lu, F., et al. (2013). Remediating organizational functioning in children with ADHD: Immediate and long-term effects from a randomized controlled trail. *Journal of Consulting and Clinical Psychology*, *81*, 113–128.

Abramowitz, J. S. (2006). The psychological treatment of obsessive-compulsive disorder. *Canadian Journal of Psychiatry*, *51*(7), 407–416.

Abramowitz, J. S., Whiteside, S. P., & Deacon, B. J. (2005). The effectiveness of treatment for pediatric obsessive-compulsive disorder: A meta-analysis. *Behavior Therapy*, *36*(1), 55–63.

Alvarenga, P. G., do Rosario, M. C., Cesar, R. C., Manfro, G. G., Moriyama, T. S., Bloch, M. H., et al. (2016). Obsessive-compulsive symptoms are associated with psychiatric comorbidities, behavioral and clinical problems: A population-based study of Brazilian school children. *European Child & Adolescent Psychiatry*, *25*(2), 175–182.

American Academy of Child and Adolescent Psychiatry (AACAP). (2012). Practice parameters for the assessment and treatment of children and adolescents with obsessive compulsive disorder. *Journal of the American Academy of Child and Adolescent Psychiatry*, *51*(1), 98–113.

American Academy of Pediatrics. (2011). ADHD: Clinical practice guidelines for the diagnosis, evaluation, and treatment of attention-deficit/hyperactivity disorder in children and adolescents. *Pediatrics*, *128*, 1007–1022.

American Psychiatric Association. (2013). *Diagnostic and statistical manual of mental disorders: DSM-5* (5th ed.). Arlington, VA: American Psychiatric Publishing.

Barkley, R. A. (1998). *Attention deficit hyperactivity disorder: A handbook for diagnosis and treatment*. New York, NY: Guilford.

Benito, K. G., Conelea, C., Garcia, A. M., & Freeman, J. B. (2012). CBT specific process in exposure-based treatments: Initial examination in a pediatric OCD sample. *Journal of Obsessive-Compulsive and Related Disorders*, *1*, 77–84.

Bloch, M. H., & Leckman, J. F. (2009). Clinical course of Tourette Syndrome. *Journal of Psychosomatic Research*, *67*, 497–501.

Bloch, M. H., Peterson, B. S., Scahill, L., Otka, J., Katsovich, L., Zhang, H., et al. (2006). Adulthood outcome of tic and obsessive compulsive symptom severity in children with Tourette syndrome. *Archives of Pediatric and Adolescent Medicine*, *160*, 65–69.

Bowen, R., Chavira, D. A., Bailey, K., Stein, M. T., & Stein, M. B. (2008). Nature of anxiety comorbid with attention deficit hyperactivity disorder in children from a pediatric primary care setting. *Psychiatry Research*, *157*, 201–209.

Brestan, E. V., & Eyberg, S. M. (1998). Effective psychosocial treatments of conduct-disordered children and adolescents: 29 years, 82 studies, and 5,272 kids. *Journal of Clinical Child Psychology*, *27*, 180–189.

Buse, J., Kirschbaum, C., Leckman, J. F., Münchau, A., & Roessner, V. (2014). The modulating role of stress in the onset and course of Tourette's syndrome: A review. *Behavior Modification*, *38*(2), 184–216.

Chorpita, B. F., Tracey, S. A., Brown, T. A., Collica, T. J., & Barlow, D. H. (1997). Assessment of worry in children and adolescents: An adaption of the penn state worry questionnaire. *Behaviour Research and Therapy*, *30*, 33–37.

Cohen, J., Mychailyszyn, M., Settipani, C., Crawley, S., & Kendall, P. C. (2011). Issues in differential diagnosis. Considering generalized anxiety disorder, obsessive-compulsive disorder, and posttraumatic stress disorder. In D. McKay & E. A. Storch (Eds.), *Handbook of child and adolescent anxiety disorders* (pp. 23–35). New York: Springer.

Comer, J. S., Kendall, P. C., Franklin, M. E., Hudson, J. L., & Pimentel, S. S. (2004). Obsessing/worrying about the overlap between obsessive-compulsive disorder and generalized anxiety disorder in youth. *Clinical Psychology Review*, *24*, 663–683.

Conelea, C. A., Walther, M. R., Freeman, J. B., Garcia, A. M., Sapyta, J., Khanna, M., et al. (2014). Tic-related obsessive-compulsive disorder (OCD): Phenomenology and treatment outcome in the Pediatric OCD Treatment Study II. *Journal of the American Academy of Child & Adolescent Psychiatry*, *53*(12), 1308–1316.

Connolly, S. D., & Bernstein, G. A. (2007). Practice parameter for the assessment and treatment of children and adolescents with anxiety disorders. *Journal of the American Academy of Child & Adolescent Psychiatry*, *46*(2), 267–283.

Daley, D., van der Oord, S., Ferrin, M., Danckaerts, M., Doepfner, M., Cortese, S., et al. (2014). Behavioral interventions in attention-deficit/hyperactivity disorder: A meta-analysis of randomized controlled trials across multiple outcome domains. *Journal of the American Academy of Child and Adolescent Psychiatry*, *53*(8), 835–847.

Davis, T. E., & Ollendick, T. H. (2005). Empirically supported treatments for specific phobia in children: Do efficacious treatments address the components of a phobic response. *Clinical Psychology*, *12*, 144–160.

Dutta, N., & Cavanna, A. E. (2013). The effectiveness of habit reversal therapy in the treatment of Tourette syndrome and other chronic tic disorders: A systematic review. *Functional Neurology*, *28*(1), 7.

Eisen, J. L., Sibrava, N. J., Boisseau, C. L., Mancebo, M. C., Stout, R. L., Pinto, A., et al. (2013). Five-year course of obsessive-compulsive disorder: Predictors of remission and relapse. *Journal of Clinical Psychiatry*, *74*, 233–239.

Evans, S. W., Schultz, B. K., DeMars, C. E., & Davis, H. (2011). Effectiveness of the Challenging Horizons afterschool programme for young adolescents with ADHD. *Behaviour Therapy*, *42*, 462–474.

Eyberg, S. M. (1988). Parent–child interaction therapy: Integration of traditional and behavioral concerns. *Child and Family Behavior Therapy*, *10*(1), 33–46.

Flessner, C. A., Freeman, J. B., Sapyta, J., Garcia, A., Franklin, M. E., March, J. S., et al. (2011). Predictors of accommodation in pediatric obsessive-compulsive disorder: Findings from the pediatric obsessive-compulsive disorder treatment study (POTS) trial. *Journal of the American Academy of Child and Adolescent Psychiatry*, *50*(7), 716–725.

Francazio, S. K., Flessner, C. A., Boisseau, C. L., Sibrava, N. J., Mancebo, M. C., Eisen, J. L., et al. (2016). Parental accommodation predicts symptom severity at long-term follow-up in children with obsessive-compulsive disorder: A preliminary investigation. *Journal of Child and Family Studies*, *25*(8), 2562–2570.

Garcia, A. M., Sapyta, J. J., Moore, P. S., Freeman, J. B., Franklin, M. E., March, J. S., et al. (2010). Predictors and moderators of treatment outcomes in the Pediatric Obsessive-Compulsive Treatment Study (POTS I). *Journal of the American Academy of Child and Adolescent Psychiatry*, *49*, 1024–1033.

Geller, D. A., Biederman, J., Faraone, S. V., Cradock, K., Hagermoser, L., Zaman, N., et al. (2002). Attention-deficit/hyperactivity disorder in children and adolescents with obsessive-compulsive disorder: Fact or artifact? *Journal of the American Academy of Child and Adolescent Psychiatry*, *41*, 52–58.

Geller, D. A., Biederman, J., Faraone, S., Spencer, T., Doyle, R., Mullin, B., et al. (2004). Re-examining comorbidity of obsessive-compulsive and attention deficit hyperactivity disorder using an empirically derived taxonomy. *European Child and Adolescent Psychiatry*, *13*, 8–91.

Geller, D. A., Biederman, J., Griffin, S., Jones, J., & Lefkowitz, T. R. (1996). Comorbidity of juvenile obsessive-compulsive disorder with disruptive behavior disorders. *Journal of the American Academy of Child and Adolescent Psychiatry*, *35*(12), 1637–1646.

Geller, D. A., Coffey, B., Faraone, S., Hagermoser, L., Zaman, N. K., Farrell, C. L., et al. (2003). Does comorbid attention-deficit/hyperactivity disorder impact the clinical expression of pediatric obsessive-compulsive disorder? *CNS Spectrums*, *8*, 259–264.

Geller, D., Petty, C., Vivas, F., Johnson, J., Pauls, D., & Biederman, J. (2007). Examining the relationship between obsessive-compulsive disorder and attention-deficit/hyperactivity disorder in children and adolescents: A familial risk analysis. *Biological Psychiatry*, *61*(3), 316–321.

Geller, D. A., Wagner, K. D., Emslie, G., Muphy, T., Caroenter, D. J., Wetherhold, E., et al. (2004). Paroxetine treatment in children and adolescents with obsessive-compulsive disorder: A randomized, multi-center, double-blind, placebo-controlled trial. *Journal of the American Academy of Child and Adolescent Psychiatry*, *43*, 1387–1396.

Halldorsdottir, T., & Ollendick, T. H. (2014). Comorbid ADHD: Implications for the treatment of anxiety disorders in children and adolescents. *Cognitive and Behavioral Practice*, *21*, 310–322.

Hennig-Fast, K., Michl, P., Muller, J., Niedermeier, N., Coates, U., Muller, N., et al. (2015). Obsessive-compulsive disorder—A question of conscience? An fMRI study of behavioral and neurofunctional correlates of shame and guilt. *Journal of Psychiatric Research*, *68*, 354–362.

Hinshaw, S. P. (2003). Impulsivity, emotion regulation, and developmental psychopathology: Specificity versus generality of linkages. *Annals of the New York Academy of Sciences*, *1008*, 149–159.

Husted, D. S., Shapira, N. A., Murphy, T. K., Mann, G. D., Ward, H. E., & Goodman, W. K. (2007). Effect of comorbid tics on clinically meaningful response to 8-week open-label trial of fluoxetine in obsessive compulsive disorder. *Journal of Psychiatric Research*, *41*(3-4), 332–337.

Jarrett, M. A., & Ollendick, T. H. (2008). A conceptual review of the comorbidity of attention deficit/hyperactivity disorder and anxiety: Implication for future research and practice. *Clinical Psychology Review*, *28*, 1266–1280.

Kazdin, A. E. (2005). *Parent management training: Treatment for oppositional, aggressive, and antisocial behavior in children and adolescents*. New York: Oxford University Press.

Kendall, P. C., Choudhury, M., Hudson, J., & Webb, A. (2002). *The C.A.T project manual for the cognitive behavioral treatment of anxious adolescents*. Ardmore, PA: Workbook Publishing.

Kendall, P. C., & Hedtke, K. A. (2006). *Cognitive-behavioral therapy for anxious children: Therapist manual* (3rd ed.). Ardmore, PA: Workbook Publishing.

Langley, A. K., Lewin, A. B., Bergman, R. L., Lee, J. C., & Piacentini, J. (2010). Correlates of comorbid anxiety and externalizing disorders in childhood obsessive compulsive disorder. *European Child and Adolescent Psychiatry*, *19*, 637–645.

Lebowitz, E. R., Omer, H., & Leckman, J. F. (2011). Coercive and disruptive behaviors in pediatric obsessive-compulsive disorder. *Depression and Anxiety*, *28*(10), 899–905.

Lebowitz, E. R., Panza, K. E., Su, J., & Bloch, M. H. (2012). Family accommodation in obsessive compulsive disorder. *Expert Review of Neurotherapeutics*, *12*(2), 229–238.

Leckman, J. F., Denys, D., Simpson, H. B., Mataix-Cols, D., Hollander, E., Saxena, S., et al. (2010). Obsessive-compulsive disorder: A review of the diagnostic criteria and possible subtypes and dimensional specifiers for DSM-V. *Depression and Anxiety*, *27*(6), 507–527.

Lewin, A. B., & Piacentini, J. (2010). Evidence-based assessment of child obsessive compulsive disorder: Recommendations for clinical practice and treatment research. *Child & Youth Care Forum*, *39*, 73–89.

Lin, H., Katsovich, L., Ghebremichael, M., Findley, D. B., Grantz, H., Lombroso, P. J., et al. (2007). Psychosocial stress predicts furutre symptom severities in children and adolescents with Touratte syndrom and/or obsessive-compulsive disorder. *Journal of Child Psychology and Psychiatry*, *48*(2), 157–166.

March, J. S. (2013). *Multidimensional anxiety scale for children*. Toronto, ON: Multi-Health Systems.

March, J. S., Franklin, M. E., Leonard, H., Garcia, A., Moore, P., Freeman, J., et al. (2007). Tics moderate treatment outcome with sertraline but not cognitive-behavior therapy in pediatric obsessive-compulsive disorder. *Biological Psychiatry*, *61*(3), 344–347.

Masi, G., Millepiedi, S., Mucci, M., Bertini, N., Pfanner, C., & Arcangeli, F. (2006). Comorbidity of obsessive-compulsive disorder and attention-deficit/hyperactivity disorder in referred children and adolescents. *Comprehensive Psychiatry*, *47*, 42–47.

McDougle, C. J., Goodman, W. K., Leckman, J. F., Barr, L. C., Heninger, G. R., & Price, L. H. (1993). The efficacy of fluvoxamine in obsessive-compulsive disorder: Effects of comorbid chronic tic disorder. *Journal of Clinical Psychopharmacology*, *15*, 354–358.

McGuire, J. F., Piacentini, J., Brennan, E. A., Lewin, A. B., Murphy, T. K., Small, B. J., et al. (2014). A meta-analysis of behavior therapy for Tourette Syndrome. *Journal of Psychiatric Research*, *50*, 106–112.

Merlo, L., Lehmkuhl, H., Geffken, G., & Storch, E. (2009). Decreased family accommodation associated with improved therapy outcome in pediatric obsessive-compulsive disorder. *Journal of Consulting and Clinical Psychology*, *77*, 355–360.

Moll, G. H., Eysenbach, K., Woerner, W., Banaschewski, T., Schmidt, M. H., & Rothenbeger, A. (2000). Quantitative and qualitative aspects of obsessive compulsive behaviour in children with attention deficit hyperactivity disorder. *Acta Psychiatrica Scandanavica*, *101*, 389–394.

MTA Cooperative Group. (1999). A 14-month randomized clinical trial of treatment strategies for attention-deficit/hyperactivity disorder. Multimodal treatment of children with ADHD. *Archives of General Psychiatry*, *56*, 1073–1086.

Nixon, R. D. V., Sweeney, L., Erickson, D. B., & Touyz, S. W. (2003). Parent-child interaction therapy: A comparison of abbreviated treatments for oppositional defiant preschoolers. *Journal of Consulting and Clinical Psychology*, *71*(2), 251–260.

Ortiz, A. E., Morer, A., Moreno, E., Plana, M. T., Cordovilla, C., & Lázaro, L. (2016). Clinical significance of psychiatric comorbidity in children and adolescents with obsessive–compulsive disorder: Subtyping a complex disorder. *European Archives of Psychiatry and Clinical Neuroscience*, *266*(3), 199–208.

Öst, L. G., Riise, E. N., Wergeland, G. J., Hansen, B., & Kvale, G. (2016). Cognitive behavioral and pharmacological treatments of OCD in children: A systematic review and meta-analysis. *Journal of Anxiety Disorders*, *43*, 58–69.

Pallanti, S., Hollander, E., Bienstock, C., Koran, L., Leckman, J., Marazziti, D., et al. (2002). Treatment non-response in OCD: Methodological issues and operational definitions. *International Journal of Neuropsychopharmacology*, *5*(2), 181–191.

Pediatric OCD Treatment Study (POTS) Team. (2004). Cognitive-behavior therapy, sertraline, and their combination for children and adolescents with obsessive-compulsive disorder: The Pediatric OCD Treatment Study Randomized Controlled Trial. *Journal of American Medical Association*, *292*(16), 1969–1976.

Pelham, W. E., & Fabiano, G. A. (2008). Evidence-based psychosocial treatments for attention- deficit/hyperactivity disorder. *Journal of Clinical Child & Adolescent Psychology*, *37*, 184–214.
Peris, T. S., Bergman, R. L., Langley, A., Chang, S., McCracken, J. T., & Piacentini, J. (2008). Correlates of accommodation of pediatric obsessive compulsive disorder: Parent, child, and family characteristics. *Journal of the American Academy of Child and Adolescent Psychiatry*, *47*(10), 1173–1181.
Peterson, B. S., Pine, D. S., Cohen, P., & Brook, J. S. (2001). Prospective, longitudinal study of tic, obsessive-compulsive, and attention-deficit/hyperactivity disorders in an epidemiological sample. *Journal of the Academy of Child and Adolescent Psychiatry*, *40*(6), 685–695.
Piacentini, J., Bergman, R. L., Keller, M., & McCracken, J. (2003). Functional impairment in children and adolescents with obsessive-compulsive disorder. *Journal of Child and Adolescent Psychopharmacology*, *13*(2, Suppl. 1), 61–69.
Piacentini, J., Gitow, A., Jaffer, M., Graae, F., & Whitaker, A. (1994). Outpatient behavioral treatment of child and adolescent obsessive compulsive disorder. *Journal of Anxiety Disorders*, *8*(3), 277–289.
Piacentini, J., Woods, D. W., Scahill, L., Wilhelm, S., Peterson, A. L., Chang, S., et al. (2010). Behavior therapy for children with Tourette disorder: A randomized controlled trial. *JAMA*, *303*(19), 1929–1937.
Power, T. J., Mautone, J. A., Soffer, S. L., Clarke, A. T., Marshall, S. A., Sharman, J., et al. (2012). A family-school intervention for children with ADHD: Results of a randomized clinical trial. *Journal of Consulting and Clinical Psychology*, *80*(4), 611–623.
Rapee, R. M., Lyneham, H. J., Hudson, J. L., Kangas, M., & Schniering, C. A. (2013). Effect of comorbidity on treatment of anxious children and adolescents: Results from a large, combined sample. *Journal of the American Academy of Child & Adolescent Psychiatry*, *52*(1), 47–56.
Read, K. L., Puleo, C. M., Wei, C., Cummings, C. M., & Kendall, P. C. (2013). Cognitive behavioral treatment for pediatric anxiety disorders. In R. A. Vasa & A. K. Roy (Eds.), *Pediatric anxiety disorders: A clinical guide, current clinical psychiatry* (pp. 269–287). New York: Springer.
Riddle, M. A., Hardin, M. T., King, R., Scahill, L., & Woolston, J. L. (1990). Fluoxetine treatment of children and adolescents with Tourette's and obsessive compulsive disorders: Preliminary clinical experience. *Journal of the American Academy of Child and Adolescent Psychiatry*, *29*, 45–48.
Roessner, V., Becker, A., Banaschewski, T., & Rothenberger, A. (2005). Tic disorders and obsessive compulsive disorder: Where is the link? In W. W. Fleischhacker & D. J. Brooks (Eds.), *Neurodevelopmental disorders* (pp. 69–99). Vienna: Springer.
Scahill, L., Riddle, M. A., McSwiggin-Hardin, M., Ort, S. I., King, R. A., Goodman, W. K., et al. (1997). Children's Yale-Brown Obsessive Compulsive Scale: Reliability and validity. *Journal of the American Academy of Child and Adolescent Psychiatry*, *36*(6), 844–852.
Spence, S. H. (1998). A measure of anxiety symptoms among children. *Behaviour Research and Therapy*, *36*(5), 545–566.
Steiner, H. (1997). *Treating school age children.* San Francisco, CA: Jossey-Bass.
Steiner, H., & Remsing, L. (2007). Practice parameter for the assessment and treatment of children and adolescents with oppositional defiant disorder. *Journal of the American Academy of Child and Adolescent Psychiatry*, *46*, 126–141.
Storch, E. A., Geffken, G. R., Merlo, L. J., Jacob, M. L., Murphy, T. K., Goodman, W. K., et al. (2007). Family accommodation in pediatric obsessive-compulsive disorder. *Journal of Clinical Child and Adolescent Psychiatry*, *36*(2), 207–216.
Storch, E. A., Jones, A. M., Lack, C. W., Ale, C. M., Sulkowski, M. L., Lewin, A. B., & De Nadai, A. S. (2012). Rage attacks in pediatric obsessive-compulsive disorder: Phenomenology

and clinical correlates. *Journal of the American Academy of Child & Adolescent Psychiatry, 51*(6), 582–592.

Storch, E. A., Larson, M. J., Muroff, J., Caporino, N., Geller, D., Reid, J. M., et al. (2010). Predictors of functional impairment in pediatric obsessive-compulsive disorder. *Journal of Anxiety Disorders, 24*(2), 275–283.

Storch, E. A., Merlo, L. J., Larson, M. J., Geffken, G. R., Lehmkuhl, H. D., Jacob, M. L., et al. (2008). Impact of comorbidity on cognitive-behavioral therapy response in pediatric obsessive-compulsive disorder. *Journal of the American Academy of Child & Adolescent Psychiatry, 47*(5), 583–592.

Swain, J. E., Scahill, L., Lombroso, P. J., King, R. A., & Leckman, J. F. (2007). Tourette syndrome and tic disorders: A decade of progress. *Journal of the American Academy of Child & Adolescent Psychiatry, 46*(8), 947–968.

Swanson, J. M. (1995). *The swanson, nolan, and pelham teacher and parent rating scale (SNAP-IV)*. Irvine, CA: Child Development Center, University of California.

Torp, N. C., Dahl, K., Skarphedinsson, G., Thomsen, P. H., Valderhaug, R., Weidle, B., et al. (2015). Effectiveness of cognitive behavior treatment for pediatric obsessive-compulsive disorder: Acute outcomes from the Nordic long-term OCD treatment study (NordLOTS). *Behaviour Research and Therapy, 64*, 15–23.

Torres, A. R., Prince, M. J., Psych, M. R. C., Bebbington, P. E., Bhugra, D., Brugha, T. S., et al. (2006). Obsessive-compulsive disorder: Prevalence, comorbidity, impact, and help-seeking in the British National Psychiatric Morbidity Survey of 2000. *American Journal of Psychiatry, 163*(11), 1978–1985.

Tryon, W. W. (2005). Possible mechanisms for why desensitization and exposure therapy work. *Clinical Psychology Review, 25*, 67–95.

Wanderer, S., Roessner, V., Freeman, R., Bock, N., Rothenberger, A., & Becker, A. (2012). Relationship of obsessive-compulsive disorder to age-related comorbidity in children and adolescents with Tourette syndrome. *Journal of Developmental & Behavioral Pediatrics, 33*(2), 124–133.

Weissman, A. S., Chu, B. C., Reddy, L. A., & Mohlman, J. (2012). Attention mechanisms in children with anxiety disorders and in children with attention-deficit/hyperactivity disorders: Implications for research and practice. *Journal of Clinical Child and Adolescent Psychology, 41*, 117–126.

Zuvekas, S. H., & Vitiello, B. (2012). Stimulant medication use in children: A 12-year perspective. *American Journal of Psychiatry, 169*, 160–166.

Chapter 17

Managing a Child With OCD Who Is Treatment Refractory

Michael H. Bloch
Yale University, New Haven, CT, United States

INTRODUCTION

Pediatric OCD affects approximately 1% of all children in the United States (Apter et al., 1996; Flament et al., 1988). When present, OCD frequently has a profound impact on the child and his/her family. Pediatric OCD can disrupt normal development and cause significant academic impairment, social difficulties, distress, and poor quality of life. Prior to the emergence of clomipramine in the 1960s, OCD was believed to be a lifelong untreatable condition with a poor prognosis (Arumugham & Reddy, 2013). However, it is now clear that many children with OCD will remit or develop subclinical symptoms over time (Geller et al., 1998). Approximately 40% of treated children with OCD have a remission of their symptoms over the long term (Arumugham & Reddy, 2013; Bloch et al., 2009; Stewart et al., 2004).

The improvement in long-term outcome in children with OCD that has occurred throughout the past half century is largely attributable to the emergence and refinement of effective first-line treatments for pediatric OCD—pharmacotherapy with serotonin reuptake inhibitors (SRIs) and cognitive-behavioral therapy (CBT). First-line interventions for pediatric OCD have safety-benefit profiles that rival treatments available for any other conditions in child psychiatry. Selective serotonin reuptake inhibitors (SSRIs) have a number needed to treat (NNT) of 4–6 and an effect size around 0.5 when compared to placebo (Bridge et al., 2007; Geller, Biederman, Stewart, Mullin, Martin, et al., 2003). CBT also demonstrates a better NNT of 2–3 and larger effect sizes around 1.2 when compared to placebo/inactive control conditions (Eddy, Dutra, Bradley, & Westen, 2004; McGuire et al., 2015).

Unfortunately, even when evidence-based interventions are delivered by expert clinicians, over a quarter of patients with OCD do not experience significant symptom improvement (McGuire et al., 2015; Pediatric OCD Treatment Study Team, 2004). Many children who respond to OCD treatments still have

The Clinician's Guide to Cognitive-Behavioral Therapy for Childhood Obsessive-Compulsive Disorder
http://dx.doi.org/10.1016/B978-0-12-811427-8.00017-4

significant residual symptoms—roughly half of children in POTS receiving combination treatment did not achieve symptom remission (Pediatric OCD Treatment Study Team, 2004).

Many of the children with OCD symptoms who do not respond to evidence-based treatments have among the poorest long-term prognoses. These children are among the most challenging and difficult to treat. Perhaps the most frustrating aspect in the care of these children is the lack of research devoted to the problem. This chapter will focus on the assessment and treatment of children with refractory OCD symptoms.

DEFINITION OF TREATMENT-REFRACTORY OBSESSIVE-COMPULSIVE DISORDER

Perhaps most challenging in generalizing treatment outcomes across trials is that these terms are inconsistently defined across trials. For instance, treatment response has been defined as a 25%, 30%, or even a 35% reduction in the Children's Yale-Brown Obsessive Compulsive Scale (CY-BOCS) score (plus/minus being "very much" or "much" improved on the CGI). Establishing a definition of treatment terms and proposed benchmarks in pediatric OCD is an attempt to move toward a consensus of reporting in the field. Previous research has used signal detection analysis to determine the optimal cut-points for treatment response (corresponding to "very much" or "much" improved on the Clinical Global Impressions—Improvement Scale) and remission (corresponding to mild illness or better on the Clinical Global Impressions—Severity Scale) although have failed to reach a consensus (Skarphedinsson, De Nadai, Storch, Lewin, & Ivarsson, 2017; Storch, Lewin, De Nadai, & Murphy, 2010). A CY-BOCS reduction greater than 25% was determined to be the optimal criteria for treatment response and a CY-BOCS score of less than or equal to 14 to be the optimal criteria for treatment remission (Scahill et al., 1997; Storch, Lewin, et al., 2010). A recent study using similar methodology suggested that a 35% reduction in CY-BOCS scores and a CY-BOCS score of less than or equal to 11 were the optimal cut-points for response and remission in pediatric OCD (Skarphedinsson et al., 2017). Given how convergent data-driven definitions of response and remission are in pediatric and adult OCD, the author currently favors working toward a consensus definition of both concepts across trials regardless of the exact cut-points chosen within a reasonable range. Table 1 provides definitions for clinical practice and research for pediatric OCD of commonly used benchmarks in the OCD literature. These represent a modified version for pediatric populations and the CY-BOCS of criteria originally proposed in adult OCD (Pallanti & Quercioli, 2006).

Among the most useful concepts in the field is that "treatment-refractory OCD" can be viewed along a continuum in stages from simply not improving sufficiently on a single first-line intervention (CBT or SSRI) to being severely symptomatic despite treatment with multiple SSRIs ($\geq$3 including

TABLE 1 Stages of Response in Pediatric OCD

Stage	Description	Pediatric Research Definition
Recovery	Not at all affected by OCD symptoms	CY-BOCS <8
Remission	Minimal OCD symptoms after treatment that do not have a significant effect on functioning	CY-BOCS ≤ 14
Response	Meaningful improvement on treatment	Improvement in CY-BOCS $\geq 25\%$
Nonresponse	Lack of meaningful improvement with treatment	Improvement of CY-BOCS $<25\%$
Relapse	Return of symptoms after a period of remission	CY-BOCS >14 and worsening of CY-BOCS $\geq 25\%$ after a period of remission
Refractory	Nonresponse and/or substantial residual despite first-line behavioral and pharmacological treatment	CY-BOCS ≥ 16 despite adequate trials of CBT and 2 SSRIs

This table depicts definitions of response in pediatric OCD. These definitions are a modified version of criteria proposed in the adult OCD literature that were modified for pediatric specific research, rating scales of disease severity, and convention of previous pediatric OCD trials (Pallanti & Quercioli, 2006).

clomipramine), CBT, and other augmentation strategies (Pallanti & Quercioli, 2006). Table 2 contains a modified version of the stages of treatment refractory OCD originally proposed by Pallanti and Quercoli for pediatric OCD. "Treatment-refractory" OCD for the sake of this chapter is defined as failing to achieve adequate symptom relief despite receiving an adequate course of CBT and at least two adequate trials of SSRIs.

EVALUATION OF A CHILD FOR "TREATMENT-REFRACTORY" OBSESSIVE-COMPULSIVE DISORDER

A thorough psychiatric evaluation is warranted whenever a child presents for treatment of obsessive-compulsive symptoms (see Chapters 2 and 4 for further discussion of diagnosing and assessing OCD). The point at which patients seek treatment for "treatment-refractory OCD" represents a time at which they should be reassessed. Ideally, this reassessment should be performed by a clinician that was uninvolved in the patient's first-line treatment. A proper,

TABLE 2 Stages of Nonresponse in Pediatric OCD

Level of Nonresponse	Treatments Utilized
1	SSRI or CBT
2	SSRI and CBT
3	2 SSRIs and CBT
4A	Multiple SRIs (including clomipramine) and CBT
4B	2 SSRIs, antipsychotic augmentation and CBT
5	Multiple SRIs (including clomipramine), antipsychotic augmentation and CBT
6	Level 5 plus experimental agents for OCD

This table presents the stages of nonresponse in pediatric OCD. These stages are a modified version of criteria proposed in the adult OCD literature that were modified for subsequent clinical trials in adult OCD and convention in pediatric OCD clinical practice (Pallanti & Quercioli, 2006). The gray shaded stages represent stages of treatment-refractory pediatric OCD.

thorough, independent evaluation of diagnostic assumptions and adequacy of prior treatment received is crucial, as available evidence suggests that the minority of patients with true treatment-refractory OCD respond to augmentation therapy. Furthermore, other than CBT, few of the augmentation strategies commonly employed in adults for OCD have met the threshold of proven efficacy (positive findings in multiple, double-blind, placebo-controlled trials). Moreover, none of these augmentation strategies have met the threshold of proven efficacy in treatment-refractory OCD in pediatric populations. The most promising evidence-based pharmacological augmentation strategies for treatment-refractory OCD (atypical antipsychotics) in adults have an even more substantial side effect burden in children, making their use in pediatric populations even less desirable. Thus an independent evaluation by a clinician experienced in OCD treatment is advisable given that (1) the likelihood of an OCD patient responding to any of these augmentation strategies is likely less than receiving any of the first-line treatments if they have not been optimally delivered previously and (2) alternate treatment strategies not considered due to diagnostic misclassification of OCD-like symptoms (see Chapter 2) or unappreciated comorbidity may be more likely to be successful (see Chapter 16).

Evaluation of a child with suspected treatment-refractory OCD should focus on verification of several factors: (1) the primary OCD diagnosis, (2) adequacy of delivery of first-line treatments for pediatric OCD, and (3) moderating factors that might influence efficacy of treatment.

(1) Verification of the primary OCD diagnosis

Many conditions can be misdiagnosed as OCD in children. In younger children, normal development (e.g., a toddler insisting on arranging objects in a particular manner before sleep or getting extremely upset if bedtime routines are not followed) and symptoms of separation anxiety disorder (e.g., a child with separation anxiety needing to repeatedly call his parents to make sure their safe) are often misdiagnosed as OCD symptoms. In older children and adolescents, symptoms of depression or generalized anxiety (e.g., ruminations—repeated intrusive thoughts about their own inadequacy, past mistakes, etc.) may become confused with obsessions. Prodromal psychotic symptoms (e.g., repetitive checking behaviors related to a delusion such as checking the locks on the doors to make sure FBI is not out to get you) and substance abuse symptoms (e.g., obsessive-compulsive behaviors related to stimulant abuse) can be misdiagnosed as OCD. Symptoms of mild autism spectrum disorder (e.g., insistence on sameness, perseverative behaviors, and restricted interests) can also often be difficult to distinguish from OCD across the life span. Complex tics of Tourette syndrome—physical movements performed in response to a physical, premonitory urge (e.g., "evening-up" tics such as the need to balance out an uncomfortable feeling in one hand by touching objects with the opposite hand if one hand has already touched it) may also be confused as OCD. Additionally, other obsessive-compulsive spectrum disorders, specifically hoarding disorder, trichotillomania, and skin picking disorder, are often misdiagnosed or treated like OCD. The misdiagnosis and treatment of hoarding disorder and body-focused reparative behaviors as OCD is particularly problematic as the behavioral therapies and pharmacological treatments for these conditions are often quite different. It should be noted that DSM-5 diagnoses, especially in children, are not completely discrete entities. Children and their families often fail to read and conform to the DSM before seeking psychiatric evaluations to treat their symptoms. Thus in the event that evidence-based treatments for OCD have been ineffective, it makes sense to examine whether any compulsive symptoms associated with these related conditions can be targeted with a different tact.

(2) Verification of adequate delivery of first-line treatments for pediatric OCD

As discussed earlier in this chapter and throughout this book, effective first-line treatments for pediatric OCD include pharmacotherapy with CBT and SSRIs. The current evidence supporting the efficacy of interventions for treatment-refractory OCD, especially in children, pales in comparison to these first-line treatments. Furthermore, the risk-benefit analysis for any of the interventions for treatment-refractory OCD proposed later in this chapter is generally considerably worse than first-line pharmacological and behavioral treatments. Therefore it is critically important that clinicians ensure optimal delivery of first-line treatments for OCD in both adults and children before considering augmentation strategies for treatment-refractory OCD. Confirming optimal delivery of first-line treatments for OCD, whether behavioral or pharmacological, requires verification of proper dose and duration of treatments.

In conducting an evaluation of a child for treatment-refractory OCD, it is critical to determine whether children and their families have received a sufficient dose of the most effective element of CBT—exposure and response prevention—for an adequate number of sessions and duration of time. All too often, clinicians convey to families that they are providing CBT for OCD, but in reality, they are not incorporating exposure and response prevention sufficiently or at all (e.g., performing cognitive therapy techniques for depression and anxiety or performing relaxation training). Helpful questions to ask the child, parent, and/or previous therapist directly to determine adequacy of past CBT trials are as follows: (1) did the child ever receive homework from the therapist?; (2) did the child ever make a list of OCD symptoms and rate them in severity?; (3) was the child exposed to a situation designed to reproduce the anxiety associated with the OCD symptoms and asked to resist performing compulsions?; and (4) were the parent(s) involved in the CBT sessions and/or homework? If the answers to any of these questions are "no," a further course of CBT from an informed provider is warranted before progressing to further treatments for refractory OCD.

Another crucial aspect of a thorough evaluation of treatment-refractory OCD is determining whether pharmacological evidence-based first-line treatments have been optimally delivered. For SSRIs, this involves determining whether a child has received an adequate dose and duration of prior treatment and whether the family has been compliant with that treatment. Table 3 presents the recommended dosing for SRIs in the treatment of OCD.

A child should not be considered treatment refractory until he has received at least two SSRIs at an adequate dose (the maximum tolerated dose) for an adequate duration of treatment (12 weeks total and at least 8 weeks at the maximal dose). Furthermore, in children, who have not been able to tolerate an SSRI at minimum recommended FDA dose either due to side effects or parental anxiety, these patients should be viewed as treatment intolerant rather than treatment refractory. There currently exists no evidence that subtherapeutic doses of SSRIs are effective in children with OCD. If CBT has already been properly exhausted as a treatment option, every effort should be made to increase the likelihood of SSRI tolerability, including improved parental education and communication regarding side effects, more gradual dosing titration of SSRI, prescription of concomitant medication to help with side effects, and use of blister packaged medication to help with contamination concerns.

TABLE 3 Serotonin Reuptake Inhibitors in Pediatric OCD

	Pediatric		Adult		
	Starting Dose (mg/day)	Typical Dose Range (mg/day)	Starting Dose (mg/day)	Typical Dose Range (mg/day)	Half-Life
Citalopram	10–20	20–40	20	40	20 h
Escitalopram	5–10	10–40	10	20–40	27–32 h
Fluoxetine	10–20	20–80	20	20–80	4–6 days
Fluvoxamine	25–50	50–200	100–300	100–300	16 h
Paroxetine	10–20	20–60	10–20	40–60	21 h
Sertraline	50	100–200	50	150–250	26 h
Clomipramine	25	50–200	25	100–250	32 h

This table recommends dosing guidelines and characteristics of serotonin reuptake inhibitors used as first-line pharmacological treatments in pediatric OCD.

Unlike in major depressive disorder, SSRIs are the only medication with FDA approval and demonstrated efficacy, thus abandoning use of these medications has additional consequences in children with OCD compared to other conditions. For instance, emergence of suicidal ideation early in the treatment of SSRIs is a common cause of discontinuation of these medications in pediatric populations. Other potential behavioral side effects early in SSRI treatment may include behavioral activation, increased anxiety, and sleep problems. Most clinicians are extremely hesitant to rechallenge children with SSRIs if they have reported past suicidal ideation with these medications likely to the detriment of their patients. Although there currently exists a black box warning on this class of medication stating that "antidepressants increase the risk compared to placebo of suicidal thinking and behavior (suicidality) in children, adolescents, and young adults," current data suggests a very favorable risk-benefit profile in this regard when it comes to pediatric OCD (Bridge et al., 2007) Metaanalysis demonstrated that the number needed to harm (NNH) (to experience suicidal ideation or behavior with SSRI that would not have with placebo) in SSRI trials of pediatric OCD was 200. This NNH = 200 for "suicidality" compares to an NNT of 5 to induce a treatment response, indicating a quite advantageous risk-benefit profile. By contrast, for pediatric depression, NNH = 111 and NNT = 9 for similar outcomes (Bridge et al., 2007). When rechallenging a child on an SSRI who has experienced past suicidal ideation with treatment, this clinician will (1) discuss the data surrounding the benefits and risks of pharmacological treatment for OCD, including the FDA warning with the family as well as alternative treatment options and the need for at least a 12-week trial of an SSRI to determine treatment efficacy; (2) liberally use additional medication to mitigate side effects and symptoms that may have led to increased suicidal ideation in the initial trial (e.g., prescribing diphenhydramine, benzodiazepines, mirtazapine, or trazodone for insomnia); (3) give the family and patient an emergency contact number to contact a clinician in case of emergency.

Lastly, it is recommended that compliance should be verified in cases that are not responsive to initial SSRI treatment. Compliance is best verified through electronic medical records or calling a patient's pharmacy to ascertain medication refill intervals. Refill intervals greater than 25% above expected should raise concerns. Compliance issues should be addressed directly with the family (as it is unlikely the child will respond to any pharmacological intervention if the medications are not taken appropriately). Compliance may be improved through thorough discussion about side effects, parental and child concerns with medication, and alternative treatment options.

(3) Screening for common moderators of treatment response

The evaluation of all patients with OCD (especially those with a history of poor treatment response) should involve assessment and screening for potential moderators and predictors of treatment outcome (Bloch & Storch, 2015). It is particularly important to examine levels of family accommodation of a child's OCD symptoms, level of insight into OCD symptoms, and presence of hoarding-related OCD symptoms (or hoarding disorder), as high levels of any of these symptoms likely suggests a poor prognosis but, more importantly, will influence a therapist's approach to behavioral treatment. Specifically, the presence of high degree of hoarding symptoms encourages the incorporation of CBT techniques targeting hoarding disorder rather than OCD. Poor insight suggests the importance of additional CBT techniques targeted at increasing insight and also perhaps motivational interviewing. Additionally, if these cognitive therapy approaches are unlikely to be successful for improving insight, concomitant or additional pharmacological treatments for OCD could be encouraged before CBT to improve symptom severity (and typically insight which is correlated to symptom severity). In this manner, a patient unresponsive to an initial course of exposure-based CBT may receive an adequate trial of an SSRI to reduce symptom severity (and ideally improve insight) before initiating a second trial of CBT. Presence of significant family accommodation emphases the importance of psychoeducation and inclusion of the whole family in CBT for OCD.

Comorbidity of tic symptoms has been demonstrated as an important moderator of pharmacological treatment for OCD. While comorbid tic symptoms appear to have little effect on the efficacy of CBT (March et al., 2007), SSRI pharmacotherapy appears to be less effective in reducing OCD symptoms in children with comorbid tics (Skarphedinsson et al., 2015). Pediatric OCD trials of paroxetine and sertraline have demonstrated a poorer response in children with comorbid tics compared to children with OCD without comorbid tics (Geller, Biederman, Stewart, Mullin, Farrell, et al., 2003; March et al., 2007). Metaanalysis of antipsychotic augmentation trials in adults with treatment-refractory OCD suggests that OCD patients with comorbid tics are significantly more likely to respond to this intervention (Bloch et al., 2006). The NNT for response of OCD symptoms to antipsychotic augmentation in subjects with comorbid tic disorders was two compared to six in subjects without comorbid tic disorders (Bloch et al., 2006). The improved efficacy of antipsychotic augmentation in treating OCD symptoms in patients with comorbid tic disorders is not surprising as antipsychotic medications are the most effective pharmacological agent in the treatment of tics (Bloch et al., 2006). Some naturalistic data suggests that antipsychotic augmentation may also be effective in children with OCD and comorbid tics (Masi, Pfanner, & Brovedani, 2013). Despite evidence for a poor response to first-line pharmacotherapy for OCD, there is some evidence that children that have OCD and a comorbid tic disorder may have a good long-term prognosis, whereby their OCD symptoms may follow the developmental trajectory of comorbid tic symptoms and improve during adolescence (Bloch et al., 2009). By contrast, in adulthood, there is some evidence that comorbid tics may be associated with poor long-term outcome in OCD cases (Wewetzer et al., 2001). The likely explanation for this phenomenon is that the adult patients with OCD with comorbid tics represent a subset of the children with OCD and tics that did not improve during adolescence.

TREATMENT OPTIONS FOR TREATMENT-REFRACTORY PEDIATRIC OCD

Cognitive-Behavioral Therapy

CBT involving exposure with response prevention is an effective first-line treatment for OCD which when practiced faithfully by experienced treatment providers works slightly better, than any pharmacological treatments currently available for OCD (Foa et al., 2005; Pediatric OCD Treatment Study Team, 2004). The combination of SSRI pharmacotherapy and CBT for OCD may be more effective than either monotherapy in both children and adults in many cases, particularly the most severe cases (Foa et al., 2005; Pediatric OCD Treatment Study Team, 2004). Current data from adult studies further suggests that CBT for treatment-refractory OCD may be more effective than antipsychotic augmentation, the most evidenced-based pharmacological strategies for treatment-refractory OCD (Simpson et al., 2013). In a clinical trial of 100 adults with significant OCD symptoms despite adequate SSRI treatment were randomized to 12 weeks of CBT, risperidone augmentation, or placebo. Patients who received CBT had significantly greater improvement than either of the other two treatment arms, which were not different from one another. Comparable OCD studies in pediatric populations are absent largely because investigators have felt that such a trial would be both unethical and uninformative given the significantly greater side effect burden of atypical antipsychotics in pediatric populations. These data underscore the importance of utilizing evidence-based CBT for OCD with exposure and response prevention at any point in the clinical course of OCD when acceptable to the patient and family.

Switching SSRI Medications

Metaanalyses suggest that SSRIs for pediatric OCD have a medium-to-large effect size (ES = 0.5) and a small NNT (NNT = 5) compared to placebo (Bridge et al., 2007; Geller, Biederman, Stewart, Mullin, Martin, et al., 2003; McGuire et al., 2015). There is no evidence from metaanalysis of existing placebo-controlled trials that there are any differences in efficacy between SSRI agents (Ackerman & Greenland, 2002; Geller, Biederman, Stewart, Mullin, Martin, et al., 2003; Varigonda, Jakubovski, & Bloch, 2016). When a patient does not respond to initial SSRI pharmacotherapy of adequate dose and duration, current treatment guidelines suggest treatment with another SSRI (or clomipramine) before considering additional augmentation strategies (American Psychiatric Association, 2007; Practice Parameter for the Assessment and Treatment of Children and Adolescenets with Obsessive-Compulsive Disorder, 2012). Based on limited data available, currently the best estimate is that only roughly one-quarter of OCD patients who fail to respond to treatment with an initial SSRI will respond to a different one (Koran & Saxena, 2002). With each additional SSRI trial, the odds of responding to the next agent become progressively smaller to the point that other treatment strategies for OCD become advisable.

Raising SSRI Dosage

Table 3 reports the starting and maximal FDA recommended doses of SSRI medications for the treatment of OCD. Current treatment guidelines suggest that SSRIs need to be used at higher doses for longer periods in children and adults with OCD compared to those suffering from depression. Metaanalysis of fixed-dose trials of SSRIs in adults with OCD has demonstrated significantly greater improvement in OCD symptoms (as measured by YBOCS) and likelihood of treatment response compared to lower doses of SSRIs (Bloch, McGuire, Landeros-Weisenberger, Leckman, & Pittenger, 2010). Although these symptom improvements are statistically significant, the incremental treatment gains of using high doses of SSRIs were modest. High dose SSRI treatment was associated with a 1.4-point greater Y-BOCS improvement compared to low dose treatment SSRI treatment (roughly a 5% greater improvement in OCD symptoms). Similarly, the NNT = 16–17 favoring high-dose compared to low-dose SSRI treatment for inducing a treatment response was similarly modest. Within fixed-dose SSRI trials in adult OCD, higher doses of SSRIs were associated with an increased rate of dropouts "due to side effects" but not an increased rate of all-cause dropout when compared to lower doses of SSRIs (Bloch et al., 2010). Fixed-dose trials comparing the efficacy of different dosing strategies in pediatric OCD are absent. Randomized, placebo-controlled trials of SSRI agents in pediatric OCD have almost exclusively employed dosing strategies that targeted the maximum FDA recommended dose. However, metaregression examining the association between maximal dose and symptom improvement in pediatric OCD trials has demonstrated a modest, nonsignificant relationship in favor of the use of higher doses (Varigonda et al., 2016). Given the currently available evidence, it would be considered best practice to start children who are treatment-naïve at the minimum FDA recommended dose and monitor symptom improvement for at least 8 weeks in order to minimize side effects and maximize compliance. If the patient does not achieve adequate symptom relief, the SSRI is titrated up to the maximum tolerated FDA recommended dose and the patient is monitored for further symptom improvement for an additional 6–12 weeks. The major exception to this conservative dosing strategy is a child where the foremost goal is to maximize acute symptom improvement (e.g., OCD leading to severe impairment in academic, social or family functioning, or contributing to acute suicidality). In these cases, it would be considered prudent to titrate the SSRI up aggressively to the maximum FDA recommended dose. With this aggressive titration (as with all cases), families should be cautioned about the increased likelihood of side effects associated with the more aggressive titration (e.g., sexual dysfunction, sleep problems, gastrointestinal issues, headache, etc.) and instructed to continue each dose escalation for a week if the side effects are tolerable.

Some clinicians also often push doses of SSRIs above the maximum FDA recommended dose in treatment-refractory OCD. Although data supporting this dosing strategy in pediatric populations is absent, there is data from adult studies suggesting the possible utility of this approach. A randomized, double-blind, controlled trial compared the efficacy of continued sertraline treatment at the maximum recommended dose (200 mg) to high-dose sertraline therapy (maximum of 400 mg daily) in 66 adults who had significant residual OCD symptoms despite 16-week treatment with sertraline 200 mg daily (Ninan et al., 2006). High-dose sertraline therapy was associated with a statistically significant, albeit modest effect (ES = 0.5, NNT for treatment response = 15), further improvement in OCD symptoms compared to continued sertraline therapy at the FDA maximum recommended dose. There were no differences in side effects or dropout rates between the two treatment arms. Escalating SSRI dose above the FDA range in children and with other SSRIs besides sertraline has been insufficiently studied. Given the slightly differing side effects and probably slightly enhanced dose-related side effects of SSRIs in pediatric populations, one should use caution especially when generalizing the dose-related tolerability from adults with OCD to children. However, raising the SSRI dose is a reasonable treatment strategy in OCD patients with a partial response to maximal dose SSRI therapy of sufficient duration that have experienced minimal side effects.

Clomipramine

Many expert clinicians in OCD believe that clomipramine is more effective than SSRIs in the treatment of OCD. In fact, metaanalyses of placebo-controlled trials in both pediatric and adult OCD demonstrate significantly larger effect size for clomipramine than SSRIs when they are compared to placebo (Ackerman & Greenland, 2002; Geller, Biederman, Stewart, Mullin, Martin, et al., 2003). The larger effect size for clomipramine is robust to adjustment for both publication year and differences in placebo response rates across studies. Despite its robustness to appropriate statistical adjustment, it remains possible that clomipramine's apparent superiority to SSRIs across clinical trials may be due to (1) more treatment-naïve subjects in the earlier clomipramine studies or (2) more stringent clinical trials methodologies in the later SSRI trials (e.g., intention-to-treat analysis, prior declaration of primary outcome measures, improved randomization and blinding techniques, etc.) rather than that clomipramine is indeed be more effective than SSRIs.

Even assuming that clomipramine is modestly more effective than the SSRIs, clinicians should still hesitate to use clomipramine until after an OCD patient has not responded to two adequate trials of SSRI medications because of the more significant side effect profile. The side effects of clomipramine that relegate it to second-line treatment behind SSRIs include increased risk of fatal overdose, cardiac arrhythmia, and lowering of the seizure threshold. More common side effects of clomipramine include weight gain, sedation, and dry mouth. Additionally, clomipramine requires EKG monitoring in children due to potential arrhythmogenic effects and blood levels at higher doses due to seizure risk (DeVeaugh-Geiss et al., 1992).

Using clomipramine as an augmentation agent to maximal dose SSRI therapy is a strategy employed by many OCD treatment experts (American Psychiatric Association, 2007; Arumugham & Reddy, 2013). No randomized controlled trials have been performed to demonstrate that clomipramine augmentation is more effective than either (a) continued SSRI treatment at the maximum tolerated dose or (b) supratherapeutic SSRI treatment. Only a single-blinded clinical trial has examined the efficacy of clomipramine augmentation in treatment-refractory OCD. In this trial, 54 adult OCD patients that did not respond to fluoxetine 40 mg were randomized to either the addition of clomipramine (75 mg daily), quetiapine (200 mg daily), or an increased fluoxetine dose of up to 80 mg (Diniz et al., 2010). Treatment with either the addition of clomipramine or an increase in fluoxetine dose was significantly more beneficial than quetiapine augmentation. Patients receiving clomipramine augmentation did nominally, but not statistically significantly, worse than those who received an increase in fluoxetine dose.

Regardless of the limited data surrounding this treatment, adding a small dose of clomipramine ($\leq$75 mg) is an augmentation strategy commonly used in clinical practice and deserves further study. Practically speaking, expert clinicians use clomipramine as both an augmentation strategy and as monotherapy in treatment-refractory OCD. Typically, when transitioning a patient from an SSRI to clomipramine (due to nonresponse), experts will use clomipramine sequentially first as an augmentation strategy and then as monotherapy. Rather than discontinuing an SSRI before starting clomipramine, clomipramine would be started at a low dose as an augmentation strategy (titrated up to 50–100 mg nightly over 2 weeks) while continuing maximal dose SSRI treatment. Six to eight weeks will then be allowed for continued treatment in order to assess the efficacy of clomipramine augmentation. If the patient fails to improve after the initial clomipramine augmentation trial, the patient will slowly be titrated over to clomipramine monotherapy (target dosing 200 mg in children and 200–300 mg in adults).

Serotonin Norepinephrine Reuptake Inhibitors

Many clinicians assume that serotonin-norepinephrine reuptake inhibitors (SNRIs) are effective in treating OCD because they have a similar mechanism of action to clomipramine. However, no randomized placebo-controlled trials support the efficacy of SNRIs in OCD. Furthermore, the limited data that does exist suggests that SNRIs may be inferior to SSRIs in treating OCD (Denys, van der Wee, van Megen, & Westenberg, 2003; Denys, van Megen, van der Wee, & Westenberg, 2004).

Antipsychotic Augmentation

Table 4 includes a list of antipsychotic agents commonly used for antipsychotic augmentation in patients with OCD. Antipsychotic augmentation involves adding a low dose of an antipsychotic medication (similar to the dosages typically utilized in tic disorders) to continuing SSRI pharmacotherapy. Evidence regarding the efficacy of antipsychotic augmentation is lacking. However, antipsychotic augmentation has a substantial evidence base of efficacy in the treatment of SSRI-refractory OCD in adults. Metaanalysis has demonstrated a significant benefit of antipsychotic augmentation compared to continuing SSRI monotherapy in randomized, placebo-controlled trials in adults with OCD (Bloch et al., 2006). The NNT was 4–5 for inducing a treatment response

TABLE 4 Antipsychotic Medications Used as Augmentation Agents in OCD

	Pediatric			Adult		
	Starting Dose (mg/day)	Typical Dose Range (mg/day)	Number of Daily Doses	Starting Dose (mg/day)	Typical Dose Range (mg/day)	Number of Daily Doses
Risperidone	0.5–1	1–2	1–2	1	1–2	1–2
Aripiprazole	2–5	5–20	1	5	10–20	1
Quetiapine	25–50	100–300	2–3	50–100	150–400	2
Olanzapine	Not recommended due to increased metabolic concerns			5	5–20	1
Ziprasidone	5–20	40–80	2	40–80	80–160	2
Haloperidol	1	1–5	2	2–5	2–20	2
Pimozide	0.5–1	1–6	1–2	1–2	2–6	1–2

This table presents the characteristics and dosing guidelines of antipsychotic medications commonly used as augmentation agents in addition to treatment with serotonin reuptake inhibitors in treatment-refractory OCD. No antipsychotic agents have demonstrated efficacy as augmentation agents in pediatric OCD.

with antipsychotic augmentation compared to continuing SSRI monotherapy. Within the nine trials included in the metaanalysis, there was no evidence of differences in efficacy between antipsychotic agents or a significant effect based on antipsychotic dosing (Bystritsky et al., 2004; Carey et al., 2005; Denys, de Geus, van Megen, & Westenberg, 2004; Erzegovesi, Guglielmo, Siliprandi, & Bellodi, 2005; Fineberg, Sivakumaran, Roberts, & Gale, 2005; Hollander, Baldini Rossi, Sood, & Pallanti, 2003; McDougle, Epperson, Pelton, Wasylink, & Price, 2000; McDougle et al., 1994; Shapira et al., 2004). Benefits of antipsychotic agents were larger in antipsychotic augmentation trials that required prior treatment with SSRI medications for at least 12 weeks before initiation of antipsychotic augmentation. This finding emphasizes the importance of optimizing SSRI pharmacotherapy in terms of dosage and duration of treatment before starting augmentation strategies.

No randomized, placebo-controlled trials exist examining the efficacy of antipsychotic augmentation in pediatric populations. Prescribers treating children with OCD and researchers have been appropriately hesitant to use/study antipsychotic agents in children with OCD because of the poor side effect profile that is especially problematic in pediatric populations. Common side effects of antipsychotic agents include weight gain, metabolic complications (increased risk of diabetes, dyslipidemia, metabolic syndrome, sedation, sexual dysfunction, constipation, dry mouth, prolactinemia, as well as drug-induced Parkinsonism). Tardive dyskinesia (a sometimes permanent side effect) is less common, but a pertinent concern with the more typical antipsychotics (e.g., haloperidol, pimozide) can also occur. However, the strong evidence from adult OCD studies of increased efficacy in adult OCD patients with comorbid tics (which constitute a greater proportion of childhood OCD cases) suggests that antipsychotic augmentation is probably effective in childhood OCD. Assuming the adult data generalizes to pediatric OCD populations, less than 20% of OCD patients will benefit from antipsychotic augmentation. Therefore given the long-term metabolic side effects of antipsychotic agents in children, it is imperative to monitor the side effects of these medications (e.g., monitoring of body weight, fasting glucose, and lipid levels every 6 months) and discontinue these medications if a child has not achieved noticeable benefit after 6–8 weeks of appropriately dosed treatment. Further caution is warranted in expediting antipsychotic augmentation in any OCD treatment algorithm, as the benefits of CBT and SSRI treatments take a while to accrue. If antipsychotic augmentation is initiated during the beginning of OCD treatment (e.g., before a patient has engaged in CBT or SSRI pharmacotherapy for 12 weeks), it is difficult to determine which treatment was truly beneficial to the patient. Thus patients are exposed to the greater side effect burden of antipsychotic agents unnecessarily.

Glutamate Modulating Agents

Recently, many investigators have begun studying pharmacological agents that effect the glutamate system because of increasing evidence that pathology within glutamate systems may be important in OCD pathogenesis (Pittenger, Krystal, & Coric, 2006). Specifically, converging evidence from genetic studies, magnetic resonance spectroscopy (Rosenberg et al., 1997), direct examination of the cerebrospinal fluid (Chakrabarty, Bhattacharyya, Christopher, & Khanna, 2005), and animal studies involving genetic knockouts (Welch et al., 2007) and optogenetics (Ahmari et al., 2013), implicates abnormalities in glutamate systems as a potential source of the emergence of OCD psychopathology. Glutamate modulating agents that have been examined in randomized, placebo-controlled trials include ketamine, riluzole, topiramate, *n*-acetylcysteine, and memantine. By in large, current trials in the area have been quite underpowered and unsurprisingly, the results have been mixed. The evidence supporting the use of these individual glutamate modulating agents is discussed in the following sections. Table 5 presents instructions for the typical dosing and monitoring of experimental augmentation strategies in treatment-refractory OCD.

Ketamine

Ketamine is a potent NMDA receptor antagonist that is FDA approved as a pediatric anesthetic agent. Numerous studies have also demonstrated that when given intravenously (0.5 mg/kg over 40 min) to adults with depressive disorders, ketamine has profound antidepressant effects. These effects typically peak 24 h after the infusion and dissipate within 1–2 weeks. Remission rates of depressive symptoms in these trials are consistently above 50% within the first week of treatment (Aan Het Rot, Zarate, Charney, & Mathew, 2012). The antidepressant effects of ketamine have been replicated in multiple treatment trials, including some with active controls. The potential benefits of ketamine treatment for depression have not been evaluated for time periods greater than 1 month.

Given the benefits of ketamine for depressive symptoms and the evidence implication glutamate pathology in OCD, a couple of trials have been conducted examining the efficacy of ketamine for the treatment of OCD. The first open trial examined the effects of intravenous ketamine (0.5 mg/kg over 40 min) in ten adults with treatment-refractory OCD as an add-on to their existing medications (Bloch et al., 2012). An extremely short-lived benefit of ketamine was observed for OCD during the first 3 h following infusion. However, none of the 10 patients exhibited a response to ketamine 1–7 days following infusion. Additionally, in the 7 patients with comorbid depression, ketamine significantly reduced comorbid depressive symptomology to a greater extent than OCD symptoms from 1 to 7 days following infusion. Four of seven patients were judged to be responders to ketamine in terms of their depression symptomology (Bloch et al., 2012). A second, saline-controlled crossover trial in 15 adult OCD subjects washed off their OCD medications as outpatients demonstrated a significant benefit of ketamine compared to placebo during the first week after ketamine infusion (Rodriguez et al., 2013). Fifty percent of OCD

TABLE 5 Experimental Agents Utilized for Treatment-Refractory OCD

Medication	Starting Dose	Dose Range	Titration	Side Effects
Glutamate-modulating agents				
N-Acetylcysteine	600–900 mg daily	2000–3000 mg divided into 2–3 doses	Increase by 600–900 mg every 2–3 days	Mild. Nausea and upset stomach
Memantine	5 mg daily	10–20 mg divided into 2 doses	Increase by 5 mg weekly	Mild. Constipation and upset stomach
Riluzole[a]	50 mg BID	100–200 divided into 2 doses	Increase by 50 mg if no response at 6 weeks	Hepatotoxicity. Abdominal pain, GI upset, dizziness, headache
Topiramate	50 mg daily	100–200 mg daily	Increase by 50 mg weekly	Cognitive impairment, dizziness, somnolence, decrease appetite
Ketamine[b]	0.5 mg/kg over 40 min intravenously		N/A	Dissociation, dizziness, hypertension, hallucinations, anxiety
Other augmentation strategies				
Clomipramine	25 mg nightly	50–100 mg nightly	Increase by 25 mg every 3–5 days	Dry mouth, constipation, sedation, seizure, arrhythmia
Mirtazapine	15 mg nightly	15–45 mg nightly	Increase by 15 mg weekly	Sedation, increased appetite
Ondansetron	0.25 mg BID	0.5–4 mg BID	Increase to 0.5 mg BID after 2 weeks	Diarrhea, constipation, hepatotoxicity

This table presents the characteristics and dosing guidelines of experimental medications studied in treatment-refractory OCD. None of these medications have demonstrated efficacy in treatment-refractory OCD and most have limited safety data in pediatric populations.

[a]Riluzole requires checking of liver function tests every 3 weeks to monitor for potential hepatotoxicity.

[b]Ketamine requires monitoring of heart rate and blood pressure during infusion to monitor for tachycardia or hypertension.

patients (compared to 0% on placebo) responded to ketamine infusion (Rodriguez et al., 2013). Additionally, there were significant carryover effects with ketamine such that the benefits of treatment lasted beyond 1 week. Larger, multisite trials are needed to evaluate the treatment efficacy of ketamine for OCD to establish the efficacy of ketamine for treatment-refractory OCD in adult populations. Ketamine is increasingly being examined as an investigational agent in adolescent populations given its long history of use in pediatric populations and remains an important potential emerging treatment in OCD pharmacotherapy. Given the rare cardiovascular side effects associated with ketamine infusion, it should only be practiced by experienced physicians in appropriate facilities with monitoring.

Memantine

Memantine is a noncompetitive NMDA receptor antagonist that is FDA approved for the treatment of Alzheimer's disease. Case report level data have anecdotally suggested the efficacy of memantine in children with treatment-refractory OCD (Hezel, Beattie, & Stewart, 2009). However, no randomized, placebo-controlled trials have been conducted in pediatric OCD. A randomized, double-blind, placebo-controlled trial in 38 adults with OCD examined the efficacy of concurrent addition of memantine (20 mg/day titrated up over 1 week) or placebo to fluvoxamine 200 mg/day for 8 weeks (Ghaleiha et al., 2013). Subjects treated with Fluvoxamine + memantine (89% response rate) demonstrated a significantly greater likelihood of a treatment response compared to fluvoxamine + placebo (32% response rate). No placebo-controlled augmentation trials have examined the efficacy in treatment-refractory OCD in adults or children. Nonetheless, memantine remains a commonly used augmentation strategy in treatment-refractory adults with OCD with a fairly modest side effect burden.

N-Acetylcysteine

N-Acetylcysteine (NAC) is a natural supplement that has been used safely for decades as an antioxidant agent and as an antidote for acetaminophen overdose. NAC is inexpensive and available over the counter due to its benign safety profile. More recently, NAC has been demonstrated to be a glutamate-modulating agent. No randomized trials have examined the efficacy of NAC for pediatric OCD. Several, randomized, placebo-controlled trials have been conducted in adults with treatment-refractory OCD. Some have demonstrated a significant benefit of NAC treatment (Afshar et al., 2012; Paydary et al., 2016) and others showed no treatment benefits (Sarris et al., 2015). Further research, specifically a larger, multisite, randomized placebo-controlled trial in adulthood OCD, is needed to establish the efficacy of NAC in treatment-refractory OCD in adult as well as pediatric populations. Given its benign side effect profile, NAC represents a possible treatment option for children with refractory OCD.

Riluzole

Riluzole is a glutamate-modulating agent that is FDA approved for *Amyotrophic lateral sclerosis* (ALS). A recent double-blind, placebo-controlled add-on trial in 60 children with OCD failed to demonstrate a benefit of riluzole compared to placebo (Grant et al., 2014). Sixteen percent of subjects in the riluzole group and 18% of subjects in the placebo group responded to treatment (Grant et al., 2014). Similarly underpowered studies in treatment-refractory OCD patients have failed to demonstrate a significant benefit of riluzole compared to placebo (Pittenger et al., 2015). Further appropriately powered randomized, placebo-controlled trials of riluzole are needed to determine its efficacy for treating OCD in pediatric and adult populations. Generally, experts use riluzole only after other augmentation strategies (e.g., NAC or memantine) have failed to lead to adequate treatment benefit because of riluzole's risk of hepatotoxicity that requires monthly monitoring of liver functioning tests.

5-HT3 Receptor Antagonists

Ondansetron and granisetron are 5-HT3 receptor antagonists that are primarily used as antiemetic agents. Ondansetron (4 mg/day) augmentation demonstrated benefit when compared to placebo when added concurrently to fluoxetine (20 mg/day) in an 8-week trial of 42 adults with OCD (Soltani et al., 2010). Another trial of 42 adults with treatment-refractory OCD demonstrated a significant benefit of granisetron compared to placebo (Askari et al., 2012). The response rate was 90% in the granisetron group compared to 35% in the placebo group. Little evidence exists for the use of either 5-HT3 receptor antagonist in children with OCD. However, the side effects from ondansetron are well known from its use as an antiemetic agent in pediatric chemotherapy. Common side effects of ondansetron include diarrhea, headache, fever, lightheadedness, dizziness, drowsiness, constipation, rash, blurred vision, and muscle spasm.

Mirtazapine

Mirtazapine is an antidepressant agent that acts as an antagonist at alpha-2, 5-HT_2, 5-HT_3, and H_1 receptors. Mirtazapine is hypothesized to be an effective antidepressant agent by enhancing serotoninergic neurotransmission through several indirect mechanisms that are different from SSRIs. No randomized, placebo-controlled trials have been conducted testing the efficacy of mirtazapine in children or adults with OCD. A randomized, placebo-controlled trial of 49 adults with OCD demonstrated that the concurrent addition of mirtazapine (15–30 mg) to the initiation of citalopram (20–80 mg/day) accelerated OCD symptom improvement up until the fourth week of treatment (Pallanti, Quercioli, & Bruscoli, 2004). After 12 weeks of treatment, no significant differences were found between subjects treated with citalopram + mirtazapine versus those treated with citalopram + placebo. Mirtazapine addition to SSRI monotherapy remains a reasonable treatment option when OCD patients present in acute distress and with prominent insomnia symptoms.

Neurosurgical Treatments for OCD

Neurosurgical techniques have been used for decades in treatment of adults with treatment-refractory OCD that causes severe impairment and distress. The common ablative procedures commonly practiced in psychosurgery for OCD include anterior cingulotomy, capsulotomy, subcaudate tractotomy, and limbic leucotomy (Greenberg, Rauch, & Haber, 2010). Although there is limited data from controlled trials that these ablative procedures are effective in the treatment of OCD, long-term studies have suggested response rates above 50% in the most severely refractory OCD patients (Greenberg et al., 2010). Furthermore, a recently completed randomized, sham-controlled study of gamma-knife anterior capsulotomy has demonstrated the efficacy of these ablative procedures for the first time in a controlled trial (Lopes et al., 2014).

Deep brain stimulation (DBS) involves the surgical implantation of electrodes that introduce targeted electrical stimulation to specific brain regions. DBS in OCD typically targets the ventral capsule/striatum or subthalamic nucleus (Blomstedt, Sjoberg, Hansson, Bodlund, & Hariz, 2013). Crossover trials comparing when implanted electrodes are on compared to off have demonstrated the efficacy of DBS for both brain regions (Goodman et al., 2010; Greenberg et al., 2010; Mallet et al., 2008). Advantages of DBS compared to neurosurgery include that the procedure is potentially reversible, a better side effect profile and that the stimulation parameters can be adjusted. Disadvantages include expense, need for battery replacement, and extensive follow-up time to manage stimulus parameters. Adverse effects of DBS are rare but have included intracranial hemorrhage, infection, electrode breakage, and stimulation-induced adverse effects such as hypomania.

Given the observation that a substantial proportion of children with OCD experience a reduction of OCD symptoms over the long term (even prior to the introduction of evidence-based treatments for OCD), most experts suggest that the use of these neurosurgical techniques for OCD in pediatric populations should be nonexistent. Neurosurgical procedures should be reserved until OCD patients are of appropriate age to provide their own informed consent and the likelihood of any developmental regression of OCD symptoms is unrealistic.

Intensive OCD Treatment Programs

Intensive CBT (i.e., daily ERP sessions for 3 weeks) has been associated with significantly improved outcomes among youth who remained symptomatic following SSRI pharmacotherapy (Storch, Lehmkuhl, et al., 2010). Over three-quarters of children with OCD responded to intensive CBT ($d=2.37$). Intensive CBT programs may be particularly beneficial in children with OCD who have not previously responded to first-line treatments (Storch, Lehmkuhl, et al., 2010; Storch et al., 2007). Several intensive, residential behavioral treatment programs now exist for children with OCD and these programs may also be particularly useful for families that have geographic barriers to obtaining exposure therapy for OCD.

CONCLUSION

Despite the generally positive short- and long-term prognoses of OCD and the effective first-line treatments available, there still exists a substantial proportion of patients who do not achieve adequate symptom relief. Furthermore, the overall financial and emotional costs to society, and for these children and their family is profound. As outlined in this chapter, the treatment options available to clinicians are nearly endless, but the data supporting these experimental strategies is scant. Fig. 1 depicts the current algorithm recommended by experts for the pharmacological management of treatment-refractory OCD in children. There are often strong financial, logistical, or emotional barriers preventing our patients (especially children) from getting optimal evidence-based treatment for OCD (e.g., OCD-specific CBT treatment or intensive behavioral treatment programs). The clinicians' duty is to advocate as strongly as possible against these barriers and verify the adequacy of previous treatment (often including services which they themselves perform). Many prescribers feel obliged to offer their patients additional hope in the form of another pill (when there may be minimal data to warrant that hope) rather than confront these barriers or the seemingly overwhelming resistance in families. When confronting the overwhelming pain, suffering, and loss faced by families living with a child with treatment-refractory OCD, clinicians often make the mistakes of (1) trying to press fast-forward and shorten the needed duration of treatment of evidenced-based interventions (e.g., trialing an SSRI for only 4 weeks); (2) engaging in experimental interventions too early (e.g., starting antipsychotic augmentation in the first few weeks of SSRI treatment); and/or (3) not adequately verifying past treatments or compliance with them (e.g., not checking on dosing of past SSRI treatment, not ensuring that proper CBT was implemented). Being present with these families and maximizing their likelihood of symptom improvement is important, but equally important is trying to maximize the child's academic, social and family functioning, and quality of life in spite of these symptoms.

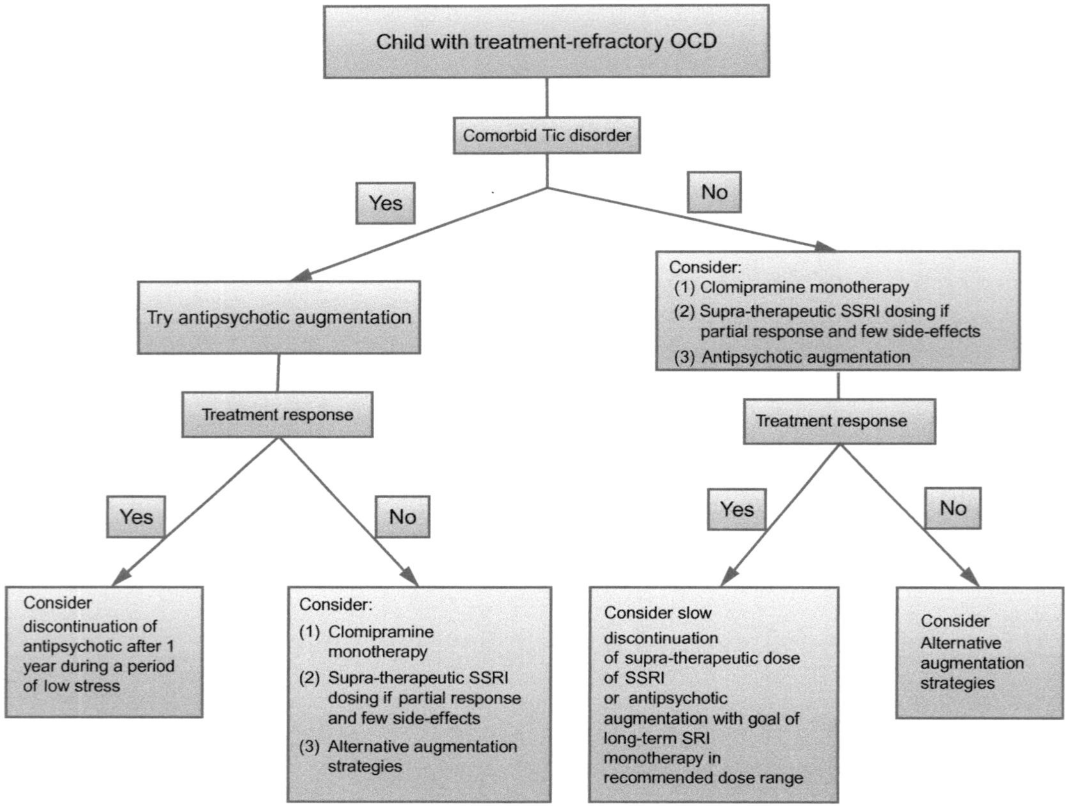

FIG. 1 Treatment algorithm for a child with treatment-refractory OCD.

REFERENCES

Aan Het Rot, M., Zarate, C. A., Jr., Charney, D. S., & Mathew, S. J. (2012). Ketamine for depression: Where do we go from here? *Biological Psychiatry*, *72*(7), 537–547. http://dx.doi.org/10.1016/j.biopsych.2012.05.003.

Ackerman, D. L., & Greenland, S. (2002). Multivariate meta-analysis of controlled drug studies for obsessive-compulsive disorder. *Journal of Clinical Psychopharmacology*, *22*(3), 309–317.

Afshar, H., Roohafza, H., Mohammad-Beigi, H., Haghighi, M., Jahangard, L., Shokouh, P., et al. (2012). N-acetylcysteine add-on treatment in refractory obsessive-compulsive disorder: A randomized, double-blind, placebo-controlled trial. *Journal of Clinical Psychopharmacology*, *32*(6), 797–803. http://dx.doi.org/10.1097/JCP.0b013e318272677d.

Ahmari, S. E., Spellman, T., Douglass, N. L., Kheirbek, M. A., Simpson, H. B., Deisseroth, K., et al. (2013). Repeated cortico-striatal stimulation generates persistent OCD-like behavior. *Science*, *340*(6137), 1234–1239. http://dx.doi.org/10.1126/science.1234733.

American Psychiatric Association. (2007). *Practice guideline for the treatment of patients with obsessive-compulsive disorder*. Retrieved from: *http://www.psychiatryonline.com*.

Apter, A., Fallon, T. J., Jr., King, R. A., Ratzoni, G., Zohar, A. H., Binder, M., et al. (1996). Obsessive-compulsive characteristics: From symptoms to syndrome. *Journal of the American Academy of Child and Adolescent Psychiatry*, *35*(7), 907–912. http://dx.doi.org/10.1097/00004583-199607000-00016.

Arumugham, S. S., & Reddy, J. Y. (2013). Augmentation strategies in obsessive-compulsive disorder. *Expert Review of Neurotherapeutics*, *13*(2), 187–202. http://dx.doi.org/10.1586/ern.12.160. quiz 203.

Askari, N., Moin, M., Sanati, M., Tajdini, M., Hosseini, S. M., Modabbernia, A., et al. (2012). Granisetron adjunct to fluvoxamine for moderate to severe obsessive-compulsive disorder: A randomized, double-blind, placebo-controlled trial. *CNS Drugs*, *26*(10), 883–892. http://dx.doi.org/10.2165/11635850-000000000-00000.

Bloch, M. H., Craiglow, B. G., Landeros-Weisenberger, A., Dombrowski, P. A., Panza, K. E., Peterson, B. S., et al. (2009). Predictors of early adult outcomes in pediatric-onset obsessive-compulsive disorder. *Pediatrics*, *124*(4), 1085–1093. http://dx.doi.org/10.1542/peds.2009-0015.

Bloch, M. H., Landeros-Weisenberger, A., Kelmendi, B., Coric, V., Bracken, M. B., & Leckman, J. F. (2006). A systematic review: Antipsychotic augmentation with treatment refractory obsessive-compulsive disorder. *Molecular Psychiatry*, *11*(7), 622–632. http://dx.doi.org/10.1038/sj.mp.4001823.

Bloch, M. H., McGuire, J., Landeros-Weisenberger, A., Leckman, J. F., & Pittenger, C. (2010). Meta-analysis of the dose-response relationship of SSRI in obsessive-compulsive disorder. *Molecular Psychiatry*, *15*(8), 850–855. http://dx.doi.org/10.1038/mp.2009.50.

Bloch, M. H., & Storch, E. A. (2015). Assessment and management of treatment-refractory obsessive-compulsive disorder in children. *Journal of the American Academy of Child and Adolescent Psychiatry*, *54*(4), 251–262. http://dx.doi.org/10.1016/j.jaac.2015.01.011.

Bloch, M. H., Wasylink, S., Landeros-Weisenberger, A., Panza, K. E., Billingslea, E., Leckman, J. F., et al. (2012). Effects of ketamine in treatment-refractory obsessive-compulsive disorder. *Biological Psychiatry*, *72*(11), 964–970. http://dx.doi.org/10.1016/j.biopsych.2012.05.028.

Blomstedt, P., Sjoberg, R. L., Hansson, M., Bodlund, O., & Hariz, M. I. (2013). Deep brain stimulation in the treatment of obsessive-compulsive disorder. *World Neurosurgery*, *80*(6), e245–253. http://dx.doi.org/10.1016/j.wneu.2012.10.006.

Bridge, J. A., Iyengar, S., Salary, C. B., Barbe, R. P., Birmaher, B., Pincus, H. A., et al. (2007). Clinical response and risk for reported suicidal ideation and suicide attempts in pediatric antidepressant treatment: A meta-analysis of randomized controlled trials. *JAMA*, *297*(15), 1683–1696. http://dx.doi.org/10.1001/jama.297.15.1683.

Bystritsky, A., Ackerman, D. L., Rosen, R. M., Vapnik, T., Gorbis, E., Maidment, K. M., et al. (2004). Augmentation of serotonin reuptake inhibitors in refractory obsessive-compulsive disorder using adjunctive olanzapine: A placebo-controlled trial. *Journal of Clinical Psychiatry*, *65*(4), 565–568.

Carey, P. D., Vythilingum, B., Seedat, S., Muller, J. E., van Ameringen, M., & Stein, D. J. (2005). Quetiapine augmentation of SRIs in treatment refractory obsessive-compulsive disorder: A double-blind, randomised, placebo-controlled study [ISRCTN83050762]. *BMC Psychiatry*, *5*, 5. http://dx.doi.org/10.1186/1471-244X-5-5.

Chakrabarty, K., Bhattacharyya, S., Christopher, R., & Khanna, S. (2005). Glutamatergic dysfunction in OCD. *Neuropsychopharmacology*, *30*(9), 1735–1740. http://dx.doi.org/10.1038/sj.npp.1300733.

Denys, D., de Geus, F., van Megen, H. J., & Westenberg, H. G. (2004). A double-blind, randomized, placebo-controlled trial of quetiapine addition in patients with obsessive-compulsive disorder refractory to serotonin reuptake inhibitors. *Journal of Clinical Psychiatry*, *65*(8), 1040–1048.

Denys, D., van der Wee, N., van Megen, H. J., & Westenberg, H. G. (2003). A double blind comparison of venlafaxine and paroxetine in obsessive-compulsive disorder. *Journal of Clinical Psychopharmacology*, *23*(6), 568–575. http://dx.doi.org/10.1097/01.jcp.0000095342.32154.54.

Denys, D., van Megen, H. J., van der Wee, N., & Westenberg, H. G. (2004). A double-blind switch study of paroxetine and venlafaxine in obsessive-compulsive disorder. *Journal of Clinical Psychiatry*, *65*(1), 37–43.

DeVeaugh-Geiss, J., Moroz, G., Biederman, J., Cantwell, D., Fontaine, R., Greist, J. H., et al. (1992). Clomipramine hydrochloride in childhood and adolescent obsessive-compulsive disorder—A multicenter trial. *Journal of the American Academy of Child and Adolescent Psychiatry*, *31*(1), 45–49. http://dx.doi.org/10.1097/00004583-199201000-00008.

Diniz, J. B., Shavitt, R. G., Pereira, C. A., Hounie, A. G., Pimentel, I., Koran, L. M., et al. (2010). Quetiapine versus clomipramine in the augmentation of selective serotonin reuptake inhibitors for the treatment of obsessive-compulsive disorder: A randomized, open-label trial. *Journal of Psychopharmacology*, *24*(3), 297–307. http://dx.doi.org/10.1177/0269881108099423.

Eddy, K. T., Dutra, L., Bradley, R., & Westen, D. (2004). A multidimensional meta-analysis of psychotherapy and pharmacotherapy for obsessive-compulsive disorder. *Clinical Psychology Review*, *24*(8), 1011–1030. http://dx.doi.org/10.1016/j.cpr.2004.08.004.

Erzegovesi, S., Guglielmo, E., Siliprandi, F., & Bellodi, L. (2005). Low-dose risperidone augmentation of fluvoxamine treatment in obsessive-compulsive disorder: A double-blind, placebo-controlled study. *European Neuropsychopharmacology*, *15*(1), 69–74. http://dx.doi.org/10.1016/j.euroneuro.2004.04.004.

Fineberg, N. A., Sivakumaran, T., Roberts, A., & Gale, T. (2005). Adding quetiapine to SRI in treatment-resistant obsessive-compulsive disorder: A randomized controlled treatment study. *International Clinical Psychopharmacology*, *20*(4), 223–226.

Flament, M. F., Whitaker, A., Rapoport, J. L., Davies, M., Berg, C. Z., Kalikow, K., et al. (1988). Obsessive compulsive disorder in adolescence: An epidemiological study. *Journal of the American Academy of Child and Adolescent Psychiatry*, *27*(6), 764–771. http://dx.doi.org/10.1097/00004583-198811000-00018.

Foa, E. B., Liebowitz, M. R., Kozak, M. J., Davies, S., Campeas, R., Franklin, M. E., et al. (2005). Randomized, placebo-controlled trial of exposure and ritual prevention, clomipramine, and their combination in the treatment of obsessive-compulsive disorder. *American Journal of Psychiatry*, *162*(1), 151–161. http://dx.doi.org/10.1176/appi.ajp.162.1.151.

Geller, D., Biederman, J., Jones, J., Park, K., Schwartz, S., Shapiro, S., et al. (1998). Is juvenile obsessive-compulsive disorder a developmental subtype of the disorder? A review of the pediatric literature. *Journal of the American Academy of Child and Adolescent Psychiatry*, *37*(4), 420–427. http://dx.doi.org/10.1097/00004583-199804000-00020.

Geller, D. A., Biederman, J., Stewart, S. E., Mullin, B., Farrell, C., Wagner, K. D., et al. (2003a). Impact of comorbidity on treatment response to paroxetine in pediatric obsessive-compulsive disorder: Is the use of exclusion criteria empirically supported in randomized clinical trials? *Journal of Child and Adolescent Psychopharmacology*, *13*(Suppl. 1), S19–S29. http://dx.doi.org/10.1089/104454603322126313.

Geller, D. A., Biederman, J., Stewart, S. E., Mullin, B., Martin, A., Spencer, T., et al. (2003b). Which SSRI? A meta-analysis of pharmacotherapy trials in pediatric obsessive-compulsive disorder. *American Journal of Psychiatry*, *160*(11), 1919–1928.

Ghaleiha, A., Entezari, N., Modabbernia, A., Najand, B., Askari, N., Tabrizi, M., et al. (2013). Memantine add-on in moderate to severe obsessive-compulsive disorder: Randomized double-blind placebo-controlled study. *Journal of Psychiatric Research*, *47*(2), 175–180. http://dx.doi.org/10.1016/j.jpsychires.2012.09.015.

Goodman, W. K., Foote, K. D., Greenberg, B. D., Ricciuti, N., Bauer, R., Ward, H., et al. (2010). Deep brain stimulation for intractable obsessive compulsive disorder: Pilot study using a blinded, staggered-onset design. *Biological Psychiatry*, *67*(6), 535–542. http://dx.doi.org/10.1016/j.biopsych.2009.11.028.

Grant, P. J., Joseph, L. A., Farmer, C. A., Luckenbaugh, D. A., Lougee, L. C., Zarate, C. A., Jr., et al. (2014). 12-week, placebo-controlled trial of add-on riluzole in the treatment of childhood-onset obsessive-compulsive disorder. *Neuropsychopharmacology*, *39*(6), 1453–1459. http://dx.doi.org/10.1038/npp.2013.343.

Greenberg, B. D., Rauch, S. L., & Haber, S. N. (2010). Invasive circuitry-based neurotherapeutics: Stereotactic ablation and deep brain stimulation for OCD. *Neuropsychopharmacology*, *35*(1), 317–336. http://dx.doi.org/10.1038/npp.2009.128.

Hezel, D. M., Beattie, K., & Stewart, S. E. (2009). Memantine as an augmenting agent for severe pediatric OCD. *American Journal of Psychiatry*, *166*(2), 237. http://dx.doi.org/10.1176/appi.ajp.2008.08091427.

Hollander, E., Baldini Rossi, N., Sood, E., & Pallanti, S. (2003). Risperidone augmentation in treatment-resistant obsessive-compulsive disorder: A double-blind, placebo-controlled study. *International Journal of Neuropsychopharmacology*, *6*(4), 397–401. http://dx.doi.org/10.1017/S1461145703003730.

Koran, L. M., & Saxena, S. (2002). Issues and strategies in treating refractory obsessive-compulsive disorder. *CNS Spectrums*, *5*, 24–31.

Lopes, A. C., Greenberg, B. D., Canteras, M. M., Batistuzzo, M. C., Hoexter, M. Q., Gentil, A. F., et al. (2014). Gamma ventral capsulotomy for obsessive-compulsive disorder: A randomized clinical trial. *JAMA Psychiatry*, *71*(9), 1066–1076. http://dx.doi.org/10.1001/jamapsychiatry.2014.1193.

Mallet, L., Polosan, M., Jaafari, N., Baup, N., Welter, M. L., Fontaine, D., et al. (2008). Subthalamic nucleus stimulation in severe obsessive-compulsive disorder. *The New England Journal of Medicine*, *359*(20), 2121–2134. http://dx.doi.org/10.1056/NEJMoa0708514.

March, J. S., Franklin, M. E., Leonard, H., Garcia, A., Moore, P., Freeman, J., et al. (2007). Tics moderate treatment outcome with sertraline but not cognitive-behavior therapy in pediatric obsessive-compulsive disorder. *Biological Psychiatry*, *61*(3), 344–347. http://dx.doi.org/10.1016/j.biopsych.2006.09.035.

Masi, G., Pfanner, C., & Brovedani, P. (2013). Antipsychotic augmentation of selective serotonin reuptake inhibitors in resistant tic-related obsessive-compulsive disorder in children and adolescents: A naturalistic comparative study. *Journal of Psychiatric Research*, *47*(8), 1007–1012. http://dx.doi.org/10.1016/j.jpsychires.2013.04.003.

McDougle, C. J., Epperson, C. N., Pelton, G. H., Wasylink, S., & Price, L. H. (2000). A double-blind, placebo-controlled study of risperidone addition in serotonin reuptake inhibitor-refractory obsessive-compulsive disorder. *Archives of General Psychiatry*, *57*(8), 794–801.

McDougle, C. J., Goodman, W. K., Leckman, J. F., Lee, N. C., Heninger, G. R., & Price, L. H. (1994). Haloperidol addition in fluvoxamine-refractory obsessive-compulsive disorder. A double-blind, placebo-controlled study in patients with and without tics. *Archives of General Psychiatry*, *51*(4), 302–308.

McGuire, J. F., Piacentini, J., Lewin, A. B., Brennan, E. A., Murphy, T. K., & Storch, E. A. (2015). A meta-analysis of cognitive behavior therapy and medication for child obsessive-compulsive disorder: Moderators of treatment efficacy, response, and remission. *Depression and Anxiety*, *32*(8), 580–593. http://dx.doi.org/10.1002/da.22389.

Ninan, P. T., Koran, L. M., Kiev, A., Davidson, J. R., Rasmussen, S. A., Zajecka, J. M., et al. (2006). High-dose sertraline strategy for nonresponders to acute treatment for obsessive-compulsive disorder: A multicenter double-blind trial. *Journal of Clinical Psychiatry*, *67*(1), 15–22.

Pallanti, S., & Quercioli, L. (2006). Treatment-refractory obsessive-compulsive disorder: Methodological issues, operational definitions and therapeutic lines. *Progress in Neuro-Psychopharmacology & Biological Psychiatry*, *30*(3), 400–412. http://dx.doi.org/10.1016/j.pnpbp.2005.11.028.

Pallanti, S., Quercioli, L., & Bruscoli, M. (2004). Response acceleration with mirtazapine augmentation of citalopram in obsessive-compulsive disorder patients without comorbid depression: A pilot study. *Journal of Clinical Psychiatry*, *65*(10), 1394–1399.

Paydary, K., Akamaloo, A., Ahmadipour, A., Pishgar, F., Emamzadehfard, S., & Akhondzadeh, S. (2016). N-acetylcysteine augmentation therapy for moderate-to-severe obsessive-compulsive disorder: Randomized, double-blind, placebo-controlled trial. *Journal of Clinical Pharmacy and Therapeutics*, *41*(2), 214–219. http://dx.doi.org/10.1111/jcpt.12370.

Pediatric OCD Treatment Study Team. (2004). Cognitive-behavior therapy, sertraline, and their combination for children and adolescents with obsessive-compulsive disorder: The Pediatric OCD Treatment Study (POTS) randomized controlled trial. *JAMA*, *292*(16), 1969–1976. http://dx.doi.org/10.1001/jama.292.16.1969.

Pittenger, C., Bloch, M. H., Wasylink, S., Billingslea, E., Simpson, R., Jakubovski, E., et al. (2015). Riluzole augmentation in treatment-refractory obsessive-compulsive disorder: A pilot randomized placebo-controlled trial. *Journal of Clinical Psychiatry*, *76*(8), 1075–1084. http://dx.doi.org/10.4088/JCP.14m09123.

Pittenger, C., Krystal, J. H., & Coric, V. (2006). Glutamate-modulating drugs as novel pharmacotherapeutic agents in the treatment of obsessive-compulsive disorder. *NeuroRx*, *3*(1), 69–81. http://dx.doi.org/10.1016/j.nurx.2005.12.006.

Practice parameter for the assessment and treatment of children and adolescenets with obsessive-compulsive disorder. (2012). *Journal of the American Academy of Child and Adolescent Psychiatry, 51*(1), 98–113.

Rodriguez, C. I., Kegeles, L. S., Levinson, A., Feng, T., Marcus, S. M., Vermes, D., et al. (2013). Randomized controlled crossover trial of ketamine in obsessive-compulsive disorder: Proof-of-concept. *Neuropsychopharmacology*, *38*(12), 2475–2483. http://dx.doi.org/10.1038/npp.2013.150.

Rosenberg, D. R., Keshavan, M. S., O'Hearn, K. M., Dick, E. L., Bagwell, W. W., Seymour, A. B., et al. (1997). Frontostriatal measurement in treatment-naive children with obsessive-compulsive disorder. *Archives of General Psychiatry*, *54*(9), 824–830.

Sarris, J., Oliver, G., Camfield, D. A., Dean, O. M., Dowling, N., Smith, D. J., et al. (2015). N-acetyl cysteine (NAC) in the treatment of obsessive-compulsive disorder: A 16-week, double-blind, randomised, placebo-controlled study. *CNS Drugs*, *29*(9), 801–809. http://dx.doi.org/10.1007/s40263-015-0272-9.

Scahill, L., Riddle, M. A., McSwiggin-Hardin, M., Ort, S. I., King, R. A., Goodman, W. K., et al. (1997). Children's Yale-Brown obsessive compulsive scale: Reliability and validity. *Journal of the American Academy of Child and Adolescent Psychiatry*, *36*(6), 844–852. http://dx.doi.org/10.1097/00004583-199706000-00023.

Shapira, N. A., Ward, H. E., Mandoki, M., Murphy, T. K., Yang, M. C., Blier, P., et al. (2004). A double-blind, placebo-controlled trial of olanzapine addition in fluoxetine-refractory obsessive-compulsive disorder. *Biological Psychiatry*, *55*(5), 553–555. http://dx.doi.org/10.1016/j.biopsych.2003.11.010.

Simpson, H. B., Foa, E. B., Liebowitz, M. R., Huppert, J. D., Cahill, S., Maher, M. J., et al. (2013). Cognitive-behavioral therapy vs risperidone for augmenting serotonin reuptake Inhibitors in obsessive-compulsive disorder: A randomized clinical trial. *JAMA Psychiatry*, *70*(11), 1190–1199. http://dx.doi.org/10.1001/jamapsychiatry.2013.1932.

Skarphedinsson, G., Compton, S., Thomsen, P. H., Weidle, B., Dahl, K., Nissen, J. B., et al. (2015). Tics moderate sertraline, but not cognitive-behavior therapy response in pediatric obsessive-compulsive disorder patients who do not respond to cognitive-behavior therapy. *Journal of Child and Adolescent Psychopharmacology*, *25*(5), 432–439. http://dx.doi.org/10.1089/cap.2014.0167.

Skarphedinsson, G., De Nadai, A. S., Storch, E. A., Lewin, A. B., & Ivarsson, T. (2017). Defining cognitive-behavior therapy response and remission in pediatric OCD: A signal detection analysis of the Children's Yale-Brown Obsessive Compulsive Scale. *European Child & Adolescent Psychiatry*, *26*(1), 47–55. http://dx.doi.org/10.1007/s00787-016-0863-0.

Soltani, F., Sayyah, M., Feizy, F., Malayeri, A., Siahpoosh, A., & Motlagh, I. (2010). A double-blind, placebo-controlled pilot study of ondansetron for patients with obsessive-compulsive disorder. *Human Psychopharmacology*, *25*(6), 509–513. http://dx.doi.org/10.1002/hup.1145.

Stewart, S. E., Geller, D. A., Jenike, M., Pauls, D., Shaw, D., Mullin, B., et al. (2004). Long-term outcome of pediatric obsessive-compulsive disorder: A meta-analysis and qualitative review of the literature. *Acta Psychiatrica Scandinavica*, *110*(1), 4–13. http://dx.doi.org/10.1111/j.1600-0447.2004.00302.x.

Storch, E. A., Geffken, G. R., Merlo, L. J., Mann, G., Duke, D., Munson, M., et al. (2007). Family-based cognitive-behavioral therapy for pediatric obsessive-compulsive disorder: Comparison of intensive and weekly approaches. *Journal of the American Academy of Child and Adolescent Psychiatry*, *46*(4), 469–478. http://dx.doi.org/10.1097/chi.0b013e31803062e7.

Storch, E. A., Lehmkuhl, H. D., Ricketts, E., Geffken, G. R., Marien, W., & Murphy, T. K. (2010). An open trial of intensive family based cognitive-behavioral therapy in youth with obsessive-compulsive disorder who are medication partial responders or nonresponders. *Journal of Clinical Child and Adolescent Psychology*, *39*(2), 260–268. http://dx.doi.org/10.1080/15374410903532676.

Storch, E. A., Lewin, A. B., De Nadai, A. S., & Murphy, T. K. (2010). Defining treatment response and remission in obsessive-compulsive disorder: A signal detection analysis of the Children's Yale-Brown Obsessive Compulsive Scale. *Journal of the American Academy of Child and Adolescent Psychiatry*, *49*(7), 708–717. http://dx.doi.org/10.1016/j.jaac.2010.04.005.

Varigonda, A. L., Jakubovski, E., & Bloch, M. H. (2016). Systematic review and meta-analysis: Early treatment responses of selective serotonin reuptake inhibitors and clomipramine in Pediatric Obsessive-Compulsive Disorder. *Journal of the American Academy of Child and Adolescent Psychiatry*, *55*(10), 851–859.e852. http://dx.doi.org/10.1016/j.jaac.2016.07.768.

Welch, J. M., Lu, J., Rodriguiz, R. M., Trotta, N. C., Peca, J., Ding, J. D., et al. (2007). Cortico-striatal synaptic defects and OCD-like behaviours in Sapap3-mutant mice. *Nature*, *448* (7156), 894–900. http://dx.doi.org/10.1038/nature06104.

Wewetzer, C., Jans, T., Muller, B., Neudorfl, A., Bucherl, U., Remschmidt, H., et al. (2001). Long-term outcome and prognosis of obsessive-compulsive disorder with onset in childhood or adolescence. *European Child & Adolescent Psychiatry*, *10*(1), 37–46.

Index

Note: Page numbers followed by *f* indicate figures, *t* indicate tables, and *b* indicate boxes.

D

E

F

M

N

O

P

R

FSC
www.fsc.org
MIX
Papier | Fördert
gute Waldnutzung
FSC® C083411

Kolibri 360 GmbH
Ferdinand-Jühlke-Straße 7
99095 Erfurt, Deutschland
produktsicherheit@kolibri360.de